AF478985

What Does It Look Like?

Sebastiaan A. Verschuren

What Does It Look Like?

Wittgenstein's Philosophy in the Light of His Conception of Language Description: Part I

Bibliographic Information published by the Deutsche Nationalbibliothek
The Deutsche Nationalbibliothek lists this publication in
the Deutsche Nationalbibliografie; detailed bibliographic
data is available in the internet at http://dnb.d-nb.de.

Library of Congress Cataloging-in-Publication Data
A CIP catalog record for this book has been applied for
at the Library of Congress

Printed by CPI books GmbH, Leck

ISBN 978-3-631-66941-9 (Print)
E-ISBN 978-3-631-70092-1 (E-PDF)
E-ISBN 978-3-631-70093-8 (EPUB)
E-ISBN 978-3-631-70094-5 (MOBI)
DOI 10.3726/b11687

Der Aberglaub', in dem wir aufgewachsen,
Verliert, auch wenn wir ihn erkennen, darum
Doch seine Macht nicht über uns. – Es sind
Nicht alle frei, die ihrer Ketten spotten.

Gotthold Ephraim Lessing

Die Aufgabe der Philosophie ist, das erlösende Wort zu finden.

"Das erlösende Wort" kann nur erlösen weil es sozusagen der Schlußstein eines Gebäudes ist. Für den der diese Voraussetzungen nicht hat ist es nicht das erlösende Wort.

Ludwig Wittgenstein

Table of Contents

Introduction

'All *explanation* must disappear, and description alone must take its place.'[1] These words from Wittgenstein's second masterpiece are as legendary as the man himself. Eleven signs, two great symbols, an entire philosophy, much folderol to one school, naught but truth and essence to another. What the one hopes for, the other challenges, a diversion that keeps legends alive and scholars kicking.

I, too, have written a book about Wittgenstein's philosophy, which I take to be saying that doing away with all explanation is not enough, but that something must take its place, namely *description*. What Wittgenstein's remark epitomizes is a true *Gedankenbewegung*, a philosophical movement of thought that does not begin with descriptions, but comes to an end in them. This movement was surely not the only one that he was anxious to engage in and to think through. Yet, compared to all the others that preoccupied him during his many years of philosophical labour, the one at issue was exceptional as it was at work in all he did to tackle philosophical problems. It dominated the whole of his philosophical thinking, each part and every share, with all bits and pieces perennially contriving a plot that I call the dialectical character of Wittgenstein's later philosophy: 'All *explanation* must disappear, and description alone must take its place.' This book is about this character with its special focus being the part and role that description plays in his philosophy. It is about the problems and difficulties that Wittgenstein faced while trying to furnish the 'final notching to his philosophical beans': *descriptions of language*.

Indeed, this book is about a topic that runs as a recurrent theme through every concern and issue that Wittgenstein, during the last twenty years or so of his life, was anxious to lay his philosophical hands on. Perhaps the most remarkable aspect about this theme *qua subject matter* in the immense literature on Wittgenstein is that it has not proved to be particularly 'in the fashion', neither among his philosophical friends nor among his foes. In the course of more than six decades of scholarly exegesis commentators have written extensively, at times even feverishly in the wake of the latest upsurge, about such topics as 'Following a Rule', 'Meaning and Use', 'Privacy of Language', 'The Inner and the Outer', and 'Seeing as', to mention only a few of them. Of course, these are the kinds of things about which Wittgenstein has thought and written himself, both extensively and intensively. But through all these more or less Wittgensteinian issues runs a conspicuous and everlasting concern, at least on Wittgenstein's own part—namely,

---

1   PI: 109. See References for the abbreviations used to refer to Wittgenstein's works.

to end up with descriptions, *and these things only*. It has been no small concern on his part, and yet, it has only been a minor *exegetical* concern among his advocates and commentators, expert or not in their adoration or abomination, neither in close connection with any of the topics themselves, nor in the form of a comprehensive investigation as this book seeks to take up as the first part of an even more comprehensive enquiry and critical evaluation. To quote Wittgenstein is so much easier than to catch him, and quotes spring readily to mind.

If Bertrand Russell ever intended to keep his aversion to the philosophy of his former pupil under his hat, he must have drastically changed his mind after Wittgenstein's untimely death.

> I have not found in Wittgenstein's *Philosophical Investigations* anything that seemed to me interesting and I do not understand why a whole school finds important wisdom in its pages. Psychologically this is surprising. The earlier Wittgenstein, whom I knew intimately, was a man addicted to passionately intense thinking, profoundly aware of difficult problems of which I, like him, felt the importance, and possessed (or at least so I thought) of true philosophical genius. The later Wittgenstein, on the contrary, seems to have grown tired of serious thinking and to have invented a doctrine which would make such an activity unnecessary. I do not for one moment believe that the doctrine which has these lazy consequences is true. I realize, however, that I have an overpoweringly strong bias against it, for, if it is true, philosophy is, at best, a slight help to lexicographers, and at worst, an idle tea-table amusement.[2]

Russell must have looked at Wittgenstein's later philosophy as what *merely* seeks to describe the use of our words and sentences. And, indeed, being looked at thus, the question arises of what there should be so difficult about anything like *that*, or exciting. Just look at the practice of our language, Wittgenstein seems to be saying, for then you will find the answer. And so it is: his *Philosophical Investigations* seems to abound in remarks that at first glance are strongly suggestive of a philosophy having ceased to be a genuinely difficult enterprise. Here are a few: 'Philosophy simply puts everything before us, and neither explains nor deduces anything' (§126); 'The work of the philosopher consists in assembling reminders

---

2   Bertrand Russell, *My Philosophical Development* (London: George Allen & Unwin, 1959), 216f. Cf.: 'It is not an altogether pleasant experience to find oneself regarded as antiquated after having been, for a time, in the fashion. It is difficult to accept this experience gracefully. When Leibniz, in old age, heard the praises of Berkeley, he remarked: "The young man in Ireland who disputes the reality of bodies seems neither to explain himself sufficiently nor produce adequate arguments. I suspect him of wishing to be known for his paradoxes." I could not say quite the same of Wittgenstein, by whom I was superseded in the opinion of many British philosophers. It was not by paradox that he wished to be known, but by a suave evasion of paradoxes' (*ibid*, 214).

for a particular purpose' (§127); 'What *we* do is to bring words back from their metaphysical to their everyday use' (§116); 'The problems are solved, not by giving new information, but by arranging what we have always known' (§109); 'Philosophy of logic speaks of sentences and words in exactly the sense in which we speak of them in ordinary life when we say e.g. "Here is a Chinese sentence", or "No, that only looks like writing; it is actually just an ornament" and so on'[3]; and, to mention one more remark here, the one that I think Russell must have had in mind particularly while speaking of a 'suave evasion of paradoxes' (cf. footnote 2): 'It is not the business of philosophy to resolve a contradiction by means of a mathematical or logico-mathematical discovery, but to render surveyable the state of mathematics that troubles us' (§125).[4]

Of course, advocates of Wittgenstein's later work may well wish to see in Russell's overt grudge against being old, antiquated, and no longer 'in the fashion' a suave evasion of the paradoxes of life. And yet, advocates, too, have their own suave evasions of asking all kinds of critical questions, and advocates of Wittgenstein not so much about descriptions as about *Wittgenstein's* descriptions; and perhaps not so much about these things as about these things *in* Wittgenstein's later philosophy. To be sure, I am not claiming that the notion of Wittgenstein's description has not been addressed in the secondary literature. All I am saying, or rather suggesting, is that this literature is conspicuously silent on (especially) the specific problems and difficulties that troubled Wittgenstein throughout his daily efforts to arrive at mere *descriptions* of language. But, I admit, this is perhaps itself a suave evasion of *claiming* that the notion of Wittgenstein's descriptions has not been of primary interest to his commentators.

Books are said to be reliable mirrors of the *Zeitgeist,* and I truly believe that even the tablespoons in Buckingham Palace envy the mirroring capacities of all those Handbooks and Companions in which Wittgenstein's own *Geist* faces its contemporary reception. *The Cambridge Companion to Wittgenstein*[5], which appeared in 1996, devoted not a single chapter, or even a page, to the question of what describing language amounts to, according to Wittgenstein. In 2001,

---

3   Boxed passage between §108 and §109.
4   Cf.: 'An investigation is possible in connexion with mathematics which is entirely analogous to our investigations of psychology. It is just as little a mathematical investigation as the other is a psychological one. It will not contain calculations, so it is not for example logistic. It might deserve the name of an investigation of the "foundations of mathematics"' (PPF: 372).
5   Hans Sluga and David G. Stern, eds., *The Cambridge Companion to Wittgenstein* (Cambridge: Cambridge University Press, 1996).

Wittgenstein – A Critical Reader (Blackwell publishers)[6] saw the light of the day; I quote the back cover: 'Exploring all of the central themes of Wittgenstein's *oeuvre*, this volume includes discussion of core topics such as meaning and use, rule following, the picture theory of language and the nature of philosophy. It also contains topics in which Wittgenstein's influence is becoming more apparent, such as intentionality and ethics. The book provides a wide-ranging collection of newly commissioned essays on Wittgenstein by internationally established philosophers [...]'. I guess that if such a Critical Reader explores 'all of the central themes of Wittgenstein's *oeuvre*' within the narrow breadth of a single book, it has simply no space left for anything so central a theme like the man's description.

In 2011, Oxford University Press followed suit with *The Oxford Handbook of Wittgenstein*[7], laying claim to being 'the most comprehensive volume ever published on Wittgenstein: thirty-five leading scholars explore the whole range of his thought, offering critical engagement and original interpretation, and tracing his philosophical development. [...]. This handbook is the place to look for a full understanding of Wittgenstein's special importance to modern philosophy.'—Certainly, if you consult this almanackic sort of place, in quest of a critical engagement or interpretation, original or not, of what it was like for Wittgenstein to do away with all explanation and to put *description alone* in its place, of how his unceasing struggles to do so has added more colour and character to his later philosophy than anything else; if you are curious to learn of the pivotally important role that, for instance, the fictitious language-games have been playing in his efforts to arrive at descriptions *at last*, and descriptions *alone*, then, the best you will find is an allusion or two at one place and some dim suggestions at another. It appears that Wittgensteinians, after more than sixty years of scholarly work, still have to catch up with Wittgenstein's ever-*lasting* concerns and troubles. But Blackwell—indeed, Blackwell again—has been magnanimously announcing a 'keynote addition'. But to what? To 'the Blackwell series on the world's great philosophers'![8]—Will it be

---

6   Hans-Johann Glock, ed., *Wittgenstein: A Critical Reader* (Oxford: Blackwell, 2001).

7   Oskari Kuusela and Marie McGinn, eds., *The Oxford Handbook of Wittgenstein* (Oxford: Oxford University Press, 2011).

8   The cover text runs as follows (16.09.2015): 'The most comprehensive survey of Wittgenstein's thought yet compiled, this volume of fifty [!] newly commissioned essays by leading interpreters of his philosophy is a keynote addition to the Blackwell series on the world's great philosophers, covering everything from Wittgenstein's intellectual development to the latest interpretations of his hugely influential ideas. The lucid, engaging commentary also reviews Wittgenstein's historical legacy and his continued impact on contemporary philosophical debate.'

more of mom's old fashioned apple pie? More of the 'absolutely necessary reading'? More of 'the definite resource for the study of this great philosopher', his soul and his bones? More explorations of his thought, this time far beyond its whole range? More penetrating insights into Wittgenstein's life from professors of philosophy and 'the most internationally eminent thinkers and intellectuals' from the sage world of commissioned academicians? Or will it be another fait accompli blessed by the imprimatur of more than a meagre thirty-five executants and interpreters?

Perhaps I do well to add one more mirror to the above list: Saul Kripke's influential book *Wittgenstein on Rules and Private Language*.[9] This book deals with no small topic, and yet, it hardly ever mentions the word 'description', never mind Wittgenstein's deep *need* for arriving at mere descriptions of language. Kripke's book has been a target of much criticism, mesmerizing, for various reasons, an entire generation of commentators for some length of time. But in the whole joined hue and cry there is little if any roaring about what counts for Wittgenstein in the end: description *alone*. To the best of my knowledge the prominent lack of this concern in Kripke's book has never been addressed and turned into a point of criticism of his 'classic' interpretation.

My concern in this book is not with Kripke's interpretation of Wittgenstein, nor with classical topics such as 'Following a Rule' and 'Meaning and Use', but rather with something far more general or characteristic of Wittgenstein's philosophy, with what I have called the dialectical character of his approach and way of thinking. What I speak of here is something that is missed once the point of Wittgenstein's descriptions is lost. And lost, I dare to say, it is more often than not in the secondary literature on the man and his philosophy. But to lose it is to miss no small point. This brings me to what Michael Dummett writes in his *The Logical Basis of Metaphysics*:

> We all stand, or should stand, in the shadow of Wittgenstein, in the same way that much earlier generations once stood in the shadow of Kant; and one of my complaints about many contemporary American philosophers is that they appear never to read Wittgenstein. Some things in his philosophy, however, I cannot see any reason for accepting: and one is the belief that philosophy, as such, must never criticise but only describe. This belief was fundamental in the sense that it determined the whole manner in which, in his later writings, he discussed philosophical problems; not sharing it, I could not respect his work as I do if I regarded his arguments and insights as depending on the truth of his belief.[10]

---

9   Saul Kripke, *Wittgenstein on Rules and Private Language* (Cambridge, Mass: Harvard University Press, 1982).

10   Michael Dummett, *The Logical Basis of Metaphysics* (Cambridge, Mass: Harvard University Press, 1991), xi.

At present my point is not that Dummett speaks of a belief here: Wittgenstein's *belief* that philosophy, as such, must never criticize but only describe. Rather my point is the question of how one should read Wittgenstein so as to believe that he says that philosophy, as such, must never criticize but only describe. For did *he* not say that 'All *explanation* must disappear, and description alone must take its place'? And did *he*, i.e. the same philosopher, not also say that 'Philosophy may in no way interfere with the actual use of language; it can *in the end* only describe it'? (PI: 124).[11]

Wittgenstein does not say that philosophy must *only* describe. But neither does he say that all explanation must disappear. What he does say is that all explanation must disappear, *and* description alone *must take its place*. Obviously, we must do away with all explanation, but doing away with this (very tempting) form of understanding is not enough in philosophy. Something must take *its place*. And *that* is something to hold on to. For if *description* must take the place of all explanation: indeed, what kind of relationship does *it* actually bear to all explanation? Should we first try to do away with all explanation, only to provide descriptions afterwards? Or is it rather by dint of description, properly done, that we should do away with all explanation? True, not anything will do as 'description alone' must take the place of all explanation, that is, description of language. But, then, not any description of language will do either. Linguists describe language, but their descriptions will not do for Wittgenstein's purpose, any more than those of psychologists, sociologists, anthropologists, biologists, or, for that matter, the advocates of ordinary language philosophy. But what about *Wittgenstein's* descriptions of language? What do *they* look like? What aspects or features of language do they actually describe, and why should it be precisely these things rather than anything else? Indeed, what about these descriptions that they, as Wittgenstein writes it in the *Investigations*, receive their light, that is to say their purpose, from the philosophical problems (cf. PI: 109). Is that light and purpose not suggestive of something specific, something uncommon, about Wittgenstein's descriptions? Michael Dummett has shown little if any interest in these questions, and yet, he was surely not a lonely bird in that respect. But is that not curious? For philosophers curious to know it surely is—if only because they look at descriptions as *preliminary steps* only, in the light of their own purpose to find redemption in terms of explanations at last. But is *that* not curious? The eye that looks at descriptions thus and begins to read itself through the *Investigations*: should that eye not feel the edge of the curiousness and begin to ask questions?

---

11 Emphasis added.

14

Well, the edge is no doubt felt, but the curiousness is blamed on Wittgenstein's *Philosophical Investigations*.

In order answer the above questions, it does not suffice to attend to what Wittgenstein has produced on the strength of remarks and statements. We must, in addition, pay close attention to his philosophical undertakings, i.e. to his hard work and severe struggles on those philosophical playgrounds where he unceasingly tries to arrive at *such description* as his own philosophy stipulates. It is one thing to promulgate that we must do away with all explanation in philosophy; quite another thing, as Wittgenstein well realized, to show what it looks like in practice to do away with *all explanation*—what the very thing looks like in practice that must take *its place*.

My fascination for these actual doings, for Wittgenstein's real philosophical *struggle*, began with *On Certainty*. In this work, shortly before he passed away, Wittgenstein writes the following: 'Am I not getting closer and closer to saying that in the end logic cannot be described? You must look at the practice of language, then you will see it' (OC: 501). This is truly an intriguing remark, exactly when it is set against the background of Wittgenstein's philosophical objective. For in spite of all his strenuous efforts to describe (the logic) of our language, Wittgenstein more often than not just failed to furnish descriptions only at the end of the day. His terse remark has a real touch of confession, and yet, it is not altogether devoid of hope. But hope, however intense and promising, has never been the kind of incentive that propelled Wittgenstein's philosophical activities. That is to say, Wittgenstein did *not* enter the philosophical stage *hoping* that he might be successful in coming out with descriptions of language alone. Rather, he entered it with a philosophical conception that has been moulded to the core by a deeply felt need that aims at '*complete* clarity'—in his own private head in the first case. What does that mean? It means, as Wittgenstein puts it, 'that the philosophical problems should *completely* disappear' (PI: 133). The modal force of this *should* does not lie in any of Wittgenstein's extraordinary powers to bring light into the dark. Ultimately inhering in his interest and deeply felt need, it rather lies in Wittgenstein's later philosophy as a whole, or, more precisely, in his conception of logic—a conception that stipulates that 'philosophy may in no way interfere with the actual use of language; it can *in the end* only describe it.' Wittgenstein's words in *On Certainty* concern this *in the end*, hence nothing less than his later conception of logic.

For some time I thought that it was only due to the subject matter in *On Certainty* and the specific difficulties it posed that Wittgenstein felt compelled to lodge a serious complaint about his long-standing philosophical aim and effort to describe our language, its logic, or so-called grammar. But the more familiar I became with his philosophical doings in such widely diverging fields of investigation as psychology and the foundations of mathematics, the more doubtful I grew. If Wittgenstein had had difficulties in furnishing descriptions of our language in *On Certainty*, then, it dawned upon me, surely no more than in any other part of his work as a whole.

Not being concerned with any particular field, then, this book is about Wittgenstein's descriptions of language as integral parts of a complex movement of thought. This being so, it not merely expounds the kinds of descriptions that Wittgenstein means to give at last; it also pays due attention to the problems and difficulties he faced while being in the business of furnishing such descriptions. Just as there is something characteristic of Wittgenstein's overall movement of thought, so there is something highly characteristic of these problems and difficulties. Of course, they are far from being the only things that troubled Wittgenstein's philosophical mind. But the ones this book seeks to expound have something special about them: they are not only stubborn but show a stubbornness that appears to be homemade. They are not so much inherent in Wittgenstein's *way of doing* philosophy as in his later philosophy, in its stipulations. Wittgenstein, in other words, saw himself systematically confronted with certain troubles; troubles pertaining to the form in which he tried to solve all philosophical problems at last. Indeed, what troubled him while *describing* our so-called everyday language are things that you will not find on the philosophical desk of any other philosopher, ancient or modern.

Acknowledgement

To finish a piece of philosophical writing is to show how much the work done remains work to be done. This book remains as much work in progress as any of its preceding stages, an early one of which was submitted as a doctoral thesis to the Philosophical Faculty of the University of Erfurt, August 2008. I am grateful to Professor Dr. Alex Burri for his help, advice, and patience. Not a Wittgensteinian himself, he nonetheless showed a great interest in my work, listening attentively to my admittedly zealous talks about Wittgenstein's conception of language description, its fundamental importance, and its amazingly odd reception in the immense secondary literature on Wittgenstein, the man, and his philosophy. I would like to express my gratitude to Hugo van den Berg whose corrections and criticism have made my English look more like English.

1. Not a common way of looking

Ich weiß, daß ich logisches Gift in mich hineintrinken muß —
um es überwinden zu können.

Ludwig Wittgenstein

1.1 In the end

A couple of years ago, on a rainy day and through a curious twist of fate, a noteworthy piece of writing fell into my hands and caught my attention: a paper with the innovative title 'What is Philosophy?' The author: Graham Priest, a modern philosopher of long academic standing; the scholarly paper in question: 'the text of an inaugural lecture delivered at the University of Melbourne, November 2003.'[12] Interestingly, it is already at the very outset that Priest bursts in upon the established order of his readership, or Melbourne audience, for that matter, in the following way:

> In the thirty or so years that I have been doing philosophy there have been two views about the nature of philosophy which have had wide acceptance. These views are the views of the later Wittgenstein and of Derrida. In the first two parts of this paper I will describe these views and explain why I find them unsatisfactory. I will then go on, in the final part of the paper, to outline a view that inspires more confidence in me.

You find these words at the bottom of p. 189 of the printed version. A few pages further on, at the top of p.195, you can find yourself reading the following: 'So much for Wittgenstein's view of philosophy.' Unfortunately, Priest does not tell his readers whether it took him also 'thirty or so years' to explain to his own satisfaction why he finds Wittgenstein's view unsatisfactory. Still, if it is true that this view has had wide acceptance, as Priest clearly thinks it had, one wonders what happened to philosophy in the twentieth century if six or so pages 'suffice to show that, and why, Wittgenstein's pessimistic account of the nature of philosophy is wrong' (*ibid*, 195).

According to Priest, Derrida's and Wittgenstein's 'account of philosophy are self-refuting, since the way they do philosophy conflicts with the way that they say philosophy is.'[13] And, as he continues:

---

12 Graham Priest, 'What is Philosophy', *Philosophy* 81 (2006), 189 (footnote).

13 Of course, if the way one does philosophy conflicts with the way that one says philosophy is, why then should it be the *account* of philosophy that is self-refuting?

Indeed, how did Priest actually evaluate Wittgenstein's view of philosophy, if only critically for his audience? His printed *critique* requires less than two pages, and its opening gambit is a statement that is worth quoting here: 'Wittgenstein's views about the nature of philosophy, as put forward in the *Philosophical Investigations*[,] derive from his view about the nature of language' (*ibid*, 189f.). Alas, Priest does not broach the question what it is to derive a view about the nature of philosophy from a view about the nature of language, but, obviously, he must in his own critical way have read Wittgenstein, and have found nothing unsatisfactory in his way of reading him, not even in the light of Wittgenstein's words in *PI* §92 saying that 'in our investigations, we are trying to understand the nature of language – its function, its structure.' Wittgenstein spent his life investigating language, trying to understand its nature as best he could. But what are we to make of these philosophical investigations if his views about the nature of philosophy, as Priest maintains, 'derive from his view about the nature of language'?

'Wittgenstein's account of philosophy is a very disappointing one. Worse, it is pretty much self-refuting', Priest says, only to continue as follows:

Of course, Priest is not particularly known as a commentator on Wittgenstein, at least not among the more established order of commentators on Wittgenstein and his work. Still, in certain respects he bears a family resemblance, whether *he* likes it or not, or whether *they* like it or not, to readers of Wittgenstein who acquit themselves less disapprovingly of his work. To be sure, I am only trading on the notion of commentators and to trade on such a thing, or on what it stands for, is to do no more than to trample upon a particular class of transgressors. In philosophical contexts the notion evokes images not unlike those that the word *politicians* evokes in the world of newspapers, or the word *newspapers* in the minds of politicians. They are always wrong or misinformed, somehow, never right, and definitely never scrupulously correct or trustworthy. Sometimes it is only a word or two that matters, but then it matters and there is a debate, great consternation, perhaps a storm at last, which tends to obtain egregious proportions. 'Commentators on Wittgenstein claim that…, but Wittgenstein…' *That* is how the philosophical community uses the notion of commentators, and 'my unhallowed hands shall not disturb' this good old wisdom. So, then, Wittgenstein mounts *arguments*, as Priests claims to have noticed, and as many a commentator before and after him has done as well. And so it is: Wittgenstein, every now and then, *did* mount arguments. And now the trouble seems to be that he should *not* have availed himself of that contrivance. After all, was he not the man who wrote the following?

> Philosophy may in no way interfere with the actual use of language; it can only describe it.

'So what has gone wrong?' I really have no idea of what *went* wrong on Priest's part, but if he claims that 'learning philosophy is not simply learning a bunch of facts; it is learning how critically to evaluate people's ideas', then, surely, among the very first things incumbent on us, students of philosophy as we are, is to quote people's words correctly. The above passage is Priest's own indelible quotation from *Philosophical Investigations*, translated by G. E. M. Anscombe (Oxford: Basil Blackwell, 1968). And if you quote from the second edition, that is, quote from this or any other non-pirated edition, i.e. correctly, the relevant section from *PI* §124 runs as follows:

> Philosophy may in no way interfere with the actual use of language; it can in the end only describe it.

Sometimes it is only a word or two that matters, but then it matters. What matters at this point are three little words.[14] I propose to attend to the more established order of commentators on Wittgenstein and his work.

Commentators recurrently mention that Wittgenstein, allegedly against the articles of his own philosophical intentions, embarked on an explanatory tour every now and then, and indulged every so often in mounting an argument or two. He, obsessive thinker as he was, was by no means averse to giving arguments in philosophy! And so it is: Wittgenstein was indeed by no means averse to giving arguments in philosophy! But there is another point to mention here, which concerns the question of how the former one can be turned into a point

---

14   Priest's quotation is on p. 192.

of criticism, to be held out against Wittgenstein's proclamation that 'we must do away with *all* explanation and description alone must take its place' (PI: 109); or against such notorious a remark as that 'philosophy only states what everyone admits' (PI: 599). The commentator's insinuation is that such nicely polished apothegms collapse under the weight of Wittgenstein's philosophical doings. But, then, there is also the commentator's own doings and these find regular expression in his books and articles without asking all kinds of critical questions first about what Wittgenstein's descriptions of language are like: How, to mention one thing here, does his activity of furnishing descriptions bear upon a miscellany of his other activities—his recurrent sojourns in argumentation not excluded. Wittgenstein argues, quite a lot actually, critical as he is of so many things we say, or fail to say, in philosophy. But does that mean that his *aim* in philosophy is primarily to establish *claims*? In his contribution to *The Oxford Handbook of Wittgenstein*, Snowdon has at any rate not hesitated to maintain the following, in the face of Wittgenstein's *Bemerkung* that philosophy can 'in the end only describe' language.

> ['Wittgenstein's] aim is primarily to establish claims of the form Not [p], or perhaps: 'we should not think that p'.[15]

One of the things we shall be considering in this book is that Wittgenstein's activity of finding his way out of philosophical perplexities does not consist in merely describing the practice of our language. That is, for Wittgenstein, philosophy, once falling into his hands, is not *reduced* to such an activity. Philosophy is not reduced to such an activity, but finds its final expression in *descriptions*. This is the import of those three little words 'in the end', which have obtained an overt and lasting place in Wittgenstein's *Philosophical Investigations*, no matter whether it is overlooked or not. Wittgenstein's anxiousness to appear at the end of the day with nothing but descriptions poses *the* point of reference, the *Bezugspunkt*, in his dialectical edifice: with respect to everything he lays his hands on philosophically, i.e., with respect to everything he undertakes to do there, says, writes and claims. To look at his activities without heeding the intimacy of connections they bear to his

---

15 Paul Snowdon, 'Private Experience and Sense Data', in Oskari Kuusela and Marie McGinn., eds., *Oxford Handbook of Wittgenstein* (Oxford: Oxford University press, 2011), 403. Cf. '[T]here is something close to self-refutation in Wittgenstein's avowed complete conception of philosophy. It is surely clear that his proposed conception of philosophy is not something that no one has doubted or denied. Wittgenstein therefore [sic] seems to go against his own idea of philosophy as leaving everything as it is by himself proposing a conception which does not do that' (*ibid*, 405).

daily efforts to come out with description at last, is to perceive them in a singularly refractory way. Thus, there is still much work to do, plenty more work indeed, once Wittgenstein throws in his legendary 'Nonsense!' at this or that stage. Of course, its bang might be heard most loudly in the vicinity of the word. But to rally near the spot where it hits the board is not without danger: one might well lose sight of the overall movement of thought, of all the various ties and connections this 'Nonsense!' bears to what in the end counts, for Wittgenstein, and counts only, for him: mere description. 'Nonsense!' surely meant something important in his hands, but its point if not its bang is completely lost once it is cut loose from what in the end redeems for Wittgenstein: only descriptions, i.e. of language.

Giving descriptions is a complex dialectical activity, at least in Wittgenstein's hands. My main contention here and elsewhere is that his idea has never been one of merely sitting down in front of our language, only to observe and to register its variety of workings in terms of descriptions. There is, as we shall see in more detail, a most important contrast at work in Wittgenstein's philosophy, a contrast between opposing urges and strivings, which is always to be respected and clearly kept in mind—should we want to grasp his philosophical *doings*. This contrast is present in almost everything that Wittgenstein has said and written, although at some time with more outward manifestation than at other times. Consider, for instance, the following remark:

> How does it come about that philosophy is so complicated a structure? It surely ought to be completely simple, if it is the ultimate thing, independent of all experience, that you make it out to be.—Philosophy unties knots in our thinking: hence its result must be simple, but philosophizing has to be as complicated as the knots it unties. (Z: 452)

This passage nicely illustrates the dialectical character of Wittgenstein's philosophy. Perhaps the first thing to notice is that he presents philosophy as a *complicated* affair, rather than as a gloomy human predicament from which there is no escape. There is a way into the muddle, but there is also a way out of it. Although the way out of it is *not* the way into it, the way out seems to close forever on us unless we begin to realize all kinds of things about our way in. What brought you there? What step did you undertake in the first place? Why believe that the problem can be *solved*?—We feel ever *urged*, according to Wittgenstein, *to explain* no sooner than the philosophical mood dawns upon us, and one of the first things to realize is that we misread this urge, this driving force on our parts: we mistake it for the philosopher in us, for our deep philosophical need rendering an inquiry worth its while. But the true philosopher in us, Wittgenstein suggests, is the need to *untie* the knots that we have tied ourselves into, knots that tighten our minds more and more with each step that our human urge induces us to make. If you realize the true nature of a philosophical difficulty, you realize that there is redemption in philosophy, and that its results *must* be simple. Redemption, yes!—but only if one declines to cut things short.[16]

'[T]hat you make it out to be.' Philosophy, on Wittgenstein's view, is *made out* to be independent of all experience. It is *made out* to be an intellectual activity that goes against the grain of our human predicament, namely to feel the strong urge to rejoice in a fair share of (stored) experiences and in explanations that ground on them. There is a big *Ought* at work in Wittgenstein's philosophy, one that we shall need to expound, one that we shall need to return to, time and again. Wittgenstein is simply not interested in 'philosophical' results that relish experiences, and it is ultimately owing to his interest that philosophy, in his hands, obtains the kind of dialectical touch and character it has there. It must be a complicated thing, because of the kind of interest with which he enters the philosophical stage. But so its results must be simple, because of that interest. Wittgenstein used a miscellany of phraseologies to make this point clear. Here is another one: 'Taking care of a philosophical problem is not a matter of pronouncing new truths about the subject of the investigation' (PO: 173). *My* aim in philosophy, Wittgenstein wants to say, unlike *your* aim as a philosopher, is not to pronounce *new* truth. Indeed, *his* descriptions *ought not* to contain new truths. But *we* constantly feel that in philosophy we must avail ourselves of new truths—so as to expedite our own redemption. Wittgenstein, however, aims at explicating what we have always known, in the face of that feeling and because of it. Of course, no-new-truths in philosophy can be obtained in various ways, by e.g. simply renouncing all explanations. But Wittgenstein wants to pronounce no *new* truths; hence *merely renouncing all explanations* is not enough as *it* does not pronounce what we have always known, unless the renouncing occurs in the end by pronouncing: no *new* truths.

An aspect such as *not* pronouncing *new* truths is no ornament of Wittgenstein's philosophy, any more than an amusing piquancy in a transient piece of prose. Wittgenstein's remark is one out of hundreds of pieces of prose in which the aforementioned contrast is being reflected over and over again, an occupation that poses the outward manifestation of Wittgenstein's individuality peculiar to the core. This leads us to his innermost interest: 'Scientific questions may interest

---

16 Cf. 'To relieve the mental cramp it is not enough to get rid of it; you must also see why you had it' (AWL: 90).

me, but they never really grip me. Only *conceptual & aesthetic* questions have that effect on me. At bottom it leaves me cold whether scientific problems are solved; but not those other questions' (CV: 91).

Although jotted down near the end of Wittgenstein's life, this remark was not meant to be a late confession. It entertains the same kind of contrast as the one mentioned before; the same kind of contrast at play in such remarks as the following, which Wittgenstein is reported to have imparted in one of his lectures from the early 1930s: 'Aesthetics is descriptive. What it does is to *draw one's attention* to certain features, to place things side by side so as to exhibit these features' (AWL: 38); 'The reasons one gives for feeling satisfied have nothing to do with psychology. These, the aesthetic reasons, are given by placing things side by side, as in a court of law. If one gives *psychological* reasons for choosing a smile, those would not be reasons in aesthetics. They would be causes, not reasons. Stating a cause would be offering a hypothesis' (AWL: 39). Of course, these remarks are plainly reminiscent of Wittgenstein's own understanding of philosophy. Thus, he speaks of placing things side by side in aesthetics, a task that Wittgenstein was anxious to carry out in philosophy, irrespective of the field or section of language under his focus. And what he predicates of aesthetics, namely that it is descriptive, is what he did not stop predicating of philosophy. 'Our method', as he puts it in *The Blue and the Brown Books*, 'is *purely descriptive*; the descriptions we give are not hints of explanations' (BB: 125).

It is to be noticed that when Wittgenstein speaks of conceptual & aesthetic questions as what really grips him, and contrasts these with scientific ones, he does not set over against the scientific field two fields of investigations *the way he found them to be*. Of course, he felt passionately attracted to philosophy, but philosophy as he found it did not sport the kind of mesmerizing awe and dialectical piquancy it obtained in his hands, if only for himself. Recall that for Wittgenstein, philosophy 'surely *ought* to be completely simple, if it is the ultimate thing, independent of all experience, that you make it out to be.' Stressing the word *ought* here, I want to say: This requirement is not what Wittgenstein came across upon his way into philosophy; it is not anything that has been characterizing the field since the days of Plato, something that lured minds such as Wittgenstein and Bosanquet into an ongoing concern with its problems only to pursue them in their own individual ways. Rather this requirement really inheres in the deepest of the interest with which Wittgenstein approached this field and that of aesthetics alike. In other words, Wittgenstein did not so much discover in philosophy a realm of inquiries offering an additional succulence to his mind and interest as that he imposed on *philosophical* questions, i.e. on things traditionally so called—, imposed on them with all his might the kind of passionate interest that rendered these questions *purely conceptual* ones for him. Wittgenstein fashioned the philosophical landscape according to his own individual 'taste'. It is here, and in much the same way with respect to aesthetics, where he felt that his core interests could be *completely* satisfied, where he could claim that everything lies open to view, where no *new* truths need to be pronounced, where the redeeming word can be had and truly savoured without delving into psychological issues or hailing evolutionary stories. 'The exciting [*aufregende*] character of grammatical unclarity' (PO: 164)—*that* is what philosophy is, for Wittgenstein.

To impose upon philosophy the kind of interest, or need, that Wittgenstein deeply felt and nourished—this, indeed, must have enormous consequences for the way one talks and thinks about philosophy, its problems, and solutions. He thought it possible to (dis)solve philosophical puzzles such that what *in the end* matters is only our looking at language and our describing its various workings. And the way language works, symbolizes, functions, Wittgenstein promulgates, *is* not hidden, does not lie beneath its surface. But Wittgenstein *is* not *interested* in things hidden. It is his interest, as we shall see in more detail, which draws boundaries.

Wittgenstein cherished an idealized notion of philosophy, one that has been moulded by that singular interest on his part. The *complete* disappearing of a philosophical puzzle, in his own private quarters in the first instance, was always of uppermost importance to him, early and later. If we feel ourselves complete duffers at the philosophical business, then, Wittgenstein would say, it is all due to our failing to look at it from the correct point of view. There shall be a lot of talk in this book about how Wittgenstein presented his own point, how he used to talk about language and philosophical problems. But, then, to be sure, there is not only this talk on Wittgenstein's own part: there is also his own *doings*, his genuine efforts and struggles to come out *in the end* with nothing but descriptions of the language-games. To these efforts we shall pay due attention as well. For everything, once seen from Wittgenstein's vantage point, looks fine and well; the practice of his own doings, as we shall see, tells quite a different story.

1.2 A closer look at the contrast

Wittgenstein always took a genuine liking to articulating his 'philosophical' interest. He was, as regards that activity, not unlike many a bygone peer and thinker. Compared to present-day philosophers, however, he is nearly a solitary figure. Not truly accustomed to self-reflections, philosophers as we are, we are prone to interpret Wittgenstein's obsessive occupation with himself as the obvious signs of a morbid mind, of a man congenitally fated to self-absorption to such grotesque proportions that, in his light, our self-aggrandizing sanity acquires an added excellence. Yet, Wittgenstein was far less self-centred than his habits of mind might lead us to believe. Much given as he was to articulating his own interest, he never meant to see it in isolation from other worldly affairs and interests, but always 'by contrast with and against the background of' one or another of the bewitching forces and influences on our philosophical minds. Wittgenstein was a human being and no less prone to misunderstanding the workings of our language than we are.

The phrase 'by contrast with and against the background of' stems from the preface to the *Philosophical Investigation*, and an apt phrase it is. For now I wish to reserve it in the way just indicated, thus with respect to different interests and persuasions. The contrast at issue looms large in several passages quoted so far, as it does in many a passage to quote in the course of our investigations. But among all these passages the following one takes pride of place.

> Of course this is not a common way of looking at things. It is a purely geometric way of looking at things, as it were. One into which cause and effect do not enter.
>
> That is, I look at this language-game as autonomous. I merely want to describe it, or look at it, not justify it. (LWPP II: 40)

Wittgenstein is truly not interested in constructing a theory about the things he looks at; he does not want to construe the workings of language *as* caught up in one or another array of causal connections. Connections yes!—but no causal ones. So what are the connections like that Wittgenstein seeks to grasp? Well, in this book we shall have ample opportunity to see him asking what they look like, as we shall have ample opportunity to expound why it is far from easy to catch up with them. But whatever they are, Wittgenstein seeks to behold them in terms in which cause and effect do not enter. Now, of course, as far as the above passage is concerned, it leaves us in doubt as to how the indicated ways of looking bear upon each other. What exactly is it to look at the language *as* autonomous? Is such a way of looking already in force as soon as one suppresses the urge to look at the language-game in terms of cause and effect? That is, do the kinds of connections that Wittgenstein seeks to describe come into view already, if only hesitantly, upon suppressing the urge to look at things in terms of cause and effect? These are important questions, and in this book we cannot possibly allow ourselves to leave them unanswered. For now let us take notice of that tiny word "as" in Wittgenstein's remark 'I look at this language-game as autonomous.' It is a word of pivotal importance as it epitomizes an absolutely indelible moment in Wittgenstein's philosophical approach. The so-called autonomy of the language-game can be traced back all the way to what he brings to bear upon language in the shape of his philosophical interest. In other words, the autonomy of the grammatical connections that Wittgenstein seeks to describe, i.e. the so-called workings of our language, is in point of fact a reification accomplished by the kind of light in which he beholds language.

The above passage indicates two ways of looking at things, but should it necessarily be taken to suggest that these two ways definitely exclude each other? Saying that he *merely* wants to look at the language-game, Wittgenstein might be taken to maintain that it is all right to look upon it in a different way, namely in the way *he* does not *want* to look at it, thus *as* caught up in some causal nexus or other. Thus, Wittgenstein's own vantage point and the ones into which cause and effect enter (and matter most), as one should like to put it, might well be mutually exclusive perspectives in one and the same head but not necessarily within a community of quiet thinkers. Indeed, why not say that each member of such a community contributes to the hunt for an encompassing grasp of language? Science works in that way, so why should philosophy be an exception? A botanist deals with a dandelion according to the tenets and dictates of his discipline if not his own personal interests, and if the biochemist operates thus, so does the ecologist, each trying to provide for a distinctive but not necessarily rival story. So Wittgenstein's words, in the above passage, might well be taken to sustain the suggestion of a peaceful if not quiet cooperation among philosophers. Whereas he merely wants to describe language, or look at it, not justify it, other philosophers just are out for *more* than descriptions only; they do want to justify the language-game. These philosophers, then, in contrast to Wittgenstein himself, are not satisfied with descriptions *only* ('the botanist'), i.e. their redeeming word does not come in terms of mere descriptions but in what goes beyond them ('the biochemist'), thus beyond the ones that Wittgenstein aims for. So Wittgenstein and his fellow philosophers, or so the suggestion, might as well amicably trudge along the same path, up to the point where the former comes to a halt and begins to relish his descriptions, whereas the champions of cause and effect, in order to gratify their needs, have to make a few *more* steps.

But that is not how it is. The point here is that the connections that Wittgenstein wants to describe, or to behold, are not what his fellow philosophers have ever dreamt of wanting to explain. They have no perception of their special nature as long as they operate within the limited reach of their own vantage point, one that has placed its bets on explanations from the beginning. The light in which Wittgenstein beholds language is the light that *his* deeply felt need or interest for no *new* truths sheds on it. It is this beholding that renders the workings of language in his hands so entirely different from how his fellow philosophers and scientists alike take it—and treat it.

Of course, Wittgenstein says that he looks at *this* language-game as autonomous, that he merely wants to describe *it*, or look at it, not justify it, his suggestion being that he is about to investigate just one particular language-game, be it a type or token. Nevertheless, his way of looking is not an ever-shifting one, that is, it should not be thought that he looks at one language-game as autonomous, at another language-game as non-autonomous—as if he were committed to settle on the fixed point of his view each time according to the characteristic features of the language-game under investigation. As we have been indicating, the so-called autonomy of the language-game is rather not a feature *of* the language-game. We definitely misunderstand the *as* in Wittgenstein's 'I look at this language-game as autonomous' if we think that it is *because* of this language *being* autonomous that he looks at it as autonomous. To think along such lines about this *as* is to misunderstand what a point of view *is*, at least for Wittgenstein. Generally speaking, he wants to describe, and, surely, to describe is what one can do as well from a point of view that ultimately aims at giving explanations. But Wittgenstein is not interested in giving explanations in the end; he merely wants to describe, and the indicated difference is what he enunciates by saying that he looks at the language-game *as* autonomous. And it is only for philosophical reasons that he looks at the language-game thus, for his description must take the place of *all* explanation and receive its light, that is to say its purpose, from the philosophical problems. Indeed, what many a passage indicates, as we shall see and enlarge upon in this book, is the downright exclusive character of the light in which Wittgenstein looks at language and tries to describe its workings. Let us consider the following passage:

> Often it is only when we suppress the question "Why?" that we become aware of those important facts, which then, in the course of our investigations, lead to an answer. (PI: 471)

The question that Wittgenstein addresses here is one that is ready to take hold of our *complete* thinking the moment we begin to philosophize. Being a ubiquitous device ruling and shaping what Wittgenstein intimates as the common way of looking at things, it lies on the tip of our tongues. Scientists revel in it and would rather sacrifice the world than renounce the question. But so it is with us, mortals as we are in the daily walk of life: we would no doubt have a hard time knowing our way about should we be forced to forsake it. The reason for this is that the question reifies within a whole series of attitudes and expectations cutting as deeply into our hold on the world as language itself does. The question partakes of our customary grip on the world at large, on its ingredients, on the people around us and on them afar. (And if an answer to it compares badly to our common conception of the world, this, indeed, does not demote the importance that the why-question has for us.) "Why?" rocks our tongues—and so it does in moments of philosophy. Should we be forced to suppress it precisely *then*, thus in a field of investigation where we have difficulties anyway in finding our way about, surely, we would sense a complete loss of control on the subject matter. We would simply stop knowing what philosophy is all about.

Of course, given the above passage, it is tempting to conjecture that for Wittgenstein philosophy begins with suppressing the why-question. But that is not exactly how it is. There is a kind of beginning with the suppression of the why-questions, but this does not mean that for Wittgenstein philosophy begins with an awareness of particular facts that suffuses his mind upon this suppression. For him, philosophy rather begins the moment a deep disquietude of a particular nature suffuses his mind. Wittgenstein does not enter the philosophical stage merely in order to become aware of particular facts, that is, to take a real interest in them and to let them play a part in his efforts to give descriptions of our language. A famous bon mot of him says that 'philosophy is a battle against the bewitchment of our understanding by the resources of our language' (PI: 109). To be sure, then, the suggestion of these words is *not* that, in order to do philosophy properly, we should first battle against the bewitching force of our language so as to keep it at bay. The suggestion rather is that philosophy *is* a battle against this bewitching force. At least that is what it is for Wittgenstein: without the bewitchment there is nothing for him to philosophize about. Without a bewitching force pressing hard on his mind there is, for him, no *becoming* aware of particular facts by suppressing the why-question. Without a bewitchment of his mind there is no *redeeming* effect of the word that he hankers after.

In the *Philosophical Investigations*, Wittgenstein, in fair and plain enough language, harps again and again on the contrast intimated here. In §109 it runs as follows: 'philosophical problems are solved … by looking into the workings of our language, and that in such a way as to make us recognize those workings: *in opposition to* an urge to misunderstand them.'[17] Thus, although Wittgenstein beholds language in a particular light, this beholding loses its point *completely* if there were not another light, precisely the one in which the why-question thrives and forces itself upon us. What the passage of the why-question entertains, then, is the contrast of which we have spoken before. Suppressing the why-questions

---

17 Translation amended.

28

brings about a change of mind, as Wittgenstein seems to suggest. Having found ourselves previously gazing at one fact or another, only to give it pride of place in a picture into which cause and effect enter, we now see for the first time those facts that do matter to us in philosophy. But this does not mean that our former frame of mind is no longer in force. On the contrary. We ourselves do not so much cultivate this frame of mind as that it obtrudes itself upon us, in moments of philosophy, only to henceforth command our thinking in its entirety. It forces itself upon us as an extremely powerful moment of understanding. The second thing to notice is that Wittgenstein, in the passage that entertains the why-question, is indeed quite suggestive of philosophy being a rather relaxed and straightforward intellectual occupation: do not bother about the why-question, just suppress it and all will be well. But how suppress it, that is, what does the suppressing, and—how keep it suppressed? And are we not supposed to destroy houses of cards (PI: 118), rather than merely *suppressing* a major source giving rise to such decrepit constructions?

These are important questions, which shall occupy our minds in the course of this book. For the moment we should emphasize the crucial importance of *the urge to explain* in Wittgenstein's dialectical enterprise: take it away, and all comes to naught. *All*, as there is no incentive left for Wittgenstein to philosophize, no need for him *to describe* our language. Wittgenstein made no bones about the fact that he is 'interested in language only insofar as it gives [him] trouble' (AWL: 97), and he did not bother to go so far as to advise that 'you must allow yourself to be dragged into the mire' (AWL: 109).[18] And yet, among his commentators, it is not an uncommon practice to counsel advice, allegedly on Wittgenstein's behalf, to the effect that we had better *not* drag ourselves into the mire. Consider, for instance, what Joachim Schulte writes.

Surprisingly, Wittgenstein offers us a 'solution': unsurprisingly, it amounts to getting rid of or escaping from the system. The solution is adumbrated in remarks like *PI* §281 ('only of a living human being and what resembles (behaves like) a living human being can one say: it has sensations; it sees;…'), §286 ('one does not comfort the hand, but the sufferer: one looks into his face'), §287 (on how one is 'filled with pity *for this man*'), §360 ('We only say of a human being and what is like one that it thinks', etc.), as well as a few scattered remarks in his later manuscripts on the philosophy of psychology. To all appearances these remarks contain the following sort of advice: in doing philosophy, avoid all ways of talking that might get you into the sort of trouble described in my

---

18 Cf. 'When philosophizing you have to descend into the old chaos & feel at home there' (CV: 74).

book. One suspects that this kind of advice might amount to suggesting that you should opt out of philosophy as long as you have a chance; or else it might catch up with you.[19]

But why believe that the remarks (to which Schulte refers) contain, 'to all appearances', the following sort of advice: 'in doing philosophy, avoid all ways of talking that might get you into the sort of trouble described in my book'? Why believe so? What is the use of walking the safe paths in life? What is the use of walking the safe paths in philosophy, if philosophy, according to Wittgenstein, is indeed 'a battle against the bewitchment of our understanding by the resources of our language'? Wittgenstein's advice, I think, amounts to this: please opt out of philosophy if you do not want bumps and boils on your *own* head; opt out of it as long as you think of it as a discipline in which safe paths exist and can be pointed to as Jacob's ladder to truth and real understanding? However, this advice is more properly regarded as a warning, for Wittgenstein himself never meant 'to escape' from 'the system'; if a way of thinking leads us astray in philosophy, his own person not excluded, he feels attracted to it like the devil and as by hellfire driven to round it up and to *destroy* it—for the sanity of his own mind and thinking.

'Wittgenstein's advice' is a choice phrase among his commentators. In his *Renewing Philosophy*, Putnam writes:

> It is precisely the big philosophical notions to which Wittgenstein wishes to apply the notion of a family resemblance. On Rush Rhees's reading (and I am convinced he is right), what Wittgenstein is telling us is that referring uses don't have an "essence"; there isn't some one thing which can be called referring. There are overlapping similarities between one sort of referring and the next, that is all. This is why, for example, Wittgenstein is not puzzled, as many philosophers are, about how we can "refer" to abstract entities. After all, we are not causally attached to the number three, so how can we refer to it? Indeed, do we know that there is such an object at all? For Wittgenstein the fact is that the use of number words is simply a different use from the use of words like *cow*. Stop calling three an "object" or an "abstract entity" and look at the way number words are used, is his advice.[20]

In this passage, Putnam not only says that Wittgenstein is not puzzled; he also explains why he is not puzzled. Moreover, we had better stop calling three an 'object' or an 'abstract entity' and look at the way number words are used—this apparently being a word of advice that Wittgenstein has sought to impart on us. Now such sayings, I think, conspire to make up something utterly fundamental

---

19 Joachim Schulte, 'Privacy', in Oskari Kuusela and Marie McGinn, eds., *The Oxford Handbook of Wittgenstein* (Oxford: Oxford University Press, 2011), 448f.

20 Hilary Putnam, *Renewing Philosophy* (Cambridge, Mass: Harvard University Press, 1992), 167f.

in the way one interprets Wittgenstein's philosophy. But was he really not puzzled? And did his advice really take on such a drastic form as Putnam suggests?

I think that the following words from Wittgenstein's *Nachlass* may serve us well in finding an answer to these questions:

> I am trying to hold the puzzlement as long as possible; Whereas you—the mathematician—get rid of it as quickly as possible.
>
> My talent consists in being capable of being puzzled when the puzzlement has glided off your mind. I'm able to hold the puzzlement when it has slipped through your hands (and you therefore think, you are clear.)
>
> The art of the philosopher is not to be cheated out of his puzzlement before it's really cleared up. (MS 157b: 30vf.)

The suggestion underlying Putnam's words 'Stop calling three an "object" or an "abstract entity" and look at the way number words are used' is this: stop being puzzled and look at the language-game. But this approach seems tantamount to cheating. To stop being puzzled in the way Putnam suggests that Wittgenstein counsels us is to let the puzzlement glide off without aspiring to know one's way about in the ways of the puzzlement. There is little if anything in Putnam's words to suggest that there is a very fine legacy to be received from knowing what Wittgenstein's calls 'a tracing of the physiognomy of every error'.[21] The good, according to Putnam, rather lies in turning one's back upon the confusion, only to devote oneself to the describing of the language-game.

But the reason why Wittgenstein devotes himself to the describing of the language-game lies in the nature of the puzzlement. Describing language-games is part of the cure. But not so according to Putnam: it comes too late. For Putnam, describing is an activity no longer informed by the puzzlement. One has already stopped being puzzled before it comes to the describing. But why describe language, now that one is no longer puzzled? And how describe it, now that one is no longer puzzled? And what did at last stop the puzzlement, when the describing of the language-game has not yet begun? To stop being puzzled in the way Putnam suggests that Wittgenstein counsels us is to let the puzzlement glide off without letting it be the ultimate incentive behind one's descriptions.

Wittgenstein *is* puzzled, not for a moment or two, nor when he chances upon Russell going to church, but throughout the entire dialectical process. That is to

---

21 'One of the most important tasks is to express all false thought process so characteristically that the reader says, "Yes, that's exactly the way I meant it". To make a tracing of the physiognomy of every error' (PO: 165).

say, throughout the activity of working his way up and through whatever stage or step it has, or comes to have. We, commentators, myself not excluded, may well be spurred to discern in Wittgenstein's proceedings a kind of symmetry, even a system, or a method or two. We do nonetheless well not to forget that for Wittgenstein *doing* philosophy has no mechanical revolvency. There is for him, most of all, no mechanical discharging of his own puzzlement. Rather than trying to destroy a malicious thing, he treats it with the utmost care as if to preserve a precious stone. In the course of his dialectical proceedings, this puzzlement comes alive, grows, and expands, obtaining a scope and dimension that take the better part of him. But while allowing his mind to be duly swamped in it, Wittgenstein never forgets its bewitching force and influence, any more than what one ends up telling the world should one lose one's control over the whole process. He nourishes his own puzzlement and feeds on it, only to dissolve it in the end. This obsessive and delicate preserving and persevering of his puzzlement is a true talent rendering his philosophy so unmistakably his and anything but mechanical. Stop being puzzled and look at the way words are being used: This, for Wittgenstein, is to obviate the need to be concerned with philosophy at all.

*

Wittgenstein, in the passage in which he addresses the question "Why?", speaks of facts, of important facts even. Facts, that is, of which we become aware when we suppress the question "Why?" and which then, 'in the course of our investigations, lead to an answer' (PI: 471). What kinds of facts Wittgenstein is thinking of here we do yet not know. But facts they are in his eyes and it is important to bear that in mind, in as much as he looks at the language-game *as* autonomous. What he seeks to describe is what we have never dreamt of explaining, in our common way of looking at things. On the other hand, what we seek to explain is surely not what Wittgenstein wants to describe. We both speak of the language-game, and yet, we do not talk about one and the same thing. But, as one may want to ask, is this way of drawing the contrast between Wittgenstein's uncommon way of looking at things and our own way of doing so perhaps not far too stark, hence confusing? Is Wittgenstein himself not at times clearly suggestive of our being most anxious to explain what he wants to describe only. Indeed, does the following passage not furnish a good example of Wittgenstein being thus suggestive?

> Our mistake is to look for an explanation where we ought to regard the facts as 'protophenomena' ['*Urphänomene*']. That is, where we ought to say: *this is the language-game that is being played*. (PI: 654)

The very notion of *Urphänomen*, which Wittgenstein brings positively into account here as far as his own philosophy is concerned, adds much to the suggestion that his way of looking is not common. The notion is reminiscent of Goethe, an author of whom Wittgenstein thought highly, and read intensively every now and then. But unlike Goethe, who took to the notion of *Urphänomen* as a fundamental element in his so-called morphology, Wittgenstein did not conceive of any fact or affair, worldly or not, as an *Urphänomen* in itself.[22] Speaking of *facts* that 'we ought to regard as *Urphänomene*', Wittgenstein's suggestion clearly is that they are not *Urphänomene* simpliciter, but hold this attribute on account of his way of looking upon things. There is an *as* at work in the above passage, as there is in 'I look at this language-game as autonomous', and, indeed, the one at work in the above passage is precisely the one that the latter entertains. The *as* makes all the difference; it renders Wittgenstein's way of looking so much different from ours. His draws limits, but no less than our view. Wittgenstein looks at the *language-game* as autonomous, that is, he does not look at the world at large as autonomous. It is only one or another part of it that he singles out for consideration and that he looks at as autonomous, for reasons of philosophy and for such reasons only. He calls such a part: a language-game.

For us, however, the world, at large, is a perfectly continuous whole: we look at it *as* governed by natural laws and causal connections, a way of looking that does not stop short of any language-game.[23] So we too draw limits. Wittgenstein did not *discover* that the language-game *is* autonomous, only to deal with it accordingly. But we, proud disciples of the common cause, did not *discover* anything to the contrary either, only to look at the world as a perfectly continuous affair. It is in the eye of the beholder that facts pass as *Urphänomene*, or not. And with the tiny *as* comes a big *ought*: 'Our mistake is to look for an explanation where we ought to regard the facts as *Urphänomene*.' If we admit that the point of this *ought* resides in the contrast between Wittgenstein's uncommon way of looking and our common way of doing so, between his need to describe and our urge to explain, we also see that he does not look at the language-game *tout court*.

But what are we to make of Wittgenstein's gesture in the above passage—'*this* is the language-game that is being played'? What does *he* point at? What *we* do see? Is it one and the same thing? Is he pointing at a fact that we want to explain and that Wittgenstein wants to describe only? Of course, the notion of language-

---

22 Of course, this claim regarding Goethe requires both explanation and differentiation, which I shall not presume to undertake in this book.

23 See Chapters 4 and 5 for more on this issue.

game has long since become common usage among philosophers and scientists alike, hence a perfect source of confusion, if only because it is not unusual at all of philosophers, so-called expert commentators on Wittgenstein not excluded, to think as much about the role of description in Wittgenstein's philosophy as astrophysicists and other black hole pundits tend to do. Generally speaking, Wittgenstein's language-games are considered to be things that he wants to describe only, to the effect that his descriptions are regarded as being no more than *preliminary steps* with respect to our explanatory accounts of these things. But Wittgenstein's descriptions of the language-games are also considered to be *preliminary steps* only, with respect to our explanatory accounts of these things, to the effect that his language-games are regarded as things that he wants to describe only and that we want to explain at last. And yet, Wittgenstein's descriptions could be said to be *preliminary steps* only within one and the same way of looking at things, namely his. Thus, a Wittgensteinian description of the language-game may be said to be preliminary in the sense that one has furnished a *sketchy* description only (see below) *within* that way of looking at things that treats the language-game as autonomous and that seeks to describe its grammatical commerce more fully than it has done so far. And, indeed, such a more fully described language-game may in turn be said to be preliminary even now, as long as it awaits integration into the kind of constellation that completes a Wittgensteinian procedure, namely one *übersichtliche Darstellung* (PI: 122) or another (see below), that is to say, a constellation for which each description is precisely designed and in which it can play its conclusive role *as a description*. So it is definitely false, and downright misleading, to speak of Wittgenstein's descriptions as preliminary steps with respect to efforts to explain the language-game. Recall here the following remark: 'the descriptions we give are not hints of explanations' (BB: 125). Not being hints of explanations, then, Wittgenstein's descriptions are not preparatory in the sense that they possess the kind of logical multiplicity that requires an explanation to render matters complete. Being the kind of descriptions they are, and being the kind of descriptions they are meant to be, the only logical multiplicity they possess is the one that requires other *descriptions* alongside themselves, just in order to contrive one *übersichtliche Darstellung* or another.

If Wittgenstein's descriptions are not hints of explanation it is because they *cannot* be preparatory in the suggested sense. Promulgating that 'all *explanation* must disappear, and description alone must take its place', Wittgenstein really speaks of all explanation that *must* disappear in the single most important sense that the *possibility* of any explanations must disappear, in philosophy. He speaks of a possibility that is guaranteed, and can be guaranteed only, by altering one's way of looking at the world. Description does not take the place of all explanation when one has merely stopped giving explanations, only to furnish descriptions henceforth. For these descriptions could still be said to be preparatory with respect to the possibility of explanation. And as long as these descriptions are operated on, one still operates within one's old way of looking. On the other hand, one's new way of looking at language should not give rise to the possibility of such descriptions to which explanations could be attached in principle, for then one has not changed one's way of looking after all, and one investigates the language-game in a way that is still altogether different from Wittgenstein's own way of doing so, in spite of appearances and in spite of whatever family resemblance that may be said to obtain between one's own terminology and that of Wittgenstein. Of course, one may well use notions such as language-game, grammatical rule, and *Lebensform*; and it is certainly not forbidden to use the notion of language even. That is, one may well make use of such notions in order to weave them into an evolutionary story about, for instance, human thinking. But the moment one brings Wittgenstein's *philosophy* into this story, one had better reminds oneself (or one's readers, for that matter) of the fact that all the family resemblance that one's notions bear to Wittgenstein's own notions transpires at level of the printed letter only.

So, then, we may well have before us the 'same' facts upon which Wittgenstein's eyes rest. And yet, we may for all his drawing of our attention fail to see what Wittgenstein sees, for he looks at these facts as part of an autonomous edifice. He is not out for new truths, but facts that, he says, we have always somehow known; so the truths upon which his eyes rest are not seen without more ado, for they are seen as part of an autonomous edifice. Although we can often find Wittgenstein pointing at one language-game or another while he is making such famous exclamations as '*this* what we call calculating'—or requesting, seeing, thanking, cursing, greeting, praying, reposting, etc., what he is drawing our attention to comes typically at such junctures in his hunt for description where he himself is still out for the particularities of the language-game. His searching has, typically, not reached its 'final notching' when he exclaims that *this* is what we call, say, calculating. That is, what he is pointing at is, typically, not even available to himself with the richness of detail of the workings of the language-game that he is anxious to have before his eyes. The very point of such gestures as 'this is what we call calculating' or 'this is the language-game that is being played', then, once addressed to us, does not lie in our having overlooked a few details but in our failure to look at certain facts differently.

Thus, even if we, in our common way of looking at things, are confronted with such richness of detail as Wittgenstein seeks to have before him, this will not readily keep us from wanting to *explain* the language-game in terms of what we take to be more primary facts. And why not? No mere facts, however great and spectacular, can tell us that we *ought* to look at them differently.

Of course, as disciples of the common cause, in whose minds and brains the question "Why?" reigns uppermost, we find it downright ridiculous to stop short of certain facts, to ask no further than the very thing to explain. And yet, for Wittgenstein, there are no matters of fact more primary, more ultimate, or more fundamental than a fact such as that *this* is the language-game that is being played and that *this* and *that* way of doing things with words is what we call e.g. calculating. For us, however, incurable votaries of asking "Why?", the language-game denotes a state of affairs that is caught up in the causal web of multifarious connections as much as anything in the world. It can be investigated from a causal point of view as it signifies a point in that web that is thoroughly continuous with whatever other point in it. Brains figure in that picture of connections, and perhaps we feel that cannot do without so-called mental episodes. But if we cannot do without them it is for their causal efficacy, for their role in the picture of causal connections. Now all this seems to suggest a kind of symmetry in the contrast between Wittgenstein's uncommon way of looking and our common way of doing so. And yet, should we, in emulation of Wittgenstein's own example, want so much as to contemplate our philosophical interest and to enunciate our own philosophical needs and way of looking at things, it would sorely lack the kind of contrast at work in Wittgenstein's own case. We would never dream of enunciating our interest to the effect that *we ought* to go beyond such facts as *Urphänomene*, simply because they do not obtain in our picture. For us, there is no urge that plays tricks on our minds, a voice that keeps inculcating the notion that we must stop short of certain *facts*, that we ought not to ask for facts beyond the facts of the thing to explain. For Wittgenstein's part, however, he cannot do without the urge to explain *himself*, for everything would be lost for him without it. There is, in other words, a strong asymmetry in the contrast at work in his way of looking at things. It cannot simply be reversed so as to obtain an appropriate presentation of the so-called common way of looking at things.

This brings us to another word on Goethe and Wittgenstein here. In his *Principles of Linguistic Philosophy*, a book originally planned to give voice to Wittgenstein's philosophy in as lucid a presentation as its author was capable of giving, Waismann writes that 'our thought here marches with certain views of Goethe's which he expressed in the Metamorphosis of Plants.'[24] Indeed, there are fascinating parallels between Goethe and Wittgenstein. As Monk writes in his biography on Wittgenstein:

---

24 Friedrich Waismann, *The Principles of Linguistic Philosophy*, ed. R. Harré (London: Macmillan Press,1997), 80.

Goethe's morphology had as its motivation a disgust with mechanism of Newtonian science; he wanted to replace this dead, mechanical, study with a discipline that sought to 'recognize living forms *as such*, to see in context their visible and tangible parts, to perceive them as *manifestations* of something within'.

Wittgenstein's philosophical method, which replaces theory with 'the synopsis of trivialities', is in this same tradition.[25]

Put thus, at least one parallel is not to be overlooked: both Goethe and Wittgenstein sought 'to replace' one thing with another thing. And yet, this phrasing tends to overlook an important difference between the two men. Wittgenstein, not unlike Goethe himself, most certainly can be said to have been disgusted with 'the scientific way of asking and answering questions.'[26] In spite of this disgust, however, Wittgenstein, and much unlike Goethe, every now and then felt the sharp edge of the urge to be won over by this way of asking and answering questions in himself. In other words, Wittgenstein, unlike Goethe, endeavoured to understand the world (of language) '*in opposition to* an urge to misunderstand its workings'— an urge of which he was not free himself. As for Goethe, *his* investigations may well be said to receive their light, that is to say their purpose, from his disgust with the Newtonian way of asking and answering questions, or at least partly so. But this disgust did not seem to have entered into his mind in the shape of an urge to ask and answer questions in this way himself. Although the urge to explain was in an important sense a serious impediment to Wittgenstein's mind and thinking, it provided him at the same time, and precisely because of it, with the power and *Pathos* that propelled his philosophical enterprise at last. 'One needs to conquer the prejudice', he writes, 'and yet, without it one is incapable of doing philosophy.'[27] Indeed, 'work on philosophy', as Wittgenstein also writes, 'is really more work on oneself. On one's own conception. On how one sees things. (And what one demands of them.)' (CV: 24). Goethe would no doubt concur whole-heartedly.

*

We should do well to cast more light on the contrast at the heart of Wittgenstein's philosophy, this time by taking up another famous credo, namely the one saying that philosophy leaves everything as it is.

---

25 Ray Monk, *Ludwig Wittgenstein – The Duty Of Genius* (London: Vintage, 1991), 303.
26 Cf. 'I am in a sense making propaganda for one style of thinking as opposed to another. I am honestly disgusted with the other' (LA: 28).
27 MS 124: 18.

There are numerous ways in which one can leave everything as it is. Wittgenstein's famous credo, though, concerns only the person who struggles with particular puzzles, namely the one who wants to justify, who feels the pull to move away from ordinary language to an allegedly more primary realm. Thus, to begin with, the credo applies by no means to the person who is simply lost to doing philosophy, whose head remains a frosty and torpid affair in the face of a philosophical conundrum. Such a person does not leave everything as it is in Wittgenstein's sense of the word, although he, out of sheer lack of cerebral sensibility, might well be said to leave much as it is. But there is another type of person to whom Wittgenstein's credo does not apply, and this person is a true Everyman: Caught up in the everyday walk of life, he merely avails himself of his words and sentences without much ado, a seemingly simple and ordinary occupation. In doing so, everything is left as it is in an important sense of the word, but when Wittgenstein, in his capacity as philosopher, wants to leave everything as it is, this activity, for that is what it is, does not consist of availing himself of his everyday language the way we do. It rather consists of *paying close attention to* this daily employment, of giving descriptions of this employment: of how our language connects up with our *Lebensform*, or this form with us and our language. Leaving everything as it is seems to be a most unchallenging, lazy if not lousy pastime, and yet, it tends to wear one out during the course of the day. Recall that Wittgenstein's descriptions of language receive their light, that is to say their purpose, from the philosophical problems. In terms of his famous credo, this means that Wittgenstein's way of describing our language leaves everything as it is only when it encroaches upon an activity prompted by the urge to move away from ordinary language (in philosophy). In other words, one needs to heed the exhortation to leave everything as it is only when one fails to do so *at the start*. Allow your puzzlement to carry your mind away from the ordinary use language and familiarize yourself with the peculiar realms and quarters where your puzzlement leads you to—the quarters where metaphysics is made and its melting pot is kept scalding. For only then, as Wittgenstein's suggests in another famous passage, have you created for yourself the condition to bring words *back* from their so-called metaphysical to the correct/normal use in language.

This passage is reminiscent of the one discussed earlier where Wittgenstein says that the *results* of philosophy *must* be simple, but philosophizing itself has to be as complicated as the knots it unties. Now simplicity, as Wittgenstein conceives it, may just come in the guise of answers that must strike a very odd if not repugnant chord in the head of many a philosopher, for they, the answers, *must* be homespun and ordinary/trivial. But, of course, what *is* homespun? What *is* trivial? The homespun (or the ordinary/trivial), at least in Wittgenstein's dialectical edifice, obviously stands in opposition to metaphysics. But, then, what *is* metaphysics? Whatever the term amounts to in Wittgenstein's philosophy, we obviously do not leave everything as it is when we become metaphysicians first and leave it at that. But we are already on our way of leaving everything as it is when we give free rein to the urge to explain first and when we take a real fancy to the dreaming episodes that metaphysicians have and cherish. And the more consciously we do this and similar things for ourselves, the more perceptive we become of the bewitching influences that our language is capable of exerting on us, hence what philosophy *ought* to be. The above passage exemplifies what I have called Wittgenstein's dialectical circle, the closing of which comes in terms of descriptions of our ordinary language only. And although many of these passages leave us with a miscellany of questions, we should by now at least be observant of the following. Wittgenstein is interested in the correct/normal use of our language, but not *without further ado*. He wants to describe, he wants to leave everything as it is, but not *without further ado*. In *PI* §116, which appears to be a refined version of the above passage, Wittgenstein articulates his philosophical aim as follows:

> When philosophers use a word—"knowledge", "being", "object", "I", "proposition", "name"—and try to grasp the *essence* of the thing, one must always ask oneself: is the word ever actually used in this way in the language-game which is its original home?—
> What *we* do is to bring words back from their metaphysical use to their everyday use.

In this passage, too, Wittgenstein speaks of bringing words back from their metaphysical use to what he here calls their everyday use. But now, as if to bring his point into sharper relief, he entertains the notion of essence: the metaphysician tries to grasp the *essence* of all kinds of things. But, then, what about Wittgenstein himself? Is he not out for essence as well? Well, contrary to the suggestion of the above passage, he definitely tries to grasp it no less than the metaphysician. Wittgenstein *also* wants 'to understand the essence of language – its function, its structure' (PI: 92)[28]—'yet *this*', as he hastens to add, 'is not what [the metaphysician] 'has in view.' What Wittgenstein has in view is the homespun, the trivial, the ordinary use of language, but not *tout court*. For the kind of essence that Wittgenstein has in view is what he does not have in view without the kind of essence that the metaphysician has in view—that is, without *the metaphysician in himself*. Whatever exactly it is that the metaphysician tries to grasp, it is what he has in view as a result of some misunderstandings of the workings of our language, its function, *its essence*. But this function, this essence, is what Wittgenstein has in view on account of these misunderstandings. It is what seems to come into view as a result of the effort to do away with the kinds of misunderstandings underlying the grand aspirations of the metaphysician. What Wittgenstein has in view, then, is an essence that is relative to the kind that the metaphysician has in view—that is, relative to the metaphysician's fancies and aspirations. What the metaphysician aspires to is an essence laying claim to being absolute, whereas Wittgenstein's answer to the metaphysician's misunderstandings lays claim to be the *real* essence. It is real and yet relative in the intimated sense, but also in the sense that the homespun/trivial is not absolute, for the real is what it is but need not necessarily be the way it manifests itself in our language.

Wittgenstein wants to leave everything as it *is*, but what *is*: the essence of language, its function, its structure, does not come into view simpliciter. The metaphysician—an old man he seems to be, no longer of this world—is ready to take hold of our more contemplative moments in life because he dwells in most of us, worldly users of our language as we are. He, then, precisely the metaphysician in the guise of Wittgenstein's Tractarian self, is dead sure that his view makes perfect sense. But so is (later) Wittgenstein himself as regards his own view, which capitalizes so much on the metaphysician's flights of fancies and aspirations. The metaphysician, though, for his part, believes that he can pursue his search perfectly well, irrespective of whether Wittgenstein's own wisdom and aspiration to leave everything as it is are being practised upon his head. Whereas Wittgenstein describes his own *purpose* as that of bringing words *back* from their metaphysical use to their everyday use, the metaphysician, for his part, does not seek to bring words *away* from their everyday use so as to grasp essence, at least not intentionally so.

Indeed, what sounds through, at times most loudly, in Wittgenstein's ruminations on his own philosophical interest is another contrast, namely, the *sure*

---

28 I have translated the word *Wesen* with "essence" so as to have a uniform and more perspicuous correspondence with *PI* §96.

success of its execution on the real playground and the sure and total bankruptcy of the philosophy of his polar opposite, i.e., the metaphysician's. Wittgenstein never presents his polar opposite as someone who *has* ever succeeded in grasping the essence of language, but always as someone who constantly plugs away at what he has in view (cf. PI: 116). Of course, Wittgenstein needs to try his hand at the redeeming word as well, but his trying is no *trying out,* as if the effect of his word is at last a matter of unreserved surprise. Presenting his own philosophy as a healthy and feasible enterprise, Wittgenstein represents that of his polar opposite as a hopeless affair, doomed to fail right from the beginning. And these two things hang together, most intimately. For what renders the metaphysician's business a predestined failure, right from the beginning, is laid down by the very *form* of Wittgenstein's dialectical thinking. The feasibility of his philosophy is as certain as the hopelessness of the metaphysician's wisdom and aspirations. Wittgenstein seeks to describe our language, but not tout court, for the *Wichtigkeit* of his descriptions is had at the expense of the metaphysician's aims and doings. Of course, all this requires further elaboration.

Wittgenstein's verdict is that the metaphysician simply labours under the *illusion* that there is such a thing as *the* possibility of language and that it falls to the lot of philosophy to grasp it, that is, its incomparable essences. As he puts it in the *Investigations*:

> We are under the illusion that what is peculiar, profound, essential to us in our investigation resides in its trying to grasp the incomparable essence of language. That is, the order existing between the concepts of proposition, word, proof, truth, experience, and so forth. This order is a *super*-order between—so to speak—*super*-concepts. Whereas, in fact, if the words "language", "experience", "world", have a use, it must be as humble a one as that of the words "table", "lamp", "door". (PI: 97)

The metaphysician is under the spell of an illusion that finds its full expanse and expression in the form of precisely the kind of investigation *it* envisages and *he* labours under. It is this spell, rather than the investigation itself, that makes it impossible for him to think of any philosophical investigation, worthy of the name, other than his own. This spell commands the metaphysician completely, priming his mind with the conception of the possibility of a philosophical investigation to the exclusion of the possibility of whatever other philosophical investigation. But as exclusive as the metaphysician holds his investigations to be, so does Wittgenstein look at his own investigations. In the above passage, he sets the super-concepts of the metaphysician over against their humble use: 'if the words "language", "experience", "world", have a use', he pronounces, 'it must be as humble a one as that of the words "table", "lamp", "door"'. Perhaps, this remark does not strike a particularly humble note itself, its modal force is nonetheless of pivotal importance and not an aspect to be belittled, for it expresses an exclusiveness on which Wittgenstein's entire later philosophy stands, thrives, and destroys.

We have just witnessed how confidently Wittgenstein writes about the feasibility of his own programme for philosophy. The possibility of his philosophy is the feasibility of the kinds of results that it has in view. Its possibility is a kind of predetermination of what these results *must* look like. And given that these results receive their light, that is to say their purpose, from the philosophical problems, the possibility of Wittgenstein's philosophy is at the same time a predetermination of the fate of all philosophies hankering after the essence of things, i.e. after their *incomparable* essences. It much seems that Wittgenstein seeks to wreak havoc with the entire motley of age-old *expectations* that philosophers have always fostered, and, no doubt, still foster.

> One of the greatest impediments for philosophy is the expectation of new, deep/unheard of/ elucidations. (PO: 179)

The results that Wittgenstein's philosophy has *in view* are unlike those of other philosophers, for he does not want to espouse *new* truth. Whereas his fellow philosophers want to reach for the (sublime) stars (cf. PI: 38, 89, 94), Wittgenstein, perfectly acquainted with these needs and strong inclinations himself, seeks to overcome them, in his own private quarters in the first place, by standing up for the polar opposite of the sublime: the humble, the trivial, the homespun (*hausbacken*), the plain and everyday run and usage of our language. But that only means that Wittgenstein does have his own expectations, namely that his manner of espousing the ordinary can be done. There is something *essential* about metaphysician's investigation—as there is about Wittgenstein's.

> It is […] of the essence of our investigations that we do not seek to learn anything *new* by it. We want to *understand* something that is already in plain view. For *this* is what we seem in some sense not to understand. (PI: 89)

> The problems are solved, not by coming up with new discoveries, but by assembling what we have long been familiar with. (PI: 109)

Of course, if it is just this plain and humble thing, this run of the mill usage of our own words and sentences, in whose drift and centre we stand and persevere all day long, and with which we seem to be familiar more than with anything else in the world, then, a philosophy that aims at having no more before its eyes than this ordinary run and usage so as to indulge in *understanding* its ordinariness seems doomed to succeed by default. Perhaps we do not see yet how this kind of success implies guaranteed bankruptcy of the philosophy of its polar opposites; on the other hand, as we should like to add, there can hardly be anything redeeming in *understanding* the ordinary run of our words and sentences. And that is precisely where Wittgenstein begins to demur and to place the crux of his 'argument'. For the main obstacle in our achieving this kind of understanding, as he suggests in the above passage, lies in our not understanding that the redeeming word in philosophy comes in the guise of the ordinary only, the humble. This obstacle is, among other things, a curious cloud of forgetfulness, one that darkens our thoughts and plunges us into a realm in which our everyday walk of life, above all our own word usage, is denied its proper importance. But this obstacle, as Wittgenstein implies above, is one that can be overcome and that is well worth overcoming. Just as we can become oblivious of the significance of the humble, of the plain and down-to-earth usage of our own language, that is, in moments of philosophy, so we can turn back to the rough ground and 'look and see' what our words and sentences do and what they ultimately pertain to. Indeed, the confident tone of voice with which Wittgenstein talks about his philosophical enterprise, a voice much reminiscent of the *Tractatus*, is surely no lullaby. It should alert us, especially when it comes to such remarks as this: 'Something that one knows when nobody asks us, but no longer knows when one is asked to explain it, is something that has to be *called to mind [besinnen]*' (PI: 89).

These words, borrowing heavily from Augustine's *Confessions*, are certainly chosen with great care, as most of Wittgenstein's words are. Nevertheless, or perhaps precisely due to his assiduousness, they give rise to various questions. For in what sense, to begin with, can we, users of our own language, be said to *know* the kinds of things that Wittgenstein seeks to have before his eyes: the humble, the trivial? Certainly, we do not know the humble *as* the humble, the trivial *as* trivial. It is Wittgenstein who calls upon such notions, employing them as pivotal characterizations of his dialectical edifice in which the so-called sublime makes up for the other pole in the kind of contrast on which it stands. This point is worth emphasizing for two reasons. First, what is the humble—the homespun, the trivial, ordinary—if the humble is what it is only in contrast to the sublime?—which is not sublime after all, but a mere house of cards in sublime disguise (PI: 118). Second, 'I look at this language-game as autonomous.' What is being looked at as autonomous is the so-called humble, the workings of an ordinary piece of language. Wittgenstein's uncommon way of looking harbours a perspective, or a frame of mind, for that matter. We, though, in the daily walk of life, having no philosophical thoughts and intentions upon our minds, do not look at our own use of words and sentences *as* autonomous.

'Their/our answers', as we saw Wittgenstein enunciating, 'if they are correct, must be homespun and ordinary/trivial. But one must look at them in the proper spirit, and then it doesn't matter.' And so it is: Wittgenstein seeks to grasp the humble, the everyday use of our language, within a frame of mind that is anything but the frame in which we, in the daily walk of life, avail ourselves of our words and sentences. Thus, when Wittgenstein, in *PI* §116, says 'What *we* do is to bring words back from their metaphysical use to their everyday use', he should not be taken to mean to say that he seeks to find his way back to that frame of mind in which he, in the everyday walk of life, just uses his own language. Wittgenstein, in other words, does not seek his way *out* of that frame of mind in which *disquieting* questions arise, hold, and bash away at it henceforth—*out* of that very frame of mind and *into* the daily spirit and everyday comedy in which these questions—almost by definition, as one wants to say—play no role. He rather seeks to find peace, unadulterated peace, *in the same frame of mind* in which disquieting questions arise, thus in the same frame of mind in which the bewitching craft of our language is felt and truly cultivated with much care—as long as the redeeming word has not been found. For only then is the so-called humble, the ordinary, the trivial, the homespun, the plain and the everyday use of language, not humbug, but *redeeming*. That is why the redeeming word does not come in the shape of *our everyday understanding* of what it is to use language.

And why not? Wittgenstein does not want to pronounce anything *new*; there is no need to make *new* discoveries, he says, for the problems are solved 'by assembling what we have long been familiar with.' He, indeed, wants 'to *understand* something that is already in plain view.' But why indeed?—Is it really clear to speak in such terms as wanting so much as to *understand* something that is *already in plain view*? Wittgenstein's suggestion is that the object of his understanding *is already* in plain view, but what about the means to understand it? Is it in plain view as well? In as plain a view as the object of understanding itself *already* is, that is, is said to be? Wittgenstein says that '[t]he problems are solved, not by coming up with new discoveries, but *by* assembling what we have long been familiar with' (emphasis mine).—But what about the assembly itself? Is *that* what we can be said to be familiar with as well? If not, how could Wittgenstein say that he does not want to understand anything *new*? On the other hand, if it is *familiar*, if it is what we have long been *familiar* with, what about wanting to *understand* it?

Do we start out being sufficiently familiar with notions such as 'being familiar' and 'being open to view' that we do not feel the need to raise questions about Wittgenstein's use of them? As regards the latter notion: Wittgenstein at times seems to take it rather absolute: our language *has* a surface and a hidden aspect, and it is up to us, philosophers, to see that we need not to dig beneath its surface. On the other hand, when it comes to the notion of being familiar it is relativized to *us*, users of our language as we are. So is what lies open to view always familiar to us? Should what is familiar to us not rather *count* as open to view? Should the things that we cannot rightly be said to have long been familiar with, but that nonetheless can rightly be said to lie open to view, drop out as irrelevant to Wittgenstein's philosophy? But what determines that something lies open view? What determines that something should be reckoned among the things that we have long been familiar with? Our eyes and ears in the first case and our elusive sense of our being familiar with life and its daily burdens in the second case? Could the one be in conflict with the other? Could they mislead each other? Can our eyes convince us that we had better see and acknowledge a certain feature concerning our language as what we have long been familiar with? Is everything that lies open to view and that we recognize as what we have long been familiar with *always* relevant to Wittgenstein's philosophy? And what are we to make of the things acquiring relevance *only* in the light in which Wittgenstein's looks at language? What should we say of language having a so-called surface and a hidden core *without* the light in which he looks at language? How can we be sure that language even has a two-layered structure? Is this true for us *in the first instance*, users of our language? Or for Wittgenstein *in the first instance*, a philosopher who is at pains to understand our daily use of language? He says: 'We want to *understand* something that is already in plain view.' But *already* for us, users of our language?—or *already* for the philosopher, who is at pains to understand our daily use of language, that is, 'in opposition to the urge to misunderstand' its workings? Wittgenstein's *already* concerns what he says in the following passage.

> On the one hand, is it clear that every sentence in our language "is in order as it is". That
> is to say, we are not *striving after* an ideal, as if our ordinary vague sentences had not
> got a quite unexceptionable sense, and a perfect language still had to be constructed by
> us. – On the other hand, it seems clear that where there is sense, there must be perfect
> order.—So there must be perfect order even in the vaguest sentence. (PI: 98)

Early Wittgenstein says: the logic of our sentences is in order as it is, for the ideal is *already* there; but the ideal is not in plain view yet, hence we need to dig beneath the surface of language. Later Wittgenstein says: the logic of our sentences is in order as it is, but there is no longer any need to dig beneath the surface, for it is *already* in plain view. The distinction between what lies open to view and what does not lie open to view is in the *Tractatus* as absolute as the ideal itself. But what becomes of this distinction, now that the ideal has turned out to be a house of cards? Logic cannot be said to lie *already* open to view with respect to the very distinction that Wittgenstein's early conception of logic once drew into language. It should be said to be already open to view with respect to his later conception of logic. But, then, what does it mean to say that logic lies already open to view if the distinction between what lies open to view and what does not lie open to view is again conceptually dependent on one's conception of logic?

Of course, if logic determines the sense of language having a surface and hidden core, it remains to be seen how this determination works out in practice. But can logic determine the sense of a distinction between familiar and unfamiliar? If not, it is still to be seen how this *lack* of determination works out in practice. Wittgenstein wants to *understand* what we have long been *familiar* with—familiarity is not enough. And Wittgenstein is entirely convinced that his philosophical aim is feasible, that it makes sense: should *he* turn out to be a complete duffer at his own philosophical business, it can only be due to his own individual failures and shortcomings, rather than to some kind of incoherence of his intellectual enterprise. In this respect Wittgenstein must be said to be as sure of the 'unassailability and definiteness' (cf. Preface *Tractatus*) of his later philosophy as early Wittgenstein was of the *Tractatus*. But this is no coincidence: it is intrinsically tied to the core interest of Wittgenstein, of which we have spoken above; an interest that is at work in the *Tractatus* as much as in the *Philosophical Investigations*.

What I am trying to bring to the fore here is what I have intimated before: the all-important difference between using language and paying attention to its use. Wittgenstein seeks to embrace the redeeming word, by paying close attention to how language is actually used in the daily walk of life. He merely wants to look at this use, humble as he says it is; he merely wants to *describe* its workings. Where does this leave us as regards these descriptions? The answers in philosophy, he says, 'if they are correct, must be homespun and ordinary/trivial.' If Wittgenstein's descriptions are to be the final answers in his philosophy, how homespun, ordinary/trivial, *are they*? 'Philosophy unties knots in our thinking: hence its result must be simple.' But if Wittgenstein's descriptions of our language are to provide the answers he is looking for, they should be said to be descriptions of a humble use. But how *simple* could these descriptions themselves be said to be? And what are we to make of the spirit in which the final answers—descriptions—should be looked at? It is the one in which Wittgenstein looks at language *as* autonomous. But we have seen that this spirit is not the one that we care for throughout the day when we, not bothered by philosophical troubles and disquietudes, use our ordinary language. But how, then, could Wittgenstein's descriptions be said to come in the humble, simple or ordinary way if they should come in the way of descriptions of the humble, simple or ordinary?

However ordinary or humble Wittgenstein's descriptions of our ordinary language-use might be said to be, they are, as we shall have ample opportunity to see in this book, not easily had *after all*.

> Suppose you say: In this way you might fail to find the nature of speaking by failing to find enough about, say, the movements of the tongue. But suppose you found out all of that sort of information about thinking, where would you be? The mistake, as usual, lies in the question, not in the answer.
>
> Then suppose it's the 'use of a word' we want to enquire about. You may say, how could I not know this? There is a point to this question – if you mean – Surely I have mastery of the technique of using 'think'. You have. There is though another task – to *describe* the technique of the use, and that is hard. (LPP: 240)

To *describe* the technique of the use of our words is hard, Wittgenstein avows. It is hard for several reasons, as we shall see in the course of this book, but one reason stands out here. It has much if not everything do with the understanding that Wittgenstein is out for: namely 'understanding something that is already in plain view'. But, as I should like to add here, one really needs to see him at work, when he is caught up in the business of trying to understand this something, for only then can one see why *it* is so hard and difficult. Unless we develop an eye for these difficulties, we will never be able to judge what doing philosophy was really like for Wittgenstein.

1.3 Three philosophical playgrounds

We have ruminated a little on Wittgenstein's anxiousness to contemplate his uncommon way of looking at things, its nature and idiosyncrasies. Philosophy, according to the tenets of his interest, has to be a complicated enterprise but a feasible affair nonetheless. To conceive it as anything but feasible is to misconceive its nature as well as its bearings on language. So, then, philosophy, at least in Wittgenstein's own hands, must for all its complicatedness be an affair that should see the end of the day with descriptions of our language, and these things only. But these descriptions, as we have been suggesting here and there, do not come with ease. On the contrary, one of the things that Wittgenstein began to realize in the course of his later mission is that furnishing descriptions of language is anything but the kind of *problem*-free effort he made it to be at the time of its overture in the 1930s. Recall here what he said, in a concessive mood, shortly before he died: 'Am I not getting closer and closer to saying that in the end logic cannot be described? You must look at the practice of language, then you will see it' (OC: 501).

There seems to be a kind of tension at work in Wittgenstein's philosophy, one that we shall try to expound in the present book, a tension between, on the one hand, the import of a programmatic statement such as 'All *explanation* must disappear, and description alone must take its place' (PI: 109) and, on the other hand, his efforts to see only *descriptions* at the end of the day. Now before proceeding, I think we do well to forge some suitable epithets first here, for there are three so-called playgrounds that our present study shall need to keep up with; three philosophical playgrounds as well as the intimacy of connections they bear to each other. Well, then, I should like to distinguish among Wittgenstein's (1) *playground of abstract consideration(s),* his (2) *playground of describing (our) language* and his (3) *playground of inventing and collating language-games.* On the first playground we can behold Wittgenstein contemplating his philosophical interest and packing its tenets into nicely polished remarks and statements of a more or less programmatic nature. Thus, statements as that the results of philosophy must 'be simple, but philosophizing has to be as complicated as the knots it unties' (Z: 452), and that 'the philosophical problems should *completely* disappear' (PI: 133), are plain products of this very playground. Such grammatical remarks or statements, as I shall denote them in this book, surely render this playground a most intriguing place indeed. But how far more intriguing a place it turns out to be when its grammatical products are seen against the background of the various actions on the two other playgrounds: places where the philosophical problems under treatment *should* completely disappear *de facto.* So we shall be looking at Wittgenstein's efforts on the playground of describing language as much as at those in action on the playground of inventing and collating language-games. But in doing so we shall constantly have to remind ourselves of the programmatic imports under which these two playgrounds lie and toil, imports coming from the playground of abstract consideration. The redeeming word is not a product from this ground. What falls to its lot is e.g. the task of *articulating* what the redeeming word in philosophy looks like. But whatever it looks like, it is a word that can be had only *by putting into practice* a promulgation as that we should 'leave everything as it is.'

Part of our concern in this book is to explore how the three playgrounds relate to each other. Wittgenstein's activities on the playground of inventing and collating language-games, for instance, are an integral part of his struggles to describe *our* language. Accordingly, he operates with a conception of language description that is as uncommon as he claims his own way of looking at language to be. It is the combined effort of the two playgrounds (2) and (3) *together*, that is, under the constant supervision of the playground of abstract consideration, that makes up his descriptions of our language. With my suggestion to distinguish among at least three different philosophical playgrounds in Wittgenstein's convoluted landscape of philosophical activities, I mean to distinguish between the mêlée of remarks, statements and sketchy descriptions in his oeuvre, some of which express how difficult philosophy *is*, some of which express how simple its results *must* be; some of which express how complicated philosophy's roads to solution *are*, or *must* be, and why there *is* a way out at last—and why it *must* be so.

Let us emphasize here that what Wittgenstein produces on the playground of abstract consideration are in the end articulations of his own deeply felt interest. Though to some large extent fashioned by his hard-won critical stance towards especially the *Tractatus*, it has in the end nothing to rest on but itself. It is ultimately as deeply 'irrational' as any other true interest. In other words, it is not founded on what the other two playgrounds have already yielded on the subject of certain results and experiences. So it is *not* a matter of (mere) fact that we end up producing gibberish when we, in moments of philosophy, dig beneath the so-called surface of our language. The primary source truly lies in Wittgenstein's deeply felt need and interest. Here is the material that determines the *form* of the happenings on those playgrounds that are ultimately responsible for the production of the redeeming word; it is this way around and not otherwise.

Consider in this regard the following remark: 'Philosophy just puts everything before us, and neither explains nor deduces anything. – Since everything lies open to view, there is nothing to explain. For whatever may be hidden is of no interest to us' (PI: 126). This remark is a real product of the playground of abstract consideration. Now notice the words *since* and *for*: Are they not symptomatic of Wittgenstein furnishing an argument or rationalization of *why* he looks at language the way he does? Well, he appears to appeal to something, to a kind of fundamental dividing line along which the world falls apart into two sharply discernible spheres, one capable of seizing hold of Wittgenstein's own interest, with the other offering a nice mouthful for scientists and like-minded philosophers to chew on. So, then, Wittgenstein appears to have fathomed his philosophical interest according to something *given*, to a critical division that he and scientists have to accept the way it is. And yet, it is rather the other way around. What separates the so-called hidden from what lies open to view is not given *tout court*. It is truly Wittgenstein's interest that draws limits here—though, to be sure, to no lesser extent than any other genuine interest. What is of no interest to him *counts*, more or less so, as hidden. Wittgenstein wants to look at the language-game *as* autonomous: this *as* draws limits. It is not a matter of contingency that what separates the hidden from what lies open to view *is* one and the same line separating the autonomous features 'of' our language from everything not so autonomous.

There is, then, really some imposition of sorts of Wittgenstein's philosophical style of thinking on what we call our language, as well as on what tradition has passed down on the subject of philosophical problems and difficulties. From the elevated highs of his own altar of abstract considerations he brings to bear upon language a conception of philosophy that, I want to emphasize, has been moulded to the core by his own, deeply felt need and interest. When Wittgenstein asks 'How does it come about that philosophy is so complicated a structure?' he does not so much give expression to what he has *found out* on the two playgrounds that jointly aim at delivering the redeeming word, as to a style of thinking that traces back to his 'philosophical' interest, to his playground of abstract considerations, where his interest finds expression in terms of *musts* and *have tos*: 'Philosophy unties knots in our thinking: hence its result must be simple, but philosophizing has to be as complicated as the knots it unties.' But, indeed, speaking of an imposition of sorts, are we now not suggesting a Wittgenstein who does not leave everything as it is after all? Well, he leaves everything as it is, that is to say, he really intends to do so, for there is no way of leaving everything as it is *tout court*, and Wittgenstein intends to do it according to how his own, deeply felt interest has laid it down.

To be sure, that the results of philosophy *must* be simple, i.e. that Wittgenstein's word of redemption *must* come in that shape, is *rather not* a matter of mere psychology. His core interest, being the ultimate source of his philosophical reflections and doings as it is, may well be construed and discussed in psychological terms. But this does not mean that Wittgenstein's articulations of this interest, i.e. the products of the playground of abstract consideration, need necessarily be construed as expressions of his psychological life and unusual personality. They are *rather not* such expressions. The same is true for Wittgenstein's redeeming word: it surely has its psychological streaks and connotations, but when Wittgenstein pronounces that the results in philosophy *must* be simple, he speaks of a requirement that is of no less a *grammatical* nature than his requirement that philosophizing has to be as complicated as the knots it unties.

The aspect of simplicity (*Einfachheit*) is what Wittgenstein emphasizes again and again in his grammatical articulations. Here is another example:

Socrates pulls up the pupil who when asked what knowledge is enumerates cases of knowledge. And Socrates doesn't regard that as even a preliminary step to answering the question.

But our answer consists in giving such an enumeration and a few analogies. (In a certain sense we are always making things easier and easier for ourselves in philosophy.) (PG: 120)[29]

Wittgenstein says that *in a certain sense* we are always making things easier and easier for ourselves in philosophy; and, obviously, the setting up of a few analogies alongside our own language-games should do anything but detract from that very sense, any more than these analogies themselves. Indeed, Wittgenstein's so-called objects of comparison—'the few analogies'—*should* be anything but fuzzy and complex themselves; they should be clear and simple:

> Our clear and simple language-games are not preparatory studies for a future regularization of language—as it were first approximations, ignoring friction and air-resistance. (PI: 130)

Remarks as these all are part of the story related by Wittgenstein's playground of abstract consideration. Quite another story, however, is related by Wittgenstein's protracted activities on the two other playgrounds: the playground of describing our language and the playground of inventing and collating language-games. On the former, as we shall expound in the course of this book, Wittgenstein finds himself tracing down grammatical structures of our language the likeness of which he cannot possibly be said to have ever seen before—kinds of structures that, notwithstanding their unfamiliar appearances, should nonetheless pass for pieces of our familiar language. On the latter ground, as we shall have ample opportunity to see as well, Wittgenstein finds himself forced to admit how little he has actually contemplated the question of what it is like to get a firm grip on his objects of comparison, in the shape of such things as clear and simple language-games. On the playground of abstract consideration, he contemplated their point and importance for the activity of describing our language-games, indispensible as he made them out to be there for his understanding of the workings of our language. Though what he did not *contemplate* there, and could not possibly have done there or anywhere, but came to *realize* more and more on the playground of inventing and collating language-games, is that precisely his own indispensible objects of comparison are *more than just difficult* to beget. Many a

---

29 Cf. 'That is also why our method is not merely to enumerate actual usages of words, but rather deliberately to invent new ones, some of them because of their absurd appearances' (BB: 28).

comment from especially Wittgenstein's more advanced stages signalizes a philosopher in deep trouble.

Many a remark from Wittgenstein's oeuvre has an origin tracing clearly back to only one of the three playgrounds that our present study has brought to the fore and means to dwell upon. But many a remark from his oeuvre has so to speak mixed sources. Recall in this regard Wittgenstein's words from *On Certainty*: 'Am I not getting closer and closer to saying that in the end logic cannot be described? You must look at the practice of language, then you will see it.' This remark entertains an interesting relation, tension if you like, between the first and second clause. In the former, Wittgenstein gives vent to the complications and difficulties he faces whilst trying to provide for mere descriptions of logic (language). But if logic—'in the end'—*cannot* be described, then, of course, this is far from anything that Wittgenstein could ever have promulgated from the elevated highs of his playground of abstract consideration. For logic, as these highs stipulated, is not only the kind of thing that can be described; it is precisely the kind of thing internally related to Wittgenstein's very conception of language description.

There is a strong sense of *surprise* in the first clause of *OC* §501. As far as the second clause of this remark is concerned—'You must look at the practice of language, then you will see it': it tells Wittgenstein what he needs to do, but what he needs to do is precisely among the things that he has been doing throughout *On Certainty*. It is precisely owing to his having looked here and there, and his having seen *this* and *that*—that he finds himself forced to lodge a complaint, as the first clause might be taken to be. The second clause bears the marks of a reminder, of what Wittgenstein has enunciated on the playground of abstract consideration, namely that *everything* of logic can be described and that nothing that is part of logic can fail to be described.

Another interesting remark to mention here is the following: 'Not empiricism and yet realism in philosophy, that is the hardest thing.'[30] This remark, too, has mixed sources. 'Not empiricism and *yet* realism in philosophy' is what Wittgenstein enunciates on the playground of abstract considerations, giving expression to the dialectical character of his philosophical approach as it does. 'Not empiricism and yet realism in philosophy, *that is the hardest thing*', on the other hand, gives vent to Wittgenstein's unceasing struggles on the two playgrounds whose combined efforts, I repeat, should ultimately furnish descriptions of our language, and these things only.

---

30 RFM: 325.

This book had singled out for its primary concern three philosophical playgrounds, but the convoluted landscape of Wittgenstein's philosophical activities should be said to be a dialectical affair of more than these three grounds only. A thoroughly convoluted thing this book would have become itself, however, should it have tried to get on board even one more playground. Wittgenstein's arguments, for example, or styles of arguing, deserve special notice, far more than I can devote to them in this book. But, as with his descriptions, their true point and significance come into view *only* when they are seen and treated as integral parts of his dialectical approach. Chasing Wittgenstein's arguments without seeing them as mere way stations on his way to furnishing descriptions, is to nurse a style of thinking that was wholly abhorrent to him. Not arguing at all in philosophy, according to Wittgenstein, is not nearly as barren as arguing only.

To be sure, then, the troubles and difficulties that this book has singled out for its primary concern are only *some* of the hurdles that Wittgenstein encountered on his way to mere descriptions. Hurdles, as I should say, that Wittgenstein faced both on and outside the two playgrounds charged with the production of the redeeming word. Ignoring many other a trouble and difficulty, then, as we shall be forced to do, does not make our task any easier. Our concern is 'merely' to lay bare, and indeed to elucidate, the details of what runs, quite *typically so*, through the convoluted landscape of Wittgenstein's philosophical activities—details among which belongs a number of *typical* troubles that he faced while craving for his descriptions.

In sum, there is something problematic about Wittgenstein's later philosophy. That is, certain things began to present themselves to his own mind, in the course of his efforts to see the end of the day with descriptions only, not so much as plain difficulties to overcome but as serious *problems* or *troubles*, kinds of knots the real nature of which that he did not fathom, and could not have envisaged, on the playground of abstract consideration. He did envisage complications there, but not of such a kind as, for instance, his complaint in *On Certainty* might be said to indicate. And my suggestion is that some of these troubles are inherent to the nature of his playground of abstract consideration. So my suggestion is that no 'critical engagement' with Wittgenstein's later philosophy is forthcoming until one begins to take his efforts seriously, namely those attempting to see the end of the day with *descriptions* only. Wittgenstein was always forthright about these efforts, as well as about the problems that he came to face.

1.4 By way of some further orientation

We miss the whole point of Wittgenstein's philosophy if we fail to take his efforts to describe seriously, but, once taken seriously, we are bound to miss the import of these efforts if we fail to see them against the background of his playground of abstract considerations. I propose, then, by way of some further orientation, to collate a few remarks and passages now, only to contrast them a little among each other. For, indeed, speaking of Wittgenstein's struggles and serious troubles, and given the shocking things that I might be taken to have been suggestive of while speaking in such terms, I had perhaps better have a look *also*, if not first of all, at his famous opening moves in the *Philosophical Investigations*. For there Wittgenstein writes the following: 'It is easy to imagine a language consisting only of orders and reports in battle.—Or a language consisting only of questions and expressions for answering Yes and No – and countless other things. —— And to imagine a language means to imagine a form of life' (PI: 19). So, then, is this not plain enough language: *it is easy*? It surely is, as I think the following words are:

> We say: "Let's imagine human beings who don't know *this* language-game". But this does not give us any clear idea of the life of these people, of where it deviates from ours. We don't yet know what we have to imagine; for the life of these people *is* supposed to correspond to ours for the rest, and it first has to be determined what we would call a life that corresponds to ours under the new circumstances. (RC III: 296)

Wittgenstein makes some disquieting observations here, clearly suggesting that the acquiring of those things on which he never ceased to place pivotal value in his later investigations, i.e. his objects of comparison in the shape of language-games, is not as easy and straightforward a matter as he seems to take it in the famous overtures of his *Investigations*. Similar echoes of plain worries and disquietudes can be heard all over the place, from various corners of his oeuvre.

> In the way we employ the word "order" and obey", gestures and words are intertwined in a web of multifarious relationships. If I am now construing a simplified case, it is not clear whether I ought still to call the phenomenon "ordering" and "obeying". (RFM: 352)[31]

Here Wittgenstein makes explicit mention of the simplified language-game, precisely the kind of thing that he has been inventing and collating in the opening sections of the *Philosophical Investigations*, where he bluntly affirms that 'it is easy to imagine a language consisting only of orders and reports in battle.' Set against this remark, it seems that he has grown sceptical if not downright despondent of the possibility of begetting what he requires so much for his understanding

---

31 Amended translation.

of our language, and cannot do without in the end: his (simple) objects of comparison.

We have been suggesting that whenever Wittgenstein begins to *give vent* to some serious problem or other, it occurs most of the time on one of the philosophical playgrounds where things need to be (dis)solved *de facto*. Thus, as regards the problems or difficulties to which he alludes in the passage quoted above, it is not anything of which Wittgenstein could have developed a clear conception *already* on the playground of abstract consideration. The latter ground confines itself to imparting remarks to the effect that it is *possible* to invent fictitious language-game, or that it is possible to invent clear and simple language-games as possibilities alongside our own language-games as other possibilities. That the invention of these fictitious entities could be seriously hampered by the troubles of which the two passages quoted might be said to be clearly symptomatic, is not so much not foreseen by this ground as simply excluded. But what should we think of the remark from the opening sections of the *Investigations*: 'It is *easy* to imagine a language consisting only of orders and reports in battle'? Is this remark not as much a product from the real philosophical battleground as the other two are? Or should we rather relegate its origin to Wittgenstein's playground of abstract consideration?

Although there is a lot of inventing and collating going on in the opening sections of the *Philosophical Investigations*, that is, of so-called clear and simple language-games, I fail to see anything battle-like in Wittgenstein's non-stop inventing of these things. Still, there is no denying that some sort of authentic battle is going on there, for Wittgenstein faces the difficult task to acquaint his readers with his freshly conceived philosophical outlook. How to reveal the purpose and method of my clear and simple language-games? When to inaugurate them? Right away at the outset, or somewhat later? How to bring them into play *against* the readers' strong and natural inclination to harp on about the need for the essence of things? How to show their importance in philosophy, their elucidatory role in the *philosophical* study of language? How to begin my book anyway?—Such and similar questions, I think, must have weighed on Wittgenstein's mind at the time he began to compose the opening moves of his book. A most uncommon way of looking it is that he needs to reveal, a way with which his readers not only will not find themselves at ease before long, but which is also *meant* to go against their views and inclinations. And the more Wittgenstein reveals, in these opening sections, the more likely his readers begin to look into the mirror of their own common way of looking at things. The process of revelation proceeds in various stages, by demonstrating a certain method, or motley of

55

methods, by introducing curious pieces of languages, on which, it is true, claims are brought to bear; by asking curious questions and by giving answers even more curious, etc. And what comes along in this wild buzzing of crazy words and things is, almost, a mere gloss in the margin: 'It is easy to imagine a language consisting only of orders and reports in battle', a remark that might well be said to give voice to the apparent ease with which Wittgenstein, in the opening sections of his book, invents and collates his clear and simple language-games.

But even if this impression is false, i.e. even if it had not been altogether *that* easy for Wittgenstein to invent his clear and simple language-game as the opening sections suggest, his remark remains significant, for it sets the stage for a method that is more than just 'another tool' within his philosophy as a whole. At least in these initial stages, Wittgenstein does not call the *possibility* of his clear and simple languages into question, and far from meaning to do so at this point he operates with a notion of possibility that is more than just interesting, for it is a remarkable thing if only because of how it finds its way *into his book*. Wittgenstein wants to investigate language, and to this end he introduces his method of inventing and collating clear and simple language-games. However, the moment he introduces the method he seems to presuppose a great deal about what he wants to investigate: the phenomenon of language. These comprise all kinds of things that drop out from his own philosophical investigations in that they are not *interrogated* on the playground of abstract considerations. Let us try to work this out a little.

The opening sections of the *Investigations* exhibit an authentic piece of philosophical composition. The reader is confronted there with a texture that is quite unlike what such texts as e.g. *On Certainty* or *Last Writings on the Philosophy of Psychology* have to offer on this score. One conspicuous feature of Wittgenstein's art of composing the opening moves of the *Investigations* is that he assembles his clear and simple language-games not so much around our own language, as is his wont in his more genuine philosophical struggles, as around the inventions themselves. Thus, no sooner has Wittgenstein given birth to his famous builders, with their truncated language, than a whole cavalcade of invented language-games follows suit: one fictitious language-game is laid down side by side with another fictitious one, and no sooner has light been thrown upon the first by the latter than another language-game is in the making, due to contribute its share of light before long. But what are we to make of this art of shedding light, for it appears to be shedding light upon each other, rather than upon *our own language* in the first place? If Wittgenstein's fictitious language-games, in the opening moves of the *Investigation*, are as tokens quite assertive but as a group conspicuously introverted, then what are we to say of his remark, further on in the same book, that his clear and simple language-games are 'meant to throw light on the *Verhältnisse* of *our language*' (PI: 131; emphasis mine)?

Of course, it is comfortable to say now that Wittgenstein's clear and simple language-games, in the opening sections of his book, throw a light on our language *indirectly*. And that is true: very comfortable it is to say *that*. But what does it mean? At as early a stage as *PI* §5, Wittgenstein says: 'It disperses the fog if we study the phenomena of language in primitive kinds of use in which one can clearly survey the purpose and functioning of the words.' These words indeed seem to be a clear invitation to direct our focus away, if only for the time being, from the full complexity of natural language towards the phenomena of language in primitive kinds of use. But this recommendation as regards our focus, as I think we should add here, is surely no recommendation to feel no longer *bothered* by the complexity of our language. That is, Wittgenstein's words do not advise us to turn our back upon the complex phenomena of language once and for all. On the contrary, precisely by way of studying the phenomena of language at the hand of primitive uses, as he suggests, do we learn to see and understand what sorts of questions we have always been prone to raise and to answer. Wittgenstein's language-games, his choice to come out with *this* one rather than *that* one at a certain stage, his tactics of moving them to and fro on the philosophical playground, all this does not come out of the blue, but comes to pass against the background of our urge to raise the kinds of philosophical questions we raise in the light of the complexity of *our own* language. What characterizes Wittgenstein's clear and simple language-games, then, as they make their first appearance in the overtures of *Philosophical Investigations*, and, interestingly, *first and only* appearance in the book as a whole, is their artificial lack of complexity, of some measure of complexity or other. Wittgenstein cultivates this lack, revels in it as it were. The *presentation* of his method should, in the matter of perspicuity, not fall behind the one that his clear and simple language-games put on display.

But if their artificial *lack of complexity* characterizes Wittgenstein's language-games, primitive or not, more than anything else, this imposed artificiality is not supposed to render these very things artificial themselves, in the non-trivial sense that they require some life-supporting contrivance to recoup for their loss of complexity. The stunning transparency of Wittgenstein's language-games is not supposed to jeopardize their viability, hence ultimately his own freshly conceived method of studying the phenomena of language at the hand of primitive kinds of use. Thus, if 'it disperses the fog if we study the phenomena of language in primitive kinds of use in which one can clearly survey the purpose and functioning of the words', the inauguration of these primitive things should not gives rise to some fog of their own, in the form of disquieting questions as regards their lack of complexity and their obvious truncatedness. But this means that where Wittgenstein's clear and simple language-game are called upon as more than just appropriate *means* in the study of 'the phenomena of language', their inauguration preys on some non-trivial conception of such phenomena, for the clear and simple language-game *are languages* after all and *qua language* no less inferior than our own (cf. PI: 18, 19). Whatever we come to learn about *the phenomena of language*, by means of inventing and collating clear and simple language-games, this method is not supposed to call into question the *possibility* of such language-games in regard of their being *phenomena of language*. But that seems to mean that there is something about the phenomenon of language that we cannot study; at least not by means of its clear and simple *possibilities* themselves, namely *that* they are possible.

We have been speaking of the manner in which Wittgenstein's philosophical style of thinking imposes itself on what we call our language, as well as on the gamut of perplexities passed down by philosophical tradition. This imposition is intimately related to Wittgenstein's infatuation with clarity, which can be exemplified in various ways. Consider the following passage.

> Think of the tools in a toolbox: there is a hammer, pliers, a saw, a screwdriver, a rule, a glue-pot, glue, nails and screws. – The functions of words are as diverse as the functions of these objects. (And in both cases there are similarities.)
>
> Of course, what confuses us is the uniform appearance of words when we hear them in speech, or see them written or in print. For their *use* is not before us clearly. Especially when we are doing philosophy. (PI: 11)

Wittgenstein speaks of the *functions* of words, which, he says, are as diverse as the functions of the tools in a toolbox. The tools have a function, but not in the toolbox itself. They have a function within a particular system, namely in our way of living. But what is the system in which *words* can be talked about *as* having a function in the sense in which Wittgenstein wants to talk about them? Should we think of the function of the word *in a sentence* as such a system? Well, sentences are among the kinds of things in which words appear uniformly, i.e. lack the diversity in function that Wittgenstein wants to harp upon for philosophical reasons. Hence his concern is with this uniform appearance, as what confuses us, therefore with something in which our confusion should finally dissolve, which is the system in which the functions of words manifest themselves in as diverse a way as the functions of tools. So what is this system?

Wittgenstein speaks of the use, of the uses of words, suggesting that *these uses* are as diverse as the functions of tools. It is not the uses of words in a sentence as a system, but these uses within language-games as systems. Wittgenstein contrasts the uniform appearance of words in sentences with the diversity of their use in language-games, suggesting all the while that the former appearance is taken in easily, whereas the latter appearance goes unnoticed *and* is not readily brought before the human eye. What Wittgenstein's words are suggestive of is something that is stated explicitly near the end of the *Philosophical Investigations*, although its theme runs throughout the book from as early a stage as its very first pages, namely the distinction between a 'surface grammar' [*Oberflächengrammatik*] and a 'depth grammar' [*Tiefengrammatik*] (PI: 664).

So words, according to Wittgenstein, have all kinds of aspects but the philosophical relevance in the present context concerns their uniform appearance in contrast to the diversity of their use. The former comes easily, of its own accord in fact, whereas the revelation of the latter appearance is what the philosopher needs to struggle for. Wittgenstein says that the use of words is not before us *clearly*, 'especially', he adds, 'when we are doing philosophy'. His suggestion is that what is not clearly before us in philosophy is *already* not clearly before us in the daily course of life, although, it seems, not in as bad a manner as it is in philosophy. His suggestion is that we can have it clearly before us, *precisely* in philosophy. But if the use of our words is not *already* before us clearly when we use them as we do (in daily life), where does this leave us as regards Wittgenstein's obsession with clarity, with his need for complete clarity. It now seems that, without further ado, we can reveal the diversity of the functions of our words only to a certain extent.

A point intimately connected with this issue concerns the following: if 'what confuses us is the uniform appearance of words when we hear them in speech, or see them written or in print', then this confusion does not impinge upon our usage of words *in the daily walk of life*. That is, our confusion about the use of words is not a confused use of words *then*. If it were, Wittgenstein would face the awkward question of what is *not* a confused use of words. What we hint at here is what we have been touching on already, namely how Wittgenstein thinks that language strikes us, as users of our colloquial language, and how he thinks that it strikes the philosopher.

Wittgenstein says: 'The clarity that we are aiming at is indeed *complete* clarity. But this simply means that the philosophical problems should *completely* disappear' (PI: 133)—a saying that is no doubt the kind of thing that he had already been saying in the *Tractatus*. Enunciating his philosophical approach, be it the

Tractatus or in the *Investigations*, without entertaining the idea that philosophical problems are things that *should* completely disappear, does not seem to have been an option for him. But in the *Tractatus* this idea took the better part of his mind as it was tied to a wrong conception of analysis. In his later philosophy, his obsession with clarity becomes again tied down, this time primarily to forms of analyses in which his clear and simple language-games play a dominant role. Indeed, in Wittgenstein's stockpile of conceptual tools, these games occupy a special position in that nothing will come of clarity and understanding unless they are clear and simple *in the first place*. They require no light themselves, for they are the bearers of light. Hence they must have an unquestionable aspect, which is precisely what they must have in respect of being stipulated possibilities among other possibilities. It thus appears that no clear and simple language-game brings the light of understanding of its own accord, for it is only in close conjunction with other clear and simple language-games that they are meant to shine and cast their light. *They*, then, are meant to shed light on the *Verhältnisse* (PI: 130) of our language, clear and simple as these games are meant to be in the first place. In other words, *they* are meant to participate in the construction of *übersichtliche Darstellungen* (PI: 122), clear and simple as these games as meant to be in the first place. *They*, then, can surely tell us much about how Wittgenstein, at the time his obsession with clarity latched on to the notion of clear and simple language-games, conceived of the conceptual textures of (our) language. 'We want to establish an order in our knowledge of the use of language: an order for a particular purpose, one out of many possible orders, not *the* order' (PI: 132). Not *the* order, then, but still one order out of many possible orders: by means in which the involvement of clear and simple language-games is absolutely mandatory in that the *philosophically constructed* alignments of their individual forms and clarities should ultimately furnish the light of understanding that Wittgenstein hankers after. These language-games, then, clear and simple as they are meant to be, should draw apart what does not lie apart in our everyday language; *they*, then, should '*emphasize* distinctions which our ordinary forms of language easily make us overlook' (PI: 132). What Wittgenstein seeks to do seems fair enough and perfectly feasible. It also seems to underscore his dictum that philosophy leaves everything as it is. How, indeed, could he fail to do so, by emphasizing in the end distinctions which our ordinary forms of language make us overlook so easily?

But it is Wittgenstein's clear and simple language-games that are being harnessed to the task of emphasizing distinctions. And over these things hovers a conception of clarity that is not everybody's clarity. 'Our grammar', Wittgenstein says, 'is deficient in surveyability [*Übersichtlichkeit*]' (PI: 122). I want to say: *that* is what language looks like in eyes of the beholder, in the eyes of Wittgenstein in his capacity as philosopher; it does not look like thus in the eyes of its users, in the daily walk of life. Another point to notice here is that what is claimed to be deficient in *Übersichtlichkeit* is the grammar of *our language*. Languages need not to be deficient in this respect at all; hence the grammar of our own language might well have been *übersichtlich* after all. So what is deficient is not the grammar of our language itself, but this grammar in respect of its *Übersichtlichkeit*. My suggestion here is that if our language had not been deficient in this respect it would not have been a different language in respect of its very workings. The deficiency is a matter of conceptual contingency in the eyes of the philosopher, and that may already reveal much about how Wittgenstein conceived the texture of our language, at the time the importance of making comparisons by means of clear and simple language-games began to dawn upon him in the early 1930s. So, then, what his method of clear and simple language-games reveals is, among other things, how he thought of the manner in which all kinds of activities and concepts lie intertwined in our language. What lies intertwined does do so as a matter of contingent fact and Wittgenstein conceived of these various kinds of intertwinedness as *knots*, as *tangles*, as things bearing a *disquieting* aspect, rather than as inherent structural properties of the complexity of our language and its use. What lies entangled can be disentangled without ceasing to be language, without ceasing to be *language*.

'It could be said that the use of the word "good" […] is a combination of a very large number of interrelated games, each of them as it were a facet of the use. What makes a single concept here is precisely the connection, the relationship, between these facets' (PG: 77). And these facets, according to Wittgenstein, can be drawn apart, for philosophical reasons. That is, the interrelated (language-) games can be drawn apart, each of them representing a single facet of the use, of the status quo in our language. They can be drawn apart, without falling apart, although each facet is, first and foremost, a matter of our language, of its complexity. The clear and simple language-games can draw apart what *does not* lie apart—*can* be drawn apart, without falling apart themselves. It is striking how thoroughgoingly Wittgenstein conceives matters of language in terms of his philosophical currency, which consists in his *preconceived* notion of clear and simple language-games.

To ask your readers not to be bothered about languages (2) and (8) consisting only of orders (cf. PI: 18), is to set the stage for a philosophical programme that aims at investigating the phenomena of (our) language without interrogating the kind of simplicity in which these phenomena are operated on as *means of comparison*. We speak of a programme prompted by a philosophically troubled mind, and yet, it asks us not to be bothered about the simplicity of its means of comparison, as if this worry does not belong to a philosophically troubled mind, and as if Wittgenstein's reply—'ask yourself whether our own language is complete'—is to be accepted just like that.

But Wittgenstein, asking his readers not to be bothered about languages (2) and (8) consisting only of orders, began before long to show signs of a bothered mind himself: 'In the way we employ the word "order" and obey", gestures and words are intertwined in a web of multifarious relationships. If I am now construing a simplified case, it is not clear whether I ought still to call the phenomenon "ordering" and "obeying"'. *That* Wittgenstein makes explicit mention of words and gestures lying intertwined in *a web of multifarious relations* is not without objective, for he brings the suggested worry to bear upon these relations, that is, on how he conceived them at the time he conceived his method of moving clear and simple language-games to and fro. His method builds on the notion that the fabric of our language hangs together like 'a combination of interrelated games' and that these games can be taken apart from each other and considered out of context. Wittgenstein's method also builds on the notion that variations on our language-games in the most simplified version can be had and operated on, that is, without automatically losing our hold on the possibility to recognize these versions *as variations* on our own way of doings things with words. But the way matters lie intertwined in our *Lebensform* seems to belong essentially to how we recognize and call all kinds things there.

Of course, much of what we say and suggest here requires further thought and due consideration. But let us, before entering upon such thoughts, mention one more point here. Wittgenstein was as obsessed with clarity and simplicity as he was with paying attention to details and with teaching differences. How do these obsessions relate to each other? Are the clear and simple language-games that Wittgenstein produces on end in the opening sections of his *Philosophical Investigations* items that pay no attention to detail? Did Wittgenstein simply ignore these details, perhaps thought of them easy to provide, as easy as the imagining of the language-game itself? Did he nonetheless think that such a provision would stand in stark opposition to his words in *PI* §5 about the method of 'studying the phenomena of language in primitive kinds of use in which one can clearly survey the purpose and functioning of the words'? Indeed, why add detail upon detail on the head of exactly those things that are meant to set the stage, if not the standard, of clearness and simplicity? What makes the opening sections of the *Investigations* so interesting, if not downright puzzling at first blush, is that Wittgenstein, in spite of his promulgation in *PI* §5, cannot be said to have developed a blind eye to detail there. On the contrary, in *PI* §51 he writes: 'In order to see more clearly, here as in countless similar cases, we must look at what really happens *in detail*, as it were from close up.' Extreme transparency and a profound concern for detail are, apparently, not supposed to be two mutually excluding points or motivations. Let us have a look at Wittgenstein's remark in *PI* §51 from close up.

The first thing to be said about this remark is a word about its English rendering, as given in the revised 4th edition by Hacker and Schulte. For the words *at what really happens* gives Wittgenstein's German a curious and unhappy twist: unlike Wittgenstein's original, they seem to suggest that we had better stop considering *invented* language-games for the time being and direct our full attention instead to what *really happens*, namely, the daily sorts of transactions in our own familiar and tangible language-games.[32] But all that is far removed from what Wittgenstein says or means to suggest. *Was vorgeht aus der Nähe betrachten* is a directive that addresses his inventions as much as our own rank and file language-games—and at present the former ones far more so than the latter ones. It is an invented language-game that Wittgenstein has thrown up for consideration in §51, and it is this same language-game that has given rise to a number of questions, which have in turn prompted Wittgenstein to remark on the importance of details.

But if Wittgenstein's remark applies to the fictitious language-games as much as to the factual ones, as I think it does, the question arises what it is like to *look* at the former ones from *close up*. Does the fictitious language-game not reach out into being to the extent it has been invented? Let us regard *PI* §53, where Wittgenstein's own call for the detail in *PI* §51 is taken care of in the following way: 'Our language-game (48) has *various* possibilities. There is a variation of cases in which we would say that a sign in the game was the name of a square of such-and-such a colour.'

Behind one and the same language-game stands a whole range of possibilities, that is, various tokens of language-games, or, as Wittgenstein would say, a family of such games. Looking at the invented language-game from close up amounts to fleshing out *various language-games*, with the original, invented language-game

---

32 Anscombe's rendering is as follows: 'In order to see more clearly, here as in countless similar cases, we must focus on the details of what goes on; must look at them *from close to.*'

as the basis for these games. We obtain one version of what we call doing A by adding a certain element to the original language-game, and we obtain *another* version of what we call doing A by adding a *different* element to the original. This way of attending to the details of invented language-games is indeed what Wittgenstein does, here and elsewhere, in those curious opening sections of the *Philosophical Investigations*.

But there seems to be another notion of detail at work in Wittgenstein's conception of language-games, invented or not. On p. 102 of the *Blue and Brown Books*, for instance, in the wake of a fresh volley of bold inventions of language-games, Wittgenstein writes, in a rather offhand manner, the following: 'We have only given a very sketchy description of the practice of our fictitious languages, in some cases only hints, but [...] one can easily make these descriptions more complete.' As this remark turns up amidst an activity bearing a marked family resemblance to the ones Wittgenstein displays in the opening sections of the *Investigations*, I take it to apply as well to the language-games making their first and flimsy appearance there, and only appearance in the book as a whole.

Wittgenstein, then, in the opening sections of the *Philosophical Investigations*, has given *sketchy* descriptions of his invented language-games only. He speaks of *hints*, not of explanations, but of descriptions, which are not hints of explanations (see above). (And he speaks of descriptions of *invented language-games* as much as of descriptions of factual and given language-games.) Here working out the details of a certain language-game amounts to putting more flesh on the bones of *one and the same* language-game—more flesh, that is, than Wittgenstein himself has bothered to provide. Indeed, more flesh, as his words in the *Blue and the Brown Books* suggest, would not necessarily make for a much better comparison between language-games. On the contrary, Wittgenstein's sketchy descriptions seem to provide him with all the light that he deems necessary for the purpose at hand. Going for more flesh just seems to go against the grain of his avowed purpose of furnishing clear and simple language-games. *More flesh* would only render them less transparent, less clear than they are, or need to be. On the other hand, if Wittgenstein's clear and simple language-games are meant to throw light on the *Verhältnisse* of our language, they need to appear with a particular physiognomy, an image *complex* enough for us to recognize as a way of doing *this* or *that* with words, what *we call* doing this or that with words in our *Lebensform*. The complexity is necessary for the light of comparison to emerge in the first instance, a light that should be directed towards our language and thrown upon its complexity. And what else could be said to be in charge of this *direction* but the clarity and simplicity of the language-games, that is, their *lack* of a certain complexity?

1.5 In the beginning

I have been suggesting that Wittgenstein never treated his fictitious language-games as, say, appendages, as embellishments to an alleged, real and solid kernel of his later philosophy. He never treated them thus simply because he was committed to treat them according to the tenets of his playground of abstract consideration. Having distinguished among three different playgrounds in Wittgenstein's philosophical battlefield, I have been suggesting that both the playground of describing language and the playground of inventing and collating language-games emerged as genuine products of the playground of abstract consideration. But so I have been suggesting that these two playgrounds are intrinsically bound up with each other: that the kind of cooperation between them has been forged and authenticated by the playground of abstract consideration. Now all this is just another way of saying that Wittgenstein looked at his fictitious language-games as pivotal parts of his descriptions of our language. He could not possibly have spared himself the trouble of inventing and collating such entities, no matter how curious the task.

Of course, a claim to the effect that Wittgenstein's fictitious language-games are anything but mere appendages to his dialectical proceedings requires detailed consideration, and so far we have done little beyond dropping a few hints and suggestions. Leaving the details for the next chapters to expound, the present one draws to a close by adding one more hint.

> A simile is part of our edifice; but we cannot draw any conclusions from it either; it doesn't lead us beyond itself, but must remain standing as a simile. We can draw no inferences from it. As when we compare a sentence to a picture (in which case, what we understand by 'picture' must already have been established in us earlier//before) or when I compare the application of language with, for instance, that of the calculus of multiplication.
>
> Philosophy simply puts everything before us, and neither explains nor deduces anything. (PO: 177)

No matter what the simile, Wittgenstein's philosophy is not what it is without a simile, part of his edifice as he says the simile is. If philosophy simply puts everything before us, and neither explains nor deduces anything, that is, if philosophy can *in the end only* describe language, it is *in the end* all due to the simile. In the beginning was the simile, and philosophy can in the end only describe language.[33] The simile does not lead beyond itself in that description is the philosopher's last word. The simile must remain standing as a simile; it cannot be explained at last, hence one fails to leave the simile for what it is if one tries to explain its appropriateness with reference to language. It is the simile that fixes the concept of language to work with; it is this way around and not the other. It is this way around and the other is nothing but twaddle and confusion. If philosophy can in the end only describe language and if the modal force of this 'can' traces all the way back to a simile, then the simile is what has been laid down *and enunciated* in the beginning. Only then is there a fixing of a concept, a means with which one can enter the philosophical stage at all and tackle problems. The simile must remain standing as a simile: this also means that there is a kind of remainder in Wittgenstein's philosophy. It is or determines the spirit with which *he* looks at language, and *wants* to look at it, for reasons of philosophy.

Wittgenstein's words '[a simile] doesn't lead us beyond itself' are a clear allusion to relativity, to a moment in his way of looking at language that is anything but an appendage. Relativity is not what Wittgenstein introduces into his investigations, so as to give *them*, say, an additional limb. No, his investigations are rather built upon relativity, which comes in the way of what does not lead us beyond itself: a simile. But in whichever way the simile comes, its attributes must be laid down *beforehand*. If you compare a sentence to a picture, you must lay down *beforehand* what you mean by that notion. If you want to look at the language-game as autonomous: you must lay down *beforehand* what that looking amounts to. If it amounts to this-and-that: your handling of language is committed to run along certain lines; and along other lines if the simile amounts to something else. The activity of laying down beforehand of what a simile signifies with respect to the phenomenon of language, i.e., the enunciation of its form and attributes, is what Wittgenstein took so much care of, among other things, on the playground of abstract consideration. It was especially in the early 1930s that he was caught up more with the activity of enunciating his interest than with solving philosophical problems *de facto*.

The notion of a simile in the above passage is not be confused with the notion of a fictitious language-game itself. Still, both notions are intimately related to each other because of what Wittgenstein has laid down on the playground of abstract consideration. The whole point of the little 'as' in Wittgenstein's remark

---

33 Cf. 'But we look at games and language under the guise of a game played according to rules. That is, we are always comparing language with a procedure of that kind' (PG: 63).

'I look at this language-game as autonomous' resides in the simile. There is no looking at the language-game as autonomous unless the notion of autonomy has been laid down first. And Wittgenstein has laid it down *such* that it makes sense to address the phenomenon of language in terms of language-games *such* that it makes sense to compare these things with fictitious language-games. Once something makes sense in Wittgenstein's hands, early and later, it makes no sense as an appendage, hence it is not to be treated as an appendage to *his* philosophical thinking. Once making sense, it is part of his dialectical edifice, in the sense that it determines the character of its proceedings, and if some part or other gives rise to more than mere teething troubles it does not stop short of what Wittgenstein has laid down and enunciated on the playground of abstract consideration, in short: Wittgenstein's vantage point. One of the things we started with in our considerations on the special character of Wittgenstein's philosophy is that he *wants* to leave everything *as it is*. How? By furnishing *in the end* descriptions *only*? This is, as we shall see, not an easy task to accomplish.

2. "Die Problematik der Philosophie ist die Problematik des Witzes"[34]

Sie glauben nämlich, man nehme der Definition ihre Bedeutung, Wichtigkeit, wenn man sie als bloße Ersetzungsregel, die von Zeichen handelt, hinstellt. Während die Bedeutung der Definition in ihrer Anwendung liegt, quasi in ihrer Lebenswichtigkeit. Und eben das geht heute in dem Streit zwischen Formalismus, Intuitionismus, etc. vor sich. Es ist den Leuten unmöglich, die Wichtigkeit einer Sache [Handlung], ihre Konsequenzen, ihre Anwendung, von ihr selbst zu unterscheiden; die Beschreibung einer Sache von der Beschreibung ihrer Wichtigkeit.

Ludwig Wittgenstein[35]

2.1 The most important questions are covered up

'I'll teach you differences.'—Wittgenstein is reported to have said that he thought of using King Lear's words as a motto for the *Philosophical Investigations*.[36] They certainly would not have cut a poor figure, for Wittgenstein was indeed anxious to teach differences, that is, on the playground of describing language as well as on the playground of inventing and collating language-games. As regards the playground of abstract consideration, Wittgenstein, among other things, far more than teaching differences there, enunciated the importance of doing so, of paying attention to particulars, of describing language-games, i.e., of 'describing one as a variation of another—by describing them and *emphasizing* their differences and analogies' (RFM: 139). And this importance, as Wittgenstein was wont to add, concerns every branch of our language, every field that troubles the philosophical mind. It is by no means confined to e.g. mathematics, or to this field more so than to the fields where we do psychological things with words.

Our concern in this chapter is with the playground of describing language, as well as with a recurring problem that Wittgenstein faced there while trying to come to descriptive terms with the logical predicament of our language. It falls to the lot of especially Chapter 4 and 5 to see what kinds of difficulties he faced on the playground of inventing and collating language-games, thus while trying to

---

34 'The problematics of philosophy is the problematics of the point.'

35 TS 211: 429.

36 Drury 1981: 171.

describe variations of the logical predicaments of our language. As we have been intimating in the first chapter, and as we shall need to explicate in time, it is only the efforts on the two playgrounds *together* that describe our own language. The internal relationship that these two grounds bear to each other has been forged and sealed by the playground of abstract consideration and only against the backdrop of this playground is it possible to unfold and to appreciate Wittgenstein's efforts and assorted movements on both grounds. The depth of his later philosophy is the depth of his descriptive concern, the nature of which is easy to misapprehend unless his recurring troubles on both playgrounds are taken into account and appropriately considered, troubles and bumps that Wittgenstein's own understanding has got by running up against the limits of language, in the light of his own stated objectives.

One of the first things for us to do is to recognize that Wittgenstein laboured under the dictum of only one playground of abstract consideration. That is, at the rear of his philosophy of, for instance, mathematics does not stand a playground of abstract consideration that is to be distinguished from the one at work with respect to his activities in the field of psychology. His concern to do away with *all* explanation and to provide for description *only* is a concern of overarching dimensions and is not confined to one field of Wittgenstein's investigations— or to one such field more so than to others. The *point* of a remark such as 'All *explanation* must disappear, and description alone must take its place' (PI: 109) is one and the same for each field of our language to which Wittgenstein finds himself attracted philosophically. To see why he is not *interested* in giving explanations in, for instance, mathematics is to see why he is not interested in giving explanations in philosophy at all. And to see why he is anxious to give descriptions instead of explanations is to see why, for instance, mathematics is in no way different a field from psychology as regards the demands he has on that very anxiousness of him. Now if we recognize that there is only *one* playground of abstract consideration, and are willing to develop a keen eye for the details of Wittgenstein's efforts to provide in the end descriptions only, it should come as no surprise that these efforts as regards mathematics appear to have strikingly much in common with those he undertakes in the field of language where we do psychological things with words. The following passage deserves our special interest.

> An investigation is possible in connexion with mathematics which is entirely analogous to our investigations of psychology. It is just as little a *mathematical* investigation as the other is a psychological one. It will *not* contain calculations, so it is not for example logistic. It might deserve the name of an investigation of the 'foundations of mathematics'. (PPF: 372)

At first blush these words seem to furnish a memorable example of a philosopher dabbling in what we might call speculative philosophy. His suggestion is that he has as yet not tried his hand in the field of mathematics, but that it could be applied there fruitfully on the model of his philosophical investigations in psychology. But, of course, the kind of *possibility* that is being contemplated here, by later Wittgenstein, is not made the subject matter of speculative philosophy. As a matter of fact, Wittgenstein was already long underway in the philosophy of mathematics before he put the above words down on paper. And, to be sure, he never tried his hand in that field of language only to *discover* that an investigation is *possible* 'in connexion with mathematics which is entirely analogous' to his investigations of psychology. There is no such kind of discovery here, any more than there is one with respect to his investigations of psychology, that is, whether they *can* indeed be carried out according to *his philosophical interest.*

Not every investigation of mathematics that bypasses *mathematical* problems is worth the name of an investigation of the 'foundations of mathematics'. However, according to the mathematician, no *such* an investigation is ever worth deserving such an impressive title. Yet Wittgenstein's work in mathematics, which is as little a mathematical investigation as his work in psychology is a psychological one, deserves to be viewed as an investigation of its foundations, at least according his own lights, because his style of bypassing mathematical problems renders his investigations *entirely analogous* to his investigations in *psychology* and not until that coordination has been established is his work in mathematics possible and worth the name. Is there anything more absurd in the eyes of the mathematician than Wittgenstein's remark? A clash is ineluctable, but I guess that it is Wittgenstein who will determine its depth and character.

Of course, mathematics differs in many a respect from psychology, but for all the charm and attraction that King Lear's words had for Wittgenstein, such a difference gained no ascendency over his philosophical interest. For what renders a *philosophical* investigation of mathematics *possible* in his eyes, as we have been suggesting above, is not an interest that is altogether different from the kind that prompts him to do philosophy in the psychological branches of our language, but one and the same interest. Wittgenstein looks at both fields with an eye that renders them cousins with each other, brother and sister if you like; but then it is at last our own philosophical proclivities that render these two fields so much akin to each other, for no sooner has the philosophical light dawned upon our minds than we think and talk in *a highly characteristic way.* '[W]hat a mathematician is inclined to say about the objectivity and reality of mathematical facts is not a philosophy of mathematics, but something for philosophical *treatment*'

(PI: 254). What Wittgenstein sets over against the mathematician's claim is not a claim of his own, an opinion which he feels he must defend against the odds occasioned by the mathematician, but a way of looking, his uncommon way of looking, which is determined to the core by his need for clarity and nothing less than 'complete clarity' (PI: 133). It is a way of looking that cannot be insensitive to what we are 'inclined to say about the objectivity and reality' of psychological facts. For what we say in that state of mind is not a philosophy of psychology, any more than the former is a philosophy of mathematics. It, too, is something for philosophical *treatment*.

In order to bring out his point, Wittgenstein has provocatively chosen to bring it to bear in the above passage upon two fields of investigation whose mutual differences could not be more pronounced. In mathematics, for instance, general agreement reigns over the results of our calculations, whereas our language-games entertaining psychological verbs do not ground to a halt should disagreement prevail—on the contrary. So Wittgenstein does not turn a blind eye to such differences—any more than he turns a deaf ear to how *we* talk about such differences in our philosophical moments. We tend to think that such differences *must* be so and *cannot* possibly have been otherwise, and, always ready to leap to explanations of such modalities, we say that the lack of general agreement in our psychological language-games has everything to do with 'the objectivity and reality of facts', with a fact such as that 'he is he and I am I'—.

Here is how Wittgenstein looks at the matter:

> "The uncertainty as to whether another person is in pain" – is it based on the fact that he is he and I am I? [...]. No, *here* I'm deceived by a picture. The uncertainty is a matter of the particular case and of the vacillating of the concept. But that is our game – we play it with an elastic tool. (LWPP I: 243; amended translation)

> It seems to me as though it would be not false but nonsense to say "I feel his pains," but as though this were because of the nature of the pain, of the person etc. as though, therefore, this statement were ultimately a statement about the nature of things.
>
> So we speak for example of an asymmetry in our mode of expression and we look on it as a mirror image of the essence of the things. (PO: 208f.)

In our present study we shall have ample opportunity to dwell on such passages as these. Now I merely quote them: because they are typical—that is, because there is a typical movement of thought at work in them, one that Wittgenstein entertains time and again in his concern with mathematics as much as in his struggles to come to descriptive terms in the psychological sections of our language. This movement is typical because we are so much inclined to think typically about the 'objectivity and reality' of both mathematical and psychological facts. In moments of philosophy, we think in highly characteristic terms about the connection between language and the world. We do mathematics the way we do and our psychological language-games are what they are, because, we cannot help thinking, of the way reality is; because our language-games mirror the essence of things and unless they do so they are done for, and we withal.

What Wittgenstein's words intimate is the unvarying character of interest behind *his* activities, an interest that renders these activities philosophical in *his* conception of the word. What prompts him to pursue the philosophy of mathematics *is* precisely what prompts him to pursue the philosophy of psychology, and vice versa. It requires no piece of mathematics itself to motivate the philosophy of mathematics any more than it requires a psychological verb to motive the philosophy of psychology. Given the kind of interest with which he enters the philosophical stage, Wittgenstein could not possibly have confined himself to doing philosophy of one particular field. What arouses his interest in mathematics is what renders him as open and disposed philosophically to other fields of our language. But, then, what do mathematics and psychology have in common? Well, both fields lead us *astray*, in moments of philosophy, Wittgenstein as well as any of us. Yet, Wittgenstein got a true nose, a mighty thirst for logical poisons—and an extravagant hunger for clarity as well. He wants nothing less than *complete clarity*, which seems a tall order. But Wittgenstein, as so often, qualifies his statements, for wanting *that much* clarity—'only means that the philosophical problems should *completely* disappear' (PI: 133).

There is a key word to be mentioned here, but it does not clarify much, I think, unless it is being mentioned and elaborated on in connection with another aspect of Wittgenstein's philosophy. The latter is 'clarity' and the key word is the extraordinary individual character of his philosophy.

> Work on philosophy – like work in architecture in many respects – is really more work on oneself. On one's own conception. On how one sees things. (And what one demands from them.) (CV: 24)

His has always been work on oneself: Wittgenstein's Tractarian effort no less than his later one. His has always been blood; his has never been a *Lehre*:[37] neither his *Tractatus*, nor his later philosophy. What is being taught at universities is Wittgensteinianism, which is a *Lehre*, a bloodless version of Wittgenstein's own personal quest, an Ism that you can practise within contemporary academic circles and teach with the same fervour and conscience as with your colleagues read Russell, Hegel, and cognitive science. Wittgensteinianism no doubt bears a little

---

37 Cf. preface to *Tractatus*.

family resemblance to Wittgenstein's own philosophy, but it bears perhaps a far greater family resemblance to Hegelian*ism*. Of course, it is no small topic that I am broaching here and my unhallowed hands shall not dare to enlarge on it in the present book. Just a few words: the above passage speaks of work on oneself, on one's own conception: *On how one sees things.* Indeed, what Wittgenstein was presenting in his first book is little more than a certain *account of a view*, and much of what Wittgenstein delivers in his second magnum opus again concerns the presentation of an *account of view*, one that has emanated from his first account and remains as intimately connected with it as anything can be. How later Wittgenstein *wants* to see things has been laid down by his famous concept of *eine übersichtliche Darstellung*[38], a concept that he, in view of that work on himself, on his own conception, deems fundamental and of which he says that it 'characterizes the way we represent things, how we look at matters' (PI: 122).[39] Indeed, a characteristic of Wittgenstein is that he presents his uncommon way of looking at things conspicuously often with a depersonalized touch: 'we', 'us' and 'our'.

The best way to characterize one's way of looking is to contrast it with other ways of doing so, which is precisely what Wittgenstein does on end. But the other ways, from his own point of view, are not such ones as keep his mind calm and his head unruffled, but precisely such ones for which he has adopted his own way of looking in the first instance, and against which he *wants* to go, primed as these various ways are with the urge to explain and justify in philosophy.

> Ramsey was a bourgeois thinker [*ein bürgerlicher Denker*]. I.e. he thought with the aim of clearing up the affairs of some particular community. He did not reflect on the essence of the state – or at least he did not like doing so – but on how *this* state might reasonable be organized. The idea that this state might not be the only possible one partly disquieted him and partly bored him. He wanted to get down as quickly as possible to reflecting on the foundations – of *this* state. This was what he was good at & what really interested him; whereas real philosophical reflection disquieted him until he puts its result (if it had one) on one side as trivial. (CV: 24)

Here is a genuine clash of interests, one that seems to concern Wittgenstein and Ramsey only: 'two households, both alike in dignity, in fair Camabridge, where we lay our scene.' And yet, Wittgenstein, in the above passage, takes to a general movement of thought of his, one that tells us as much about his own private

---

38 'Perspicuous representation' and 'surveyable representation' are the usual English renderings of Wittgenstein's phrase. I shall, throughout this book, more often than not stick to the German original.

39 See especially Chapter 4 for more on this concept.

household of thinking as about the public household of his times, here presented in the very person of Ramsey *as a thinker*. If Ramsey was bourgeois, well then, he did not work *against* the general drift of his times, a time that Wittgenstein did not mean to deny an eye for clarity, any more than a certain sensitivity for doing philosophy that aims at elucidatory work. But Ramsey was bourgeois: 'The idea that this state might not be the only possible one partly disquieted him and partly bored him.' These words pinpoint the place where Wittgenstein's and Ramsey's personalities kept clashing, thus not in spite of the fact that Ramsey was out for clarity as much as Wittgenstein himself, but precisely owing to it. For Ramsey's understanding of clarity was inherent to his bourgeois way of thinking, to his bourgeois way of looking at the world. He did not aim at seeing the present state as one possibility among other possibilities; on the contrary, other such possibilities partly disquieted him and partly bored him. Wittgenstein, for his own part, with his fundamental concept of an *übersichtliche Darstellung*, precisely aimed at doing *that*: seeing our own logical predicament as a possibility alongside other possible predicaments. Exactly the present state of affairs—in our language, notably—partly disquieted him and partly bored him, and the more it impressed upon him the appearance of being the *only* possibility the more disquieting it was to his mind. We shall have much opportunity to elaborate on these general points in this book. For now let us have a look at how Wittgenstein speaks of the status of contradiction in the following passage.

> It is not the business of philosophy to resolve a contradiction by means of a mathematical or logico-mathematical discovery, but to render surveyable [*übersichtlich*] the state of mathematics that disquiets us – the state of affairs *before* the contradiction is resolved. (And in doing this one is not sidestepping a difficulty.)
>
> The bourgeois status [*bürgerliche Stellung*] of a contradiction, or its status in the bourgeois world [*bürgerlichen Welt*] – that is the philosophical problem. (PI: 125)[40]

The bourgeois thinker reacts to contradiction as follows: 'Oh my God! It destroys *everything*, our hard-won present calculi!' The image of a contradiction *disquiets* the bourgeois thinker enormously, whereas the opposite, i.e. the radical disallowance of a contradiction, *disquiets* a thinker as Wittgenstein. Ramsey aims at clarity, no doubt, but he is the kind of thinker whose conception of clarity aims at seeing the present state on a foundation that tolerates no other possibilities. So where Ramsey sets off, Wittgenstein begins to demur, a reaction in which the bourgeois thinker sees little more than trivialities and to which he reacts with a shrug of the shoulders and 'you are not being constructive'-type responses. What

---

40 Amended translation.

Wittgenstein says about Ramsey in the above passage is a recurring *theme* in his work and it is notably reminiscent of what he has been saying, endlessly, with respect to the mathematicians. Here are some of these sayings.[41]

> 'Mathematical logic' has completely deformed the thinking of mathematicians and of philosophers, by setting up superficial interpretation of the forms of our everyday language as an analysis of the structures of facts. Of course in this it has only continued to build on the Aristotelian logic. (RFM: 300)[42]

> Philosophical clarity will have the same effect on the growth of mathematics as sunlight has on the growth of potato shoots. (In a dark cellar they grow yards long.) (PG: 381)

> If a philosopher draws the attention of a mathematician to a distinction, or a misleading mode of speaking, the mathematician says 'Yes, we know all that already, it isn't really very interesting.' What he does not realize though is that when he is troubled by philosophical questions, it is just because of those very unclarities [*Unklarheiten*] that he passed over in the past with a shrug of the shoulders. (TS 219: 10)

> A mathematician is bound to be horrified by my mathematical comments, since he has always been trained to avoid indulging in thoughts and doubts of the kind I develop. He has learned to regard them as something contemptible and, to use an analogy from psycho-analysis (this paragraph is reminiscent of Freud), he has acquired a revulsion from them as infantile. That is to say, I trot out all the problems that a child learning arithmetic, etc., finds difficult, the problems that education represses without solving. I say to those repressed doubts: you are quite correct, go on asking, demand clarification! (PG: 382)

Demand clarification! But what is demanded *here* is not really wanted by modern western civilizations, not really understood, and modern academic circles contribute as much to this general attitude and culture of passing over unclarities with a shrug of the shoulders as any other institutionalized form of thinking and philosophy. 'Our children already learn in school that water *consists* of the gases hydrogen & oxygen, or sugar of carbon, hydrogen & oxygen. Anyone who does not understand is stupid. The most important questions are covered up [*zugedeckt*]' (CV: 81). There is no doubt a demand for clarity in our time and

---

41 Cf. the passage from Chapter 1.

42 Wittgenstein speaks of '"The disastrous invasion" of mathematics by logic' ['"*Der unheilvolle Einbruch*" *der Logik in die Mathematik*'] (RFM: 281), a clear reference to—and nice turning of—Frege's famous words: 'Und damit komme ich auf das zu sprechen, was der Wirkung meines Buches bei den Logikern im Wege steht. Es ist der verderbliche Einbruch der Psychologie in die Logik.' Gottlob Frege, *Grundgesetze der Arithmetik* (Hildesheim, Zürich, New York: Georg Olms Verlag, 1998), XIV.

culture, but *that* demand concerns 'the present state'; it is constructive; it aims at building, as mathematicians and scientists do.

> Our civilization is characterized by the word progress. Progress is its form, it is not one of its properties that it makes progress. <u>Typically</u> it constructs. Its <u>activity</u> is to construct a more and more complicated structure. And even clarity is only a means to this end & not an end in itself.
>
> For me, though, clarity, transparency, is an end in itself.
>
> I am not interested in erecting a building but in having the foundations of possible buildings transparently before me.
>
> So my aim is another one compared to the scientists', and my movement of thought is different from theirs. (CV: 9)

It is part of Wittgenstein's aim to subjugate his hunger for clarity to reflections such as the above passage exemplifies. His anxiousness to achieve clarity does not stop short of that anxiousness itself, as if that state of mind provides a driving force behind his philosophical activities without expressing the need to reach clarity over its own state and condition. One of Wittgenstein's favourite means to elucidate his own aims and interest is to contrast them with those of other people. And the dupes are more often than not scientists, i.e., *the scientific way of thinking*, which 'elbows all others aside' (CV: 69). Its aims and enduring interests are clear enough by themselves, at least according to Wittgenstein's suggestion in the above passage, and, obviously, clear enough to make clear what his own aims and interest are: *not* anything of the scientists'.

Scientists erect buildings; clarity is not their aim, but clarity must nevertheless be a factor in their aims and interests, and thus a point in common with Wittgenstein. Although clarity is not an end in itself for the scientists it still might turn out to be something that Wittgenstein can catch up with only to push it a little further, beyond the scientists' aims. Yet, Wittgenstein's 'aim is another one compared to the scientists', and [his] movement of thought is different from theirs.' This rider makes all the difference: Wittgenstein destroys. What renders his own aim intrinsically different from virtually everything that we are accustomed to, in science and philosophy, as well as in the daily course of life, is that Wittgenstein does not so much think in the 'true versus false'-category as that he plies his whip in terms of 'sense versus nonsense' first and foremost. Clarity is an end in itself for Wittgenstein, hence clarity is not enough; that is to, clarity *cannot* be enough, for there can be clarity only where darkness and obscurity reigns first, as it did in Wittgenstein's own mind no less than in the heads and minds of his contemporaries. His demand for clarity is work *on himself*, something that clearly demands great courage: 'It is all one to me whether the typical western scientist understands or appreciates my work since in any case he does not understand the spirit in which I write' (CV: 9).

The dark and obscure was Wittgenstein's own self in relation to the time in which he lived, in relation to the language he used and spoke; in relation to music and architecture, his own ancestry, his friends and foes, his family, his own biography, his own dire need for love, his own style of thinking and writing, his future life and death.

The relation of Wittgenstein to his times is well-captured by the one word *Entgegengesetzt*. Speaking of the spirit of his own time as one that is 'alien and uncongenial [*unsympathisch*]' to him, he continues as follows:

> For in these times genuine & strong characters simply turn away from the field of the arts & towards other things & <u>somehow</u> the value of the individual [*der Wert des Einzelnen*] finds expression. Not, to be sure, in the way it would at times of Great Culture. Culture is like a great organization which assigns to each of its members his place, at which he can work in the spirit of the whole, and his strength can with a certain justice be measured by his success as understood within that whole. In a time without culture [*Zeit der Unkultur*], however, forces are fragmented and the strength of the individual is wasted through the overcoming of opposing forces & frictional resistance [*entgegengesetzte Kräfte & Reibungswiederstände*]; it is not manifest in the distance travelled but rather perhaps in the heat generated through the overcoming of frictional resistances. (CV: 8f.)

Wittgenstein's philosophy was work on oneself, on how *he* saw things, in opposition to [*entgegen*] how the time in which he lived saw things and looked at the world. He would not have claimed of himself to be a strong character, I think, but strong he surely was of mind to comprehend that he would definitely have been crushed by the *Zeit der Unkultur* if his talent for answering conceptual questions had not come to pass and granted him a ground to stand on, and the means to express his own individuality to the core. His talent had given him 'a job' to work on himself, on how he saw things, in opposition to [*entgegen*] all kinds of forces that were at large in some form or other in the dark and obscure of his time, and still are in our present *Lebensform*, in the language we employ. His was work on himself, on how he saw things, in opposition to all the mesmerizing forces that obtrude themselves upon the mind and lead it astray the moment ones becomes contemplative. There are many remarks and passages in Wittgenstein's oeuvre in which the word "*entgegen*" turns up and in which the connection with the import of his words in the above passage has been somewhat lost, or ceased to be obvious.

> One cannot guess how a word functions. One has to *look* at its application and learn from that.

But the difficulty is to remove the prejudice which stands opposed to [*entgegensteht*] this learning. It is not a *stupid* prejudice. (PI: 340, translation amended)

[The philosophical problems] are, of course, not empirical problems; but they are solved through an insight into the workings of our language, and that in such a way that these workings are recognized: *in opposition to* [*entgegen*] an urge to misunderstand them. (PI: 109, translation amended).

The *urge* to misunderstand makes *all* the difference; it renders Wittgenstein's aim 'another one compared to the scientists', his 'movement of thought different from theirs' (CV: 9). 'His labour in philosophy is as it were an idleness in mathematics' (RFM: 302), he says, but it is not that kind of labour if his philosophy in the psychological field is not 'motivated' by an entirely analogous idleness. This reminds us of Wittgenstein's dictum that an 'investigation is possible in connexion with mathematics which is entirely analogous to our investigations of psychology.'

> What does mathematics need a foundation for? It no more needs one, I believe, than propositions about physical objects—or about sense impressions, need an analysis. What mathematical propositions do stand in need of is a clarification of their grammar, just as do those other propositions. (RFM: 378)

One needs to notice the rhetoric here, the typical Wittgensteinian *turning* of a phrase or way of thinking. It is the mathematician who declares that mathematics is in need of a foundation; hence he would be rather baffled at reading the question with which the above passage opens. But how much more baffled he would be to read it in connection with something that he has never *questioned*, and never would, namely that mathematical propositions stand in need of a clarification. The mathematician has long since noticed that the products of his own discipline stand in need of a clarification, but, and that is Wittgenstein's point, he fails to see how this need could ever be met without making their connection to a particular foundation clear. The mathematician truly may believe that he is clear, that he cares about clarity and strives after it, whereas he, according to Wittgenstein's lights, *is not clear at all*. So where the mathematician with his conception of clarity is anxious to clarify his propositions *by* bringing them to bear upon 'a' foundation, he will soon come across Wittgenstein and hit upon *his* conception of clarity. To come across Wittgenstein is to see him clearing up the ground on which one is erecting a building, be it in the name of logical atomism, formalism, or intuitionism. The building: a house of cards.

> What we are destroying are only houses of cards, and we are clearing up the ground of language on which they stood. (PI: 118)

Wittgenstein subjugates every field of our language to a *Pathos* that is the same each time. To destroy nothing but houses of cards *and* to clear up the grounds of language on which they stood is not what Wittgenstein could have performed for one field of our language only. His interest is very different from the one with which the mathematician enters the philosophical stage and turns contemplative. The latter's interest commits him to write a books on the foundations of his own discipline whilst his mind grows weak at the mere thought to think philosophically about the psychological branches of his language. The former's interest, on the other hand, has not a single field or section of language of its own, prompting his mind to move systematically to and fro within each of its frontiers, within *and* between them, without gassing.

There is nothing contingent under Wittgenstein's philosophical sun *as far the broad round* of his dialectical movement is concerned. On whatever field Wittgenstein does do his ploughing, he leaves its marks (the earthworms can tell us much about its characteristic cuts and bearing). If the broad round of Wittgenstein's dialectical edifice is given by his dictum 'All *explanation* must disappear, and description alone must take its place' (PI: 109), so is the main outline of his philosophical problems given by another dictum: 'Not empiricism and yet realism in philosophy, that is the hardest thing. (Against Ramsey)' (RFM: 325). The kind of realism that Wittgenstein aspires to see in philosophy is to be achieved ultimately in terms of descriptions of our language *only*, that is, not only with respect to his investigations on the so-called foundations of mathematics, but with respect to any other field of our language falling under his attention. It is the broad round of his dialectical movement in which the nature of his descriptions inheres, and it is this same broad round of a dialectical thing to which we need to pay attention should we want to see what he faces on the theme of recurring problems whilst trying to come out with descriptions, with these things only, and with these things in the end.

2.2 The *Witz* of the language-game

Our focus in the present chapter is on that stage of Wittgenstein's dialectical process where he has at long last done away with Empiricism—except for the part that is to close the dialectical circle: his description of language. To have done away with it except for this seemingly minor 'addition' seems to virtually have done away with it. And yet, as we have been suggesting, Wittgenstein, within shouting distance of coming out with descriptions only at the end of the day, faces particular troubles that are very difficult to overcome—troubles that keep turning up, irrespective of his field of investigation, be it mathematics or our indeterminate ways of doing psychological things with words. Wittgenstein has not done away with Empiricism as long as language keeps troubling him, which is exactly what it does in a way that cannot be expounded fully without reference to his notion of describing language *in the end*. Not until Realism has taken the place of Empiricism has Wittgenstein done away with the urge to lodge Empiricism in philosophy. Modelling the words 'Not empiricism and yet realism' on his own dictum 'All *explanation* must disappear, and description alone must take its place' (PI: 109), I suggest that expounding Wittgenstein's troubles is a task intrinsically bound up with the effort to expound what the Realism is that *he* aspires to achieve. But so I suggest that it would be a grave mistake to expound what Wittgenstein's Realism amounts to *without* getting involved into all kinds of questions concerning his efforts to see the end of the day with *descriptions* of our language only.

The hardest thing in philosophy is the difficulty to close the dialectical circle *against* the urge to lodge Empiricism there. And my suggestion is that the process of *closing* this circle by mere descriptions comes to a halt *at a certain stage*. In other words, Wittgenstein gets stuck in his efforts to overcome certain troubles which he in all likelihood did not foresee when he began working out his later way of looking at language. He gets stuck on both the playground of describing language and the playground of inventing and collating language-games. And what he gets stuck in are not certain troubles in the field of mathematics and certain troubles of an utterly different kind in the field of psychology, but troubles that from one field to whatever other field appear to have strikingly much in common with each other. Wittgenstein's dialectical edifice, whose architect he was and whose implementation *he* did not consider to be *some* alternative way of doing philosophy after the demise of the Tractarian way of doing so, is built on something that *turned out* to be *problematic*. But, of course, what are the troubles that beset Wittgenstein's efforts to appear with descriptions only at the end of the day? Let us first try to outline what is at issue here, and leave the famous 'second' for the sections to come.

Wittgenstein's troubles are Wittgenstein's troubles. They are inherently related to his own philosophy, to what we have been calling his uncommon way of looking at things. For his philosophy *is* a struggle against the bewitchment of our language by the resources of our language (PI: 110).[43] He struggles against all kinds of prejudices but notably against those that draw before our philosophical

---

43 Cf. 'Philosophy, as we use the word, is a fight against the fascination which forms of expression exert upon us' (BB: 27).

eyes an Empiricist picture of its workings. To Wittgenstein it is a patent fact that, in our philosophical moments, we look at language through such pictures. It is a fact that he exploits philosophically—in the sense that there can be no philosophy for him without this fact. *That* philosophy, in Wittgenstein's sense of the word, faces difficulties on its way of overcoming the bewitchments lies partly in his determination of his philosophy, for he wants to fight against this bewitchment. But now, that Wittgenstein was to face serious troubles and genuine blockages in this fight is something that requires further reflection. For although philosophy is a struggle against the bewitchment of our language, it is, according to Wittgenstein's lights, certainly not a hopeless affair, something that philosophers are doomed to lose no matter how much they try. The battle can be won, but one needs to change one's point of view:

> If one doesn't want to SOLVE philosophical problems – why doesn't one give up dealing with them. For solving them means changing one's point of view, the old way of thinking. And if you don't want that, then you should consider the problems unsolvable. (LWPP II: 84)

Philosophical problems are solvable: the fight against the bewitchment of our language can be won, provided that one gives up on 'the old way of thinking' by changing one's point of view. That the fight can be won is a determination on the part of Wittgenstein's philosophy, and my point is that this determination has brought along problems of its own making: problems the full scope of which Wittgenstein did not divine at the time he enunciated his uncommon way of looking at things. What are these problems, troubles? Wittgenstein, most determined as he was to wage a battle against the bewitchment of our language, soon found himself keeping count of a recurring trouble in a formulation that I could not resist appropriating as the title of the present chapter. '*Die Problematik der Philosophie ist die Problematik des Witzes*'[44]. This remark, then, not unlike the famous 'not empiricism and yet realism, that is the hardest thing in philosophy', has a significance that is not confined to one or another field of Wittgenstein's investigations. Once in the business of giving descriptions, he sees himself raising one and the same type of questions—the tokens of which he has found out very difficult to answer indeed. The question: What is the point (*Witz*) of *this* language-game? That is to say: What is its *real* point? Precisely such questions are anything but easily answered, as Wittgenstein *came* to see and had to admit.

---

44 'The problematics of philosophy is the problematics of the point' (MS 150: 12).

Wittgenstein's important notion of *Witz* has found little resonation on the part of his commentators. This general lack of interest may reflect the general neglect, in the secondary literature, of Wittgenstein's notion of language description, which amounts to a blind spot for the kind of convoluted difficulties that he faced, not only on the playground of describing language-games, but also on the playground of inventing and collating them. This oversight seems to be substantial, as it touches upon a most crucial part of what Wittgenstein deems the hardest thing in philosophy. Now in order to get a feel of what is at issue here, let us consider the following remark:

> A use of language has normally what we might call a *point*. This is immensely important. Although it's true this is a matter of degree, and we can't say just where it ends. (LFM: 205)

This is the kind of remark that had better alert us to Wittgenstein's frequent use of the notion of *Witz*; or, indeed, of cognates such as *Wichtigkeit, Bedeutung, Bedeutsamkeit* and *Interesse*. (I shall avail myself of the words "*Witz*", "*Wichtigkeit*", and sometimes of the word "point".) Wittgenstein's playground of abstract consideration says that a use of language has normally what we might call a point. So on this playground there is no use of telling what the point of a language-game is. One needs to set out for the playground of describing language and 'to look and see' there. Here, as on the playground of inventing and collating language-games, Wittgenstein finds himself time and again confronted with the question of what is the *Witz* of the language-game at hand. He wants to *describe* the language-game and if we want to have a concise answer to the question of why it is 'immensely important' to bear in mind that 'a use of language has normally what we might call a point', it should be this: no descriptive account of this use is forthcoming as long as one fails to discern a *Witz*. But why should it be so difficult to make out the *Witz* of the language-game? The relevance of this question should be clear.

> So I am inclined to distinguish between the essential and the inessential in a game too. The game, one would like to say, has not only rules but also a *point* [*Witz*]. (PI: 564)

What Wittgenstein points out here is that there is an *indeterminacy* in his way of looking at things. To grasp the rules of the game is not yet to grasp *the game*. For two games can have one and the same set of rules and yet be totally different. It is with the overcoming of such differences that Wittgenstein is constantly confronted in his comparisons of language with rules of the game. The 'mere circumstance' that there is an unmistakable indeterminacy in his uncommon way of looking is not problematic, for the indeterminacy sets the stage for how he wants to look upon things and to work on himself. Rather what is problematic, that is, what has turned out to be so, is the overcoming of the indeterminacy *by* leaving our language *as it is*. The trouble arises when one attempts to provide descriptions of language only. Now what does the trouble look like in practice? The following passage, I think, gives us an exemplary answer.

> "But when I imagine something, something *goes on*, doesn't it?!" Well, something goes on —and then I make a noise. What for? Presumably [*wohl dazu*] in order to communicate what went on.—But how is telling done? When are we said to tell anything?—What is the language-game of communicating?
>
> I should like to say: you regard it much too much as a matter of course that one can tell anything to anyone. That is to say: we are so much accustomed to communication through [*Sprechen*], in conversation, that it looks to us as if the whole point of communication lay in this: someone else grasps the sense of my words—which is something mental: he as it were takes it into his own mind. If he then does something further with it as well, that is no part of the immediate purpose of language.
>
> One would like to say "Telling brings it about that he knows that I am in pain; it produces this mental phenomenon; everything else is inessential to the telling." As for what this queer phenomenon of knowledge is—there is time enough for that. Mental processes just are queer. (It is as if one said: "The clock tells us the time. What time is, is not yet settled. And as for what one tells the time for—that doesn't come in here.") (PI: 363)[45]

Wittgenstein, famous for broaching philosophical issues, here throws out a couple of thorny questions, only to leave his readers to think about the answers for themselves. The questions are: 'But how is telling done? When are we said to tell anything?—What is the language-game of communicating?'

Wittgenstein does not appear to be at pains to answer these curious questions. In the sections following the above passage, right up to the back cover of his book, he seems to keep as low a profile as he might be said to be keeping in the passage itself. And yet, if we look in vain for answers in that book, or in his oeuvre as a whole, we should notice that Wittgenstein faces a set of closely connected questions the answers to which he finds extremely difficult to supply himself. He tries to encourage his disciples and more dedicated readers to look and see for themselves, no doubt. But Wittgenstein's exhortation, in the passage quoted above, concerns a matter of pivotal importance to his dialectical edifice, the real intricacy of which he did not seem to have foreseen fully if at all on his playground of abstract consideration—the intricacy, namely, of answering

---

45 Cf. 'I make a plan not merely so as to make myself understood but also in order to get clear about the matter itself. (I.e. language is not merely a means of communication.)' (Z: 329).

questions of what the language-game *really looks like*. What is at work in *PI* §363 is a typical movement of thought (of which further examples will be given shortly), a movement that distinguishes between, on the one hand, the point of the language-game as it strikes us in the daily walk of life—and tends to do so with increased intensity in our philosophical moments, and, on the other hand, the *real point* of the language-game. But, of course, how did Wittgenstein manage to broach such a complicated matter in the first instance?

How, to keep to the above passage here, did Wittgenstein ever come so far as to see that there is something utterly bewitching in moments of philosophy, as he seems to be suggesting, about communication through language—: *so* bewitching that we fail to catch up with its so-called *real* point? That is, if 'we are so much accustomed to communication through *Sprechen*, in conversation, that it looks to us as if the whole point of communication lay in this: someone else grasps the sense of my words—which is something mental: he as it were takes it into his own mind', how then did Wittgenstein, *in spite of not* knowing what its real point is, at least conspire to perceive that the whole point of communication is *not* what we normally take it to be?

Not having the answers to his own questions at his disposal, Wittgenstein not only cannot possibly have broached the above issue on the basis of these answers, he might as well have asked himself whether he would have recognized them as correct should they have surreptitiously fallen into his hands on the playground of describing language. But how then salvage the real point of communication through language? Does the philosophical quest *in the end* really turn on merely 'looking and seeing'?—or, for that matter, on reminding oneself of how language *really* works?

In spite of its special focus on 'the language-game of communicating', *PI* §363 is noticeably general in its tendency. It exemplifies a point that Wittgenstein introduced only a few pages before, namely that we, in moments of doing philosophy, are so much *drawn* into believing that 'language always functions in *one* way, always serves the same purpose: to convey thoughts – which may be about houses, pains, good and evil, or whatever' (PI: 304).[46] Obviously, Wittgenstein finds fault with this one-sided way of looking at language. But he finds fault with any way of looking at language that imposes a one-sided way of functioning on its workings.

---

46 Cf. 'Misleading parallel: the expression of pain is a cry—the expression of thought, a proposition.
 As if the purpose of the proposition were to convey to one person how it is with another: only, so to speak, in his thinking part and not in his stomach' (PI: 317).

But could it not be said that Wittgenstein looks at language from a one-sided point of view himself?

We are interested in language as a procedure according to explicit rules, because philosophical problems are misunderstandings which must be removed by clarification of the rules according to which we want to use words.

We consider language from a one-sided point of view only. (PG: 68)[47]

Indeed, Wittgenstein is interested in language from a one-sided point of view, but his way of looking leaves something most important open, namely the *Witz* of the language-game. If you look at language as what 'always functions in *one* way, always serves the same purpose: to convey thoughts – which may be about houses, pains, good and evil, or whatever', then, you operate on the basis of a *preconceived* idea of what the *Witz* of the language-game is, no matter what the game. Wittgenstein, however, while comparing language with explicit rules, operates from a vantage point that wants to teach differences and that is at pains to describe 'one language-game as a variation of another—by describing them and emphasizing their differences and analogies.'

Wittgenstein *compares* language—for reasons of philosophy, and for these reasons only—with a procedure according to strict rules. He does not *impose* on the workings of language the notion that it *functions* according to rules. He, at least, does not mean to impose on language such a notion and he does not conceive his own way of looking as an approach to that effect either.

[R]emember that in general we don't use language according to strict rules—it hasn't been taught us by means of strict rules, either. *We*, in our discussions on the other hand, constantly compare language with a calculus proceeding according to exact rules.

This is a very one-sided way of looking at language. In practice we very rarely use language as such a calculus. (BB: 25)

Of course, if 'our ordinary use of language conforms to this standard of exactness only in rare cases why then do we in philosophizing constantly compare our use of words with one following exact rules?' (BB: 25). Although the answer that Wittgenstein gives to his own question should come as no surprise now—'the puzzles which we try to remove always spring from just this attitude towards language' (BB: 26)[48]—we do well to have a closer at it and to dwell on its point.

The attitude of which Wittgenstein speaks *is* our common way of looking at language, in moments of philosophy. We believe that the rules of language must be exact, for we think that language fails to function where exactitude fails to

---

47 Amended translation.

48 This answer anticipates *PI* §§130–131, which we shall address in the next chapter.

86

rule. We also believe that our attitude is the only correct one, for we think that one's point of view must conform to what language *is*, and language, in spite of its daily appearances, is not what it is unless its rules *are* exact. There is a *must* at work on the part of language and this *must*, we tell ourselves, must be felt and fostered on our part as philosophers, that is, in our attitude towards language, in our way of looking at the objects of our investigations. Any other attitude passes by these objects, and right from the beginning. So our attitude towards language sends us in pursuit of exactitude, in pursuit of something we think must be found in reality, but what we are in pursuit of then, according to Wittgenstein's lights, is only a house of cards. His uncommon way of looking at things deals with this kind of thinking of us about how a point of view must conform to what language is.

To compare language with a calculus proceeding according to exact rules is to look at its workings *as* autonomous, and it is from this point of view that Wittgenstein seeks to come to terms with the language-game *as* he finds it. Whatever he *finds* as regards certain features on the part of the language-game, it should have no negative effect on his way of looking at the language-game. Should Wittgenstein chance upon a language-game that turns out to have both arbitrary and non-arbitrary aspects, well, *that* is what he needs to come to terms with from his very way of looking at language as autonomous. It would have no negative effect on his way of looking and to think that it must have such an effect is to misunderstand what his point of view amounts to. If on the part of a language-game no exact rules can be made out, thus from a point of view that compares language with a calculus proceeding according to exact rules, well, *that* just is how the language-game presents itself *from his point of view*, a fact that Wittgenstein needs to come to (descriptive) terms with from that point of view. And to think otherwise is to misunderstand what his way of looking amounts to, if not any way of looking.

Wittgenstein, then, does not adapt his point of view according to the so-called nature of the language-game. He does not first look at its workings in order to find out what features it involves, only to adapt his point of view according to these ascertained features. Rather, he looks at the language-game as autonomous and if it *turns out* to have some non-autonomous characteristics it is exactly on account of a *predetermined* notion of what autonomy amounts to for *language*, that Wittgenstein is at all able to come to descriptive terms with its so-called workings. Autonomy is not a feature *of* the language-game. Wittgenstein merely looks at it *as* autonomous, not because the language-game *is* autonomous, but because of the philosophical problems.

Oskari Kuusela has a different take on these matters. Consider, for instance, what he says on the following words from the *Investigations*.

> To invent a language could mean to invent an instrument for a particular purpose on the basis of the laws of nature (or consistently with them); but it also has the other sense, analogous to that in which we speak of the invention of a game.
>
> Here I am stating something about the grammar of the word "language", by connecting it with the grammar of the word "invent". (PI: 492)

Here is what Kuusela makes of it:

> What the comparison of the invention of a language with the invention of instruments and games brings into view [...] is two different aspects of the concept of language: a sense in which its rules may be arbitrary and a sense in which they may be non-arbitrary. Both these aspects may be important for a clear understanding of the concept of language in that envisaging language under one aspect only may lead to forcing particular cases of language use into a mould in which they do not fit, and overall constitutes a simplistic conception of language. Equipped with such a simplistic conception one may then remain unable to resolve philosophical problems whose resolution requires the recognition of other aspects too.[49]

Wittgenstein, according to Kuusela, suggests that the concept of language has the two aspects of arbitrariness and non-arbitrariness, and that both are philosophically relevant, hence that we, lest our philosophical concern with language and its workings go astray, had better bear both of them in mind. Of course, to bear both aspects in mind does not mean, according to Kuusela's Wittgenstein, that they must be brought into account on every occasion. Rather, he just urges us to be alert to the particular features of the language-game at hand, and to guard against the temptation to handle each and every case in the light of either one or the other aspect exclusively.

But Wittgenstein's words in *PI* §492, I think, go much against the grain of Kuusela's suggestion. It is not because the concept of language has the two aspects that we need to bear them in mind in our (philosophical) investigations of language and its workings. It is rather the other way round. Kuusela's suggestion is that it makes sense to compare the invention of a language with the invention of instruments and games *because* of the 'intrinsic' nature of the concept of language, whereas Wittgenstein's suggestion is that such comparisons reveal us many an interesting thing about what the concept of language could mean, and

---

49 Oskari Kuusela, 'Gordon Baker, Wittgensteinian Philosophical Conceptions and Perspicuous Representation: the Possibility of Multidimensional Logical Descriptions', *Nordic Wittgenstein Review* 3/2 (2014), 82.

how it is operated on, by scientists and philosophers alike. Kuusela conjures up a Wittgenstein who has first investigated language, or the concept of language, only to discover that it makes good sense to compare the invention of language with the invention of instruments and games. But Wittgenstein's suggestion is precisely that the point of our investigations of language is determined by what we compare it with, wittingly or not. Wittgenstein effectively says: 'Tell me what you compare language with, and I tell you how you conceive the grammar of the word "language"'.

The peculiarity of Kuusela's argument is compounded by the way in which he tries to give support to his own interpretation. 'Envisaging language under one aspect only may lead to forcing particular cases of language use into a mould in which they do not fit, and overall constitutes a simplistic conception of language.' But the first part of this sentence begs the question and the second part gives rise the following question: Why should *two* aspects not also constitute a simplistic conception of language? The last sentence—'Equipped with such a simplistic conception one may then remain unable to resolve philosophical problems whose resolution requires the recognition of other aspects too'—speaks for itself: it exacerbates the begging and gives rise to similar questions.

In the foregoing we have been distinguishing between the so-called real point of the language-game and the point of the language-game as it *strikes us* in the daily course of life. Of course, the latter point is as real a point as the *real* point is of the language-game, for it is reality for us, users of our language as we are. But so it is a reality for Wittgenstein, the philosopher, namely as what leads us astray in philosophy only to disguise the real point of the language-game more than ever before. Wittgenstein should not find fault with the point of the language-game as it strikes us in the daily course of life. Wanting to leave everything as it is, he ought not to quarrel with our being 'so much accustomed to communication through language, in conversation.' What he should quarrel with, though, is that philosophers 'regard it much too much as a matter of course that one can tell anything to anyone.' The point of the language-game as it strikes us in the daily course of life is what it is and should not be treated as what misleads us then, hence as what requires an uprooting from our language. But no sooner has the philosophical mood dawned upon us than this same point begins to overwhelm our entire thinking process about the nature of any number of language-games. There is a picture at work in our language, one that we, philosophers, tend to take *au pied de la lettre*: 'the whole point of communication lay in this: someone else grasps the sense of my words—which is something mental: he as it were takes it into his own mind.' Indeed, there now is an Inner and an Outer.

We take the point of the language-game as a matter of course, the point as it strikes us in moments of philosophy, to this effect that we not so much fail to observe any alternative possibility as that the need to think about other possibilities does not even dawn upon us. We slide into a thinking process that leads us to build nothing but houses of cards. Though we do not yet see how the language-game is to be brought to bear upon mental processes—they just are queer—we are certain that they *must* play the part of the beating heart in the language-game.

> "Right; but there is a Something there all the same, which accompanies my cry of pain! And it is *on account of this* that I utter it. And this Something is what is important – and frightful." (PI: 296, emphasis mine).

Misled by what we take to be its *Witz*, we are eager to outline the language-game in a way in which *Wittgenstein* sees no more than the spontaneous erecting of just another house of cards. Outlining matters thus, we dabble feverishly and un-hampered in what he calls Empiricism. Processes in the medium of the mind are being looked at as taking essentially part of the language-game, whereas, in Wittgenstein's hands, they drop out from its *logical* commerce altogether. Empiricism, then, as Wittgenstein understands the term, has its ultimate source in our own language, in the characteristic ways it captures our minds in moments of philosophy. Empiricism, in philosophy, denominates a doctrine whose propositions do not turn out to be false, but nonsense for the most part. Exposing statements as nonsensical is, of course, part and parcel of Wittgenstein's dialectical process, but, as I shall try to show later on, it does not occur by virtue of those things that should draw this process to a close: descriptions of the language-game.

Of course, if we are 'so much accustomed to communication through [*Sprechen*], in conversation, that it looks to us as if the whole point of communication lay in this: someone else grasps the sense of my words', then the intimated phenomenon of iridescence must be widespread and should not be expected to confine itself to the more philosophically orientated corners of our intellectual life. Here is an excellent example from Oliver Sacks' book *Seeing Voices*:

> Joseph [a congenitally deaf boy of eleven] longed to communicate, but could not. Neither speaking nor writing nor singing was available to him, only gesture and pantomime, and a marked ability to draw. What has happened to him, I kept myself asking? What is going on inside, how has he come to such a pass? He looked alive and animated, but profoundly baffled: his eyes were attracted to speaking mouths and signing hands—they darted to our mouths and hands, inquisitively, uncomprehendingly, and, it seemed to me, yearningly. He perceived that something was "going on" between us, but he could

not comprehend what it was—he had, as yet, almost no idea of symbolic communication, of what it was to have a symbolic currency, to exchange meaning.[50]

Michael Tomasello, in two recent books of his own hand and direction, obliges with further intriguing examples of how unwittingly the whole idea of communication is operated on, by his own part as much as by others, and of how strong the phenomenon of iridescence is that fools him, us, all of us.[51]

*

Back to Wittgenstein's remark 'A use of language has normally what we might call a *point.*' Its clue, as should be clear by now, is not that we, in our philosophical moments, are forgetful of such a use having a point; rather, the clue is that we tend to associate ourselves in these moments with a point that is not its *real* point. We become *forgetful* of something pivotally important and before long we find ourselves facing the perplexing world of mental processes. I deliberately introduce the notion of forgetfulness, for it is one of those grammatical fixtures in Wittgenstein's philosophy in terms of which he *characterizes* a most important feature of his dialectical circle. Just as there is a way into the philosophical muddle, so there is a way out of it. But the way out is not paved on flagstones of novel truths, but on paths constituted by our *reminding ourselves* of what we have always known, namely, the use of our words in the daily course of life. To become forgetful in moments of philosophy is a thoroughly human affair and perfectly comprehensible. Though not necessarily being a sign of an exasperating habit or a contagious disease, our forgetfulness requires a rigorous healing for all that. Just be meticulously attentive to how you got where you are now philosophically, knotted and all, and observe that before long on your way into the muddle you have become *forgetful* of how our language works in daily life. Remind yourself of how we use this or that particular word in the everyday walk of life; remind yourself of it—and do not stop *looking* at the practice of language!

Wittgenstein's notion of forgetfulness deserves to be singled out in connection with the kind of Realism that *he* strives for, hence with his difficulties in reaching it. That he wants Realism *in philosophy* is reflected in many of his remarks.

---

50 Oliver Sacks, *Seeing Voices: A journey Into the World of the Deaf* (Berkeley and Los Angeles: University of California Press, 1989), 39.
51 Cf. Michael Tomasello, *Origins of Human Communication* (Cambridge, Mass: The MIT Press, 2008) and his *A Natural History of Human Thinking* (Cambridge, Mass: Harvard University Press, 2014).

Thus, he wants to leave everything *as it is*, and he wants to understand, though *not anything new*, but something that we, users of our language, have somehow always known. Wittgenstein's need for Realism *in philosophy* is also reflected in his famous dictum that he is 'interested in language only insofar as it gives [him] trouble'[52], or in the fact that he wants to describe our language—in opposition to the urge to misunderstand its workings. In short, that Wittgenstein wants Realism *in philosophy* is reflected in his uncommon way of looking at things. Wittgenstein looks at our language both as what leads us astray in philosophy and as what can help us out of the muddle. One might consider it rather trivial to say that there is a way into the muddle as well as a way out of it, but this seeming truism tells us an enormous lot about how Wittgenstein looks at language, as well as about the kinds of aspects that language begins to reveal from his vantage point. For language, seen from this point, obtains a kind of two-layered structure, one that Wittgenstein circumscribes as a relationship of surface grammar (*Oberflächengrammatik*) and depth grammar (*Tiefengrammatik*).[53] In other words, if there is a way into the muddle it is owing to something *of language* that leads us into it and if there is a way out of the muddle it is owing to something else *of language* that leads us out of it. But that is what language begins to look like from Wittgenstein's vantage point. What leads us astray are all kinds of aspects that he begins to treat as partaking of an existing structure: the surface grammar of our language. And, of course, it would make little sense to speak thus, as Wittgenstein well realizes, unless this kind of grammar finds itself placed over against something that passes for the so-called depth grammar.

So there is something *of language* that leads us astray, in philosophy, something that, in Wittgenstein's dealings with it, reifies in the shape of something that our language *anyway* seems to have in the daily course of life, namely a surface grammar, a structure that *hides* something else of our language, and which seems to be there anyway as well: a so-called depth grammar, language's real stuff and proper workings: something that we have somehow always known, and that Wittgenstein is anxious to have before his eyes in a form in which we have never seen it before. What we have somehow always known should as it were guarantee that the kind of Realism that Wittgenstein strives for in philosophy is more than something that his philosophy of language begins to reify. So the notion of our becoming forgetful in philosophy, together with the notion of our having the means, will, and capacity in philosophy to remind ourselves of what we have somehow always known in the daily course of life, guarantee that there

---

52 AWL: 97.
53 Cf. PI: 664.

is a sure and characteristic way into the philosophical muddle as much as a sure and redeeming way out of it. Indeed, if it is owing to Wittgenstein's uncommon way of looking at language that it obtains a two-layered structure, one wonders how language could ever function without a misleading veneer. For if there could be no depth grammar of our language in the daily course of life without a surface grammar that leads us astray in moments of philosophy, the veneer seems to be necessary to the real workings of our language without taking part in it.

But now, if we become indeed forgetful in moments of philosophy of how we use our colloquial language, forgetful, that is, of something whose knowing Wittgenstein considers important if not decisive within his dialectical edifice, what should we make of our knowing it somehow in daily life? I raise this question in the light of *PI* §363, but it is what raises itself, I think, not only with respect to that paragraph but also, and with no lesser alacrity, with respect to so many other passages in which Wittgenstein tells us that we have been misled by the kind of apparent *Witz* that our language has forced upon us. To stay with the present case: if we are so much *accustomed* to communicating through *Sprechen*, in conversation, it surely is in the daily course of life that we are thus accustomed. But then the suggestion is that it is already in the daily course of life that the real *Witz* of the language-game does not catch up with us in its true shape. So what about reminding ourselves of it in moments of philosophy, if this very point is already obscure if not hidden from us in the daily course of life? It is in moments of philosophy that we need to catch up with the real *Witz* of the language-game; only then will our description of the language-game be a description of its real workings. Only then do we get Realism in philosophy, instead of Empiricism (to stay with the present concern). And yet, or so it seems, we do not even discern the real point of the language-game in the daily course of life. And we do not obtain Realism in philosophy if we, in spite of our belief to have come to *descriptive* terms with the language-game at last, have framed these descriptions through an invented *Witz*.

We shall shortly pay more attention to how Wittgenstein characterizes our language: how it strikes us as users of our language in contrast to how it strikes us in our philosophical moments. For now let us note Wittgenstein's appeal to the notion 'being accustomed' in the passage quoted above: 'we are so much accustomed to communicating through *Sprechen*, in conversation, that it looks to us as if the whole point of communication lay in [...].' Wittgenstein wants to teach differences, but his words 'we are so much accustomed to' are a customary turn of phrase in his hands (see below), a seeming resourceful means to which he resorts suspiciously often so as to circumscribe a source of confusion, not only with respect to the language-game of communication through *Sprechen*, but with respect to *many* language-games.

But how did he recognize that we are so much *accustomed* to communication through *Sprechen*? Wittgenstein suggests that matters might well have been different, i.e., that we need not have been *that much* accustomed to communication through *Sprechen* as we actually are. But what does it look like to be *less* accustomed to communication through *Sprechen* than we actually are? How are we to imagine this? How should we depict it in detail? Here I raise some typical Wittgensteinian questions, if only in order not to lose our own critical grip on his philosophy.

We have seen that Wittgenstein, in *PI* §363, raises questions that he does not answer, neither in *PI* §363 itself, nor at any other place in the *Investigation*. Interestingly, he does not present *PI* §363 as exemplifying a certain problematic stage in his own efforts to emerge in the end with descriptions only. He does not present it thus to his readers in the *Investigations*, nor are there signs that he, at the time of composing the book, construed it himself as posing a serious problem. On the other hand, the *Bemerkung* forming the title of the present chapter precisely concerns such questions as Wittgenstein leaves unanswered, not only in *PI* §363, but in hundreds of other remarks and passages in his oeuvre. I should like to close this section by merely quoting some of these passages, all of which, I think, could be subsumed under the heading under which I have presented and discussed *PI* §363. In these passages, Wittgenstein raises questions that he cannot leave unanswered as they coalesce around his conception of the true nature of the language-game. To be sure, then, a question such as what 'the interest is of his inner state of gladness' seems easy to answer, that is, as long as we move on in our 'old way of thinking'. But now think of answering it from: Wittgenstein's uncommon way of looking at things.

> "I know that he was glad to see me." *What* do I know? What consequences does this fact have? I feel certain in my dealings with him. But is that knowing?
>
> But what is the difference between surmising and knowing that he was glad?

> If I know it I'll assert it without signs of doubt, and others will understand this statement. Well yes, it does have certain practical consequences; in a pinch something can be deduced from it, but that seems merely to be its shadow.
>
> What is the interest of his inner state of gladness? (LWPP II: 82)

> "I know that he enjoyed seeing me." – What follows from that? What of importance? [*Was von Wichtigkeit*?] Forget that you have the correct idea of the state of his mind! Can I really say that the importance [*Wichtigkeit*] of this truth is that it has certain consequences? – It is pleasant to be with someone who is glad to see us, who behaves in such and such a way (if one knows a thing or two about this behaviour from previous occasions).

So if I *know* that he is happy, then I feel secure, not insecure, in my pleasure. And that, one could say, isn't knowing. – Still it is different if I know that he is seeing what he claims to be seeing.

"I know that he was sincerely pleased to see me." (LWPP II: 49)

One wonders, "What does 'I'm afraid' really means; what do I aim at when I say it?" And, of course, no answer is forthcoming, or only an inadequate one.

The question is: "In what sort of context does it occur?"
No answer is forthcoming if I try to settle the question "What do I aim at?", "What am I thinking when I say it?" by repeating the fear utterance and at the same time attending to myself, as it were observing my mind out of the corner of my eye. In a concrete case, I can indeed ask, "Why did I say that, what was I up to?" – and I could answer the question too; but not on the ground of observing what accompanied the speaking. And my answer would supplement, paraphrase, the earlier utterance.

What is fear? What does "being afraid" mean? If I wanted to explain it in a *single* showing – I would *act* fear. (PPF: 75–77)

"I have already remembered three times today that I must write to him." Of what importance [*Wichtigkeit*] is it what happened then?! – On the other hand what is the importance, what the interest [*Interesse*], of the statement itself?

It permits certain conclusions. (LWPP I: 128)

Wittgenstein's work abounds in passages as these. They press for the redeeming word, at the furthermost frontiers of his philosophical investigations. They comprise no descriptions of the language-game themselves. Rather they rally around a characteristic, recurring trouble to describe their workings. And Wittgenstein does not seem to get himself beyond his most advanced point. He keeps asking questions of this type: What do I know when someone is in pain?—Or, closely related, ones such as: 'What do we take notice of in life' (LWPP II: 81) and 'is the fact that someone else is really glad to see me important to me because it has different consequences' (LWPP II: 84). Wittgenstein's German—'*Woran liegt mir?*'—should be taken in account here, for it is difficult to translate and yet it catches his recurring trouble so well.

2.3 Intermezzo: Wittgenstein – the psychologist

We have been considering a few passages in which we find Wittgenstein raising some highly curious questions—questions that we do not raise in our daily affairs and that, indeed, cast a very uncommon light on these affairs. Confronted with such passages, of which we shall give several more examples, one may well wonder what Wittgenstein's way out looks like, thus out of such predicaments into which he has manoeuvred himself again and again, at least with respect to his philosophical concerns in the psychological branches of our language. But if he had serious difficulties in answering his questions, as I think he had, and if these questions do not come out of the blue, but are intrinsically related to his way of looking at things, we may as well wonder what his way into his logical predicaments looks like. Of course, his way of looking at things is an uncommon way, according to his own judgement. But what exactly is there about this way that Wittgenstein finds himself continually confronted with questions that are difficult to answer? I say 'continually', for, as we have outlined in the beginning of the present chapter, there are indeed striking parallels between Wittgenstein's philosophical predicaments in the field of mathematics, on the one hand, and the ones he faces in the psychological branches of our language, on the other hand; predicaments, to be sure, with respect to his untiring efforts to see the end of the day with descriptions of our language, and these things only.

In order to obtain more insight into the nature of Wittgenstein's predicaments, we need to throw a light on him as psychologist. Wittgenstein, *the philosopher*, looks at language from a *logical* point of view, not because language *is* a logical phenomenon, but because its workings present themselves to us first and foremost as phenomena vibrant with empirical features. For Wittgenstein, in his engagement as philosopher, our language *is* an empirical affair *and yet* a phenomenon that he wants consider from a logical point of view. Indeed, he says 'Not empiricism [*Empirie*] and yet realism in philosophy', for *that* his philosophical concern is of a purely logical nature has everything to do with the kinds of problems that he seeks to solve: philosophical problems and these problems only. They define what language is for Wittgenstein in the first instance, namely a place where such problems arise, but so they also define what language is for Wittgenstein in the last instance, namely a phenomenon by whose resources these problems should be solved. The light in which language is to be seen to his end is a logical one. Language presents itself to us as an empirical phenomenon, but that should not hinder us from looking at it from a logical point of view. To look at it from an empirical point of view *because* it is an empirical phenomenon is to call for an appointment with Wittgenstein.

'The characteristic thing about all philosophical problems', Wittgenstein says, 'is that they arise in a peculiar way' (AWL: 90). But one might as well say that it is a characteristic thing about Wittgenstein that he circumscribes the arising of all philosophical problems in a peculiar way. He looks at our language as a phenomenon on which all kinds of psychological forces work, but equally he sees it as a rich and powerful source of such forces and energies itself. There is a striking amount of psychologising going on in Wittgenstein's philosophy of his own position as well as that of his main opponent, the Empiricist. That he 'is interested in language only insofar as it gives [him] trouble' (AWL: 97)[54] cannot be emphasized too much. So how do philosophical problems arise? That is, how does *Wittgenstein characterize* their arising, and how does he circumscribe our language as it troubles him, for it is against the background of these circumscriptions that we should try to see his descriptions of language-games. Wittgenstein's concern, even if it is consistently a *logical* one, has its origin in our language as a *psychological* phenomenon. He presents it as a phenomenon that *tempts* us in moments of philosophical reflection, a phenomenon that *leads us astray* and *bewitches* us. Of course, we all know this, and yet, it cannot be emphasized too much, and in the following I shall do no more than touch upon some aspects of a topic that can be treated accurately only by a book-length treatise: Wittgenstein – the psychologist; for there is still a lot to say and to do here. Wittgenstein's psychological interest stands out properly only in the light of his logical concern, and his logical concern stands out properly only in the light of his psychological interest.

When Wittgenstein says that he 'should like to be able to describe how it comes about that mathematics appears to us now as the natural history of the domain of numbers, now again as a collection of rules' (RFM: 230), he expresses not only psychological as well as logical interests in the phenomenon of mathematics, but also the extent to which he as a philosopher is fascinated by such a phenomenon and seeks to come to descriptive terms with the way it is.

> The substitution of "identical" for "the same" (for example) is another typical expedient in philosophy. As if we were talking about shades of meaning, and all that were in question were to find words to hit on the correct nuance. And that is in question in philosophy only where we have to give a psychologically accurate account of the temptation to use a particular mode of expression. What we are 'tempted to say' in such a case is, of course, not philosophy; rather it is its raw material [*Rohmaterial*]. So, for example, what a mathematician is inclined to say about the objectivity and reality of mathematics is not philosophy of mathematics, but something for philosophical *treatment*. (PI: 254)

Philosophy is not what we are inclined to say in our contemplative moments. It rather deals with what we are inclined to say in such moments, namely as its raw material, as something that leads us further astray and that we need to treat accordingly. Let us observe, then, how Wittgenstein *characterizes* this material, and how he *circumscribes* its arising, its hold—on us.

---

54 Cf. 'You are lost and your *Sätze* lose their sense if you dare to push your descriptions beyond the boundaries of our aims, into empty space' (MS 133: 43).

Look at the blue of the sky and say to yourself, "How blue the sky is!" – When you do it spontaneously – without philosophical purposes – the idea never crosses your mind that this impression of colour belongs only to *you*. And you have no qualms about exclaiming thus to another. And if you point at anything as you say these words, it is at the sky. I mean: you don't have the pointing-into-yourself feeling that often accompanies 'naming sensations' when one is thinking about the 'private language'. Nor do you think that really you ought to point at the colour not with your hand, but with your attention. (Consider what "to point at something with one's attention" means.) (PI: 275)

In ordinary life one is never troubled by a gap between the sign and its application. (AWL: 90)

"A thought – what a strange thing!" – but it does not strike us as strange when we are thinking. A thought does not strike us as mysterious while we are thinking, but only when we say, as it were retrospectively, "How was that possible?" How was it possible for a thought to deal with *this very* object? It seems to us as if we had captured reality with the thought. (PI: 428)

The feeling of an unbridgeable gulf between consciousness and brain process: how come that this plays no role in reflections of ordinary life? This idea of a difference in kind is accompanied by slight giddiness – which occurs when we are doing logical tricks. (PI: 412)

It's strange that in ordinary life we are not troubled by the feeling that the phenomenon is slipping away from us, the constant flux of appearance, but only when we philosophize. This indicates that what is in question here is an idea suggested by a misapplication of our language. (PR: 83)

These remarks and observations would be well at place in a book on the psychology of human attention and inclination. However, at work is not a psychologist from the scholarly tradition but Wittgenstein, a philosopher whose interest in psychology is absorbed in particular by such phenomena as feelings, attention, and inclination. Interestingly, his observations are not based on psychological research; they are rather of the introspective sort, which does not prevent him from claiming unmitigated generality. 'To go down into the depths you don't need to travel far; you can do it in your own backgarden' (CV: 57). Wittgenstein regards the psychological processes in his own backgarden as what transpires in a lot of backgardens. Another point is that Wittgenstein gives his observations on the phenomena of human feelings and inclinations an uncommon twist, namely by bringing them to bear upon the phenomenon of our language. If, in our moments of philosophy, we feel urged to look at something in a certain way, or if we are so much tempted to say this or that in these moments, it is owing to these urges and temptations having deep-seated roots and ramifications in us, in our language and *Lebensform*. 'The problems,' Wittgenstein says, 'arising through a misinterpretation of our forms of language have the character of depth. They are deep disquietudes; they are as deeply rooted in us as the forms of our language, and their significance is as great as the importance of our language' (PI: 111). This is indeed a recurring theme. 'Evidently there is an aspect [*Zug*] of the language-game which suggests [*nahelegt*] the idea of being private or hidden – and there is also such a thing as hiding of the inner' (LWPP II: 36). It is the language-game, Wittgenstein emphasizes, which *nahelegt* the idea of being private or hidden. *Our* language-game has an aspect that plays tricks on us in that it leads us astray, completely, in our contemplative moments.

The tricks are being played on us, *not* in ordinary life, as Wittgenstein puts it, but in moments of philosophy. True, the above list is not long; its general drift is open to view for all that: the world (of language) strikes us so much different in our philosophical moments. The world (of language) strikes us with a most *disquieting* aspect, in these moments, but *not* in our ordinary life. But, again, that is how Wittgenstein presents it—Wittgenstein: the psychologist. And Wittgenstein the philosopher is most anxious to overcome such disquieting moments, or he is done for.

Wittgenstein is a restless soul, his mind steeped in deep disquietude. He seeks to find his way out, but not out of the philosophical frame of mind by finding his way back into the everyday spirit of life. Rather, he seeks to find his way out of his disquietude whilst remaining in the same frame of mind in which the disquietude emerged and obtained ascendancy over its ordinary constitution.[55] Wittgenstein seeks to find his way out by leaving everything as it is. He seeks his way out, that is, by appealing to how our language *is*, but within that frame of mind in which the world or his own language looks so queer, so mysterious.—I say *appeal*, Wittgenstein avails himself of another notion: *remind* yourself of this and that, and look and see!

At first blush, it much seems that what Wittgenstein has in mind is nothing less than unadulterated Realism in philosophy. Yet, as we have been suggesting, leaving everything *as it is* is not a straightforward exercise for Wittgenstein, but a complex dialectical movement of thought. His Realism is bound up dialectically with how our language confounds our minds in moments of philosophical reflection, and it is for that reason, and that reason only, that Wittgenstein looks

---

55 Cf. 'Here I would like to make a general observation concerning the nature of philosophical problems. Philosophical unclarity is tormenting. It is felt as shameful. We feel: we do not know our way about where we *should* know our way about. And yet, it *isn't so*. We can get along very well without these distinctions *and* without knowing our way about' (RC III: 33).

at the language-game as autonomous. His Realism acquires sense only *in opposition to our urge* 'to rest content' with what our language tends to instill in us in terms of realistic images and impressions. How language *strikes us* in ordinary life is not for Wittgenstein to appeal to in respect of his efforts to find his way out, and neither is the way language *strikes us* in moments of philosophy. Neither the Realism of our ordinary life nor the Realism of the Empiricist is Wittgenstein's Realism, simply because to him neither is Realism *in philosophy*.

Recall in this connection also the concept of the simile that Wittgenstein regards as part of his edifice[56]. The simile, in whatever form it is being called upon, serves as a mediator between Wittgenstein and language, between him in his engagement as philosopher and our language as his subject matter, a means that Wittgenstein brings into account for reasons of philosophy *only* in order to solve philosophical problems, only in order to find his way out of his disquietude. The simile is there, right from the beginning, because of the disquietude, which was there initially. Right from the beginning, the simile lays down that Wittgenstein's foray into the Empiricist's frame of mind is not his way out of the disquietude. However, the simile equally lays down that his seeking refuge in the ordinary frame of mind is not his way out of the disquietude either. But then, if a simile is part of Wittgenstein's (dialectical) edifice, if it stands so to speak between him on the one hand and language on the other hand, it stands to reason that the simile does not behold language *as it really is*, only to mediate between this reality and Wittgenstein in his role as philosopher. The simile is rather brought to bear upon language, but not on it *as it is*, for that is what Wittgenstein seeks to have before his eyes out of philosophical concerns. Accordingly, he brings a simile to bear upon our language, and it is through *the workings* of its enunciations that he seeks to leave the workings of (our) language as they are.

You do not leave language as it is, i.e. you do not obtain Realism in philosophy, if you want 'to refine or complete the system of rules for the use of our words in unheard-of ways' (PI: 133). But neither do you obtain Realism in philosophy if you want to bring this system to bear upon processes in the medium of the mind. That is what the Empiricist wants, and seeks to do, all in the firm belief that he thereby leaves everything as it is. But all the Empiricist does, according to Wittgenstein, is to show the world how much he has actually misunderstood language. His programme looks so thoroughly realistic, and yet it deeply misconstrues the reality of language. Indeed, it is no coincidence that Wittgenstein

---

56 *Here*: a picture, for instance, with which Wittgenstein *should like to compare* our language. Cf. Chapter 1.

exclaims 'Not empiricism and yet realism in philosophy, that is the hardest thing.' His own Realism is dialectically bound up *above all* with the tendencies inspiring the Empiricist's programme because our language is so suggestive of that direction. And that is to say that Wittgenstein's Realism is dialectically bound up *above all* with these tendencies because they are so much at work in Wittgenstein himself. Both the Empiricist and the Realist intent to leave everything as it is, and yet, for the Realist there is no way of doing it *tout court*. The Realist seeks to do it in opposition to the urge to do it in the Empiricist's way, which Wittgenstein acknowledges all too well in himself.

> The impression that we wanted to deny something arises from our setting our face against the picture of an 'inner process'. What we deny is that the picture of an inner process gives us the correct idea of the use of the word "remember". Indeed, we're saying that this picture, with its ramifications, stands in the way of our seeing the use of the word as it is. (PI: 305)

Wittgenstein does not deny that our language is awash with all kinds of pictures. He does not deny their existence any more than the 'existence' of mental processes. All he denies is that the way the Empiricist operates on such pictures gives us a realistic image of the workings of our language. The picture is there, absorbed into the forms of our language; it is there, with its ramifications, and Wittgenstein does not mean deny its existence. But if the picture is there, so is the use of the word *as it is*, a use that Wittgenstein does not mean to deny either. For the *workings* of our language are not given by the way the picture lies absorbed into the forms of our language: it is not the picture, with its ramifications, but the use of the word *as it is*, and the picture, with its ramifications, stands in the way of our seeing 'the word as it is'. The philosopher leaves language *as it is*, though not by leaving the picture as it lies absorbed into the forms of our language as it is, but by working his way up against its alluring aspects. Of course, the picture then stands in the philosopher's way of finding his way out, by seeing 'the use of the word as it is.'

Notice that Wittgenstein, in the above passage, does not *describe* our language. All he does is to *circumscribe* certain features of it. To describe language, in Wittgenstein's sense of the word, does not mean to describe how a picture, with its ramifications, lies absorbed into the forms of our language. To describe language, in his sense of the word, is to describe word usage, and to describe it *as it is* is to describe it against the urge to misunderstand one picture or another as it lies absorbed into the forms of our language. The picture *alone* does not give the philosopher the *correct* idea of the use of the word as it is, but, indeed, the picture, with its ramifications, is a solid piece of reality of our language for all that. The above remark presents a stage in Wittgenstein's dialectical proceedings where he prepares himself for the task of giving *descriptions* of our language, by providing *circumscriptions* of that reality first. And these circumscriptions deserve our full attention, for they characterize how Wittgenstein sees our language.

The Empiricist is the philosopher in us, to the extent that all kinds of pictures lie absorbed into the forms of our language. He enters Wittgenstein's dialectical stage more often than not as the complete dupe of one urge (*Trieb*) or another. The Empiricist truly believes to be following his own *interest* in philosophy, and yet, by Wittgenstein's wits, he has merely fallen prey to a powerful *urge* that he mistakes for the vibrations of his own true interest. Incidentally, Wittgenstein's notion of an urge (*Trieb*) bears an interesting family resemblance to Freud's psycho-analytical notion of *Trieb*. The urge presents itself to us as a strong desire longing for undivided satisfaction, a desire whose true nature and origin remain hidden from our everyday eyes.

The Empiricist, then, is no stranger to Wittgenstein. On the contrary, nothing troubles his mind more than his own individual urges and inclinations, as what he needs to work on for himself. In order to be *able* to do philosophy in his own (uncommon) way, Wittgenstein does not need to go into the open first so as to see and notice what kinds of bewitching forces are in town, ready to obtrude themselves upon the citizens' mind on the first philosophical occasion. On the contrary, being a full member of a community of language speakers himself, he does not stand above the myriads of similes and pictures with their ramifying connections in our language. He undergoes no less than any other member the bewitching influences that our language keeps exerting on us, in our more philosophical moments. But, to be sure, that is how Wittgenstein presents the matter: *he* often takes to 'we' and 'us', for the presentation of *his* philosophy.

> In order to get clear about the meaning of the word "think", we watch ourselves thinking; what we observe will be what the word means! – But that's just not how this concept is used. (PI: 316)

We watch ourselves thinking, believing, having intentions, knowing this and that; we watch ourselves calculating, we watch ourselves suffering pains and nourishing hopes, we watch ourselves doing all kinds of things, *while philosophizing*. But the important point here is: *that* is how Wittgenstein presents the matter, *characterizes* it. Of course, it need not to be less true for all that.

The Empiricist, in Wittgenstein's recurring characterizations, is a person who is just *inclined to look so much into him- or herself.* Interestingly, Wittgenstein often characterizes this looking as a vantage point on language, over against which he sets his uncommon way of looking at things. Wittgenstein wants to leave our language as it is by looking at its workings *from without*; the Empiricist, for his estimation, fails to see how language could ever be left as it is without looking at its workings *from within*. This is not to suggest that Wittgenstein and the Empiricist have one and the same thing before their eyes, namely the so-called workings of our language, with this minor difference that the former looks at them from without and the latter from within. The truth rather is that the Empiricist does not look at the language-game as an autonomous whole; he seeks to explain its workings ultimately in terms of processes in the medium of the mind—workings that, according to Wittgenstein, are to be exposed as a house of cards. But does that mean that there is no such thing as looking at language from within? If not, how then could there be anything like Wittgenstein's looking at language from without?

Phrases such as 'looking into one self' and 'looking at the language-game from without' are characterizations from Wittgenstein's playground of abstract consideration. Here are some further examples of remarks in which the former notion and its cognates figure prominently.

> Indeed, when we look into ourselves as we do in philosophy, we often get to see just such a picture. Virtually a pictorial representation of our grammar. Not facts; but, as it were, illustrated turns of speech. (PI: 296)

> The 'inner' is a delusion. That is: the whole complex of ideas alluded to by this word is like a painted curtain drawn in front of the scene of the actual word use. (LWPP II: 84)

> (You keep on steering towards an inner ostensive explanation.) (PI: 380)

> The very fact that we'd so much like to say "*This* is the important thing" – while we point for ourselves to the sensation – already shows how much we are inclined to say something which is not a piece of communication. (PI: 298, amended translation)

> Hence we want to see the absurdities both of what the finitists say and what their opponents say – just as we want in philosophy to see the absurdities both of what the behaviourists say and what their opponents say. Finitism and behaviourism are as alike as two eggs. The same absurdities, and the same kind of answer. Both sides of such disputes are based on a particular kind of misunderstanding – which arises from gazing at a form of words and forgetting to ask yourself what's done with it, or from gazing into your own soul to see if two expressions have the same meaning, and such things. (LFM: 111)

Wittgenstein employs the notion of looking into oneself in various ways, sometimes in order to explicate a certain strong tendency of us in moments of philosophy, sometimes in order to tell how *he* looks at language, namely from without, sometimes only to make clear what his difficulties are in describing a particular language-game. We can see that sometimes his stance towards this notion is negative, when he e.g. says that the 'inner' is a delusion, but at other times it is positive, precisely when he expresses that there *is* a real or actual word use: 'the whole complex of ideas alluded to by this word [i.e. the 'inner'] is like a painted curtain drawn in front of the scene of the actual word use.' When Wittgenstein employs the notion in a negative sense, he seems to be suggesting that there is no Inner and Outer, but when the sense is positive, his suggestion often seems to be that there is *a kind* of Inner and Outer. But what is it like to want to look *into oneself*, if the word "inner" is a delusion? And is there no Outside, when the Inner is a delusion? And if the Inner *is* a delusion, why then say anything such as the following: 'Is the reason for this that the language-game is something outer?' (LWPP II: 63). For the moment, I merely want to raise these questions and to leave them for what they are.

Philosophy leaves everything as it is. Philosophy is a battle against the bewitchment of our understanding by the resources of our language. We are not bewitched in the daily course of life, and yet, our language is vibrant with a miscellany of forms and elements without which it would lose its lustre when they fail to exert a *bewitching* influence on our understanding, in moments of philosophy. But that is how Wittgenstein presents it. He seeks redemption, again and again, redemption from the deep disquietudes that *he* feels, not in the daily course of life, but in moments of philosophy, which was his daily course. He aims at redemption, but not by seeking his way out of a moment of philosophical disquietude into a quiet moment of the day, any more than by trying to eliminate *a picture* from our language, for then he does not leave everything as it is. But neither does Wittgenstein seek redemption by shielding himself, while doing philosophy, *against* the bewitching influences of such pictures so as to be able to do philosophy in a supposedly carefree and unhampered sort of way. Rather he is keen to see and to understand how such pictures ramify in our language, driven as he is to see and to describe the physiognomy of their misleading appearances in philosophy. He is keen to do that, just in order to eliminate the disquieting aspects that our forms of language begin to pose to his own contemplative mind.[57] And the crowning achievement in all these efforts of him takes the form of descriptions of our language, i.e., in the way of surveyable *representations* (in which fictitious language-games necessarily partake as possibilities alongside the possibilities of our language-games).[58] Thus, then, is how Wittgenstein leaves everything as it is: by *representing* certain elements of our daily language, by creating

---

57 Cf. 'The solution of the problems consists in eliminating the disquieting aspects to which certain analogies in our grammar give rise' (MS 157b: 14r).
58 See Chapter 4 for more on this.

a certain order, not *the* order, any more than an order *in* our language, but an order in that frame of mind in which the philosophical disquietude arose and took shape. Wittgenstein, while working himself towards giving such a *representation* at last, presents (*circumscribes*) language already in a certain way, namely as the kind of material to work on philosophically. And my point here is not that he had better not do *that*, but that he does do it; and that the way he does do it is something that deserves our attention.

Wittgenstein 'is interested in language only insofar as it gives [him] trouble' and he leaves language as it is to extent to which he is troubled by it. The extent to which he leaves language as it is is relative, first and foremost, to how *he circumscribes* a trouble. Aiming at philosophical peace of mind, on account of the bewitching or disquieting aspect that a form of language exerts on him, he aims at it with respect to his own circumscription of what troubles him. Such circumscriptions need not be fixed irreversibly (and typically are not at the time of Wittgenstein's first encounters with the disquieting aspect), but the road towards redemption is open the moment he has settled on a *redemptory circumscription* of the disquietude, which is not so much elusive itself as long as it has not been circumscribed satisfactorily as that the absence of such a circumscription is part of the disquietude. In other words, the depth of Wittgenstein's descriptions of language does not so much inhere in the felt disquietude as in how he succeeds in fixing the disquietude in terms of a circumscription first. The raw material for Wittgenstein to work on is not so much the disquietude itself as its repair by means of his own circumscription.

Once more: Wittgenstein does not consider it to be part of his philosophical concern to find fault with the way our own language is, any more than with the myriads of similes absorbed into its forms, as if they comprise material to be substituted by something else, by something less bewitching. His task is not substitute a blank for a bewitching simile, as if the blank and substitution are without bewitchment. Contrast this with how Russell looks at these matters.

> Before we can understand language, we must strip it of its mystical and awe-inspiring attributes. To do this is the main purpose of the present chapter.[59]

It is debatable whether Russell succeeds in his mission of stripping language of its mystical and awe-inspiring attributes. Wittgenstein, for his part, regards such purgatory attempts as the best proof of a philosophically muddled mind.

---

59 Bertrand Russell, *An Inquiry into Meaning and Truth* (London and New York: Routledge, 1995), 23.

Noticing that an entire mythology is laid down in our language[60], he respects it and leaves its ramifying array for what it is, in accordance with his dictum that 'Philosophy may in no way interfere with the actual use of language; it can in the end only describe it' (PI: 124).

> A picture that is firmly rooted in us may indeed be compared to superstition, but it may be said too that we always have to reach some sort of firm ground, be it a picture, or not, so that a picture at the root of all our thinking is to be respected & not treated as a superstition. (CV: 95)

Rather than extricating similes or entire mythologies from our daily language (whatever that means), Wittgenstein considered it to be part of his mission to show how extraordinary sway such similes begin to hold on our thinking when the philosophical mood dawns upon us. He was at pains to understand how pictures, deeply rooted in our language, turn into disquieting elements, how they fool us and obtrude upon our minds in moments of philosophy and, before long, command our complete thinking. Nourishing a life-long fascination for the sources of our philosophical entanglements, he was keen to circumscribe the characteristic *appearances* that our language obtains in philosophical reflections, for it was primarily relative to his own circumscriptions of these appearances that there was, for him, work on himself, on the way he saw things.

Let us take stock with respect to our present considerations. Wittgenstein, within the realm of his philosophical moments, wants to draw on certain things in the medium of our daily life that, he claims, go more or less unnoticed there. He says that 'The meaning of words, what stands behind them, doesn't concern me in normal conversation. Words flow along and transitions are made from words to actions and from actions to words.'[61] Of course, what we should remind ourselves of is not everything that does not concern us in normal conversation. What concerns us in the daily course of life is the well-being of our parents and children, the health of our pet cats and dogs, that is, all kinds of things that constitute the topic of our talks and conversations. Being mindful that our words and sentences should not lose their point and significance in conversation is not beyond our daily concern, albeit not on a par with the well-being of our parents. Wittgenstein speaks in this connection of things standing *behind* our words, things that, obviously, are constitutive of their point and meaning. We, in the daily course of life, just apply our words and what our talk passes by are all kinds of non-trivial *facts*.

---

60 Cf. PO: 199.
61 RPP II: 603.

> The *facts* of human natural history that throw light on our problem, are difficult for us
> to find out, for our talk *passes them by*, it is occupied with other things. (In the same way
> we tell someone: "Go into the shop and buy…" – not: "Put your left foot in front of your
> right foot etc. etc., then put coins down on the counter, etc. etc.") (RPP I: 78).[62]

Wittgenstein wants to understand the *workings* of our language by drawing on a miscellany of things that we gloss over by everyday talk. This gives rise to the questions of what it is to understand our language on account of the things that lie outside the scope of our daily sense of understanding of its workings. Wittgenstein is concerned to have before his eyes the arrays of connections that seem foreign to our common grasp and understanding, connections that we not only do not associate with our technique of using words, but which, once confronted with them, we would not be readily prepared to associate with language either. Unnoticed as these connections go in our use of language, we should in our philosophical efforts to make them explicit not expect to encounter something that we know how to handle without further ado. Here I am characterizing the kind of difficulty alluded to above, and to which we shall return below.

What does our language look like in the daily course of life? What does it look like in our philosophical strivings? And what does it look like after a philosophical cure? We do well to explicate three different but intimately related points [*Witze*] in Wittgenstein's dialectical edifice:

1) The point that a use of language has for us in the daily course of life.
2) The sublimation of this point in moments of philosophy.
3) The point that a use of language has according to Wittgenstein's uncommon way of looking at things.

What, from Wittgenstein's point of view, goes along with these three points are three different notions of language: (1) Language as we use it in the daily course of life; (2) Language as the Empiricist explains it in moments of philosophy; (3) Language as Wittgenstein describes it in his moments of philosophy.

Given that the Empiricist signifies Wittgenstein's main foil and foe in the enunciation of his own perspective, we might say that we have a polar contrast between, on the one hand, the *Witz* of the language-game as seen in the light of the medium of the mind, and, on the other hand, the *Witz* that is to lend the eye the kind of hold for Wittgenstein's description of the language-game. The latter *Witz* has turned out to be most difficult to descry; the former *Witz* is not what the Empiricist needs to search for as it catches up with him before long. He tends

---

62 Cf. 'One sees the terminology, but fails to see the technique of applying it' (RPP I: 911).

to sublimate the kind of *Witz* that a use of language anyway has, for us, in the daily course of life.

Wittgenstein, then, presents our language as having a particular kind of reality for us, its users, in the daily course of life. But so he presents it as having a particular kind of reality for the Empiricist in his philosophical moments, namely a sublimated version of the reality that language in any event has for us, its users. Though Wittgenstein's Realism concerns both kinds of realities, it is neither the former nor the latter. Reminding is a procedure directed by his *philosophical* concern, but so it is informed by all kinds of urges and feelings that play no substantial role if any in our ordinary life, emerging as they rather do in our contemplative moments. Generally, then, to remind oneself of what one has somehow always known, in Wittgenstein's sense of the word, is to embark on an activity that plays no role in our ordinary life, which also has little commerce with the kind of forgetfulness that one comes to underlie in philosophy.

2.4 The system

If a picture of the indicated kind of entanglement among three different modes of realities is what we can extract from Wittgenstein's work, as I think we can, then, his recurring emphasis on the procedure of reminding ourselves in philosophical moments takes on a rather puzzling aspect. For whatever it is that we should remind ourselves of, the procedure seems to play an important if not essential role in securing the possibility of closing Wittgenstein's dialectical circle, of putting the coping stone on his edifice. But where this procedure concerns the kind of realistic workings of our language that Wittgenstein seeks to describe, it concerns a kind of Realism that appears to lie beyond our conscious grasp in the daily course of life. So there seems to be a kind of tension in Wittgenstein's philosophy, one that should invite us to have a closer look at how the following two points relate to each other: Wittgenstein's notion of the system in a remark as 'We don't want to refine or complete the system of rules for the use of our words in unheard-of ways' (PI: 133) and his notion of reminding ourselves in moments of philosophy.

In the *Investigations*, Wittgenstein says that 'The work of the philosopher consists in marshalling recollections for a particular purpose' (PI: 127), only to leave us in the dark as regards the question of the matter of which we should remind ourselves. Baker and Hacker, in their analytical commentary on the *Investigations*, feel rightfully prompted to raise the following question: 'What recollections do we have to assemble (marshall, arrange)?' Less on the mark, though, I think, is their answer: 'Descriptions of the ways in which we use words (cf. BT

419 below)'[63]. Indeed, this answer should already strike a rather puzzling chord in the light of BT 419: 'To study philosophy is really to recollect. We remind ourselves that we really use words in this way.' According to this remark, it is word *use* of which we need to remind ourselves, that is, this use in the daily course of life. We remind ourselves of this use 'for a particular purpose.' It seems that Baker and Hacker have inadvertently mixed up two things: the use of our words, on the one hand, and descriptions of this use, on the other hand. That is, the use of our words in daily life, on the one hand, and the kind of descriptions that Wittgenstein means to furnish of this use in moments of doing philosophy, on the other hand; descriptions, then, that receive their light, that is to say their purpose, from the philosophical problems (PI: 109). For those descriptions that Wittgenstein means to furnish of this use have neither place nor purpose in the daily course of our lives and those descriptions that we might be said to give of this use in that course do not receive their purpose from the philosophical problems.

But is it really word use alone of which we need to remind ourselves? As a matter of fact, the *Bemerkung* quoted by Baker and Hacker is only one among dozens of remarks and passages in which Wittgenstein testifies to the importance of reminding ourselves. But then notice how miscellaneous the items are that he makes mention of in respect of this palpable importance.

> [R]emember that in general we don't use language according to strict rules—it hasn't been taught us by means of strict rules, either. (BB: 25)

> Remember what a hard time children have believing (or accepting) that a word really has//can have//two completely different meanings. (PO: 187)

> Philosophy could be taught (cf. Plato) just by asking the right questions so as to remind you – to remind you of what? In this case, that a man does not say "I'm depressed" on the basis of observed bodily feelings.

> And here one must remember that all the phenomena that now strike us as so remarkable are the very familiar phenomena that don't surprise us in the least when they happen. They don't strike us as remarkable until we put them in a strange light by philosophizing. (PG: 169)

> Learning philosophy is *really* recollecting. We remember that we really used words in this way. (TS 213: 419)

> The appearance of the awkwardness of the sign in getting its meaning across, like a dumb person who uses all sorts of suggestive gestures – this disappears when we remember

---

63 Gordon Baker and Peter M. S. Hacker, *Wittgenstein: Understanding and Meaning. Part II – Exegesis §§1–184* (Oxford: Wiley-Blackwell, 2009), 271.

that the sign does its job only in a grammatical system. (In logic what is unnecessary is also *useless*.) (PG: 133)

Reading these remarks, one may well be struck by how out of the ordinary Wittgenstein's use of 'reminding ourselves' at times is. We use the notion ourselves in the daily course of life, in a variety of ways, and Wittgenstein seems to have added some variations on these ways, for a particular purpose. And the same, I think, could be said of his notion of becoming forgetful. Wittgenstein really claims that we become *forgetful* in philosophical moments. We become forgetful of all kinds of things the reminding of which he, obviously, deems utterly important. Wittgenstein wants to leave everything *as it is*, but he means to do so only in moments of philosophy. So leaving everything *as it is* does not appear to be within his reach as long as he fails to remind himself of what he becomes forgetful of in moments of philosophy. One might disparage Wittgenstein's remarks on our becoming forgetful in philosophy; hence disparage the importance of our reminding ourselves of all kinds of things then. One might want to pass over these remarks with that famous shrug of the shoulders (see above). And yet, becoming forgetful in moments of philosophy appears to have much if not everything to do with the famous way into the philosophical muddle and reminding ourselves in philosophy appears to have much if not everything to do with the famous way out of it. And so it is: Wittgenstein's remarks articulate certain *psychological* processes and happenings concerning his dialectical circle.

But now, given that Wittgenstein wants to describe our language *as it is*, thus *only insofar as it troubles him*; wants to give descriptions of *its workings*, hence descriptions that receive their light, that is to say, their purpose from the philosophical problems (cf. PI: 109), from exactly those things that do not trouble us at all in the daily walk of life, we had perhaps better ask ourselves at once what are we to make of his so-called Realism? For what do we know about our language *as it is*, about its workings, when we use our words the way we do? What is our so-called language *as it is*, in the absence of the light in which Wittgenstein wants to leave everything *as it is*? If it is something that we become forgetful of in our philosophical reflections it seems that it has a kind of reality of its own in daily life, no matter whether the light in which Wittgenstein looks upon language shines or not. This brings us to the last of the passages quoted above.

Of what kind of reminder is Wittgenstein speaking here? I included it for the simple reason that a grammatical system stands out against the other items as quite an odd thing. For what do we, as users of our language, know about the so-called grammatical system in which our signs supposedly do their job? Is the kind of system that Wittgenstein has in mind really a mere matter of fact, something with which we are somehow acquainted in the daily course of life, but of which we tend to become forgetful in our philosophical moments, hence need to remind ourselves of, i.e. of it and its point? It does not seem to be so, at least not according to the following passages.

> What *we* want is to attend to the system of language. (PG: 171)

> The sign (the sentence) gets its significance from the system of signs, from the language to which it belongs. Roughly: understanding a sentence means understanding a language.

> As a part of the system of language, one may say, the sentence has life. But one is tempted to imagine that what gives the sentence life is something in an occult sphere, accompanying the sentence. But whatever accompanied it would for us just be another sign. (BB: 5)

> Explain to someone that the position of the clock-hands that you have just noted down is supposed to mean: the hands of this clock are now in this position.—The awkwardness of the sign in getting its meaning across, like a dumb person who uses all sorts of suggestive gestures—this disappears when we know that it all depends on the *system* to which the sign belongs.
>
> We wanted to say: only the *thought* can say it, not the sign. (Z: 228)[64]

Wittgenstein's notion of the (grammatical) system of language played a pivotal role in his philosophical reorientation in the early 1930s. To be sure, it made its appearance already in the *Tractatus* (cf. TLP: 5.555), without much ostentation though, but nonetheless with an air and importance that we had better not overlook. Upon having found his way to philosophy again, Wittgenstein used the word "system" 'very very frequently', as he is reported to have said[65], and he

---

64 Cf. Z: 236.

65 G. E. Moore frequently attended Wittgenstein's lectures during this time. The following, which is from the notes he took, clearly attests to the importance that Wittgenstein attached to the notion of system.

> As to what he meant by saying that, in order that a word or other sign should have meaning, it must belong to a "system", I have not been able to arrive at any clear idea. One point on which he insisted several times in (II) was that if a word which I use is to have meaning, I must "commit myself" by its use. And he explained what he meant by this by saying "If I commit myself, that means that if I use, *e.g.* 'green' in this case, I have to use it in others", adding "If you commit yourself, there are consequences". Similarly he said a little later, "If a word is to have significance, we must commit ourselves", adding "There is no use in correlating noises to facts, unless we commit ourselves to using the noise in a particular way again—unless the correlation has consequences", and

added significantly to its prominence by placing it—and it alone!—over against exactly such conceptions of language towards which we gravitate so much in philosophy. The purpose of this parade of conceptions was to make the philosophical significance of language *as* a grammatical system clear, for it is, in contrast to so many other conceptions of language, not anything that we tend to espouse in philosophy, although it precisely what we *must* do so at long last. What is the meaning of a word? What is the sense of a sentence? What makes up the meaning & sense of our words and sentence? Is it the world of facts? Some particular facts perhaps? Why not anything such as our feelings or mental episodes? It is against the background of these questions as well as the answers that we tend to give in philosophy, among which the Empiricist's answers and questions take pride of place, that Wittgenstein worked out the philosophical importance of the notion of language *as* a grammatical system, an activity that did not so much solve philosophical problems itself as that it established the very framework within which the nature of these problems and their solutions was laid down and articulated.

---

going on to say that it must be possible to "led by a language". And when he expressly raised, a little later, the question "What is there in this talk of a 'system' to which a symbol must belong?" he answered that we are concerned with the phenomenon of "being guided by". It looked, therefore, as if one use which he was making of the word "system" was such that in order to say that a word or other sign "belonged to a system", it was not only necessary but *sufficient* that it should be used in the same way on several different occasions. And certainly it would be natural to say that a man who habitually used a word in the same way was using it "systematically".

But he certainly also frequently used "system" in such a sense that *different* words or other expressions could be said to belong to the *same* "system"; and where, later on, he gave, as an illustration of what he meant by "Every symbol must essentially belong to a system", the proposition "A crochet can only give information on what note to play in a system of crotchets", he seemed to imply that for a sign to have significance it is *not* sufficient that we should "commit ourselves" by its use, but that it is also necessary that the sign in question should belong to the same "system" with other signs. Perhaps, however, he only meant, not that for a sign to have some meaning, but that for *some* signs to have *the significance which they actually have in a given language*, it is necessary that they should belong to the same "system" with other signs. This word "system" was one which he used very very frequently, and I do not know what conditions he would have held must be satisfied by two different signs in order that they may properly be said to belong to the same "system". (PO: 52f.)

112

Language *as* a system *is* a point of view, one that Wittgenstein wants to entertain *only insofar* as language troubles him: *only* in moments of philosophy, when e.g. the phenomenon of word-meaning tends to be seized upon in especially the Empiricist's mode of looking at the world. As we have been suggesting, the Empiricist's mode of doing so has on more than one occasion served as the polar opposite in Wittgenstein's enunciations of his own point of view. Thus, to mention some pair of opposing items, it is with respect to a characterization such as that the medium of the mind is hidden that the system of language counts as open to view; and when the medium of mind is said to be queer or occult, it is language as a grammatical system that should pass for being ordinary and homespun in its workings. It is also with respect to the notion of the grammatical system of language that the antagonism between description and explanation acquires its proper light. If philosophers feel so strongly urged to explain in terms ultimately referring to mental episodes, it is through our preoccupation with the system that the description of language 'receives its light, that is to say its purpose, from the philosophical problems.' And, to mention one more polar opposition here, one of pivotal importance as we shall see in the course of this book, whereas the Empiricist deems the medium of the mind the incomparable thing par excellence, it is language as a grammatical system that allows of various possibilities.

Wittgenstein's *notion* of the system of language is a typical product of what we have called his playground of abstract consideration. It is at home in his grammatical *remarks* and *statements*. It is not at home in the description of language itself. In other words, it does not partake of the elements constituting the coping stone of his dialectical edifice. But it is *at work* on both the playground of describing language and the playground of inventing and collating language-games, finally dropping out here and there from the terms describing the language-games.

A typical product of his playground of abstract consideration, Wittgenstein's notion of language as a system, including such polar contrasts as aforementioned, ultimately reflects the interest with which he approaches language. So when he pronounces that 'it is *in language* that it's all done' (PG: 143), it is to be noticed that Wittgenstein never discovered, in the sense in which scientists make discoveries, *that* it is all done in language. It is all due to his way of looking at language *as* a system that it is all done in language. He did not first discover that it is all done in language only to proclaim himself to be a person interested in language in which it is all done. Wittgenstein's interest rather determines what counts as language *in which it is all done*. What stands against language as a system are not conceptions of language in which he is not interested, but exactly those that render him interested in language as a system in the first place. We just feel deeply urged to think that language is vacuous should it not ultimately refer to mental episodes, and Wittgenstein does not turn his back upon this urge to explain, upon the kinds of conceptions of language it seeks to inculcate in us. Rather he takes a sincere interest in this urge, just in order to overcome it, just to dismiss the conceptions of language it fosters as styles of thinking that are misconceived right from the beginning. Language *as* a grammatical system plays a pivotal role in this overcoming and dismissing, that is, by means of descriptions at last.

And this brings us back to Wittgenstein's requirement of leaving everything as it is, a requirement that he means to carry through no less than he once thought to have done so in the *Tractatus*.[66] In the 1930s, upon having recognized that his early work felt short of having left everything as it is, Wittgenstein realized that it could be done *only* by looking at language as autonomous, as a system, as a medium in which it is all done. But how are these two things supposed to go together: to leave everything *as it is* and to look at the language-game *as* autonomous?

The relevance of this question springs from our realization that the *system* of language is not given to us in the sense in which our language can be said to be given, but rather stands or falls with Wittgenstein's way of looking at language. If we need to remind ourselves of how we use our words in the daily course of life, we may well come to see that we do it thus-and-so. But to remind ourselves of our word *use* is not to remind ourselves of the system in which it is all done. To remind ourselves of the latter is rather to remind ourselves of the importance of paying attention to word *use*. Language *as* a system, language in which it is all done, is the hallmark of Wittgenstein's way of looking at language, one that is utterly foreign to our daily grasp of language. Language *as* a system cannot even be said to escape our daily attention.

> Certainly I read a story and don't give a hang about any system of language. I simply read, have impressions, see pictures in the mind's eye, etc. I make the story pass before me like pictures, like a cartoon story. (Of course I do not mean by this that every sentence summons up one or more visual images, and that that is, say, the purpose of a sentences.) (PG: 171)

> I said that it was the *system* of language that makes the sentence a thought and makes it a thought *for us*.
>
> This doesn't mean that it is while we are using a sentence that the system of language makes it into a thought for us, because the system isn't present then and there isn't any need for anything to make the sentence alive for us, since the question of being alive doesn't arise. But if we ask: "why doesn't a sentence strike us as isolated and dead when

---

66 See next chapter for more details on this and related points.

we are reflecting on its essence, its sense, the thought etc." it can be said that we are continuing to move in the system of language. (PG: 153)

> The system of language, however, is not in the category of experience. The experiences characteristic of using the system are not the system. (Compare: the meaning of the word "or" and the or-feeling). (PG: 170)

Saying that the system of language is not in the category of experience, Wittgenstein clearly implies that this system is not what he discovered, nor what he could ever have discovered. And saying that it is 'the system of language that makes the sentence a thought and makes it a thought *for us*', i.e. philosophers[67], and adding that 'this doesn't mean that it is while we are using a sentence that the system of language makes it into a thought for us', i.e. users of our language, he intimates a difference that he seems to have conceived as utterly unproblematic at the time of his philosophical reorientation but that might well be pinpointed, in the light of his troubles to describe the system of our language, as perhaps *the* source of these troubles. (I am referring here to such troubles as we have pronounced in Section 2 of this chapter and to which we shall shortly return.) What a sentence is for us, i.e. users of our own language, is not what it is for the philosopher, but all the philosopher has by way of his material to work on, and with, is 'the resources of our language' (PI:109). The system is not in the category of our experience, that is, in the category of all those things that *we*, users of our language, have and associate with questions concerning the sense and significance of sentences, namely images, moods, feelings, emotions, sensations, intentions, etc. But even when these things were not attendant upon our employment of our language, the system is still not present in this use. It is not, simply because it is present only for the philosopher, present in the sense of his having a way of looking at language, a kind of light in which *he wants* see things, i.e. *wants* to come to descriptive terms with what language poses to him in moments of philosophy: a thoroughly disquieting thing.

Language *as* a system, then, typifies first and foremost Wittgenstein's vantage point on language. It is what he adopts and fosters in his philosophical moments, bringing it to bear upon our language each time *as* the polar opposite of all those vantage points that our urge to explain brings into view and seeks to implant in our helpless minds, Wittgenstein's own not excluded.

> Language is not defined for us as an arrangement fulfilling a definite end. Rather "language" is for me a name for a collection and I understand it as including German,

---

67 That is, for Wittgenstein!

English, and so on, and further various systems of signs which have more or less the same affinity with these languages.

Language is of interest to me as a phenomenon and not as a means to a particular end. (PG: 190)

'Language' is only languages, plus things I invent by analogy with existing languages. Languages *are* systems. (PG: 170)

The only thing that is of interest to me is the content of a proposition and the content of a proposition is something internal to it. A proposition has its content as part of a calculus. (PG: 63)[68]

When Wittgenstein, in the passage quoted above, says that we had better remember 'that the sign does its job only in a grammatical system', he means to say that we had better turn our *Betrachtung* around (on the pivot of our *real* need, as he adds in the *Investigations* §108[69]). And being just a reminder, it does not resolve philosophical problems itself. There is work to do once our *Betrachtung* has been turned around, not every kind of work though, but work nonetheless, for the mere act of turning our *Betrachtung* around does not do away itself with the urge to explain language. On the contrary, this urge is now felt, for the first time, *as* what it *really* is.

The kind of work to do should be internally related to Wittgenstein's way of looking. He needs to give descriptions of our language, but not any kind of description will do, for the ones at issue need to bear internally to language *as* a system. Only when this internal relation holds does his description receives its light, that is to say its purpose, from the philosophical problems. If 'it is *in language* that it's all done', then the descriptions relating internally to language as a system will show that it is indeed all done in language. They should give us understanding at last, thus without giving rise to the need for explanations as complementing elements.

Wittgenstein's descriptions make up the coping stone in his edifice, a building of dialectical proportions whose form is first and foremost determined by his looking at the language-game as autonomous. To give descriptions of our language

---

68 The preponderance of the personal pronoun clearly suggests that Wittgenstein is at pains to articulate *his* vantage point, *his* 'own conception, how he sees things'. Cf. "'A *proposition* is a unit of language." "After all, what constitutes propositions is the combination of words which might be otherwise combined." But that means: what constitutes propositions *for me*. That is the way I regard language' (PG: 170f.).

69 Cf. Chapter 3.

116

is *prima facie* straightforward, and yet, Wittgenstein faces severe difficulties, due to his need to describe our words and sentences as part of a *certain* system. Of course, it seems fair enough to articulate something like 'The only thing that is of interest to me is the content of a proposition and the content of a proposition is something internal to it. A proposition has its content as part of a calculus.' Fair enough, that is, at the level of abstract considerations. But what does it look like in practice: operating on that particular interest? Attend to our language and ask yourself, in opposition to the urge to explain that is pressing hard on your mind, what items and connections should make up the system or the calculus in which it is all done.[70] If the content of the proposition is not anything like a meaning in our heads or a feeling in our hearts, if the content is nothing of that sort, but inherent to the system to which the proposition belongs, and if this system is autonomous, hence is something that does bear connections to the 'objective world', although not in any obvious sort of way[71]—if this system, in short, is something that inheres in his way of looking at language, at what sends us in pursuit of chimeras the moment we turn philosophical, and if it is for that reason that Wittgenstein looks at the language-game as autonomous, as a system that is not in the category of experience, then where does this kind of determination leave us as regards our descrying the system *in practice*, hence as regards our giving descriptions of language, as the coping stone in one's philosophy? It is reasonable to articulate one's way of looking at things, by way of a beginning, but how to bring one's philosophy to an end, given one's interest?

The content of the proposition is, for Wittgenstein, not anything like a meaning in our heads or feelings in our hearts. He, with *his* determination of sense, seems to have dissociated himself entirely from what we as users of our language normally associate with its words and sentences, from what we e.g. call the sense or meaning of any given morsel of language in the daily course of life. He has so to speak dissociated himself from such things first, on what we have called the playground of abstract considerations, only to bring this dissociation in the form of a certain system of language to bear on our language, on it as the material to work on, on it as the material to come to descriptive terms with at last, but also as the material that has urged him to move away from it at first, for the kinds of things that *we* as users associate with our language precisely begin to operate so bewitchingly on our helpless minds the moment we turn philosophical.

---

70 At this juncture it does not matter whether we speak of a calculus or the system—or just in terms of the language-game.

71 Cf. Chapter 5.

Speaking of a dissociation that Wittgenstein brings to bear upon language, I might as well have said: there is an indeterminacy in his way of looking at things. We shall shortly return to its point.

The system, we said, is not so much open to view as that it *counts* as open to view; but the system has *turned out* to be rather hidden in the course of Wittgenstein's persistent efforts to describe our language. It has turned out to be hidden in a sense that Wittgenstein does not seem to have fully foreseen on the playground of abstract consideration. *Something of decisive* importance in Wittgenstein's later philosophy, as one wants to say, has *turned out* to be quite troublesome. His uncommon way of looking at language commits him to pay attention to how we use our words, but what should be counted among a use if the system of which it is part counts as recogniz*able* but is not easy to recognize? If only one knows the system (say, the language-game), if only one has a firm hold on that thing, for then it seems possible to tell where a certain use begins and where it ends. We may well remind ourselves of a particular aspect, or of one item or another belonging to the system, but the system itself does not seem to belong to the items of which we can remind ourselves. So whereas some items lie open to view, the system itself seems anything but open *to view*. But if the system does not lie open to view, how should we know that the items we find ourselves considering belong to one and the same system? If our eyes fall upon an interesting set of items and our minds begins to consider it as what makes up a particular language-game, how could we possibly be certain that we have not overlooked an item or two? It is fair enough to *determine*, as Wittgenstein does, that the use settles it all, but sooner or later the question arises: What settles the use? The trouble that I am intimating here is expressed by remarks such as the following:

> We certainly see bits of the concepts, but we don't clearly see the declivities by which one passes into other. (RFM: 302)

> What matters is precisely *what* settles the sense of a proposition, what we choose to say settles its sense. The use of the sign must settle it but what do we count as the use?— (RFM: 366f.)[72]

> *That* we use the sentence is clear; *how* we use it is the question.
>
> *That* we use the sentence doesn't yet tell us anything, because we recognize the enormous variety of use. Thus we see the problem in *How*. (RPP I: 366–367)

These remarks may strike a rather innocuous chord, and yet they address a general concern, something that turns up in Wittgenstein's philosophy time and

---

72 Amended translation.

again, irrespective of the kind of field of language under his attention: *'Die Problematik der Philosophie ist die Problematik des Witzes.'*

Shortly before he died, Wittgenstein asks himself 'What am I after?'—and he replies: '[t]he fact that the description of the use of a word is the description of a system, or of systems. – But I don't have a definition for what a system is' (LWPP I: 294). Could Wittgenstein have forgotten here what giving descriptions amounts to in philosophy? Is he *reminding* himself of what he had laid down in the early 1930s and had been operating on henceforth, namely that the description of the use of a word is the description of a system (or of systems)?

Be that as it may, the fact is that Wittgenstein could not anticipate on the playground of abstract consideration what the effort of describing languages looks like *in practice*, that is, what the effort amounts to and all that one has to come to terms with. And it seems that the above remark gives at least expression to the difficulties that Wittgenstein had to cope with on the playground of describing language. Of course, not having a definition at hand does not mean that one is using a notion illegitimately or wrongly. But it does make it more difficult to penetrate the kind of *enunciations* that Wittgenstein was promulgating in the 1930s. On the other hand, how could a definition have helped Wittgenstein on the playground of describing language? It is not even clear that Wittgenstein wanted to have a definition. What is clear is that he considers the system as something self-contained, a fact that finds expression in his regarding each and every language-game as autonomous, as something in which it is *all* done, as something in which a word or proposition acquires meaning on account of being part of it. Indeed, the *notion* of a system is rather abstract, whereas our language seems to be concrete, perhaps only because it is the object that is being looked at as a system. The notion of a system is not in the category of our experience. In any case, should there exist a system in our experience, it does not hold Wittgenstein's interest, for reasons of philosophy—unless it leads us astray.

The difficulty that Wittgenstein's remark addresses can be characterized as follows: his descriptions of our language as a system invariably face an *indeterminacy* in our language. Wittgenstein faces the difficulty to determine what belongs and what does not belong to the language-game. But this indeterminacy lies in the eye of the beholder, more particularly in Wittgenstein's later eyes. It lies in his uncommon way of looking at things, in that he looks at the language-game as autonomous, at language as a system in which it is all done. The so-called indeterminacy of language is the shadow that Wittgenstein's uncommon way looking casts on it. Again:

Language is of interest to me as a phenomenon and not as a means to a particular end. (PG: 190)

The only thing that is of interest to me is the content of a proposition and the content of a proposition is something internal to it. A proposition has its content as part of a calculus. (PG: 63)

To be sure, remarks such as these do not exclude the possibility that *concepts* function in language as means to a particular end. There are such concepts, as Wittgenstein well knows.[73] So to remind ourselves of this is not to point out that what he says in the above remarks is just wrong or not fine-grained enough. They stem from the period of Wittgenstein's reorientation in philosophy, a time at which he was long since aware of the fact that our language involves *concepts* that do serve a particular end. Nevertheless, he began to look at (our) *language* as a phenomenon and not as a means to a particular end. Wittgenstein began to look at language thus only insofar as it troubles him, and the troubles to which he seems to succumb especially are those provoked by the so-called basic concepts from sectors such as mathematics and psychology.[74] The more basic our concepts are, the more Wittgenstein is confronted with the question of what the *Witz* of the language-game is. It is not up to the philosopher to *decide* that question, for if it is all done in language, the answer must be *found* there: in our language. It should be found within the category of our language itself, as what one must attempt to sort out by looking at its practice, by noticing the *Witz* of a language-game—by reminding oneself of one thing or another. But how does Wittgenstein know that he has given the correct answer in the end? There is no higher authority to which he might appeal; his only recourse is our language itself, the medium in which it is *all* done. Indeed, prejudices lie in wait, as we shall shortly see, lie in wait precisely so at the very last stages in Wittgenstein's efforts to close the dialectical circle, for they, the prejudices, are as it were acquainted with what he requires for his descriptions: in the end the answer to the question wherein the whole point of a particular use lies. This answer is the means to overcome the indeterminacy that he has been running up against all the time.

'What did the hypothesis of the importance [*Wichtigkeit*] of glance do for us? – It offered us a picture of definite multiplicity' (RPP I: 430). With the *hypothesis* at hand you have a means to describe the language-game. Language, in its light,

---

73 Cf. 'Why do we count? Has it proved practical? Do we have our concepts, e.g. the psychological ones, because it has proved to be advantageous? And yet we do have *certain* concepts just for that reason; they were introduced for that reason' (RPP I: 951).
74 Cf. Chapter 5 apropos basic concepts.

now suddenly appears to be determinate. And yet, the hypothesis is only a hypothesis. The indeterminacy that one's way of looking casts on language should not be met by a hypothesis, a means that may well fire the imagination, but by reminding oneself of one thing and another, and by paying close attention to the practice of our language. But how to know that one's reminding is correct? If you do not know whether you have reminded yourself correctly, why reject the hypothesis? Is it because you do not know whether the *hypothesis* leaves everything as it is? And how do you know that? One needs to reject the hypothesis in the end, because this requirement lies in one's indeterminate way of looking at language, in the way one *wants* to look at its workings and do work on oneself. The requirement itself is thought of as what can in the end be met by processes such as looking at the practice of language and by reminding oneself of one thing or another—processes that are thought of as determinate means to meet the indeterminacy in one's way of looking.

In sum, the source of Wittgenstein's saying that '*Die Problematik der Philosophie ist die Problematik des Witzes*' is, ultimately, the indeterminacy of his uncommon way of looking at things. It is the source of his difficulties in describing the grammatical commerce of our language *and*, at the same time, the ultimate expression of how he *wants* to consider its workings, namely by leaving everything as it is. The indeterminacy of one's way of looking determines that there is work to be done; the kind of indeterminacy determines the kind of work. Wittgenstein's difficulties lie in the *how*; their source in the *that*. *That* the sign does do its job within the system of language is not what he observes or could have discovered, in the manner scientists observe and discover things. Caught up in the business of observing *how* a sign functions[75], Wittgenstein cannot possibly be curious to be taught—by language—*that* a sign functions as part of a certain system only. The *that* pertains to a form of looking and this form is not in the category of language itself. The system-in-which-it-is-all-done *is* the kind of attitude that the philosopher fosters towards language, the ground on which he stands and from whose vantage point he wants to understand language's life and logic. We, in the daily walk of life, do not give a hang about the system of our language, as Wittgenstein says, which means that we, as users, do not give a hang about *the workings* of our language as *he* seeks to have them before his eyes.

---

75 Recall: 'One cannot guess how a word functions. One has to look at its use and learn from that' (PI: 340).

2.5 Two types of prejudices

'You are simply looking at the sentence as a move in a given game.'[76] Thus said Wittgenstein in the early 1930s, or perhaps we should say: observed. His remark turns up after a relatively long struggle to find his way back into philosophy, which appears to have been a kind of *Selbstfindung*, a process of higher contemplation in which he kept an attentive eye on his own doings and anxiously watches over the tendencies of his restless mind, with the sole intention of getting hold of a new way of looking at things. Wittgenstein seems to have noticed how his mind as it were kept looking at the sentence, only to tell himself that that is how he had better look at it himself henceforth. And now that the novel vantage point has at last been found: is it not worth a try? But, then, what does it look like: solving philosophical problems from your newly won vantage point, Wittgenstein? For your act of *Selbstfindung* has so far been a rather abstract affair. Hence the question of what it looks like in practice: to look at the sentence *as* a move in a *given* language-game? For the *as* epitomizes an unadulterated indeterminacy. What Wittgenstein's remark suggests is that the sentence is a kind of *given* entity, but also that the game itself is a *given* entity. The sentence is what he wants to look at *as* a move in a certain game. But what is the game? What *is* the language-game in which the given sentence plays the role it plays there? But *what* role does it play? Unless the game is known in which it plays its role it seems hopeless to answer this question. It is all well and good to catch up with a sentence, with what we call a sentence in the daily course of life, but what about the so-called language-game in which it should be looked at as a move? Is it as much *given* as the sentence itself? Language does not inform the philosopher that its sentences ought to be looked at as moves in certain games. Rather it is for him to find his way of looking, and, once found, to commit himself to the important task of articulating his way of addressing his subject matter beforehand—only to carry this way through in the face of those facts he finds and stumbles upon. But is Wittgenstein the philosopher not running the risk, now that he is eager to look upon the sentence as a move in a 'given' game, to *determine* the borders of the language-game according to how he picks upon the sentence, i.e. how *he* takes it, how *he* looks at it? In the following we shall try to make plausible, by means of several passages from Wittgenstein's own hand, that his main difficulty in describing the language-game is intimately tied to the indeterminacy discussed above. He wants to leave everything as it is; hence he ought not to give

---

76 PG: 153.

way to any temptation to *render* our language determinate. Let us begin with considering the following.

> Nothing is more difficult than facing concepts *without prejudice*. (And that is the principal difficulty of philosophy.) (RPP II: 87)

> Nothing is more difficult than facing concepts without prejudice—For the prejudice is a system, that is, a form of understanding, even though it is not the correct understanding. But to be without prejudice means: not to park the weight at some place or other, but to keep it in balance.[77]

Knowing of the role of prejudices in Wittgenstein's philosophy, we should not be surprised to see him saying that facing concepts without prejudice is *the principal difficulty* of philosophy. But neither should we be surprised to see him circumscribing the difficulty to the effect that it is a matter of keeping the *Verhältnisse*[78] of our language in balance. Indeed, this metaphor appears in scores of remarks and statements of Wittgenstein's own hand, and the first to recall here is the one saying that he looks at the language-game as autonomous. To look at the language-game thus is to look at its *prima facie* image as a veritable challenge. This image does not inform us how the *Verhältnisse* really are. It shows a relationship of the language-game to the world that it does not bear and that requires reconsideration in philosophy. This reconsideration looks at the *prima facie* image of the language-game as involving all kinds of building blocks that we deem necessary for the proper functioning of our language but that on closer scrutiny need to drop out from the final picture, a process that calls for a reorganizing of the remaining material precisely so as other building blocks lie in wait to be brought into account; blocks, that is, which we have never been accustomed to see in connection with our language-game, with its essence, with how it relates to us and we to it, in the daily course of life.

In the remaining part of this chapter I want to address two types of prejudices on which Wittgenstein has amply expanded. The first type can be seen at work on the mind of the Empiricist, for he fails to keep the *Verhältnisse* in our language in balance, in the sense that he puts the weight of its workings in charge of the medium of the mind. The second type of prejudice comes into play *only after* the axis of one's *Betrachtung* has been turned around, for not knowing now what belongs to the use of an expression, in short what the function of a word is, one

---

77 MS 136: 18b.

78 A fitting word, I think, in connection with Wittgenstein's circumscription of the difficulty. It should also remind us of his own words in *PI* §130, namely 'to throw a light on the *Verhältnisse* of our language.'

tends to bring elements into play that do not belong to the language-game, or, given that one has correctly recognized an element as taking part of it, of putting too much weight on its role.

The two types of prejudices are intimately tied to each other, for as long as our philosophical efforts operate under a prejudice of the first type, we experience no difficulties in knowing what Wittgenstein calls the beginning and the end of the language-game (see below). But no sooner have we turned the axis of our whole *Betrachtung* around than in another twinkling of an eye have we lost our hold on the language-game: we now fail to see wherein its very point lies. The prejudice of the second type reflects the indeterminacy that Wittgenstein's way of looking at language casts on its workings. In other words, turning the axis of one's *Betrachtung* around amounts to relinquishing one's determinate way of looking, which prescribes the *Verhältnisse* in language. This prescribing does not come out of the blue, but obtrudes on our philosophical minds in the form of one picture or another lying in our language. Indeterminacy in one's way of looking is not problematic in itself. Rather, it is the first step on the way towards the solution, but also the soil on which prejudices of the second type tend to grow and arise. Now recall here what we have seen Wittgenstein proclaiming in his lectures on the foundations of mathematics: 'A use of language has normally what we might call a point. This is immensely important. Although it's true this is a matter of degree, and we can't say just where it ends.' In this passage, Wittgenstein makes mention of the end of the language-game. But what are we to make of its beginning? What *marks* this beginning *as it is*? Indeed, Wittgenstein means to leave everything *as it is*, but what do we, daily users of our own language as we are, know about so-called beginnings and so-called ends of so-called language-games?

Let us consider the following passage with its terminology of ends and beginnings of language-games, which presents no exception in Wittgenstein's grammatical enunciations.

> What I do is not, of course, to identify my sensation by criteria: but to repeat an expression. But this is not the *end* of the language-game: it is the beginning.
>
> But isn't the beginning the sensation—which I describe?—Perhaps this word "describe" tricks us here. I say: "I describe my state of mind" and "I describe my room". You need to call to mind the differences between the language-games. (PI: 290)

To be sure, a passage such as this one is not a description of language itself; it furnishes rather a few grammatical remarks with respect to Wittgenstein's efforts to describe its grammatical commerce. Thus, a remark such as that 'but this is not the *end* of the language-game: it is the beginning' is a valuable turn in Wittgenstein's dialectical proceedings, for not being itself a description of language, it

124

rather helps to pave the way towards description by administering a first hold or orientation on the language-game in terms of its so-called beginning. But then notice how an ordinary expression from the daily flux of our language comes to represent to Wittgenstein's lights the very *beginning* of a language-game. He *sets* it as the beginning; and he does do it, not without further ado, but in opposition to the urge to look at the language-game in the Empiricist's way, wherein the sensation takes necessarily part in the language-game, indeed even presents its beginning, with the expression of the sensation making up its end. From Wittgenstein's uncommon way of looking, however, the sensation should precisely drop out from the logical commerce of the language-game, i.e. from the system in which it is all done. Wittgenstein furnishes a *reminder* in the above passage when he says that 'What I do is not, of course, to identify my sensation by criteria: but to repeat an expression.' But the reminder does not tell us or him how the language-game really looks like; it merely states that a certain item should be taken *thus* rather than *so*, a taking that sets the item as a firm hold for the kind of work to come yet. So there is *as a matter of fact* nothing in or about this reminding itself to have the expression count as the *beginning* of the language-game. In other words, the reminder does not remind us of what the language-game is, nor of anything such as that the expression *is* its very *beginning*. It is rather against the background of the Empiricist's way of arranging the world that one particular item, in Wittgenstein's hands, reifies *as* the beginning of the language-game, and to that extent helps to set the stage for the request to describe the language-game.

If Wittgenstein's remark reminds us of something *as it is*, it does not remind us of how a *language-game* works, but only of something that is put to use in his dialectical efforts to grasp the actual order of this thing. More generally, Wittgenstein's reminders are put to use *as* parts in a particular building, his dialectical edifice, *as* so-called *as-it-is* pieces—as things behind which Wittgenstein's interest is at work to see his way out of his disquieting state of mind. These *as-it-is* pieces should make up the system, the thing in which it is all done, the language-game. But these *as-it-is* pieces do not tell him what the system is, the thing in which they are what they are. Wittgenstein's philosophical interest informs him that he *ought to* turn his back, ultimately so, upon processes in the medium of the mind and that he needs to pay attention to how we use our words and sentences. If it is *all* done in language, i.e., if *that* is how he looks upon language, this looking informs him that, should he reach out to one mental episode or another as what he feels he cannot do without in his understanding of the workings of the language-game, he ends up bulging in stuff and nonsense. So whilst being about to expose the Empiricist's conception of the language-game as a house of cards,

Wittgenstein does *not* avail himself of a detailed *understanding* of what the real *order* of the language-game is—simply because that expository business is part of his efforts to have that very order before his eyes. This business, integral part as it is of his dialectical efforts, sets the stage for what he is ultimately aiming at. He no doubt throws a look, every now and then, at how we use our own words and sentences—that is, whilst exposing the house-of-cards appearance of the language-game. But whatever these occasional looks give him as regards insight, it is, as we should observe, not an understanding *yet* of how the language-game works. Much is still missing at this dialectical stage of finding his way out, and much turns out to be open-ended for Wittgenstein.

I have just brought the notion of understanding into account; a notion that deserves our full attention, for Wittgenstein certainly wants to understand.[79] But he wants to do so, not by explanations, but by descriptions only, and in opposition to 'an urge to *misunderstand* the workings of our language' (PI: 109, emphasis mine). He says that 'the prejudice is a system', 'a form of understanding' (cf. above passage). It is not likely that the prejudice, the moment it begins to force itself upon our philosophical minds, does do so as a complete system, as a full form of understanding. But it appeals to us at daybreak, no doubt, and before the end of the day it appeals to us as what we as Empiricists have meticulously worked out as system, as a form of understanding that holds our minds in thrall more than ever before. The point now is that Wittgenstein, who seeks to understand by means of descriptions, and these things only, cannot be said to be free from the lures of the prejudice until he has finally settled with *his* descriptions. He seeks to do away with the form of understanding that the prejudice *is*, or seeks to impose on us, but the only thing that can ultimately take the place of this form is the kind of understanding that he is out for. It is in the course of his efforts to give description, that is, in the course of his efforts to come out at the end of the day with description *only*, that he seems to be most vulnerable to the lures of the prejudice, for he does not understand *yet*. Only understanding holds out against the prejudice at last, and the only form of understanding in Wittgenstein's dialectical edifice comes by way of its very last course of stones: description of language.[80]

Wittgenstein remains in complete darkness about the language-game *as it is*, about its *actual* order as it takes part in our language, as long as he fails to grasp its *Witz*, and as long as this vexing situation persists the prejudice keeps

---

79 See Chapter 4.
80 More on this issue in Chapter 4.

exercising its strong influence on his mind.[81] Without the *Witz*, he fails to see all that is involved in the language-game in respect of its various components as well as in respect of the question how they relate to each other. What Wittgenstein faces, after having salvaged a language-game from its plunge into the medium of the mind, is not a language-game itself but a few scratches of word use backed up by a few reminders: a more or less incomprehensible heap out of which he is to salvage the language-game *as it is*. He is to make it up *as it really is*, and not as he believes it to be. But as long as no alternative *Witz* steps in and guides his efforts, the appeal of the medium of the mind is quick to fill in the existing vacuum by providing him with a powerful *Witz*. In its light, the language-game is tidy and perfectly comprehensible; it has a clear beginning and a clear end, and, importantly, it sits so well and easily (we rightly believe) with our everyday grasp and understanding of our life and language. The *Witz*, as one might say, works like a glue: it holds things together and arranges the material of our language-game in a way that strikes us as the *realistic* order. It strikes us as the *only* possible order. And yet, the *Witz* administered by a picture of the mind arranges matters in a way in which Wittgenstein sees nothing but a house of cards. But, to be sure, this 'insight' alone does not do away with the powerful lures of the prejudiced *Witz*.

Wittgenstein's effort to appear at the end of the day with description only is anything but powered right from the beginning by the kind of *Witz* that is so important for *his* Realism. It is the question of what the real *Witz* is, rather than the answer to it, which guides and determines his various philosophical doings—*against* the urge of the *Witz* that sends him contemplating the realism of the Empiricist. And this pursuit of an answer bears the danger of fatigue. Not discerning what the real *Witz* of the language-game is, hence not seeing how to close the dialectical circle at last, one becomes vulnerable to the threat to settle on one preference or another, perhaps on an invented *Witz*, one that offers itself as a fitting choice by giving the overall account a realistic look or feel. One just is strongly driven by the single-mindedness to close the dialectical circle, just as the Empiricist is driven to give the medium of the mind its proper and lasting place in the whole of his intellectual fabric. But in contrast to Wittgenstein, the Empiricist presides over a powerful *Witz* guiding his enterprise right from the beginning. The difficulty of describing language-games, then, as far as it pertains to the threat to settle eventually on one preference or another, turns up relatively late in

---

81 Cf. 'And there will be constant lapses from description into explanation here' (RFM: 216).

the dialectical process of Wittgenstein's philosophy. It is one thing to salvage the language-game from its plunge into the medium of the mind; it is an altogether different thing to *complete* this heroic effort by seeing what the language-game really is. There is no salvaging *yet* as long as we keep staring at a blank, or this blank back at us, one that has taken the place of a powerful *Witz* that had sent us in pursuit of a chimera and that keeps smiling at us, always ready to free us from our self-imposed struggle.

Of course, having just spoken in terms of the threat to settle on one preference or another, I have again entertained Wittgenstein's conception of a prejudice, namely of the second type. These prejudices, as I have been suggesting, are as omnipresent in his later work as are the prejudices of the first type. They concern the field of mathematics as much as the field of psychological verbs and avowals. The following imagery summarizes many a thing at stake in Wittgenstein's struggles, nicely exploiting, for instance, the important idea of keeping things in balance, of not placing too much weight on any kind of element or relation. The sweeping character of the imagery clearly suggests that Wittgenstein's efforts to complete the salvaging process are not confined to one field of our language only; or to one such field more so than to other fields.

> It is difficult to put the body of fact [*Tatsachenkörper*] right side up: to regard the given as given. It is difficult to place the body differently from the way one is accustomed to see it. A table in a lumber room may always lie upside down, in order to save space perhaps. Thus I have always seen the body of fact placed like *this*, for reasons of various kinds; and now I am supposed to see something else as its beginning and something else as its end. That is difficult. It as it were will not stand like that, unless one supports it in this position by means of other contrivances. (RFM: 254)[82]

Wittgenstein, in order to overcome the indeterminacy of his vantage point, must at last settle with a determinant in our language, in the form of such an item as e.g. a purpose or usefulness in subtle balance with another item so that the *Witz* of the language-game is not exclusively a matter of usefulness.[83] But this

---

82 Cf. 'The difficulty of renouncing all theory: One has to regard what appears so obviously incomplete, as something complete' (RPP I: 723), see also RPP I: 257.

83 Wittgenstein writes:
> What I have to do is something like describing the office of a king;—in doing which I must never fall into the error of explaining the kingly dignity by the king's usefulness, but I must leave neither his usefulness nor his dignity out of account. (RFM: 357)

Wittgenstein wants so much as to take the trouble to work out what mathematics *is* and this seemingly heroic effort conceives its main difficulty to lie in finding the right

determinant ought not to be imposed on our language, on *the given*. However elusive, it must be made out as real, as what partakes of the language-game. Unless Wittgenstein succeeds in regarding the determinant as part of the given, he cannot be said to have left language as it is. He looks at the so-called given from a certain point of view, that is, at a particular segment of the world *as autonomous*, a view under which the language-game needs to be placed differently from the way we are accustomed to see it, a placement that severs it from the familiar connections it bears to the world, connections without which the language-game loses its hold on the world and we our accustomed image of the language-game. By entertaining the imagery of the *Tatsachenkörper* that will not stand right side up *unless one supports* it in this position by means of other contrivances, Wittgenstein precisely signals how difficult it is to regard the given *as given*, the given *as the system* in which it is all done.

Of course, if Wittgenstein's imagery exemplifies a certain highly unattractive kind of difficulty, we may well make use of it so as to illustrate how the difficulty arises. For the very *Tatsachenkörper* has its place in our *Lebensform*, not as an isolated thing, but as a language-game connected with other language-games.[84] It stands there, in our lives, and it is what it is *for us* (perhaps) also because of the array of ramifying connections it bears to so many other things in our lives and *Lebensform*. If Wittgenstein is now supposed 'to see something else as its beginning and something else as its end', he deprives it of the kinds of connections that it has *for us*. There is a vanishing or changing of what *we* have always connected with it and its bearings on our *Lebensform*. While trying to put the thing right side up, there is a vanishing or changing of its original *Witz*, and this vanishing or changing amounts to a dismembering of the thing itself, of something that just *has* an inviolable 'normative' quality for us in the daily course of life. We are

---

balance, in not putting too much weight at the door of one aspect to the detriment of another aspect. So his suggestion is that he fails to give a *realistic* account of mathematics should he fall into the error of explaining, as he puts it, 'the kingly dignity by the king's usefulness'. On the other hand, he is again in danger of falsifying mathematics should he leave out the usefulness of its propositions altogether, or the dignity of the king's position. In other words, the *Witz* of a mathematical proposition lies neither in its usefulness alone nor in its dignity only; it rather lies in a delicate balance between these two items; a balance that, to be sure, need not be one and the same for every mathematical proposition. Indeed, it is *rather not* one and the same, as Wittgenstein keeps emphasizing. I shall return to the above passage in part II of the present study.

84 And if the thing stands there more or less isolated, well *that* is the connection it bears to us and our *Lebensform*.

now left beholding what does not even have an order, let alone the one that we connect with the original; a mere pile of bits and pieces on which we have no sensible hold unless we bring a new *Witz* into account. But this new *Witz* should not be *our* addition, that is, anything like an invention or preference that we, philosophers, feel urged to bring into account *in order to obtain a sensible* hold on the thing—in order, that is, to put our restless mind to rest.

Now suppose that we truly believe to have succeeded in seeing the body right side up. What do we see? In what way is *this* body, which we are not accustomed to behold thus in the daily course of life, connected with *the rest of our lives*, with how we, users of our language, conceive the world? It seems to stand out there as pretty odd and perfectly *isolated*. To put the *Tatsachenkörper* right side up is, as I should like to say, to produce a genuine *Fremdkörper*, something that we would not easily (if at all) associate with what *we*, in the daily course of life, call doing mathematics (say). But if that is precisely what hinders us from believing that we have finally put the *Tatsachenkörper* right side up, that is, if the *image* of the supposed result keeps striking us as what does not fit with the rest of our lives, with what *we call* doing this or that thing with words, what should ever tell us that we have successfully managed to put the body right side up? What tells us that we have at last closed the dialectical circle? A pair of closed eyes?

It is difficult to regard the given *as* given: this sums up Wittgenstein's difficulty in *describing* our language-games. It is a difficulty that turns out to have a highly unattractive aspect, the real depth of which Wittgenstein did not fathom at the playground of abstract consideration. What emerged there in the 1930s is a picture saying that something *of language* is lying in the foreground and that something *of language* is lying in the background, a picture telling us that what lies in the foreground leads us astray *in philosophy*—leads us astray *there and then*, only to add to our sense that what lies in the foreground *hides* what lies in the background. One should like to say that what leads us astray in philosophy reifies in Wittgenstein's hand as the surface of our language, and, of course, given a surface there must be something lying behind it. Anyway, Wittgenstein avails himself of the imagery of language having a two-layered structure in order to give expression to how *difficult* it is to regard the given as given. It does not readily give expression, at least not in his own perception, to some serious doubts about the feasibility of his later philosophy. He says that 'nothing is hidden' (PI: 435), a slogan that earmarks his way of looking at language. What it earmarks is that it is *all* done in language, that in *his* 'study of symbolism there is no foreground and background; it isn't a matter of a tangible sign with an accompanying intangible power of understanding' (PG: 87). Indeed, as one should like to say, it is precisely due to this way of looking at language that it obtains a two-layered structure, a foreground and a background. The intangible power of understanding remains, for all the difficulties that Wittgenstein encounters while describing the symbolic character of the tangible sign, excluded from the system in which it is all done; it is owing to that kind of exclusion that it is so difficult to regard the given as given, to see *how* it is all done there.

Nothing is hidden *and yet* our concepts *are* concealed. This paradox, then, is only apparent, for *that* nothing is hidden is not a claim about language but a statement earmarking a way of looking at it. But, to repeat my point, it is precisely owing to that way of looking that language *reifies* into a two-layered structure, reifies to the effect that the relevance of Wittgenstein's way of looking concerns something that finds itself hidden behind a so-called surface grammar. The slogan 'Nothing is hidden' leaves open how difficult it is to reveal the real workings of our language, and that it *turned out* to be far more difficult than Wittgenstein once thought it to be himself became a recurring theme of his reflections, one that seems to have gained additional attention in especially his more advanced years. 'In order to overview these concepts', he says, 'you must compare them differently than their surface grammar suggests. You must conceive other parts as homologous: One must compare what looks like a jawbone with a foot. Concepts are concealed.'[85] Here, too, then, Wittgenstein's imagery of the *Tatsachenkörper* to be turned right side up is at work, as it is in the following remark: 'It is so difficult to pinpoint the family tree of *Erlebnisse*. Because it is difficult to put the old concepts upside down.'[86]

What is so interesting about such remarks, alluding to a highly unattractive difficulty as they do, is that they exploit it in order to express that there is a real word use, a real sense. The recurring difficulties worked their way into Wittgenstein's consciousness, but they did not settle there as deep worries, at least not according to the following passage.

> What do I believe in when I believe that man has a soul? What do I believe in when I believe that this substance contains two carbon rings? In both cases, there is a picture in the foreground, but the sense lies far in the background; that is, the application of the picture is not easy to survey. (PI: 422)

> The 'inner' is a delusion. That is: the whole complex of ideas alluded to by this word is like a painted curtain drawn in front of the scene of the real word use. (Amended translation) (LWPP II: 84)

---

85 MS 134: 126.
86 MS 134: 124.

It is the *indeterminacy* in Wittgenstein's uncommon way of looking that gives rise to such typical remarks as these. It is a way of looking that sets its face *against* how things strike us in moments of philosophy, *against* the urge to explain language, *against* one or another form of understanding that obtrudes itself upon us then, only to take complete hold of our thinking henceforth. And the more these forms have roots in our own language, be it in the character of a picture or a simile, the more difficult it appears for Wittgenstein to turn the *Tatsachenkörper* right side up. Empiricism in philosophy materializes more often than not in the guise of a sublime version of how things strike us in the daily course of life, of how we look at the world then, of our own experiences of using our words and sentences the way we do. In other words, setting one's face against the urge to explain *in philosophy* amounts to setting one's face against what strikes us as natural owing to the elusive though determinate appeal of our mental episodes.

Setting his face against the urge to explain in philosophy, Wittgenstein, by the time he seeks to close his dialectical circle in terms of descriptions, faces the unattractive difficulty to put the *Tatsachenkörper* right side up, that is, *at last* against the way we are accustomed to see things in the daily course of life. Wittgenstein starts his philosophical journey with 'Nicht *Empirie und doch Realismus in der Philosophie*', but by the time he needs to emerge with descriptions only, thus after having shown how much of a house of cards Empiricism is in philosophy, he still faces *die Empirie*, the way things strike us in the daily course of life. Near the end of the day, he still faces the unattractive difficulty to put the *Tatsachenkörper* right side up against the accustomed appearance of how language works, for that appearance is not Empiricism but *Empirie*. Hence: '*Nicht Empirie und doch Realismus in der Philosophie, das ist das Schwerste.*'[87] Wittgenstein, by the end of the day, faces the unattractive difficulty to come to terms with something the likeness of which he has never seen before, with something *the whole of which* he cannot reasonably claim to remind himself of, with something that in contrast to the daily image of the *Tatsachenkörper* does not obtrude itself upon our minds but instead calls out for contrivances lest it fall to nothingness in our philosophical hands; with something, at last, that does anything but sit well with the rest of our *Gepflogenheiten* in the daily walk of life. True, Wittgenstein wants to leave everything as it is, that is, he does not mean to substitute the *Tatsachenkörper*

---

87 Anscombe's rendering of Wittgenstein's famous words is not altogether without harm *and yet* I make use of it every now and then myself! Cf.: 'The limits of empiricism [*die Grenzen der Empirie*] are not assumptions unguaranteed, or intuitively known to be correct: they are ways of comparing and acting.' (RFM: 387): *Here* to render the original '*Empirie*' with 'empiricism' is not only incorrect but *highly* misleading.

right side up for the one that plays its accustomed role in our lives. Even so, putting the *Tatsachenkörper* right side up amounts to *representing* all kinds of things of, and concerning, our language to something that we are not accustomed to behold and deal with in the daily walk of life. The ultimate origin of this conflict between what things look like and what things really look like, which is the conflict between what things look like in the daily course of life and what things should like in philosophy, is, as so often, Wittgenstein's uncommon way of looking at things, at the heart of which stands his conception of logic. Logic is not *Empirie*. *Empirie* is how we use language. Empiricism is the false lesson we draw from *Empirie*, in moments of philosophy. *Empirie* is the material that Wittgenstein needs to look at, and wants to come to terms with at last, but he does it from a point of view saying that logic is not *Empirie*. He does it from such a point of view because we tend to draw false lessons from *Empirie*, in moments of philosophy, his own person not excluded.

'How hard it is for me to see what is *right in front of my eyes!*' (CV: 44); 'God grant the philosopher insight into what lies in front of everyone's eyes' (CV: 72). And, indeed, at last some deep kind of worry seems to have settled down in Wittgenstein's mind: 'Am I not getting closer and closer to saying that in the end [*am Schluß*] logic cannot be described? You must look at the practice of language, then you will see it' (OC: 501).

3. Wittgenstein's Copernican Revolution, Part I

The first thing the intellect does with an object is to class it along with something else. But any object that is infinitely important to us and awakens our devotion feels to us also as if it must be sui generis and unique.

William James

3.1 By way of a prologue

Fleshing out fictitious language-games has turned out to be quite a troublesome affair, or at least a far more challenging task than Wittgenstein's playground of abstract consideration has stipulated it to be. It *has turned* out to be so, as I should like to emphasize here, irrespective of whether Wittgenstein found himself doing philosophy in the psychological domains of our language or in a field such as mathematics. He considered every part of our language from his uncommon way of looking, and it is owing to that looking that he was committed to fleshing out fictitious language-games, an activity that he could not possibly dodge should his philosophical hand grow weak, weary or tentative at the request. So, in order to understand Wittgenstein's difficulties on the playground of inventing and collating language-games, we need to see what kind of ground it actually is and how it pertains to the playground of abstract consideration. It is this task that I wish to pick up and to carry out in the present and the next chapter.

What lies at the heart of both chapters is Wittgenstein's notion of the language-game as a *logical* possibility. We play a certain language-game thus-and-so, but we need not play it thus—or at all. Our way of doing it is only one possibility among other possibilities and these other possibilities are conceivable and can be described—and need to be described should we want to *understand* our own logical predicament. This, roughly, is the notion of possibility as it underlies Wittgenstein's playgrounds of inventing and collating language-games (as well as his playground of describing language); a notion that is surely not everybody's cup of tea. It is indeed something peculiar, an as uncommon a thing as Wittgenstein's way of looking, which is not everybody's cup of tea either. In order to examine the notion, we shall need to address his Tractarian conception of logic first, not in order to get distracted by every detail, but still with enough brush and focus so as to come out with an appropriate foil for the story to be told in this and the next chapter. Wittgenstein's conception of the language-game as a logical possibility did not come out of the blue, but out of a period in which he began to tear down his Tractarian enterprise and to clear up the ground on which it stood. This chapter, which together with the next one contrives to make up a kind of diptych, shall not dare to sketch the *birth* of the language-game as a logical possibility in as dismal a light in which the right tablet relates the story of Wittgenstein's difficulties on the playground of inventing and collating language-games.

What Wittgenstein seeks to flesh out on the playground of inventing and collating language-games are so-called objects of comparison. He wants to leave everything as it is, and he seems to be in perfect compliance with that proclamation when he articulates his aims as follows.

> Our clear and simple language-games are not preparatory studies for a future regularization—as it were first approximations, ignoring friction and air-resistance. The language-games are rather set up as *objects of comparison* which, by similarity and dissimilarity, are meant to throw a light on features [*in die Verhältisse*][88] of our language. (PI: 130)

Obviously, it is due to these language-games being clear and simple that *they* throw a light on our language, rather than our language on them, complex and deficient in *Übersichtlichkeit* as it is. Indeed, as we shall need to expound, Wittgenstein does not take to our language so as to *understand* his objects of comparison, but to them *as means to understand* our language. They are means to *understand*, but not just some among other *such means* within one and the same approach, namely Wittgenstein's. They bear an intimate connection to his uncommon way of looking at language, and being the very means they are meant to be, his objects of comparison cannot be ignored or degraded should their constructing turn out to be troublesome. They bear an importance of pivotal momentum, one that Wittgenstein conceived long before he began to try his own hand at the challenge of fleshing them out. In other words, Wittgenstein did not anticipate the pivotal importance of these objects on the playground of inventing and collating language-games. This playground is rather built upon this importance, whereas its activities need to bring this importance out and into account, for the ultimate purpose of obtaining *eine übersichtliche Darstellung* that produces that kind of understanding which consists in 'seeing connections' (cf. PI: 122).[89]

Wittgenstein began to reflect on the importance of objects of comparison at a time that is to be distinguished from the time he seriously began trying to flesh

---

88 Recall that throughout this book I shall stick to Wittgenstein's '*Verhältnisse*'. 'Features' (fourth edition) is not a better rendering than 'facts' (third edition); both are misleading. Cf. '*die Begriffsverhältnnisse liegen sehr kompliziert*' (RPP II: 454).

89 I shall return to this 'received' translation below.

them out. Their importance was grasped when he was still much accustomed, out of sheer Tractarian habit, to a style of abstract thinking that he did not yet consider sufficiently *homespun* to his new taste and interest. It is fair enough to think along such lines as that language's logic is not unique, but always a possibility among other possibilities; it is fair and abstract enough to think thus, by way of a novel approach. But how does it work out, at e.g. the playground of inventing and collating language-games? The divergence of *styles of thinking* that I am alluding to should help to explain why Wittgenstein can often be seen expressing an authentic sense of surprise at the bold resistance of his objects of comparison to come out in the form through which they can play the role assigned to them in the first place. They should be presented such as makes a comparison among languages possible, thus not in abstract space, but on the playground of inventing and collating language-games. Wittgenstein's requirement that we should compare languages with each other seems fair enough, but is it not peculiar that it is *languages* that we need to compare with each other? True, we compare all kinds of things with each other, all day long, with each other and to each other, presenting all the while the results of these activities through the means that our language has at its disposal. But how should we proceed when languages themselves come to lie under comparison, when the challenge is to compare *our* language with other languages, the one *we use* when we compare tables and chairs with each other—with such ones that we do not, or cannot use, for such a purpose? Wittgenstein, to be sure, does not so much mean to compare language-games with each other as such things conceived from his uncommon way of looking. For he compares only insofar as his language troubles him.

Wittgenstein's fictitious language-games should be fashioned with a particular form or physiognomy, one that we can recognize as a way of doing *this* or *that* particular thing with *words*, in spite of their more or less deviant character in respect of our language, in respect of our own way of doing things with words, in respect of what *we call* doing mathematics and doing *this* and *that*. So no *comparison* comes to pass between fictitious language-games and our own, factual language-games unless Wittgenstein succeeds in dressing up his fictitious possibilities beyond a mere suggestive level of doing something particular with words. No small thing is at stake here, for a collapse of Wittgenstein's comparisons does not amount to a mere blemish on his later way of doing philosophy. On the contrary! Unless he succeeds in carrying his objects of comparison beyond the abstract idea of being possibilities among other possibilities, he might well be said to have made 'all logic into nonsense'—to use his own words here.[90]

We have just outlined whence the light on the *Verhältnisse* of our language needs to come. Let us merely add here *PI* §131 to our quotation of *PI* §130 above, by way of a further shot at the present topic.

> For we can avoid ineptness or emptiness in our assertions only by presenting the model as what it is, as an object of comparison—as, so to speak, a measuring-rod; not as a preconceived idea to which reality *must* correspond. (The dogmatism into which we fall so easily in doing philosophy.) (PI: 131)

Though covering only a little segment, *PI* §§130–131 succeed in mentioning a vertiginous number of matters: simple and clear language-games, objects of comparison, correspondence, light to be thrown on the *Verhältnisse* of our language, ineptness or emptiness to be avoided, the model, a measuring-rod, a preconceived idea, reality, dogmatism, *must*, philosophy: these being all kinds of notions that, apparently, relate to each other most intimately. The point that I wish to make with respect to the two passages, and to explicate in the present chapter, is that they take something for granted, something pivotal and absolutely fundamental, namely that the so-called clear and simple language-game can indeed be provided in the form giving them the importance and effectiveness that Wittgenstein ascribes to them, precisely so in *PI* §§130–131. Thus, his suggestion is that whatever obtrudes itself upon us in moments of philosophy: we should try to take hold of it, rather than it of us in the long run, by *presenting it as an object of comparison*. So it may be a picture that obtrudes itself upon our philosophical minds, it may be something else, but whatever it is that begins to knock on our philosophical doors, Wittgenstein suggests, we cannot but must present it as an object of comparison. But, then, an object of comparison it is with respect to the phenomenon of language if it appears in the very character of a *language-game*. It is the possibility of the suggested 'transformation' of something like a picture into an object of comparison which Wittgenstein seems to have taken for granted in the 1930s.

Before seeing Wittgenstein struggling on the playground of inventing and collating language-games, we first need to address the *raison d'être* of this playground, which means that we shall need to return to Wittgenstein's playground of abstract consideration. Indeed, *PI* §§130–131 are typical products of this playground. But this means that the aforementioned 'presupposition' underlies Wittgenstein's entire discussion to which the two passages belong; the discussion that

---

90 See Chapter 4.

begins at *PI* §89 and ends with *PI* §133. In this intriguing series of closely related remarks and statements, Wittgenstein throws a critical light on his *Tractatus*, but so he discusses how we should look at philosophical matters now. Obviously, that critical light and his subsequent discussion are inextricably bound up with each other. For my present concern with *PI* §§89–133, I shall not need to consider all that Wittgenstein discusses there, a task that appears to be much easier to carry out than when I had planned to include every single item. Still, it is the extraordinary strength of build and connection that Wittgenstein's remarks in *PI* §§89–133 bear to each other that might well render a task as my present one a bit of poor stammering, for the suggested strength is much reminiscent of the hardness of the *Tractatus'* crystalline purity.

3.2 Crystalline purity

The notion that should take pride of place in our efforts to grasp Wittgenstein's *Tractatus* is that of the crystalline purity of logic. If Wittgenstein's new ideas, as he puts it in the preface to his *Philosophical Investigations*, 'could be seen in the right light only by contrast with and against the background of [his] older way of thinking', well then, as I would say, nothing will come of that contrasting unless it is built around his Tractarian notion of the crystalline purity of logic, the incomparable essence of language and thinking. To miss this notion is to miss what Wittgenstein's first philosophical exertion was all about, and a book-length story could be told in favour of the view that Wittgensteinian scholarship appears to have established a long tradition of exegetical efforts to come to terms with virtually everything of the *Tractatus* except for its very notion of the crystalline purity of logic.[91] James Conant, with his so-called resolute reading of the *Tractatus*, has, in spite of his sustained and repetitive efforts to pursue a radically

---

91 A story in which, of course, the more interesting exceptions of lack of attention to Wittgenstein's notion should not be left out. Here I am thinking especially of Leo K. C. Cheung's 'The Unity of Language and Logic in Wittgenstein's *Tractatus*', *Philosophical Investigations* 29/1 (2006), 22–50; Marie McGinn's "The Single Great Problem": Wittgenstein's Early Philosophy of Language and Logic', in A. Pichler and S. Saatela, eds., *Wittgenstein: The Philosophy and his Work* (Bergen: Wittgenstein Archive Bergen), 99–132; also clearly appreciative of Wittgenstein's notion is Peter Hylton's 'Functions, Operations, and Sense in Wittgenstein's *Tractatus*', in W. Tait, ed., *Early Analytic Philosophy: Frege, Russell, Wittgenstein: Essays in Honour of Leonard Lynsky* (Chicago: Chicago University Press, 1997), 91–106.

new interpretation, only fallen in line with this remarkable tradition.[92] Brian McGuinness is another contributor, one of the early hours in fact, and although not avowedly pursuing a Conantian reading of the *Tractatus*, the following passage exemplifies that he has *something* important to share with one of the latest upsurges in Wittgensteinian scholarship.

> [...] in the first part of the *Tractatus*, notably in the 3's and early 4's, we seem to be told that the essence of a proposition is to be a picture, while in the later parts we are told that its essence is to be a truth-function, that is to say a result of applying the operation of simultaneous negation to elementary propositions. The 'picture theory' requires further elaboration, and the truth-function account of what it is to be a proposition seems to involve circularity by presupposing a prior understanding of what it is to be an elementary proposition. But a more serious difficulty is that the two accounts seem to be quite separate things, and, if this is so, cannot both be adequate accounts of what it is to be a proposition.[93]

In this passage, McGuinness speaks of the *Tractatus* as a work that expounds two accounts of the essence of a proposition. According to one account, the essence of a proposition lies in its being a picture, whereas the other account sees the essence lying in its being a truth-function. McGuinness has these two accounts appear to him as quite separate things, as I would have myself; two accounts that, *if true*, he adds, cannot both be adequate accounts of what it is to be a proposition.

But if that is how things strike us, then why not try to give the impression a chance to dissolve itself? If the two accounts cannot both be adequate, for the simple reason that each one purports to account for the *essence* of the proposition, had we then not better wonder how a work as the *Tractatus* could engender such an awkward impression? Indeed, how to work further with it? How could it be secured? How could it keep holding a firm grip on a mind that should work its way up and higher on Wittgenstein's famous ladder, only to leave one quite puzzled in the way McGuinness seems to be? How could the impression recur again and again, at each attempt to get more out of the book, only to confirm what we have picked up before and against the obvious odds of all those passages so much at pain to inoculate in us what Wittgenstein calls the comprehensive logic of language? Perhaps the idea of this comprehensiveness at first enters upon our mind in the shape of an impression too. But if one then tries to read the book against the background of this impression, if only as an exercise in an alternative attempt to come to terms with the intellectual challenge, one soon notices that

---

92 For an in-depth criticism of Conant's resolute reading see 'Johannes Climacus reads the *Tractatus*', *Wittgenstein-Studien* 5 (2014), 57–87.

93 Brian McGuinness, *Approaches to Wittgenstein* (London: Routledge, 2002), 65f.

Wittgenstein has not at all expounded 'quite separate things' of one and the same item, i.e. the proposition, but an 'aspect' or two neither of which can be had and appreciated fully without the other.

The comprehensiveness of Tractarian logic, which is the incomparable essence of language, does not consist of two or more things as it were amalgamated into a certain unity or wholeness—two or more things (essences), each incomparable and simple in its own way. Thus, just to confine ourselves to two things here: *that* the elementary proposition and the world must have something in common for the proposition to be a picture of the world is not *one* thing, i.e. something that Wittgenstein conceives to be so, only to conceive the possibility of the elementary proposition to build propositions with other elementary propositions to be quite another thing. Rather, Wittgenstein conceives 'each thing' as absolutely essential for the other thing. The *possibility* of the elementary proposition as a picture should on the Tractarian view not involve anything that is not already involved in the *possibility* of the elementary proposition to build complex propositions with other elementary propositions, and so the other way around. When the former possibility bears upon the other possibility in a truly connective way: well, each thing must then appear from the perspective of the other thing as *accidental.* The intimacy of 'connection' that early Wittgenstein *required* with respect to everything that 'comes to partake of' the elementary proposition, of language, is: simplicity. Logic is *utterly* simple: it is not simple when it comprises two or more essences each one of which is clear and simple in its own way. Logic is simple in the only way it can be simple. Only when it presents the incomparable essence of language, of thinking, is it simple in the way it can be.

Simplicity, *absolute* simplicity, is the hallmark of Wittgenstein's early grip on logic. Yet, this grip is more than a hold on logic only. Early Wittgenstein is at a loss for knowing what philosophy comes to unless he takes as his starting point the enunciating of the absolute simplicity of logic. To be concerned with this simplicity (i.e. purity) is to be concerned with no small thing indeed.

> Thinking is surrounded by a nimbus.—Its essence, logic, presents an order, in fact the a priori order of the world; that is, the order of *possibilities*, which the world and thinking must have in common. But this order, it seems, must be *utterly simple.* (PI: 97)

Simplicity is not a particularly Wittgensteinian infatuation. As Lovejoy relates in his famous *The Great Chain of Being*:

> "Simplicity, noblest ornament of truth," wrote John Toland, characteristically; and one can see that to him, and to many of his time and temper, simplicity was in fact, not

merely an extrinsic ornament, but almost a necessary attribute of any conception or doctrine which they were willing to accept as true, or even fairly to examine.[94]

Simplicity, for early Wittgenstein, was not a philosophical trapping, an ornament of truth, any more than *almost* a necessary attribute of what he was most anxious to have before his eyes. Rather, it was an absolutely necessary 'attribute' of what he sought to grasp and to enunciate in the *Tractatus*.

> The solution of the problems of logic must be simple, since they set the standard of simplicity. Men have always had a presentiment that there must be a realm in which the answers to questions are symmetrically combined—a priori—to form a self-contained system. A realm subject to the law: Simplex sigillum veri. (TLP: 5.4541)[95]

Where simplicity fails to reign in logic, perspicuity does not obtain. In other words, simplicity and clarity are two sides of the same coin. And simplicity is not had in early Wittgenstein's eyes if logic leaves open loopholes. So logic must be exact, not exact in one or another way, but exact in the only way logic can be. So logic must be absolutely exact, and is, on that account, *self-contained*, so much so as to have its connection to us, mortal beings as we are and users of our language in daily life, appear somewhat problematic; and problematic enough, as Wittgenstein came to recognize in the early 1930s, to rethink the whole affair of logic from bottom up.

Early Wittgenstein had to find his way into philosophy, far more so than his later self. He was not without *any* orientation at the time of his grand reorientation in the early 1930s. What he brought along then and relied much upon was the result of a long and arduous process that did not come to an end until he was finished with philosophy, and philosophy with him, in the late 1910s. He never saw in philosophy a readymade task, the prêt-à-porter stuff and problems that fill the books and minds of professors of philosophy, and that keep their careers going. Wittgenstein, for his own part, was not so much set to task by philosophy as that *he* set *it* to task, and he did so twice: the first time through an intensity of interest that finally defined itself as what seeks the redeeming word in the grasp and articulation of a purity of the highest kind, a simplicity that permeates the entire world of facts without being an empirical thing itself. Wittgenstein avowed

---

94 Arthur O. Lovejoy, *The Great Chain of Being* (Cambridge, Mass: Harvard University Press, 1964), 9.

95 Recall here what Wittgenstein would write many years later: 'Philosophy unties knots in our thinking: hence its result must be simple, but philosophizing has to be as complicated as the knots it unties' (Z: 452).

to grasp this thing, come what may, and in spite of the fact that he did not find it in as obvious and open a form as he may perhaps have wished it to be. This thing—What is it? It is 'the order of *possibilities*', he says, 'which the world and thinking must have in common' (PI: 97). Well, then, to be concerned with this order, with this utterly simple thing, is not so much to be concerned with logic as with what early Wittgenstein christened *Logic*.

> That utterly simple thing, which we have to enunciate here, is not a likeness of the truth, but the truth in its entirety. (Our problems are not abstract, but perhaps the most concrete that there are.) (Translation amended). (TLP: 5.5563)

Wittgenstein's Tractarian infatuation is a concern with the so-called self-contained system.[96] It is a concern with something that he found infinitely important, with something that must be presented as *sui generis* and unique. Frege and Russell, for all their insights and important achievements in logic, ultimately failed to grasp its true nature. They may well have believed to have thought its matter and concern through and through, what their minds went through, however, were only the consequences of what their heads had settled on without a second thought, namely that logic is a body of doctrines after all. It is different from science, to be sure, but only in degree, they truly believed, for logic deals with the most general features of reality. And that is where Wittgenstein sets in: he breaks with both Russell's and Frege's conception of logic precisely where they believed themselves sure and unassailable. Thus, in the *Tractatus*, he writes that 'The correct explanation of logical propositions must assign to them a unique status among all propositions' (6.112). And in a letter to Bertrand Russell, he claims that 'Logic must turn out to be totally different from any other science' (WC: 22.6.12). Here 'Logic' stands for the investigation of logic; it is not a *Lehre*[97] but the kind of philosophical occupation as Wittgenstein was to lay it down and out in the *Tractatus*. Since early Wittgenstein thought that logic must be totally different from any other science, he nourished no doubts as to whether science could mingle with the task of enunciating the self-contained system, and, in consequence, with solving philosophical problems. But if early Wittgenstein wanted logic to be so much different in this respect, so did his later self. And yet, logic, in his early hands, looked totally different from what it came to look like later on. For it had lost its nimbus, it exalted status, as it had to come down to earth, to 'the rough ground'. It *had* to be a complete occupation with things as *homespun* as anything can be, in the ordinary walk of life.

---

96 Cf. TLP: 5.4541, quoted above.
97 Cf. preface *Tractatus*.

That both early and later Wittgenstein's grasp of logic share the peculiarity of being utterly different 'than any other science', in spite of having fairly little in common with each other, is something that deserves our full attention. To see how this is so, and to see how the notion of fictitious language-games enters into the story of Wittgenstein's reorientation, is the task that we have set ourselves in this chapter. The following words form Malcolm's *Memoirs* are a good starting point.

It is most important to notice that Wittgenstein, in this reported placing of his early enterprise against his later philosophy, contrasts their *points of view* with each other. And these points of view, as Malcolm words clearly suggest, do not sit well in one and the same setting. On the contrary, the *Tractatus* is claimed to have provided a perfected account of a point of view that is the *only* alternative to the one of his later investigations. Here we have a suggestion that we should hold on to as it shines through in nearly everything that Wittgenstein has written about in his early and later philosophy (in respect of their mutual similarities and dissimilarities). Later Wittgenstein's vantage point did not come out of the blue, but is *his own* true and only heir to his Tractarian way of looking at the world; and if we want to understand how these two views bear upon each other in the suggested, exclusive way, we should try to single out one item. It should be an item which his later view has laid down at the bottom of its own approach, namely as the polar opposite of precisely that kind of item that his early view had made fundamental to its approach. It should be an item which later Wittgenstein, i.e. the person who in the early 1930s was to become the later Wittgenstein, recognized as deeply confused *and* as the linchpin of his early philosophical enterprise more than anything else. This linchpin is what enabled him to do philosophy at all, and it came in the guise of his own presentiment that here *must* be 'a realm in which the answers to questions are symmetrically combined—a priori—to form a self-contained system.' So the mutually exclusive character of Wittgenstein's early and later way of looking might be formulated in terms of the following polar

---

98 Norman Malcolm, Ludwig Wittgenstein: A Memoir. With a Biographical Sketch by G. H. von Wright (London: Oxford University Press, 1958), 69.

opposition: Logic, according to the *Tractatus*, must be *sui generis* and unique; logic, from his later point of view, must be *sui generis*. Indeed, logic, according to Wittgenstein's later lights, is still totally different from any other science, and yet, as he now wants to make clear: it is *sui generis* only when it represents language as one possibility among other possibilities. In other words, there is a big MUST at work in Wittgenstein's later philosophy, as there was in his early philosophy. It could hardly have been otherwise if his *Tractatus* had provided a perfected account of a view that is the *only* alternative to the viewpoint of his later work.

Should early Wittgenstein have been deprived of his own private presentiment that 'there must be a realm in which the answers to questions are symmetrically combined—a priori—to form a self-contained system': he would have been finished philosophically, as we have been suggesting. But how, then, given this point or fact, could there ever have been a later Wittgenstein? If Wittgenstein's later philosophy is his own true and only heir to his early philosophy on account of his having seen what the linchpin of his early philosophy was, why was he not finished philosophically at the time he began to perceive things more clearly? The answer is quite simple: Wittgenstein did not so much recognize what the linchpin of his early philosophy was as that he *made out* a certain thing to be the linchpin of that philosophy. This making-out developed into a philosophical concern itself: what brought his early philosophy to a full stop is what rendered itself the origin of a fresh and novel way of coping with the world philosophically.

This point, which we shall develop in the present chapter, is reflected in the fact that Wittgenstein conceived his later philosophy as radical as his early conception, as destructive of any other conception of philosophy as his early conception of philosophy was meant to be. The deathblow to his early philosophy is the deathblow to what conceived itself to be the only philosophy possibly. But this deathblow need not necessarily be as destructive as the receiver of the blow once conceived itself, any more than it needs to *conceive itself* as such. But that is precisely how Wittgenstein went to work. Nothing, he determined, could be considered a deathblow to his former philosophy unless it develops itself into the only alternative possible. Only such an alternative could win him over to doing philosophy again. In other words, Wittgenstein, for all the faults he recognized in his *Tractatus*, held on to its ambiguous character. He would make, at the time of his reorientation, statements such as that 'a wrong conception of the way language functions destroys, of course, the *whole* of logic and everything that goes with it, and doesn't create some merely local disturbance' (PR: 63); and yet, what was not jettisoned along with his logic in its entirety was his grand and ambitious vision of philosophy, which released itself from his early conception of logic only to come to Wittgenstein's aid in his efforts to think about a new conception of logic and the functioning of language. His ambitious vision of philosophy hovered a good deal over the whole process of his reorientation until Wittgenstein gradually settled upon a new conception of logic, a conception so markedly different from his former one and yet so much like its peer as regards its ambition.

It was Wittgenstein's Tractarian presentiment of the ideal that determined his conception that language is in order as it is, but after the demise of this presentiment the notion that language is in order as it is remained alive and kicking, only to have its share in the development of his novel conception of logic. Indeed, it was now up to this novel conception to give expression to his early notion that language is in order as it is. This notion, then, deserves our attention as it went along with another notion of early Wittgenstein, one that survived the demise of his *Tractatus* as well, namely that philosophy is a concern with our language: it is the source of all our philosophical problems and the resource through which they can be solved without remainder. To enter the philosophical stage with a conception of language telling that not *all* philosophical problems arise out of a misunderstanding of its workings, or with a conception telling that not all philosophical problems can be solved in the light of its workings, is to have embarked upon a misconceived notion of both language and philosophy, and right from the beginning.

It was Wittgenstein's Tractarian presentiment of the ideal that inculcated in him the idea that to show *what* the ideal looks like is to show *that* you have solved all philosophical problems *im Wesentlichen*, as he puts it in the preface to the *Tractatus*. The notion of 'all philosophical problems' is primarily a Tractarian construct. That is, it is inherently related to Wittgenstein's presentiment of the ideal, of the crystalline purity of logic, which gives rise to the question of how the notion is to be understood with respect to a conception of language in which light this ideal is itself a house of cards. Wittgenstein, prior to solving philosophical problems, has never been on a grand *Tour de Philosophie* so as to ascertain an overview of its kind and number in the field at large; he has never been on such a tour just to reassure himself that he has taken on board of his philosophy enough armament and appropriate means so as to be able to deal with 'all that is great and important'. No such tour Wittgenstein undertook on behalf of the *Tractatus*, and nothing of the sort he did with respect to the *Philosophical Investigations*. As far the *Tractatus* is concerned, Wittgenstein might well be said to have solved *not* even a single philosophical problem in the book. He gave 'a perfected account of a view' in whose light, he believed, philosophical problems have been solved *im*

Wesentlichen. To enunciate this view is to provide for everything necessary *to see* that nothing less than all philosophical problems have been solved *im Wesentlichen*. What stands in contrast to this enunciating is the *solving* of philosophical problems, which is a tiresome and piecemeal process, a concern that Wittgenstein did not bother to undertake in the book itself. Russell thought otherwise.

3.3 About a *That* and its *How*

Both early and later Wittgenstein, as I have been suggesting, held philosophy to be a concern if not infatuation with nothing less than *all* philosophical problems. Of course, this does not mean that philosophy is committed to solving each and every philosophical problem. Rather, it means that the vantage point on language from which philosophy is being practised treats philosophical problems as solvable *sans exception*. And solvable they are from Wittgenstein's vantage point, early and later, thus from two such points that bear to each other in the polar opposite way.

What I have been suggesting as well is that much of this significant fact is reflected in *PI* §§89–133, where Wittgenstein has chosen to enunciate his later conception of language against the background of his former conception of language first and foremost. And a highly characteristic piece of prose it is indeed, these paragraphs. Tractarian philosophy is long passé, but this is not to say that every form of criticism of Wittgenstein's youthful work is so. One can still criticize the *Tractatus* in various ways, but Wittgenstein did it thus-and-so. The point here is that Wittgenstein did not so much mean to dispose of his Tractarian conception of language on the basis of his hard-won, later conception of language as that he tried to show that the bankruptcy of the former leaves one doing philosophy on the basis of a so-called real need, and this thing only, a need that stands out against the need underlying his Tractarian project.

In *PI* §§89–133, Wittgenstein shows himself thoroughly critical of various Tractarian aspects as regards the way language functions, but instead of treating these things as *mistakes*, that is, as local disturbances in a conception of language that might be considered as correct at large and that could be held on to come what may, he is anxious to trace their origins back to one common source. Some one single item is *made* responsible for various mistakes: *that* is Wittgenstein's hand, the characteristic stamp on his criticism of the *Tractatus*. Importantly, what he singles out in this respect is not considered to be a *mistake* itself.

> "Language (or thinking) is something unique" – this proves to be a superstition (not a mistake!), itself produced by grammatical illusions. (PI: 110)

Early Wittgenstein nourished his presentiment of the self-contained system, a conception of the workings of language that emphasized the order of all possibilities, of something that must be *sui generis* and unique. In the 1930s, he revived his former presentiment so as to scrutinize its nature as the ultimate common source of each and every detail of his Tractarian work. The fundamental importance of the presentiment was out of the question for early Wittgenstein, but what was out of the question on that account, as he began to realize in the 1930s, was nothing less than *the nature* of the presentiment in the form of a requirement. The extent to which the presentiment understood itself was the extent of the success in which the *Tractatus* hailed its own erection. And the extent to which Wittgenstein began to understand the nature of his Tractarian presentiment in the 1930s was the extent to which began to tear down its logical ideal. The ground on which it stood 'proves to be a *superstition* (not a mistake!), itself produced', Wittgenstein adds, 'by grammatical *illusions*' (emphases mine). But that phrasing should not blind us to the fact that that is how Wittgenstein saw it: *he* exposes the *Tractatus* thus; *he* brings psychology into account, that is, *he* takes to such a psychological turn of phrase.

Wittgenstein's suggestion is that there is a momentum beyond the self-understanding of the *Tractatus*, one that only needs to be recognized by an observant philosopher of his later class, to the detriment of his own Tractarian cause. But, perhaps, to put matters thus is to see them already too much in the light of his later philosophy. Be that as it may, the point is that Wittgenstein, in the 1930s, even if gradually at first, began to subject his Tractarian enterprise to a number of highly critical questions that he had to develop first—questions that fashioned a space of awareness that eventually encapsulated the whole of the logical space in which the *Tractatus* understood itself and its own accomplishment. What these questions brought home to Wittgenstein was the realization how much his former foray into philosophy was made dependent on what committed him to his presentiment of the self-contained system in the first place. This presentiment committed him to articulate the incomparable essence of language. However, what committed him to his presentiment itself was a question that Wittgenstein now felt compelled to answer and to articulate. The former articulation understood itself as an act to give a perfected account of a philosophical view, whereas the latter articulation understood itself as a complete deracination of this self-understanding and the beginning of an alternative view at the same time.

Another salient characteristic of Wittgenstein's proceedings in *PI* §§89–133 concerns the following. Although it was *he* who wrote the *Tractatus*, although it was *he* himself who once slipped into a certain way of looking at language,

148

unwittingly, to be sure, he now begins to look at what happened to *him* as what might well have happened to *all* of us philosophers. It was no doubt *his* early self who once contrived the *Tractatus*, a work championing a certain view on language into which *he* slipped. Yet, later Wittgenstein would rather not see anything idiosyncratic in this part of his biography, any more than in what he constructed on the basis of his early *faux pas*. What is more, although the *Tractatus* was the work of a single man, later Wittgenstein enunciates the slippery road into its construction as exemplifying only one slippery road among so many others. All this is remarkable as later Wittgenstein nevertheless presents himself as a philosopher who is utterly critical of his former tendency to *generalize*.

> The tendency to generalize the case seems to have a strict justification in logic: here one seems *completely* justified in inferring: "If *one* proposition is a picture, then any proposition must be a picture, for they must all be of the same nature." For we are under the illusion that what is sublime, what is essential, about our investigation consists in its grasping *one* comprehensive essence. (Z: 444)[99]

Here, too, Wittgenstein leaves no doubt about the ultimate importance of the fact that he had been underlying a great *illusion* in the *Tractatus*, and that he considers his first contribution to philosophy to be no more than one house of cards only—one house of cards among so many others.

> Where does this investigation get its importance from, giving that it seems only to destroy everything interesting; that is, all that is great and important? (As it were, all buildings, leaving behind only bits of stone and rubble.) But what we are destroying are only houses of cards, and we are clearing up the grounds of language on which they stood. (PI: 118)

At first blush, this passage might well have found a respectable place in the *Tractatus*. Indeed, that work, too, 'seems only to destroy everything interesting; that is, all that is great and important.' And early Wittgenstein, as we can imagine him saying, might well have retorted that 'what we are destroying are only houses of cards, and we are clearing up the grounds of language on which they stood.' And yet, the above passage contains a detail that renders it less suitable for the *Tractatus* after all. The point is that Wittgenstein's later philosophy does not see itself among 'everything interesting; that is, all that is great and important.' It sees its own importance to lie in the activity of destroying houses of cards, and the clearing up of the grounds of language on which these things stood. The *Tractatus*, on the other hand, stands on its own feet, shines in its own glory, no matter

---

99 'One comprehensive essence': the *Tractatus* speaks of 'the all-embracing logic which mirrors the world [*die allumfassende, welt-spiegelnde Logik*]' (TLP: 5.511).

whether it sets out to destroy houses of cards or not. Its glory is not in the least demoted should it refrain from the activity of solving philosophical problems. Its importance is absolute, whereas Wittgenstein's later *philosophy* derives its whole importance from actually solving them, from practising philosophy. Indeed, *PI* §118 is one of those subtle moments in the series of the passages running from *PI* §89 to *PI* §133 where Wittgenstein merely contributes to a highly general tendency. Speaking of *all* that is great and important, he seems to suggest that there is hardly anything special about the ideal of the *Tractatus* and the demise it has suffered at his own hand, for it is now just one house of cards among the great and important houses that philosophers have erected, and still try to erect.

And that, to say the least, is curious. For in his exposition of what his later philosophy amounts to, it is his early Tractarian effort to grasp the incomparable essence of language that function there as the single most important foil to the presentation of his current aims and doings. It enters the stage as the only foil, only to end up there as *one* house of cards among *all* that is great and important. It surely is something great and important, but not *all* that is great and important; it *is* a house of cards, but no more than *one*. And yet, in its role *as* a house of cards it points beyond itself, for now it is representative of a fate that *all* that is great and important must share. Wittgenstein's early and only philosophical edifice *turned out* to be a house of cards, but that every other philosophical thing of importance *must* suffer the same fate eventually is a curiosity, and a most important commitment on Wittgenstein's later part at the same time.

What I am suggesting is an important difference between the *Tractatus* as a house of cards and *everything else* that Wittgenstein means to address as such in the *Investigations*. In the *Investigations*, he does not throw up the *Tractatus* as one of the first things to destroy and to clear up *the grounds of language* on which it stood. That is, he does not throw up (the ideal of) the *Tractatus* there thus, only to address the next house of cards—as if what comes next in the series of houses of cards to be destroyed is addressed from a vantage point on language in whose origin and development the destroying of the *Tractatus* has not played a *fundamental* role. Wittgenstein does not so much *destroy* the (logical ideal of his) *Tractatus*, that is, in the *Investigation*, as that he *exposes* it there *as* a house of cards. He destroyed it in the 1930s and to destroy the *Tractatus* by the means and methods of the *Investigation* is to avail oneself of precisely those things that Wittgenstein had developed and laid down in the 1930s, thus at the time of his factual destroying of the ideal of the *Tractatus*. So you can destroy the *Tractatus* by way of the *Investigations*, as a kind of comical exercise. Wittgenstein, then, destroyed the *Tractatus* in the 1930s, but the so-called *grounds of language* on

which it stood and which he was most anxious to clear up then were just about to
be cleared up through a new conception of (logic) language that the destroying
of his Tractarian ideal was about to give rise to itself. The means and methods
that Wittgenstein developed and laid down in the 1930s have found a decent and
firm place in his *Investigations*. But they have more than anything else added to
development of a novel conception of logic as the ground on which his *Investigations* came to stand itself.

Consider *PI* §110 again, this time in its full length.

> "Language (or thinking) is something unique" – this proves to be a superstition (not a
> mistake!), itself produced by grammatical illusions.
> And now the *Pathos* retreats to these illusions, to the problems. (PI: 110)

This passage, playing a part in the critical *exposition* of Wittgenstein's Tractarian
feat, indeed appears to criticize it from his *later vantage point*. Wittgenstein im-
pugns his early feat here, no doubt; still, he draws on a distinction that deserves
our attention. For the distinction—between his having made mistakes all over
the place in the *Tractatus* on the one hand, and his having slipped towards this
place due to certain illusions, on the other hand—is not what Wittgenstein so
much draws *within* his later way of looking at language as that this way draws on
the distinction. You can criticize Wittgenstein's *Tractatus* from the vantage point
of his later conception of language, but in doing so you are caught up in an activity that draws on distinctions that Wittgenstein conceived and began to articulate
in the 1930s vis-à-vis his *Tractatus*, distinctions that he laid down as the basic
points of criticism of that work, and as the groundwork for his later conception
of language at the same time. Not making any *additional* point, then, the above
passages draws on what Wittgenstein hardened, in the 1930s, into a certain *characterization* of his early philosophy, a move with immense consequences for the
way he went on construing and characterizing matters out of which his later way
of looking at language grew to maturity.

So what I am suggesting is that the above passage is one among several passages in *PI* §§89–133 indicating how much Wittgenstein's later investigations
bear *internally* upon his early conception of language. One might be so bold
as to state that Wittgenstein's Tractarian view belongs, in an important sense
of the word, to his later way of looking at things. What he sets over against his
erstwhile preoccupation with enunciating the ideal is not a philosophical investigation that *has* turned its back upon this preoccupation once and for all. Rather
his later investigations draw on precisely what Wittgenstein in the 1930s made
out to be the linchpin of his former philosophy. Early Wittgenstein really thought
that he was practicing philosophy, but what rendered his Tractarian elucidations

possible turned out to be a set of illusions. So what should become of philosophy now, given that his Tractarian accomplishment traces back to illusions? Well, philosophy, according to Wittgenstein's suggestion, should now draw on the kind of concern that has characterized his former elucidatory work as having been made possible by *illusions*. This characterization, then, is not left for what it is; it rather establishes the foundation of investigations worthy of a name: the true and only heir to his former hold on philosophy.

The *Tractatus*, I said, stands on its own feet, within a glory of its own making. But Wittgenstein's later investigations should be inspired by a fire of no lesser kind than the one that once forged his Tractarian enterprise. I speak of fire; Wittgenstein of *Pathos*. But whence this fire? For the *Tractatus*, great and all important as it conceived itself to be, took its *Pathos* from what the author believed to have seen, namely that 'Language (or thinking) is something unique'. This kind of seeing, which was a seeing *right* into[100] the heart of everything, was Wittgenstein's first and only hold on language and the world at large, hence on his conception of what philosophy is beholden to *at first*, namely: elucidating the order of all possibilities, 'which the world and thinking must have in common'. The *Pathos* of the *Tractatus* inspired a move upwards, the erection of a grand system, having its ultimate source in a certain mystical feeling that is what it is because it concerns something *sui generis* and unique, for it concerns *that* the world *is*.[101]

What should become of philosophy, now that 'Language (or thinking) is something unique' proves to be a superstition (not a mistake!), itself produced by grammatical illusions? If it proves to be that, the whole grand system should turn out to be a house of cards. But if what is great and important proves to be that, then, the mesmerizing awe and inspiration that the exclamation 'Language (or thinking) is something unique!' once exercised on our minds retains its *Pathos*, notwithstanding our recognition that no *building* can be done with it. Its *Pathos* prompted us to build on it, so it has not vanished, now that we see that no building could ever have been done through it. In other words, there is work to do for the philosopher. Indeed, '[w]hat we are destroying are only houses of cards, and we are clearing up the grounds of language on which they *stood*' (emphasis mine). We may well come to recognize that what is great and important is a house of cards, but this leaves *all kinds of questions* untouched about the grounds of (our) language on which it stood. So there is work to do for the philosopher: he should be anxious to clear up the grounds on which the building *stood*. There

---

100   Wittgenstein's notion is '*durchschauen*', cf. PI: 90.
101   Cf. Chapter 4.

is a certain need now, one that the philosopher has never felt before. So the work, the clearing up of the grounds on which the house of cards stood, receives its *Pathos* from the *Pathos* that 'Language (or thinking) is something unique' *still* exercises on us, in moments of philosophy. Illusions prompted us to erect a building, but let us now, Wittgenstein suggests, see and clear up how these very things root in us and our language, until the *Pathos* has been overcome at last.

Philosophy has no *Pathos* of its own; 'it receives its *Pathos* from the *Pathos* of the propositions which it destroys.'[102] This does not mean that Wittgenstein's philosophy reduces to a preoccupation with only those illusions that have made his early work possible in the first instance, but what *does* reduce to these illusions is the systematic role that their revealing has played in forging Wittgenstein's conception of philosophy as what has no *Pathos* of its own making.

But, again, that is how Wittgenstein forged the matter himself, for *he* began to couch certain Tractarian things in terms of illusions and it was not so much they, in that revelation, that now forced *him* to think about philosophy along the lines of what was to become his later philosophy as that it was he *himself* who began to groom his mind for that very conception of philosophy. The internal connection that Wittgenstein's later vantage point on language bears to his Tractarian vantage point is inconceivable without the systematic role to which *he* has hitched his later reading of 'the true nature' of his *Tractatus*. Having found that his Tractarian notion of the uniqueness of logic was illusionary, he now regards any new notions that appear to be *sui generis* and unique in philosophy with the utmost suspicion. And exactly that bears out a conception of language, of its workings, under which *all* philosophical problems are to be treated now. But if the *Tractatus* turns out to be a house of cards, why should *everything* else we ascertain in philosophy turn out as a possible house of cards as well? If the *Tractatus* is made out to be such a thing, why should *all* that is great and important be such a thing as well? I merely ask.—

Let us now pick up an earlier thread, namely the important idea that our colloquial language is, logically speaking, in order as it is.

> Philosophy may in no way interfere with the actual use of language; it can in the end only describe it. (PI: 124)

---

102   'Die Philosophie bezieht ihr Pathos von dem Pathos der Sätze, welche sie zerstört' (VoW: 121f.). Cf. 'Philosophy, as we use the word, is a fight against the *fascination* which forms of expression exert upon us' (BB: 27, emphasis mine).

<blockquote>It is not our aim to refine or complete the system of rules for the use of our words in unheard-of ways. For the clarity that we are aiming at is indeed complete clarity. But this simply means that the philosophical problems should completely disappear. (PI: 133)</blockquote>

Neither the Wittgenstein of the *Tractatus* nor the Wittgenstein of the *Investigations* intended to interfere with the workings of language. 'All propositions of our colloquial language', early Wittgenstein articulated in *TLP* 5.5563, 'are actually, just as they are, in perfect logical order'; and later Wittgenstein concurred, kept to this early spirit, and did not intend to interfere with its intention. Yet, what it is like for a sentence to be in order as it is, according to the doctrines of the *Tractatus*, is not what it is like for a sentence to be so according to the creeds of the *Investigations*. The suggested difference is tremendous. Consider the following passage from the *Investigations*:

<blockquote>That is to say, we are not striving after an ideal, as if our ordinary vague sentences had not yet got a quite unexceptionable sense, and a perfect language awaited construction by us.—On the other hand it seems clear that where there is sense there must be perfect order.——So there must be perfect order even in the vaguest sentence. (PI: 98)</blockquote>

Neither early nor later Wittgenstein strove after an ideal—after a logically perfect language that was to take the place of our colloquial language. But what withheld early Wittgenstein from this pursuit is altogether different from Wittgenstein's later rationale. His early self thought that there was no need to strive after the ideal as each and every language already encompasses it. Our colloquial language may well strike us as more or less imperfect, but, early Wittgenstein thought, this appearance is only a matter of its incidental character, which hides its real and ideal workings. These workings are ideal, not only for our language, but for every language; ideal, that is, in the *only* way in which any language can be language at all. Since the ideal is already there, it would be misguided to believe that we must strive after it. But this simply means that early Wittgenstein would not know what to make of the notion of our everyday language being in order as it is without the ideal. Indeed, without it, he would clearly not have known what to do in philosophy either. These things are intimately connected with each other.

But what is there for philosophy to do? If 'all propositions of our colloquial language are actually, just as they are, in perfect logical order', philosophers need not create an ideal and their striving after it is a waste of time.

<blockquote>We want to say that there can't be any vagueness in logic. The idea now absorbs us that the ideal *'must'* be found in reality. At the same time, one doesn't see *how* it occurs there, and doesn't understand the nature of this "must". We think the ideal must be in reality; for we think we already see it there. (PI: 101)</blockquote>

That there *must* be an ideal is clear, *how* the ideal obtains in reality is not clear yet. But the difference precisely defines the task for the philosopher. As soon as he has seen *that* the ideal must obtain in reality, he sees a *how*: How does it obtain there? Early Wittgenstein keenly felt the difference between the *that* and the *how* as something to be overcome feverishly. But, importantly, it could live productively in his mind because he did not see to the bottom of the nature of the *must*. And whatever Wittgenstein came to see on the subject of *how* the ideal obtains in reality, it could never reveal to him on what his entire philosophical enterprise and doings ultimately rested. It was not until much later that the real nature of his early *must* began to dawn upon him.

Early Wittgenstein not only did not see into the very heart of the *must;* he then also lacked the means to make himself aware of its distinctive nature; and, owing to that specific shortage, of his own philosophical enterprise at large. The difference between his having been aware of requiring something and his later awareness of what this requiring amounted to, is *conceptual* in nature, at least for later Wittgenstein. But if such conceptual means were made available to later Wittgenstein, they certainly did not enter into his mind in the guise of some attractive set of analytical devices that he chanced upon while reading some philosophical books. No, he forged these means and devices himself in the 1930s, but not in order to add them to his later philosophy, or to what was to become this philosophy in due course. Rather, the kind of insight he gained into the nature of his former way of looking became a decisive building block in the establishing of his later way of looking. In this way, what his early self sorely lacked on the subject of awareness of the ultimate nature of his own philosophical enterprise loomed over his later philosophy as the deepest insight into *its* own nature and doings.

James Conant champions a somewhat different view on Wittgenstein's notion of *laying down* requirements. In a short contribution to the *New History of German Literature*, he writes the following:

> Later Wittgenstein came to realize that his earlier method of clarification embodied an entire metaphysics of language, which illustrated that the most crucial moments in the "philosophical conjuring trick" are those that are apt to appear as most innocent.
>
> It turned out to be much more difficult to avoid laying down requirements in philosophy than his earlier self had imagined.[103]

---

103   James Conant, 'A Ladder Turns into a Fly-bottle', in David Wellbery, Hans Ulrich Gumbrecht, Anton Kaes, Dorothea von Muecke, and Judith Ryan, eds., *New History of German Literature* (Cambridge, Mass: Harvard University Press, 2004), 871.

The last sentence is of particular interest. It appears to be a stock phrase of Conant's resolute reading of the *Tractatus*, that is to say, whenever he addresses topics such as the continuities and discontinuities between Wittgenstein's early and later philosophy.[104] In his paper 'Wittgenstein's Later Criticism of the *Tractatus*', for instance, he writes that for later Wittgenstein,

> the most crucial moments in the philosophical conjuring trick are the ones that are apt to strike one as most innocent (*PI* §308).[105] This directly bears on the evolution of his later philosophy in two ways. First, it is tied to his later apprehension that it is much more difficult to avoid laying down requirements in philosophy than his earlier self had ever imagined – where this is tied in the later work, in turn, to the need to develop a form of philosophical practice that can diagnose, identify, and clarify the precise moments in which such requirements on thinking are first unwittingly laid down, well prior to their manifesting themselves to the thinker as commitments of any consequence. Second, it required a set of procedures for the conduct of the new activity of diagnosis, identification, and subsequent clarification that would not themselves prove to carry further unwitting commitments in their train (introducing yet a further metaphysics, now newly built into the successor conception of clarification).[106]

Conant's suggestion clearly is that not only later Wittgenstein but that the Wittgenstein of the *Tractatus* had already at his disposal a conception of *laying down* requirements in philosophy. True enough: early Wittgenstein cannot be denied to have had no a conception at all of what it is to lay down requirements. But, then, in the *Tractatus* he did not so much try to avoid laying down requirements as that he *deliberately* and zealously laid down the requirement that there must be the order of all possibilities, the ideal, which is the incomparable essence of language. Importantly, however, Wittgenstein laid down this requirement of overarching proportions without understanding its true nature (cf. PI: 101). It was not until his grand reorientation in the 1930s that he began to realize and understand the nature of his Tractarian feat. In other words, it was not a matter of his having inadvertently slipped into laying down a requirement in the *Tractatus*, that is, *in spite of* his conceptual awareness of what it is to lay down such things. His early conception of what it is to lay down requirements is scarcely

---

104   The phrase turns up for the first time, I think, in Conant's and Diamond's 'On Reading the *Tractatus* Resolutely: Reply to Meredith Williams and Peter Sullivan', in M. Kölbel and B. Weiss, eds., *Wittgenstein's Lasting Significance* (London: Routledge, 2004), 84.

105   Wittgenstein phrases his point in *PI* §308 in a way that lacks Conant's pleonastic overtones.

106   James Conant, 'Wittgenstein's Later Criticism of the *Tractatus*', in Alois Pichler and Simo Säätelä, eds., *Wittgenstein: the Philosopher and his Work* (Frankfurt am Main: Ontos Verlag, 2006), 195. Cf. (Conant: 2007: 78), (Conant 2010: 64f.).

156

anything over which Wittgenstein presided beyond his deliberate and cognisant act of laying down such a thing in the *Tractatus*. Indeed, his requirement was not so much laid down 'in philosophy', as Conant puts it, as that he just failed to see what philosophy could ever amount to without this requirement. Importantly, it was his vital hold on language *and* philosophy at one and the same time, and it was not until much later that he saw on what he had made the possibility of his first overtures in philosophy ultimately dependent. Conant fabricates a continuity between early and later Wittgenstein by crediting the first with something over which only the second presided.

Conant, in the longer passage quoted above, qualifies his words as follows: 'this is tied in the later work, in turn, to the *need* to develop a form of philosophical practice that can diagnose, identify, and clarify the precise moments in which such requirements on thinking are first unwittingly laid down, well prior to their manifesting themselves to the thinker as commitments of any consequence' (emphasis mine). But what are we to make of this sort of need? For one thing, later Wittgenstein's conception of what it is to lay down requirements goes hand in hand with his conception of what it is to finally do away with the urge to contemplate incomparable essence. A little diagnosing here and there does not do away with this urge itself, any more than it does in combination with the other items of which Conant makes mention: identifying and clarifying. Thus, it is part of Wittgenstein's extensive efforts 'to transform' e.g. the picture standing behind such an urge into a language-game, to be set up alongside our own language (see below). Moreover, if early Wittgenstein entertained already a conception of laying down requirements in Conant's sense of the word, how then should only later Wittgenstein have keenly felt the need to develop the kind of philosophical practice of which Conant speaks? What is it like to entertain such a conception if it is not tied to a bare minimum of needs such as 'diagnosing, identifying and clarifying' a requirement? If early Wittgenstein championed a notion verging on what he expounds in the *Investigations* as the laying down of requirements, it much seems that early Wittgenstein should already have admitted the possibility of a language that is unlike the workings of the ideal, which he was precisely about to spell out.

Let us return to the important difference between the *how* and the *that*. The *that* precedes the *how*: without the *that* early Wittgenstein would have been at a loss for seeing what philosophy is all about and what its task amounts to. Its task was set, completely, by what lived in his mind as a requirement in the shape of a certain ideal that, he thought, '"*must*" be found in reality'. This ideal also informed early Wittgenstein of the idea that 'All propositions of our colloquial language are actually, just as they are, in perfect logical order.' The task, then, that early Wittgenstein faced was that of seeing *how* all these propositions are in *perfect* logical order. 'Logic', he said, 'takes care of itself; all we have to do is to look and see how it does it' (NB: 13.10.14). But both early and later Wittgenstein thought that logic is in order as it is; both thought that logic must take care of itself and that, importantly, all we have to do is 'to look and see how it does it'. But what early Wittgenstein did not see, and came to recognize only much later, was that all there was for logic to do at the time he wrote the *Tractatus* was not to take care of itself, but to look and see how the author *himself* took care of it. He thought that logic can take care of itself only when it comes as the ideal, of what '*"must"* be found in reality'. And as he did not yet see 'how it occurs there', he was convinced that there was a critical task incumbent upon him, the *only* task he thought he should try for all he was worth, namely enunciating 'a realm in which the answers to questions are symmetrically combined—a priori—to form a self-contained system. A realm subject to the law: Simplex sigillum veri' (TLP: 5.4541).

This realm, i.e. the crystalline purity of logic, was not what Wittgenstein *discovered*: 'it was a requirement' (PI: 107). It provided the ultimate footing on which he and his early philosophy stood; it was the key expression of his philosophical concern and core interest, lending his investigation its character and awe-inspiring depth. Whatever else Wittgenstein might be said to have imposed on the world during his investigations, it came in the wake of that singular *must*, of what made his investigations possible in the first instance: logic *must* be of crystalline purity; it *must* be the incomparable essence of language, of thinking; it *must* be the order of all possibilities. This requirement, then, was the single great ordering principle, subjugating everything else that Wittgenstein might be said to have come out with regarding 'further requirements'. He believed he was addressing the *how* of logic, of the ideal, but what his elucidatory activities amounted to was the enunciating of the form of *the* requirement he had laid down himself. Early Wittgenstein genuinely thought to have perceived a precondition of the greatest purity. As matter of fact, he had only been looking at the world through a mode of presentation that, owing to its alleged perspicuity, only darkened his mind about the true nature of his doings. What lay in his mode of presenting the world on the subject of certain attributes is what Wittgenstein took for features inhering in the world itself. He conferred on the object of his investigations such attributes as inhered first and foremost in his mode of presenting it.[107]

---

107   Cf. PI: 114.

The following passage illustrates well the difference between the *that* and the *how* concerning Wittgenstein's requirement:

> Thought, language, now appear to us as the unique correlate, picture, of the world. These concepts: proposition, language, thought, world, stand in line one behind the other, each equivalent to each. (PI: 97)

The purpose of Wittgenstein's early investigations could not possibly have been to show *that* the concepts of which he speaks in the above passage stand one behind each other, each equivalent to each. It could not, as this way of standing was precisely Wittgenstein's ultimate hold on his philosophical investigations, a hold that he imposed on language and the world. It was impossible for Wittgenstein's early investigations to show that the above concepts did not stand behind each other after all. What his investigations could show, however, what was indeed the only thing for them to show, was *how* this standing-behind-each-other occurs in reality. Wittgenstein's investigations derived their complete importance from expounding the form of his *that*, from articulating what he in fact himself imposed on language and the world, unwittingly, to be sure. It is by the *how* that the *that*—this infinitely important and profound *that*—obtained its lasting hold in Wittgenstein's philosophical concern. The *how* is the form of the *that*, but Wittgenstein, misconceiving the true nature of his early requirement, took this *how* to be the form of the world, as the only possible form, as *the* ideal order of possibilities: a super-order. It is in the same vein that we should say and add: *That* language must take care of itself was not under investigation. Rather, 'we must recognize *how* language takes care of itself' (NB: 43).

Now the difference between the *how* and the *that*, I think, not only elucidates the character of Wittgenstein's early philosophy but also the character of his famous turn as he *systematizes* it himself in the *Investigations*. But so does the difference help us see the fundamental character of his later philosophy, as we shall shortly see. The minutiae of his *Tractatus*, of his so-called picture-theory, thus matters of the *how* rather than of the pivotal *that*, have no doubt played an important role in the critical evaluation of his early enterprise by his later mind. And yet, the famous turn of Wittgenstein's mind pivoted much more on the character of his early *that* than on matters of the *how*. The *that*, the very first movement in the conjuring trick (PI: 308): this prompted Wittgenstein to espouse the so-called picture-theory and to enunciate its minutiae henceforth. His first sojourns in philosophy were rather quickly paved by a certain image that foisted itself onto his youthful mind only to commit him to a task to which he thought he had committed himself. It was the moment of this uncritical acceptance by an otherwise highly critical mind that set *everything* rolling into the direction of what has come down to us as his *Tractatus*.

In the following passage, Wittgenstein pinpoints the moment that sent him in pursuit of chimeras.

> We now have a *theory*, a 'dynamic theory' of the proposition; of language, but it does not present itself to us as a theory. For it is the characteristic thing about such a theory that it looks at a special clearly intuitive [*anschaulichen*] case and says: "*That* shews how things are in every case: this case is the exemplar [*Urbild*] of *all* cases."——"Of course! It has to be like that" we say, and are satisfied. We have arrived at a form of expression that *strikes us as obvious*. But it is as if we had now seen something lying *beneath* the surface. (Z: 444)

As Wittgenstein would have it here, he was tempted by a theory which did not present itself to him as a theory. It made him look at a clearly intuitive case only to bias his vision henceforth. Thus, once under the spell of this case, Wittgenstein failed to see that it could *not* apply to all cases. In his failure to see that one case or another could be out of tune with the special case, he had actually long lost sight of what has come to pass; he had committed 'himself' without apprehending the real nature of this commitment. In other words, Wittgenstein did not see that his avowal of adherence—"Of course! It has to be like that"—concerned only a mode of presentation.

Notice that Wittgenstein, in the passage at hand, entertains the important notion of satisfaction. The avowal "Of course! It has to be like that" does not mean that there is no work left to do. On the contrary, for what comes along with this lethal state of satisfaction is blank dissatisfaction, namely, with *how* matters of daily appearance now strike us: they do not dovetail at all with how we think *all* things must be. So we had better dig down now, we tell ourselves, and further down beneath the veil of appearance, down to the point where our real concern lies!

> '*The essence is hidden from us*': this is the form our problem now assumes. We ask: "*What is* language?", "*What is* a proposition?" And the answer to these questions is to be given once for all; and independently of any future experience. (PI: 92)

The kind of work we think we need to do, now that we have seen 'something lying beneath the surface', concerns the aforementioned *how*. In other words, our first state of satisfaction concerns the *that*, whereas ultimate satisfaction will be attained only when we have finished with expounding the details. Wittgenstein's efforts to fathom out the moment he went astray in the *Tractatus*, then, crystalized into the idea that he was utterly impressed by a comparison but did not recognize the comparison as such. This failure drove him straight into the kind of dogmatism of which he speaks in *PI* §131. As he puts it elsewhere:

> I had used a simile; but through the grammatical illusion that a certain *one* thing, something *common* to all its objects, corresponds to a concept-word it did not seem like a simile.[108]

This passage reminds us of what we have been emphasizing before, namely that Wittgenstein distinguishes between mistakes and grammatical illusions. He makes no secret of the fact that he had been making numerous mistakes in the *Tractatus*, but so he is anxious to make clear that the source of all was not a *mistake* itself. Rather it was an illusion. 'I had used a simile', he says in the above passage, but 'it did not seem like a simile.' What Wittgenstein says here may seem insignificant, and yet, it marks is the *beginning* of his Tractarian feat beyond the point where his early self conceived it to lie at the time he wrote the work. *That* is how Wittgenstein diagnosed his early steps into the world of philosophy, an activity in which the notion of a *grammatical illusion* begins to play a pivotal role, and never ceased to do so in his thinking henceforth.

From Wittgenstein's diagnostic point of view, a grammatical illusion is the *Tractatus'* end and rock bottom, the *unwitting* beginning of his Tractarian feat. His diagnosis, then, goes beyond the analytical means and methods that his Tractarian effort had sought to establish as the only philosophical means and methods possible. It is important to emphasize this point precisely so with respect to the question how Wittgenstein's later philosophy bears upon his Tractarian feat. For whatever early Wittgenstein may be said to have taken on board without having perused its nature first, later Wittgenstein makes sure to present that eccentric person in his own idiosyncratic way, in which the distinction between mistakes and illusions takes pride of place.

It seems that Wittgenstein avails himself of the notion of a grammatical *illusion* as a diagnostic tool without throwing much grammatical—or diagnostic—light on the tool itself. But, if true, that only shows how fundamental a notion it is in his diagnostic toolbox. And that means that one demotes the importance that the notion has for him should one want to go so far as to dissect it in turn; that is to say, to dissect it in trite a term such as 'presupposition', or 'assumption', or 'hypothesis' or even 'postulate'. To be sure, then, Wittgenstein did not lose sight of the true nature of the simile, ultimately in consequence of his having entertained

---

108　'Ich hatte ein Gleichnis gebraucht; aber durch die grammatische Täuschung, dem Begriffswort entspräche *Eines*, das *Gemeinsame* alle seiner Gegenstände, erschien es nicht als Gleichnis' (TS 220 §93).

an *assumption* as regards concepts. To render an assumption ultimately responsible for the rise of the *Tractatus* is to leave Wittgenstein asking what drove him to move ahead on the basis of an assumption in the first place. Was it due to another assumption? Was it because of an illusion behind *that* assumption? And what are we to make of that illusion? These questions should help us to appreciate the point of Wittgenstein's words: 'I had used a simile; but through the grammatical illusion that a certain *one* thing, something common to all its objects, corresponds to a concept-word it did not seem like a simile.' If an assumption—or, for that matter, a hypothesis or postulate—ultimately 'constitutes' an illusion, if that is how far later Wittgenstein got to bottom of his *Tractatus*, one well wonders why an illusion should have mediated between the alleged assumption and the very place where it left Wittgenstein and his early philosophy.

3.4 Another *That* and *How*

We have been distinguishing between a *that* and a *how* in Wittgenstein's early philosophy. What we need to realize now is that there is a *that* and a *how* at work in Wittgenstein's later philosophy as well, a division between a kind of determination on the one hand and a working out of its requirements on the other hand. To realize this is exactly to see how Wittgenstein's later philosophy bears upon his first. Neither his first nor his later philosophy came out of the blue; the first did not as it emerged on the basis of a certain simile that kept obtruding itself upon Wittgenstein's mind; and the later did not as it came out of the first—in a way that has everything to do with *how* this first philosophy managed to leap to its feet. Wittgenstein's diagnostic move that he 'had used a simile; but [...] it did not seem like a simile' does not express, as we have been emphasizing, just *some* point in the fabric of his diagnostic efforts to clear up and characterize the very moment he went astray in the *Tractatus*. Rather, it concerns something that played a truly pivotal role in his reorientation in philosophy. The weight and significance of Wittgenstein's diagnosis becomes apparent when we look at what he proposes by way of a therapeutic move: if it is simile that obtrudes itself upon your mind: use it as a simile; pay your tribute to the thing by giving it a pivotal place in the elucidatory work to do. Obviously, Wittgenstein is at pains to leave the simile as what it is; it is what our language *must* be compared with, rather than what its workings *must* match up with. Wittgenstein's turn is not a radical turn away from what once foisted itself onto his mind in the shape of a certain picture, a turn away from such an influence so as to be able to do philosophy without being hamstrung. On the contrary, philosophy has become a complete obsession with doing away with the urge to explain, with one urge or another to look at the world in a certain way, in our contemplative moments.

Doing away with such an urge is doing away with it in the light of what our language is. You need to take language to task as the means to do away with what obtrude itself upon your mind in moments of philosophy. Doing away with what obtrudes itself upon your mind is elucidating *how our* language works, the language in which all kinds of similes and pictures reside anyway but take on a disquieting aspect in moments of philosophy. The simile forces you to look at language as what *must* work in a certain way and cannot work otherwise: doing away with this obsessive *must* is treating the simile as a simile—that is, a simile with respect to the language in which it tends to obtain a disquieting aspect in moments of philosophy. You want to leave everything as it is: well, begin by leaving the simile as what it is: use it as a proper means of comparison, a treatment under which our language is being looked at as what epitomizes possibilities among other possibilities. So there is a *how* at work in Wittgenstein's later philosophy: the *how* of the *that* that treats the simile *as what it is*. This *how*, then, no longer pertains to an absolutely self-contained activity as the *Tractatus* is and nicely presents, a mere enunciating of what the *that* imposes on language and the world. The *how*, in Wittgenstein's later philosophy, has at last become an activity of truly looking and seeing, a genuine concern of describing *how* this or that language-game of us works and obtains in our *Lebensform*, in contrast to other possible ways of working. But this means that this *how* does not obtain *tout court*, any more than it did in the *Tractatus*. Not unlike its predecessor, it is primed by a particular *that* telling what *logic* amounts to. And in *that* sense the relation between the *that* and the *how* in Wittgenstein's later philosophy is as fundamental as it was the *Tractatus*.

We shall shortly see how Wittgenstein's later conception of logic enters into this sketchy description of the relation between the *that* and the *how*. It is a *that* that has taken the place of the *that* of Wittgenstein's Tractarian enterprise, a *that* that is no longer answerable to *any* incomparable essence. The *that* informs one's way of looking at language and the world. But in philosophy, later Wittgenstein would think, it is more often than not language itself that forces us to look at its workings in a certain way. *That* there is an incomparable essence is clear, early Wittgenstein thought, *how* it transpires in reality is what the philosopher needs to clarify. Logic is the incomparable essence of language, i.e. the order of all possibilities, and being what it is, namely not a (thing =) possibility among other possibilities (= things) itself, it does not even amount to being *any-thing*; it is an

Unding, in contrast to *its* application.[109] Always symbolizing one possible system among other possible systems, the application of logic obtains in the spatial and temporal dimensions in which we live and thrive. So there are actually two *hows* in the *Tractatus*: *how* the incomparable essence obtains in reality and what ('*how*') its application looks like. The first *how* is what Wittgenstein was anxious to expound; the latter *how* is what he did not bother to say more about than he deemed absolutely necessary with respect to the mission incumbent on him, namely the expounding of the first *how*.[110]

What drops out in Wittgenstein's conversion of his early *way of looking at* language into his later *way of looking at language* is not only the notion of the *Unding* in the character of the incomparable essence of language as the *Tractatus* had expounded, but any notion that philosophers might feel urged to expound as the ultimate and *incomparable* essence. As a result, what this dropping out left Wittgenstein facing is not the *how* of the application of the incomparable essence as the *Tractatus* conceived it, which occurs through the medium of elementary propositions and these things only, but a certain *how* that is exactly determined by the effort to do away with the urge to look at the workings of language as what obtains in one way only. Thus, although Wittgenstein's later concern is with the system of our language, this system is not the kind of system of which he speaks in *TLP* 5.555[111]. It is heir to this system. 'It is all done in language', later Wittgenstein says; it was not *all* done in the kind of system of which he speaks in *TLP* 5.555. It was *not*, because this system concerns *the application* of the incomparable system, a *comparable* periphery tracing back to the incomparable essence of language, to something that lies 'outside' the so-called spatial and temporal dimensions of our language, of any language.

What I am suggesting is that there is a *must* at work in Wittgenstein's later work as much as there had been in his early work. The *must* of the enthralling picture that says that the workings of language must obtain in a certain way, and that way only, is what Wittgenstein wants to see dissolved completely: thus not the picture itself, but the very *must* of the picture, and this *must* not thus or so,

---

109   I leave Wittgenstein's apt epithet for his Tractarian logic—'*Unding*'—without translation (cf. the boxed passage between *PI* §108 and *PI* §109). See next chapter for more on the *Unding*.

110   See next chapter for more on this point.

111   'It is clear that we have a concept of the elementary proposition apart from its special logical form.
       Where, however, we can build symbols according to a system, there this system is the logically important thing and not the single symbols' (TLP: 5.555).

but in the *only* way in which he conceives it possible, namely by employing the picture as a means of comparison. One's obsession to look at (our) language in a certain way *can* be broken, that is, completely. The obsession is man-made, a mere artefact that arises in our philosophical moments owing to the way our language is organized and we, human beings, participate in it. The obsession that language *must* in the end be answerable to an incomparable essence can be broken by transforming the enthralling picture into an object of comparison, a therapeutic move through which the workings of our language no longer present themselves as one 'possibility' only, but as one possibility among other possibilities. The *must* at work in Wittgenstein's later way of looking at language, then, is not the *must* of a *thesis* claiming that the language-game *is* a possibility among other possibilities. Rather, it is a *must* that merely enunciates, in the grammatical mode of the word, that the obsessive hold of language on our philosophical minds is break*able*: a *must* that inheres in Wittgenstein's later way of looking at language. Wittgenstein looks at our language as the medium in which the urge to explain *is* dissolv*able*, a medium through which the urge arises and takes shape in our philosophical moments: a medium in which this same urge must at last be dissolved through *our* seeing the language-game alongside other possibilities. The obsession *can* be broken, and broken it *must be* in a mind such as that of Wittgenstein, for *he* does not find peace unless *his* urge has been broken.

One does not see right away what is involved in this *can*, in this *must*. Language is not compar*able simpliciter*; it is comparable in Wittgenstein's later philosophy *because* the urge to explain is break*able*. Wittgenstein does not so much exploit language's comparability as that he preconceives *a* comparability, for reasons of philosophy. Philosophical problems are solvable, in the medium of our language, ultimately because their sources in the shape of misunderstood similes and pictures can be dealt with by looking at (our) language-games as possibilities among other possibilities. Perhaps, one prefers to turn the matter around: our urge to explain is a breakable affair because philosophical problems are solvable, something that Wittgenstein did not discover but, rather, 'adopted' as his *unquestionable stance* towards philosophy and its problems. Be that as it may, language is a comparable phenomenon for Wittgenstein. And one does not see right away what is involved in this preconceived idea of comparability.

Wittgenstein, in the *Tractatus*, does not know what it is like to leave language as it is without looking at logic as what must come in the (incomparable) shape of crystalline purity. But later Wittgenstein, having recognized the true nature of his Tractarian requirement, does not know either what it is like to leave language as it is, that is, *without more ado*. Early and later Wittgenstein were anxious to leave everything as it is, and both looked at philosophical problems as solvable without exception. Every philosophical problem is dissolvable in the face of what language *is*, rather than in the face of a future regulation of its logic. But what becomes of logic, if it no longer comes in the form of an incomparable essence? One might think that Wittgenstein, having recognized the true nature of his Tractarian requirement in the 1930s, begins to leave language as it is *for the first time*. But we need to realize that the notion of language being *logically* in order as it is, is primarily a Tractarian construct, a notion that Wittgenstein held on to at the time of his reorientation, come what may. So we need to realize that *his way* of leaving language as it is, is ultimately informed by the *that* of his later vantage point, a *that* which involves a requirement no less than his early *that*. Later Wittgenstein is bent on considering the humble *instead* of the sublime. He wants to *describe* the humble, but the way he seeks to do so is informed by his later conception of logic. In other words, the so-called humble, the *Hausbacken*, is rather not given *without more ado*. No longer wanting so much as to grasp the sublime, after having seen that it is a house of cards, does not leave one facing anything like the so-called humble, that is, *without more ado*. The humble is more like the Humble.

My reason for paying so much attention to Wittgenstein's dictum 'to leave everything as it is' has everything to do with my concern to see how his latter *how* bears on his early *that*. Neither early Wittgenstein nor his later self *observed* that language is in order as it *is*. What informs Wittgenstein's dictum is not a discovery, a truly perceptive moment of the eye telling him that our language is *logically* in order as it is. On the contrary: *that* language is *logically* in order as it is—is just the eye through which language is being looked at. *That* language is *logically* in order as it is, is not anything that Wittgenstein has *understood* first so as to make sure that his vantage point makes for a correct *how* language works. The *that* epitomizes no *understanding*: neither the *that* of his early philosophy nor the *that* of his later philosophy. The *that*, not being a piece of understanding itself, informs how language is to be understood. And that means that the *that*, by itself, cannot inform how language is to be understood. *That* language is logically in order as it is, is the eye through which language is being looked at, but without more ado it is barren and impotent.

Wittgenstein speaks of the necessity of turning our *Betrachtung*[112] around, which is to occur 'on the pivot of our real need' (PI: 108). Speaking thus, he is again suggestive of this: it does not occur on his having discovered how language

---

112   I prefer to stick to Wittgenstein's '*Betrachtung*' throughout this book.

166

really is. His *Betrachtung* should now pivot on a certain *need* that, obviously, is altogether different from the one that championed his *Tractatus*. We shall turn to this need shortly. The important thing for us to realize here is that this need involves a requirement on language no less than Wittgenstein's Tractarian need did. If the latter need has ceased to *determine* his way of looking at language, it has ceased to do so because another need has taken *its* place, a need that precisely seeks to do away with a need such as has been responsible for the construction of his Tractarian edifice. A need such as that of Wittgenstein's early philosophy does not dissolve once it has been replaced by another need. It dissolves, and Wittgenstein's later philosophy precisely aims at its dissolving, only in the face of the *how* of his later *that*. It does not dissolve in the face of that *that* itself: *that* logic is merely one possibility among other possibilities. *That* logic need not come in the way it obtains in our language is not a matter for us to show or to prove. For *that* logic need not come thus informs Wittgenstein's new way of looking at language. What remains is to see *how*. But that means that Wittgenstein looks at language in a way in which a certain *must* is at work, a *must* determining the sense of the *how* in whose light a need such as his Tractarian one should ultimately dissolve.

The logical space, then, in which Wittgenstein's later investigations operate, has no room for anything incomparable. Whereas logic in the *Tractatus* epitomizes the incomparable essence of language, in the *Investigations* it epitomizes the comparable essence of language, which means that each and every language-game is to be described as one possibility among other possibilities. Each and every language-game is compar*able* because its logic epitomizes the comparable essence of its workings. And what I have been suggesting is that Wittgenstein did not seem to have foreseen at the time he was about to consolidate his later vantage point what it really is like to compare *languages* with each other, what it really is like to flesh out a fictitious language-game, to flesh it out alongside one of our own language-games as another possibility. Of course, Wittgenstein would not consider his later treatment of language as an exercise in metaphysics.

3.5 *PI* §108

Wittgenstein's growing awareness in the early 1930s of what rendered his Tractarian project in the end possible, namely his blindness to the real nature of his requirement on logic, was at once the deathblow to his first philosophical effort and the germ of his later way of looking at things. But, as I have been suggesting, this awareness was rather a product of his own making. For Wittgenstein *characterized* the underlying cause of his early efforts in terms of a genuine blindness. At first he had no means to characterize it thus, no mind or reason, nothing but his good old resolve to get to the bottom of the various *mistakes* that he began to uncover one after another. He could not resort to that work itself so as to avail himself of some means or other so as to see that his project had a highly dubious origin. He had to forge the conceptual means himself and in so doing a whole battery of conceptualizations began to assert itself and to build up a framework in which *his own* criticism of the *Tractatus* matured and took its final shape. It was Wittgenstein who wrote an idiosyncratic work called the Tractatus, and it was he again who wrote a narrative no less idiosyncratic, a narrative called his criticism of the Tractatus. *His* criticism is anything but a conventional move, i.e. a good-boy exercise that has at last reached a depersonalized form and that can be had and assimilated into a Handbook. Wittgenstein was the author of the *Tractatus* and it was he himself who began to criticize it. It was *his* diagnostic move that groomed his mind for a course that began to assert itself as championing a philosophical mission equal to the task that his early view had claimed for itself. The deathblow to his Tractarian view did not mean the end of philosophy. A mighty pile of rubble Wittgenstein surely faced at first, but the means responsible for the destruction and the first clearings of the grounds on which it stood, hovered over it like a gracious spirit, much determined to establish itself as the Full and Only Heir to his own, peculiar Tractarian philosophy.

Of course, Wittgenstein's turn away from his Tractarian project and toward his later philosophy has both historical and systematic aspects. From a historical point of view, it was a rather slow and laborious process, lasting a couple of years. From a systematic point of view, however, the turn appears to be a *singular* movement of thought, if not of the hand. In the famous *PI* §108, for instance, Wittgenstein addresses his readers as much as he did before, suggesting that they should at last carry out a philosophical feat for themselves much in emulation of his own good example. Indeed, he seems to be addressing his readers *as if* their own mind has been pivoting all the time on a kind of urge to contemplate essence much reminiscent of his own Tractarian doings. And *as if* the readers' turn away from the view championing such a Tractarian feat towards a view that Wittgenstein calls his 'uncommon way of looking at things' should not last as long as it lasted for him in the 1930s. And why not? Why should it *cost* us as much as it had once cost Wittgenstein himself? Why should it cost us anything? Do we not have Wittgenstein's Genius, his experiences, his blood, sweat, and tears; and his polished words at last, in which we trust? And, what is more, does he not come to our aid himself, encouraging us here and counselling advices there? So why should we not be able to see that all we need to do is just to turn our *Betrachtung* around *once and for all*. Having done so, we have finally got rid, *once and for all*, of the urge to contemplate essence, of any preconceived idea that otherwise keeps exercising its bewitching influence on our philosophical mind.—Let us try to see for ourselves what Wittgenstein says, or does not say, in *PI* §108.

In *PI* §§89–133, Wittgenstein seeks to make a purely systematic point. Although he constantly addresses his own Tractarian project as a foil for his present concern, and although many a biographical streak of his own thoughts from the 1930s-manuscripts could be said to have entered into this dense exposition, he deals with every item from a purely systematic point of view.[113] *PI* §108 takes a special position as it represents a turning point in *PI* §§89–133. Roughly, the passages preceding §108 are written in a rather diagnostic mood, whereas the passages following §108 take up the effort of articulating a novel approach and concern. *PI* §108 is worth quoting fully:

> We see that what we call "proposition", "language", has not the formal unity that I imagined, but is a family of structures more or less akin to each other.——But what becomes of logic now? Its rigour seems to be giving way here. – But in that case doesn't logic altogether disappear? – For how can logic lose its rigour? Of course not by our bargaining any of its rigour out of it. – The *preconception* of crystalline purity can only be removed by turning our whole examination [*Betrachtung*] around. (One might say: the examination must be turned around, but on the pivot of our real need)'.

The so-called preconception of crystalline purity can *only* be removed, Wittgenstein says, by turning our whole *Betrachtung* around. Here the word 'only' [*nur so*], which corresponds to the 'only' [*nur so*] in *PI* §131, marks a turning point that must strike a highly curious chord if all that Wittgenstein needs to impugn were a minor *assumption*. But the move, in the radical form in which Wittgenstein expounds it, is of a high design and fully considered: owing to the *illusions* on which the *Tractatus* was erected. What transpires in §108 is the discharging of *the* conflict that Wittgenstein has been building up from §89 onwards. He brings his former *need* to contemplate incomparable essence into account only to place it over against the so-called *real need*, which seems to strike a psychological chord no less than his Tractarian need does and that should apparently now cover the field of philosophical problems to no lesser extent than its counterpart once claimed for itself, namely, the entire field.—But, then, the Tractarian need was Wittgenstein's own infatuation in the first instance, a need that he nonetheless presents to his readers as our need, over against which he places not his real need, but 'our real need'.

---

113   Which is anything but conventional.

Of course, in *PI* §108, Wittgenstein is about to articulate a philosophy that *he* wants to practise himself and in fact already practises, that is, *also* in *PI* §108. But while articulating it, he again begins to introduce a philosophy that he means to promulgate as the only possible philosophy. In the *Tractatus* he already wanted to make it clear that there is such a thing as the only correct method of philosophy, namely the one that *TLP* 6.53 speaks of. (Wittgenstein does not practise this method in the *Tractatus* himself, nor does he ask the reader to apply this method to the sentences in the book, as if this is how the reader should come to see that the elucidatory steps of the book fall short of being philosophy itself and that all that remains is the method itself. The reader should indeed in the end see that the method is the only correct one, but he should see it *through the book*.) There is another parallel between the *Tractatus* and the *Investigations*: in both cases we find Wittgenstein promulgating a method, or motley of methods, which he feels the reader will not straightforwardly recognize as what philosophy is all about and amounts to. But, then, precisely in this very respect there is a clear difference between early and later Wittgenstein. For the method that Wittgenstein promulgates in the *Tractatus* has, at last, everything to do with the very presentiment of which he speaks in *TLP* 5.4541, a presentiment that not only *he* senses but which *men* have always had, namely 'that there must a realm in which the answers to questions are symmetrically combined—a priori—to form a self-contained system.' The presentiment has given to rise to the deep need, on the part of early Wittgenstein, to enunciate this realm; a need that not only early Wittgenstein but also his later self presents as a need in which *we* can recognize ourselves as philosophers. But over against this need later Wittgenstein 'posits' a need—the so-called real need—that goes every bit *against* the need to enunciate incomparable essence. It is as if he can no longer appeal to quite a universal thing, a kind of *natural* urge or tendency in us, philosophers as we think we are. In other words, Wittgenstein again needs to wear himself out while articulating his philosophy, but this time he can no longer count on the readers' own urge or tendency as what will speak for itself, if only with some aid, and what he can rely on as the ultimate basis for a mutual understanding. He now faces the awkward task to present and to develop his new philosophy, which comes at first in the shape of a new vantage point on language, *against* the readers' bold need in which they have always recognized the inchoate but true philosopher in themselves.

Thus, although Wittgenstein constantly resorts to his early 'private' need to grasp the so-called crystalline purity of logic, he presents this very need in due course, not as a highly peculiar need, but as one that should be reckoned among those human needs that philosophers have always had and still nourish, namely to grasp *the essence of things* (PI: 116). And this systematic twist to what is at first a purely biographical matter does not stop short of *PI* §108. For Wittgenstein precisely brings *his Tractarian* need into account there—only to refer to it as *our* need. But this need, as Wittgenstein seeks to emphasize here, is the sort of thing on which *our Betrachtung* had better cease to pivot. It should pivot, now, on *our* real need. But whence *this* need?

To see what Wittgenstein's real need is, a need that he thinks at least some readers are capable of having themselves, we do well to recall here what the turn of which he speaks in §108 is *not*. It is not anything that leaves his Tractarian need (or any need to contemplate incomparable essence) for what it is, for it seeks to overcome such a need. But the turn is not what overcomes this need in one fell swoop, as if the turn is capable itself of doing away with it *once and for all*. In the first chapter I have been suggesting that we misunderstand what Wittgenstein's later philosophy amounts to if we think that the philosophical *urge* to grasp the incomparable essence of language no longer plays any role there. True, later Wittgenstein no longer *aims* at grasping whatever incomparable essence. But having renounced his early aim only means, in his case, that his later aim faces a *powerful urge* that he once mistook for his self-avowed interest. The urge did not present itself to him as a force taking hold of his philosophical mind only to manipulate its course of ratiocinations henceforth. Rather, it presented itself in disguise, by inculcating in him the sure conviction that all there is for a philosopher to do, namely grasping incomparable essence, is what *he* has set himself as his philosophical aim. His early aim has been renounced; what remains is what has led him to espouse it in the first place. The aim has been renounced; what remains is a powerful urge to be overcome. The aim has been renounced, but it is the need to overcome the powerful urge that has led one to renounce the aim in the first place. Wittgenstein, then, with a remark such as that 'philosophy is a struggle against the bewitchment of our understanding by the resources of our language' (PI: 109) only endorses that he (we) should be on the alert for what takes hold of his (our) thinking in philosophy. And endorsing it, he already tells much about the nature of his later investigations.

No longer wanting to grasp the incomparable essence of language, then, is impotent against so powerful an urge as to grasp it. The urge is still there, in spite of our having seen its real nature, an urge that, according to Wittgenstein's lights, has everything to do with the way our language is organized, with the way we relate to it in the daily course of life. Of course, over the *Tractatus* there already hovered an awareness that language does do queer things with our philosophical minds, but this awareness obtained its later depth and spiritual force only after

Wittgenstein had characterized the linchpin of his early philosophy as a motley of illusions, against which his *Tractatus* itself had nothing to offer as regards a cure. But now, a certain kind of generalization has found its way into the very core of Wittgenstein's later philosophy, for if language once sent Wittgenstein in pursuit of *the crystalline purity of logic*, it now presents itself an institution that tends to send him in *pursuit of chimeras*. Furthermore, language did not only send *Wittgenstein* in pursuit of the crystalline purity of logic, it sends *us* in pursuit of *chimeras*. What happened to him in the *Tractatus* is what could happen to us as well, and what he was after in the *Tractatus* is now seen as just one of the many things that language sends us pursuing. Wittgenstein's later vantage point on language seeks to deal with whatever sends us in pursuit of chimeras, but its origin lies in the exposure of one extravagant chimera only, in one single item that Wittgenstein has made out as a chimera: the crystalline purity of logic.

Wittgenstein, having recognized the true nature of his early philosophical need, did not set out so as to explore his soul in search for a substitute, a kind of devout and *natural* conation ready to be harnessed as 'his truly real need'. He rather recognized that the urge to contemplate incomparable essence is a brute force always to be reckoned with the moment we turn philosophical. He recognized that this is the kind of force to stay with, only to try to do away with it in the end. The urge to contemplate incomparable essence, once its true nature has been recognized, gives rise *itself* to the need to do away with it. It gives rise to the need to understand the workings of language *in opposition to* the urge to grasp its workings under the injunction of some *must* or other to contemplate incomparable essence. So whereas the force of such a *must* has everything to do with the way we relate to our language in the daily course of life, as later Wittgenstein thinks, his truly real need is a *philosophical* thing par excellence. It is not what each of us carries around, as part of his or her 'human constitution', a somewhat latent but nonetheless noticeable inclination to come powerfully true during a moment lost in philosophical meditation. Wittgenstein's real need, in other words, is not a need *sui generis which just happens* to be the polar opposite of the urge that sends us in pursuit of chimeras. Wittgenstein rather *wants* to go against this urge, and so his truly real need is ultimately the expression of a decision. It is, above all, the expression of a radically different way of looking at language.

I said that Wittgenstein has been building up a conflict, one that comes to a head in *PI* §108. Thus, as he says in *PI* §107: 'The more closely we examine actual language, the greater becomes the conflict between it and our requirement.' The resolution of this conflict *is* that of seeing the necessity to change one's need. Once you have your *Betrachtung* turning around the pivot of your real need, you have it running against the urge to grasp incomparable essence. Only when you have it turning around this way does philosophy become 'a struggle against the bewitchment of our understanding by the resources of our language.' Philosophy, as Wittgenstein practised it in the *Tractatus*, has never been a struggle of this nature. He then laboured, without realizing it, on the wings of a powerful bewitchment. He laboured 'under the illusion that what is peculiar, profound, essential, in our investigation, resides in its trying to grasp the incomparable essence of language' (PI: 97). Early Wittgenstein operated within a dimension that was structurally entirely determined by this illusion, a dimension outside of which, he says, 'we cannot breathe' (PI: 103). His growing awareness, in the 1930s, of the true nature of this dimension brought home to him the insight not so much that it is possible to breathe outside as that outside is the *only* place where the philosopher can breathe. That is, what Wittgenstein realized is that there is no breathing *outside* without the dimension where a *philosophical* life and living has ceased to be possible (in spite of all academic appearances). The urge to contemplate essence, then, is not only a force still to reckon with but also the kind of thing lending the dimension in which Wittgenstein's later investigations take place its ultimate stamp and structure. In other words, Wittgenstein's historical turn does not so much create a new dimension, one in which his philosophical practice now takes place, leaving the old one for what it was, as that it merely creatively 'enlarges' the existing dimension. Our language keeps providing the mesmerizing dimension into which we tend to fall and where we think we can breathe only, but the need that seeks to overcome it lest *it* take the better part of us, has been structured, in Wittgenstein's own case, by his bygone Tractarian fall in the first place.

We have elaborated a little on early Wittgenstein's urge to contemplate the incomparable essence of language, an urge that he mistook for his philosophical need, the only true need in philosophy. In so doing, we have said something about how this urge bears upon language, how it prompted Wittgenstein to look at language as having an external form that clothes the thought (as he puts it in *TLP* 4.002). Indeed, his Tractarian urge did not so much prompt him to be concerned only with what lies 'beneath the surface' of language as that it stood at the beginning of such a structural division of language. But what about Wittgenstein's real need? We have said something about how it and his early need relate to each other, but very little so far about how his real need bears upon language, upon the kind of thing that tends to send us in pursuit of chimeras: *our* language. We said that the real need is a philosophical need *sui generis*, a need that Wittgenstein contrasts with the bold, natural urge that once propelled his Tractarian life and interest. True, this urge constituted a way of looking at language as much as the real need is meant to do now, and it is important to emphasize that what Wittgenstein places over against his early need is one need only, which means that he advances, as before in the *Tractatus*, no more than one way of looking only. But, again, the question now is how Wittgenstein's real need bears upon language. It is all well and good to have unmasked the need that once drove one's philosophical doings, and it is all well and good to tell that these doings had better pivot on one's real need. But what does all this tell us about the latter need's relation to our language? How, in other words, does Wittgenstein's real need relate to his later conception of logic?

We have been intimating an answer to this question at more than one stage in our proceedings, with respect to *PI* §110, for instance, quoted above, where we saw Wittgenstein speaking of the *Pathos* that now 'retreats to these illusions, to the problems.' Wittgenstein's real need is no doubt a concern if not infatuation with clarity, but to leave it at that is to beg the question, for Wittgenstein's Tractarian need was already a concern if not infatuation with clarity. So the question is how Wittgenstein's real need differs from his Tractarian need for clarity. The answer is that the former is quite an impotent thing without a need as the one that propelled his *Tractatus*. 'Quite impotent', I say, but perhaps I had better say *utterly impotent* at once. Why? Because Wittgenstein's real need just is a concern with conceptual clarity *only* in the light of such *misunderstandings* about our language as lead us pursuing chimeras, the 'great and important' things. Wittgenstein's real need is activated the moment the need to explain *in philosophy* comes into action, which occurs at every turn as our language just is not the kind of institution to miss the opportunity of exercising its bewitching craft on our minds and of sending us in pursuit of something 'great and important'. So Wittgenstein's real need bears upon our language through the urge to explain its workings, at least that is how he presents it in *PI* §§89–133. But where does this leave logic? Or, as Wittgenstein puts it, 'What becomes of logic now?' (PI: 108). What role does logic now play in the elucidatory activities of the philosopher? I should like to answer these questions by bringing into account the idea of colloquial language.

The role that colloquial language has played in Wittgenstein's *historical* reorientation in philosophy can, I think, be distinguished from the role it plays in *PI* §§89–133, the place where Wittgenstein presents his reorientation in a decidedly *systematic* manner. Wittgenstein, throughout the historical process of reformulating a new way of looking at language, no doubt did not fail to refrain from looking at our colloquial language every now and then. That is, after having realized that he had to arrange a good many things from bottom up, he did not

174

go into himself first so as to explore his soul, only to *look* at language after he had come out of himself with a novel way of looking at it. But if he did not refrain from looking at colloquial language during the process of his reorientation, one might well wonder what role if any this looking played in the formulation of a new way of looking at language. I raise this question, not in order to answer it (here), but in order to pay attention to the role that our colloquial language plays in Wittgenstein's *systematic* presentation of his turn. For in *PI* §§89–133, Wittgenstein appeals regularly to our language, to its colloquial forms and uses, in a way that is interesting.

In *PI* §107, Wittgenstein writes: 'The more closely we examine actual language, the greater becomes the conflict between it and our requirement. (For the crystalline purity of logic was, of course, not something I had *discovered*: it was a requirement).' And right on the heels of that remark he writes in a conclusive manner: 'We see [*erkennen*] that what we call "proposition", "language", has not the formal unity that I imagined [*vorstellte*], but is a family of structures more or less akin to each other' (PI: 108). Obviously, there is an important contrast at work in both of these passages, a contrast that Wittgenstein has been building up in the shape of a *conflict* (see above). His suggestion is that we cannot but adopt a novel way of looking at language, one that pays tribute to what we see [*erkennen*], rather than to what he as a young man once imagined [*vorstellte*]. The contrast is indeed intriguing, if only because it is puzzling.

The question, I think, is: How could there ever be a conflict here? For if you are about to let *some examples* count, that is, *against* your previous conception of logic, are you then not already in the grip of another conception of logic? Well, *another* conception of logic need not necessarily be already at work here. Still, to let some examples count does not so much seem to loosen the grip that your previous conception of logic has on you as that this loosened grip renders it possible to let these examples count. There is a conflict, to be sure, but I would rather circumscribe it as one that obtains between early Wittgenstein and his later self. For consider how early Wittgenstein would have reacted to the examples that his later self brings into account against him. He, in the firm grip of the requirement the real nature of which did not dawn upon him until much later, was anxious to articulate the crystalline purity of something that he saw lying 'beneath the surface' (PI: 92)[114]. In other words, the *forms of our colloquial language* could not

---

114   But notice that it is indeed curious to speak of the crystalline purity of logic as what lies 'beneath the surface' of language, for this logic is the *Unding*: it has no spatial dimensions. More on this point in the next chapter.

possibly touch him; they could never have called his early elucidatory work to a halt.

On the contrary, it was precisely the sentences in their colloquial and jagged forms in which he saw his elucidatory activities more than justified. Early Wittgenstein might already have seen [*erkennen*] that what we call "proposition", "language" *is* 'a family of structures more or less akin to each other'; he might well have seen *any* kind of structure. And yet, he should for all that seeing and recognizing not have felt less confident and self-assured in his aim and doings than he actually was, trying to grasp the incomparable essence of language as he did.

However, matters should be evaluated differently with respect to a mind that is in the process of being seized upon by the requirement that language must invoke incomparable essence. Such fresh moments of seizure leaves the mind in a most disquieting state indeed, for the requirement makes one see the crystalline purity already, whereas colloquial language imparts anything but that appearance.

> A simile that has been absorbed into the forms of our language produces a false appearance which disquiets us. "But *this* isn't how it is!" – we say. "Yet *this* is how it *has to be!*"
> (PI: 112)

This passage describes a true conflict, namely between how language strikes us and how we think language must be. And *if* that was the kind of conflict that early Wittgenstein struggled with at first, he resolved it through giving way to the *Must*; how language struck him was correct for all that. Indeed, from Wittgenstein's later point of view, he resolved the conflict because he had been toppled over into the dogmatism of the *Tractatus*. But that means, among other things, that *early Wittgenstein* would never have accepted that a mere *Is* ("But this isn't how it is!") can be held out *against* so powerful a force as the modal *Must* is ("Yet this is how it has to be!").

Early Wittgenstein resolved the conflict between "But *this* isn't how it is!" and "Yet *this* is how it *has to be!*" by going underground. That is, he saw no way out the conflict but by giving way to the sublime: "Yet *this* is how it has *to be!*" And if we now ask how later Wittgenstein resolved the matter, we need only look at *PI* §112 and observe how *he* presents the predicament of his early conflict, namely in such terms as his Tractarian mind did not preside over and could not straight away: 'A simile that has been absorbed into the forms of our language produces a false appearance which disquiets us.' Wittgenstein's suggestion is that if only we become aware of what it is that disquiets us in moments of philosophy we will also see that our need or urge to overcome the conflict by going underground—

by going to whatever sublime and unworldly place—is as much a product of our language as the conflict is its result. There is a simile at work on us, philosophers, a simile that 'has been absorbed into the forms of *our* language' (emphasis mine). Indeed, the word "simile" is what we have met before, namely in Wittgenstein's comment that he 'had used a simile; but through the grammatical illusion that a certain *one* thing, something *common* to all its objects, corresponds to a concept-word it did not seem like a simile.' The simile, then, is part of our language, but its *false appearance* is not what we are confronted with in the daily walk of life. It is what comes true and begins to occupy us the moment we turn philosophical; it is what *disquiets* us then. The simile is part of our language, and philosophy leaves everything as it is, hence it leaves the simile for what it is, as part of our language. The real need tries to do away with the false appearance of the simile, thus not by administering a purgative to our language so as remove its cause, namely the simile itself, but through treating the simile *as what it is* (see below).

Wittgenstein, in the systematic presentation of his turn, indeed seems to let a few examples count against his former way of looking at language—only to have his *Betrachtung* now pivot on a so-called real need henceforth, come what may. A philosophical problem, once seen in the light of this need, is no longer a genuine *problem*, but only one more knot in our philosophical thinking, caused by some misleading aspect of our language or other. So for our way out of the muddle it is crucially important to realize that the problem is only a knot, something into which we have worked ourselves, inadvertently, hence something from which there is a way out—if one so desires. The way out is merely one's personal way out. It is not what happens to one, but what needs to be done, by movements of thoughts that one, in our modern way of being on the move, is not accustomed to perform, any more than encouraged to learn and to contemplate seriously. For science is everywhere, above all its popularizations, setting standards for the proper way of thinking and functioning in our civilized societies. Standards and techniques that lead us into the muddle the moment the philosophical mood dawns upon us.

But if language is now to be treated by a need that has been systematized with respect to one thing (i.e. the urge to contemplate *Tractarian essence*) first and foremost, it needs to be looked at and treated as one possibility among other possibilities, thus irrespective of the part of language falling under our attention, and irrespective of the kind of muddle at issue. Each and every part of our language is ultimately to give way, not to the pressure that the *Must* of a false appearance exercises on us, but to the pressure under which *it* must lose its mesmerizing hold on us in moments of philosophy. How? By our relocating this *Must* from something that language must invoke as part of its workings to something with which these workings *must* be compared.

We have just been bringing two things together, namely the kind of generalization of which I have spoken and the role that logic plays in Wittgenstein's later way of looking at language. Speaking of a generalization, I was also thinking of the following transition from *PI* §115 to *PI* §116:

> A *picture* held us captive. And we couldn't get outside it, for it lay in our language, and language seemed only to repeat it to us inexorably. (PI: 115)

> When philosophers use a word – "knowledge", "being", "object", "I", "*Satz*", "name" – and try to grasp the *essence* of the thing, one must always ask oneself: is the word ever actually used in this way in the language in which it is at home? –
> What *we* do is to bring words back from their metaphysical to their everyday use. (PI: 116)

If it had only been one picture that held early Wittgenstein captive, his later self seems to have characterized the destiny of the whole of philosophy in the light of what that single thing once did do to him in his early life. For language now seems to be full of misleading pictures and analogies, similes and other latent traps, ready to take us in at every turn in our philosophical moments. What is more, if a certain picture takes hold of us, it does not do just this or that with our minds; it rather prompts us to grasp the essence of a certain thing, something great and important—something *incomparable*. And if we then need to bring words back from this metaphysical grasping of things to their everyday use, we should not grasp the incomparable essence of what lies already open to view. No, we should regard the grammars of our words as what they are: possible grammars among other possible grammars. This brings us back to *PI* §108.

Wittgenstein asks: 'But what becomes of logic *now*? Its rigour seems to be giving way *here*. – But *in that case* doesn't logic *altogether* disappear? – For how can logic lose its rigour? Of course not by our bargaining any of its rigour out of it.' The added emphases in this passage should draw our attention to what Wittgenstein accomplishes here, namely a transition from his Tractarian conception of logic to our more *hausbacken* notion of that word in respect of its very rigour. The undeniable vagueness of (our) language did not prompt early Wittgenstein to bargain any of the rigour out of logic, for then language could not even be spoken of as a vague thing. So the antithesis between rigour and vagueness is to be held up at all costs, should one not want to lose one's grasp on the (empirical) world right from the beginning. But the antithesis, in Wittgenstein's early conception, gave way to a difference between the vagueness of language as being purely a matter of its surface and the crystalline purity of logic as a hidden entity, at work behind all languages. Later Wittgenstein, any more than his former self, did not try to bargain any rigour out of logic, now that he has seen the real nature of the Tractarian antithesis between (the) rigour (of logic) and (the) vagueness (of language). That is, language does not cease to be vague, now that he has seen that the rigour of logic is not anything beneath the surface of language as something true of all languages. But that means that language can still *not* be spoken of as being vague *unless* there is a polar opposite. So logic keeps its rigour, but not of the kind as the *Tractatus* conceived it to be, but precisely such as has been absorbed into the forms of our language in the shape of one ideal or another. Wittgenstein says: 'we misunderstand the role played by the ideal in our language' (PI 100).

Wittgenstein's Tractarian antithesis between the rigour of logic and the vagueness of our language runs along the vertical axis. It has at last become all a matter of the horizontal axis, with everything open to view. Some of our language-games *are* indeterminate; some of them are of the more definite type, but we misunderstand the role played by the ideal in our language.

3.6 *PI* §§130–131

The turn away from the need to contemplate essence towards the real need does not do away with the former need. This turn rather brings home to our consciousness the full force of that need, what it does do to us and leads us to philosophically; and this realization demarcates the status quo for the purpose of the turn: to do away with the need to contemplate essence, i.e. to disarm it. This activity is what Wittgenstein designates as a 'struggle against the bewitchment of our understanding by the resources of our language.'[115] The turn, then, lays down a course of investigations that is founded on Wittgenstein's insight that he had been bewitched all the time, an insight that is impotent itself against the force that this bewitchment keeps exercising in moments of philosophy.

Let us now again turn to *PI* §§130–131, for they bear a most intimate connection to Wittgenstein's turn. Wittgenstein speaks of a model (*Vorbild*) there, of something that can come in either one or another way but not in both ways at one and the same time. In one way, *it* takes hold of our philosophical minds only to *prescribe* our course of looking at language henceforth; in the other way, *we* take hold of it as a means of comparison, as a means of describing our language, a means that determines our course of looking at language in no less fundamental

---

115   Cf. 'We are struggling with language. We are engaged in a struggle with language' (CV: 13).

a way than when the model takes hold of *us*. Thus, according to Wittgenstein, what foists itself onto our philosophical minds is one picture or another. That is, the *Vorbild* foists itself onto our minds in the shape of a picture that makes us forget its real nature (but see also below). In other words, the picture completely swamps our philosophical minds in the form of a prejudice to which we think reality *must* correspond. But so the picture can entertain these same minds of us in the form of an object of comparison. And only, according to Wittgenstein's suggestion, *only* when we take to the picture in the latter way, and entertain it accordingly, can we do away with the influence that the picture otherwise exerts on us. We need as it were *to turn* the picture away from the influence that it otherwise exerts on us. To take to the picture *as* an object of comparison is the very first step to obtain a firm hold on its bewitching influence, but no more than a first step. For it also needs to be set up as an object of comparison.

Wittgenstein, then, asks us to do something very specific with the picture. Not doing anything with it is not an option, for then the picture does do something with us, something specific. Indeed, without more ado, it does not inculcate in us what the world is like; rather it inculcates in us the firm image of the only way the world could be. With the picture upon our mind we feel that *this* is how things *must* be. The 'must' at stake here is the dogmatic urge to exclude every possibility but the one that the picture furnishes. And this exclusion yields 'ineptness or emptiness in our assertions'. In order to avoid this, that is, in order not to *end up* facing 'ineptness or emptiness in our assertions', all we can do is to take to the picture and, instead of giving way to the way it tends to take to us, treat it as an object of comparison. And advancing thus, we end up facing, not one possibility, but one possibility alongside other possibilities, with the picture furnishing the possibility that it otherwise inculcate in us as the only possibility. So what emanates in the shape of certain features that we cannot help thinking language *must* have, should end up living in the shape of features characterizing a language(-game). These features, then, which at first come as certain attributes characterizing a picture through which we look at language, should in the end characterize some language-game other.

PI §§130–131 undergirds Wittgenstein's conception of philosophy as 'a struggle against the bewitchment of our understanding by the resources of our language.' More precisely perhaps, it rather explains why philosophy is such a struggle. For philosophy will take up arms only insofar as language gives us (him) trouble, thus when some picture or other begins to exercise its dogmatic influence on our (his) mind(s). The picture begins to exercise its influence and the means that Wittgenstein brings to bear against this influence are his clear and simple language-games. These means relate to the picture intimately, for what should characterize these language-games are precisely those attributes of the picture that we need to bring into account on the playground of inventing and collating language-games, thus within a dimension that not only does not exist in the eyes of the dogmatic picture but which this picture simply excludes as possible. In other words, there is a kind of stubborn tugging at 'one and the same picture', for *it* tries to foist its influence onto us, whereas *we* try to convert it into a means of description. And it is not until the redeeming effect of the language-game has taken the place of the kind of influence that this picture exercises on us that we have finished with it. It keeps exercising its *dogmatic* influence as long as the object of comparison falls short of coming in the shape with which our language can and must be compared: a *language*-game. As for Wittgenstein himself, it belongs to his style and audacious character of thinking to move constantly, willingly, and unabashedly on the verge of being toppled over into a way of doing philosophy bent on grasping the incomparable essence of language and the world. Without this precarious moving to and fro between two fundamentally opposing styles of doing philosophy, there is nothing for him to struggle for; nothing for him to philosophize and to describe.

The struggle, then, is one of *turning* a dogmatic picture into *a means of description*. But why description? Why call it thus? Well, that is how Wittgenstein conceives it. True, he speaks of the *Vorbild* that is to be presented 'as what it is, as an object of comparison' (PI: 131, my emphasis), his suggestion being that one should do no more than giving way to what the thing *anyway* is. But, then, as I want to say, if the *Vorbild* has its roots in a *Bild* (picture) that 'lay in our language' (PI: 115), the picture (*Bild*) does not lie there as a *Vorbild*, thus as an object of comparison itself. The picture in our language *is what it is*: a picture; and it either operates on our philosophical minds *as* a prejudice or we operate on it *as* a *Vorbild*: an object of comparison. Wittgenstein is suggestive of leaving language *as it is*, of wanting to do this at as early a stage as possible: to present the *Vorbild* *as what it is*. Wanting to leave everything as it is, he surely does not mean to reap our language of the pictures that lie in it, in some way or other. He seeks to leave these pictures for what they are, but if a picture begins to foist itself onto us, and we need to present it *as what it is*, then, as I want to say, it is owing to what it does do otherwise with our minds that the picture needs to be presented as a *Vorbild*. It is not because the picture *is* a *Vorbild* that we need to present it as such, for it is not *that* in our language; it is because of what the picture does do otherwise with us, namely sending us on a dogmatic *Tour de Philosophie*.

Wittgenstein's therapeutic move in *PI* §§130–131 entertains a requirement as much as the dogmatic move itself. For where the dogmatic move presents language, *through a picture*, as what must be so and so only, the therapeutic move presents language, *through the same picture*, as what *is* so. The latter move presents (our) language as one possibility among other possibilities, but only because it presents the picture *as* what it *must* be, rather than as what it *is*, lest we are sent off flying on dogmatic wings. Only another Must can hold out against a dogmatic Must.

To be sure, then, Wittgenstein's objects of comparison do not throw that famous light on the *Verhältnisse* of our language unless they materialize in the shape of language-games. What obtrudes upon our minds is a *picture* rather than a language-game. That is to say, what obtrudes upon our minds is not a language-game itself, ready to be operated on *as such*, by us, who seek redemption from the dogmatic urge to look at our language in a certain way. Rather, it is a *picture* that appeals to us and it is what *we* should in turn appeal to and take care of *such* that it can be brought to bear upon our language as an object of comparison. In other words, the dogmatic picture should be fleshed out as a piece of language, as a recognizable piece of doing this or that thing with words. It is ultimately the appearance that the object displays, a recognizable face or physiognomy, rather than an object as abstract as a mere plan, which renders it effective and redeeming as an object of comparison with respect to the phenomenon of *language*.

What this means is that there is a most significant supposition at work in *PI* §§130–131, namely that what obtrudes upon our minds in the shape of a picture can be neutralized by converting it into a fictitious language-game. Wittgenstein seems to have taken the possibility of such a conversion for granted. It was not until much later, as we have been suggesting, that he appreciated the full scope of *fleshing out* fictitious language-games. We may well wonder now what should be called into question as regards Wittgenstein's uncommon way of looking if his fictitious language-games fall short of materializing in the shape that brings light on earth.

4. Wittgenstein's Copernican Revolution, Part II

Aus Trägheit verlangt der Mensch bloßen Mechanism oder bloße Magie. Er will nicht thätig sein – seine productive Einbildungskraft brauchen.

Novalis

4.1 Parallel cases

From time to time Wittgenstein appealed to the Copernican Revolution so as to illustrate the point of his frequent use of examples and similes. In the 1930s, for instance, he is reported to have said the following:

> Now you may question whether my constantly giving examples and speaking in similes is profitable. My reason is that parallel cases change our outlook because they destroy the uniqueness of the case at hand. For example, the Copernican revolution destroyed the idea that the earth has a unique place in the solar system. (AWL: 50).

> The obsessions of philosophers vary in different ages because terminologies vary. When a terminology goes some worries may pass, only to arise again in a similar terminology. Sometimes a scientific language produces an obsession and a new language rids us of it. When dynamics first flourished it gave rise to certain obsessions which now seem obsolete. Something may play a predominant role in our language and be suddenly removed by science, e.g., the word "earth" lost its importance in the new Copernican notation. Where the old notation had given the earth a unique position, the new notation[116] put lots of planets on the same level. Any obsession arising from the unique position of something in our language ceases as soon as another language appears which puts that thing on a level with other things. When there was only one dynamics philosophers asked how they could reduce everything to one mechanism, and became obsessed. With the discovery of several other dynamics, the obsession disappeared. (AWL: 98)

Wittgenstein's similes came on end, in forms derived from the everyday hodge-podge of our own language to forms derived from the resources of his powerful imagination—the latter often clad in attires which Mother Nature had never seen before among her own creations. Wittgenstein was well aware of his strong fancy for inventions, just as he was well aware of the necessity to explain his imaginative mind before his students. Norman Malcolm, in his memoirs on Wittgenstein, ascribes the following to him.

---

116   Cf. 'Every particular notation stresses some particular point of view' (BB: 28).

> What I give is the morphology of the use of an expression. I show that it has kinds of use of which you had not dreamed. In philosophy one feels *forced* to look at a concept in a certain way. What I do is to suggest, or even invent, other ways of looking at it. What I do is to suggest possibilities of which you had not previously thought. You thought that there was only one possibility, or only two at most. But I made you think of others. Furthermore I made you see that it was absurd to expect the concept to conform to those narrow possibilities. Thus your mental cramp is relieved, and you are able to look around the field of the use of the expression and to describe the different kinds of uses of it.[117]

Obviously, one preponderant objective of Wittgenstein's similes is to break the spell that the so-called unique case exerts on our minds. Saying that parallel cases change our outlook, he clearly suggests that there are other possibilities, things that we fail to take into account as long as our spellbound condition lasts. Of course, to be enthralled by the unique case does not necessarily mean that one is blinded to any kind of difference. Thus, early Wittgenstein, to keep to his own example here, was far from being reluctant to acknowledge differences that any philosophically uncorrupted mind would declare to exist without further ado. And yet, his early readiness to do so is not on a par with his later preoccupation to 'teach differences'. At present it suffices to say that although early Wittgenstein attached even great importance to differences, he was not interested in considering them. He rather wanted to look beyond them, or through them, up to the point where he believed he beheld the unique case: the crystalline purity of logic. To get stuck in one's interest in differences without *wanting* so much as to look beyond them was, for early Wittgenstein, a sure sign for having failed to realize what philosophy is all about. Differences, he thought, are part of the overt vagaries of our language, or languages. They belong to the contingencies of language, and should not be confused with the essence of its workings. To be sure, the unique case is not itself *language*, but the *essence* of all languages, possible and actual, hence the object of the philosopher's chief concern and deepest interest.

In the above passages, and in line with *PI* §§89–133, Wittgenstein brings the rationale of his similes to bear on a general account of how our philosophical reflections tend to start. According to him, our philosophical attitude towards the world is in the first instance primed by an obsession with the unique case, rather than by an interest in beholding parallel cases. And much in line with his remarks from the *Investigations* is Wittgenstein's own position while addressing his students or readers on the role of his similes. For while talking about

---

117   Malcolm, *Ludwig Wittgenstein: A Memoir. With a Biographical Sketch by G. H. von Wright*, 50.

the importance of changing one's 'outlook', he talks from an outlook already changed. Unlike his audience, Wittgenstein is already convinced of the fundamental importance of similes in philosophy. His suggestion, at least as far as the above passages are concerned, clearly is that all is well *once* our mind is free to look around and to take in parallel cases. Indeed, his suggestion is that once our mind is free to look around the field that parallel cases can be seen lying about there and taken in without much ado. And that is not out of keeping with the spirit of the *Philosophical Investigations* either, where similes and parallel cases abound, at least so in its opening sections, bursting in as they do at Wittgenstein's wishes only to be operated on as he pleases.

Wittgenstein's similes are more than just similes. He considers the unique and the so-called parallel cases as indicators of alternative ways of looking at the world, hence of doing philosophy. He wants to teach differences, although he tends to cut up philosophy, its history not excluded, as a field of inquiries set by, and moving between, two alternative outlooks that 'present themselves' as polar opposites of each other: the world (of language) seen as having a working that at last comes down to one possibility only, and the world (of language) seen as invoking one possibility among other possibilities. It is conspicuous that in this tendentious presentation the unique case is time and again characterized as what tends to appeal to the philosophical mind first, only to render it totally obsessed. The mind that strives after the unique case *is* obsessed, as Wittgenstein puts it the above passages; the mind that strives after a parallel, though, is free to look around and to pick on similes and concrete, parallel cases as it pleases. However, as we shall see in this and the next chapters, Wittgenstein's later mind is far less free from obsession than the above passages wish to have it, for it is most anxious to see alternative ways of doing things with words. His later outlook is an *obsession* with seeing various possibilities, just as his early outlook was an obsession with articulating the *Unding*, the unique case.

And why not? The form of Wittgenstein's later outlook is from the outset primed by his interest in seeing connections among parallel cases, which means that he is committed to seeing such connections, i.e., to finding parallel cases and to exhibiting them properly in one *übersichtliche Darstellung* or another. But this interest, as we have seen in the former chapter, does not stand alone, basking as it were in its own glory. Wittgenstein's later outlook battens on the powerful urge to look at the workings of language as what must be traceable to an incomparable essence. His change of outlook, the so-called turn of which he relates in *PI* §108, does not do away itself with the urge to contemplate incomparable essence. The turn rather aims at overcoming the firm hold that this urge exercises on our minds in moments of philosophy. Indeed, Wittgenstein's turn endorses this urge as what tends to take hold of our minds *first*, come what may. It endorses it not so much as what one has to reckon further with, in moments of philosophy, as what one needs to feed on at last, as a powerful force or mind to overcome.

Wittgenstein, then, once having turned his *Betrachtung* (cf. PI: 108) around, has not abruptly ceased to feel 'forced to look at a concept in a certain way'; he is at first as much under the continuing influence of similes in our language as any other user of it is, things that have been absorbed in the forms of our language and in moments of philosophy '[produce] a false appearance which disquiets us' (PI: 112). Indeed, what disquiets Wittgenstein more than anything else—that is, the Wittgenstein *after* the turn, and not in the least due to the turn—are appearances of the workings of language as the only possible workings. Compare this with how language must have struck him at the time he wrote the *Tractatus*: it looks so variegated, so amazingly rich and copious in form and possibility, an appearance that began to work most disquietingly on a philosophical mind as his. Why? Because he had been seized by an outlook telling him that language works in one way only. If our language strikes the later Wittgenstein as if its forms and workings were the only possible ways in which they could come, how far more disquieting these appearances must strike him after the turn. He speaks of a mind free to look around, but he also promulgates that 'philosophy is a struggle against the bewitchment of our understanding by the resources of our language' (PI: 109). In effect, it is not until one has turned one's *Betrachtung* around that philosophy *is* such a struggle. One may well *be* 'forced to look at a concept in a certain way', but it is not until one *wants* to look at it in another way that the forced way of looking is really *felt*. The disquietude of which Wittgenstein constantly speaks ultimately inheres in his way of looking at things. (To *feel* forced to look at a concept in a certain way in philosophy: indeed, this point should help us to see what *he* means by 'philosophy'.)

Wittgenstein's reported language give rise to more critical observations. For if an obsession with the unique case keeps our philosophical outlook strongly in thrall, that is, an obsession of the kind with which early Wittgenstein himself looked at language and the world at large: where does this leave us as regards the question of breaking the spell? How *could* a so-called parallel case 'change' the 'outlook' of the obsessed mind if it would inculcate it but as a *parallel* case? For the obsessed mind there are no *parallel* cases, and for those who have already changed their outlook, the purpose of the parallel case is not to change one's outlook. The parallel case, as we shall shortly see, plays its role first and foremost in an *übersichtliche Darstellung*, that is to say, in a certain order where it finds itself alongside (through so-called intermediate cases) the language-game under investigation. It plays its role in Wittgenstein's effort to *understand* the language-game under investigation, an effort that does not aim at understanding its workings in any way, but according to the tenets of his fundamental concept of an *übersichtliche Darstellung*. In other words, this concept concedes already the possibility of parallel cases, the possibility of doing things with words other than how we do it ourselves, in the daily course of life. It concedes it as much as Wittgenstein's notion of 'struggle' does in the passage from *PI* §109.

'Parallel cases change our outlook because they destroy the uniqueness of the case at hand.' So nothing *is* a parallel case unless it destroys the uniqueness of the case at hand? But if the uniqueness of a particular case has been destroyed by a parallel case: how could there be other parallel cases? Perhaps we do well here not to take Wittgenstein at his word in these reported sentences. On the other hand, if it is true that he articulated his own mind according to the gist of above passages, we had better wonder about his appeal to science here: 'When there was only one dynamics philosophers asked how they could reduce everything to one mechanism, and became obsessed. With the discovery of several other dynamics, the obsession disappeared.' Well, is this an appeal to science or to the history of science? Is it meant to highlight that the unique case *in philosophy* is on a par with the role of the unique case in science? Is the philosophers' obsession with the unique case quite like the scientists' obsession with the unique case? Be that as it may, the history of Wittgenstein's own career, I think, is poorly elucidated with reference to such examples from (the history of) science. Wittgenstein's own obsession with Tractarian logic did not cease at the sight of a parallel case, at the sight of some parallel logic or other. At the pinnacle of his Tractarian obsession, he would have treated the possibility of such logics as something that *must* trace back to what is in the end not itself a possibility among other possibilities, namely the *Unding*. Indeed, if it is really a historical fact of science that the obsession with one dynamics *disappeared* with the *discovery* of several other dynamics, one wonders what it is like to *discover* parallel cases in *philosophy*.

Wittgenstein's suggestion in the above passages is that the unique case is alright in itself as a case. What parallel cases destroy is not the unique case itself but our obsession with its alleged uniqueness. In other words, if we begin to accept other cases as parallel cases, thus as cases standing on the same level as the so-called unique case, we may well be said to have accepted the unique case as a parallel case among certain other cases. And this is precisely what Wittgenstein seems to suggest in the passages in which he appeals to the notion of the Copernican Revolution. But whilst expounding the objective of his similes in this way, he rides on a simile itself, one that goes awry with respect to the logic (i.e. the unique case) of the *Tractatus* and its demise in the early 1930s. Thus, Copernicus may well be said to have hurled the earth Demiurge-like onto a heap of parallel cases, even so the earth was left for what it is. Indeed, renouncing its unique position, it started to live as one planet among other planets, i.e., without having undergone any alteration first in respect of either its entrails or its surface. Wittgenstein, on the other hand, did not stumble upon a parallel case only to set it up alongside Tractarian logic. That is, he did not change his outlook *by* setting up parallel cases alongside the *Unding*, the crystalline purity of logic. Parallel cases *were* rather to be set up alongside things (i.e. language-games) already drawing on an altered conception of logic, one that precisely allows for various possibilities and comparisons between them. In other words, logic, not meant to function in the *Tractatus* as one possibility among other possibility, never managed after the demise of the *Tractatus* to rise to the rank of being one possibility among other possibilities. It was an *Unding*, and remained an *Unding*, ever since its first appearance on the philosophical scene.

Indeed, Sraffa, as the story goes, may well have forced Wittgenstein to acknowledge one or another thing as a sign, but this acknowledging did not prompt Wittgenstein to look at the sign as a parallel case exemplifying a logic to be treated on the same level with Tractarian logic.[118] Rather, the acknowledgement added to if not initiated the demise of Tractarian logic. In other words, Wittgenstein's notion of putting parallel cases alongside the so-called unique case seems to require a teaching of differences: to break the obsession with the unique *within an outlook already changed* is not to be confused with breaking the obsession so as to change one's outlook.

4.2 Whose possibility?

'*Unding*', as we have seen in the preceding chapter, is later Wittgenstein's apt epithet for the kind of logic hailed by the *Tractatus*. But, to be sure, young Wittgenstein had already himself deemed this logic an *Unding*, in a most important sense of the word. For him, logic presents 'an order: namely, the a priori order of the world; that is, the order of *possibilities*, which the world and thinking must have in common' (PI: 97). This order, then, is a some-thing that does not live up to being one possibility among other possibilities itself. And not 'being' such a thing, it is not a thing itself. Still, this *Unding*, in spite of being 'non-spatial and

---

118   'I had to acknowledge this and that as signs (Sraffa) and yet could not state a *Grammatik* for them' (MS 157b: 5v).

atemporal', did not altogether appear to early Wittgenstein as a nothing either. It did not appear to him as 'an abstraction', as he puts it, but 'as something concrete, indeed, as the most concrete, as it were the *hardest* thing there is' (PI: 97).[119] And so it is: early Wittgenstein, unaware of the illusions railroading his mind, simply failed to see how the sentences of our language, which he conceived to be logically in order as they are, could be sentences *at all*: how each sentence could signify a possible sentence among other possible sentences *tout court*, i.e. without the *Unding*. He failed to see how our language as a possibility, hence how every other language as another possibility, could ever be realized without the *Unding*, the order of all possibilities. For later Wittgenstein, then, the epithet *Unding* bears a negative connotation it did not have for early Wittgenstein. Tractarian logic truly is an *Unding* as it emanates ultimately from grammatical illusions, of which his early mind was unaware and of which this same mind simply failed to have the conceptual means to identify them as such. Logic, according to later Wittgenstein, should not be seen as standing in sharp contrast to 'the spatial and temporal phenomenon of language', to what signifies one possibility among other possibilities; rather it is to be seen and described 'as part' of these dimensions itself, that is, of the phenomena of our human life.

One could tell an intriguing story about Wittgenstein's *Tractatus* under the aspect of his conception of logic in relation to the spatial and temporal phenomenon of language. But an even more interesting story could be told, I think, about the change this relation underwent from the *Tractatus* to the *Philosophical Investigations*. I am not going to tell that story, but a few clues and hints are necessary for the kind of story that I should like to tell. Let us return once more to the *Tractatus*, in which Wittgenstein not only speaks of logic but also of *its* application.

> The application of logic decides what elementary propositions are.
> What lies in its application logic cannot anticipate.
> It is clear that logic may not conflict with its application.
> But logic must have contact with its application.
> Therefore logic and its application may not overlap one another. (TLP: 5.557)

Whatever Wittgenstein meant by the *application* of logic, it is something that he could not possibly have said more about—in the *Tractatus*—than what the above passage discloses in this respect. The reason for this restriction was logic itself, for to be interested in logic is to be interested in something that 'is prior to

---

119   Another allusion to Wittgenstein's Tractarian conception of logic as an encompassing whole. For try for all you are worth: the hardest thing will not give way to your hammering, and if one piece breaks off after all, *everything* falls apart.

every experience—that something *is so*' (TLP: 5.552). That is, Wittgenstein did not *find* logic as what is prior to every experience—that something *is so*. Rather: *that is* how Wittgenstein determined the matter in the *Tractatus*. His perspective on logic was internal to logic as *the subject matter* of his investigations. But what is logic if it fails to retain any contact with the world in which we live, with the spatio-temporal extension of our lives? If logic itself is devoid of such extension, then there must be some residue or projection of logic in the spatio- temporal world of human beings, something that owing to our being *in* the world must itself come as one possibility among other possibilities. It is this very attribute of logic that Wittgenstein calls *its* application. His Tractarian perspective on logic *determined* that its application, contrary to logic itself, *is* a matter of one possibility among other possibilities; it determined that the question of 'what elementary propositions are' could not be answered in one fell swoop with the question of what logic itself is. Logic pre-empted the possibility of contemplating its application from the perspective as determined by logic in the *Tractatus*. Tractarian logic is an *Unding*, whereas *its* application is anything *but that*; it is real, a *thing*, something that transpires within the spatio-temporal extension of our lives and the world we inhabit. But that is how logic determined it: that it must have *contact* with its application. This contact obtains between the *Unding* and the thing(s), between the non-spatial and atemporal on the one hand, and the spatio-temporal extensions of our lives, on the other; between the hardest, most concrete and the soft. And the interface between these two 'spheres' is infinitely thin, as Wittgenstein's German *"berühren"* so markedly suggests.

'Logic is prior to every experience—that something *is so*.' But the heir to Tractarian logic has (in an important sense of the word) not ceased to be prior to every experience—that something *is so*. Logic, for later Wittgenstein, has merely ceased to be an *Unding*. A seemingly small difference, which we should not take too small. For logic to cease to be an *Unding* does not mean for logic to disappear altogether. Rather, it means that logic, according to later Wittgenstein, must take on the role of a *Darstellunsgform*, a form of presentation. It must take on this role on account of his so-called real need, a need that is interested *only* in the overcoming of the urge to explain, that is, the disappearing of philosophical problems. For logic to cease to be an *Unding* does not mean for logic to disappear altogether. Rather, it means that the urge to settle on whatever kind of *Unding* should be overcome by a conception of logic that presents the language-game as one possibility among other possibilities, *without* presenting these possibilities as predicated on a possibility that fails to be a possibility among other possibilities: an *Unding*. Logic, in this form, remains its a priori character, but it has lost its nimbus.[120]

One might say that Wittgenstein's philosophical turn is more like a *shift* of attention. Logic, according to the *Tractatus*, plays its constitutive role *non-spatially and atemporally*; logic, in the *Investigation*, plays its constitutive role 'within' the same world in which we eat, drink, and avail ourselves of our daily language. 'It is *in language* that it's all done', as we have seen Wittgenstein putting things succinctly in the 1930s[121]; and, as his *Investigations* put it: 'nothing *extra*ordinary is involved' (PI: 94). Logic, in other words, has at last reached up to being a *thing* (see above); it has got a face, a physiognomy, one that lies perfectly open to view and that need not necessarily be the way it figures in our *Lebensform*. 'Language is just a phenomenon of human life' (RFM: 351), of the spatio-temporal extensions of the world in which we live. But now, although the shift in Wittgenstein's conception of logic—from logic being constitutive on account of being an *Unding* to something that 'takes part' in the same spatio-temporal phenomena in which it plays its constitutive role—, although this shift left him operating on our language in a way unhampered by the problems under which his early conception of logic suffered and ultimately collapsed, it gives rise to problems of its own, problems whose true scope and intricacies Wittgenstein did not seem to have anticipated when he was intent on a fresh and novel start in philosophy. Language just 'is enormously complicated'.

Later Wittgenstein, not unlike his early self, did not *fully* anticipate the consequences of his conception of logic. He went to great lengths contemplating the crucial role of fictitious language-games, but he did not anticipate what is involved in the construction of these things, objects of comparison as he articulated them to be and objects of comparison as he meant them to use.

I draw a distinction between contemplating the importance of fictitious language-games and the importance of fleshing them out. To face trouble in the latter activity does not necessarily demean the importance of the former activity; one may well bring this importance into account long before one tries one's hand on the playground of inventing and collating language-games. And Wittgenstein always brought this importance into account, at several times and occasions, in one form or another, sometimes even in the form reminiscent of an argument.

---

120   Cf. 'The a priori needs to become a form of presentation. That is, what needs to be taken from the concept as well is its Nimbus' (MS 157b: 3v).
121   PG: 143, see below.

Language is being used,—whether it utilizes words for physical objects or words for sense impressions.

But aren't sense impressions what we are immediately aware of? Aren't they the immediate objects to which everything we say must finally refer?

The picture of building blocks. Everything we build consists ultimately of these blocks. But it is a false picture since we are not contrasting 'these' building blocks with any others. (PO: 413)

In this intriguing passage, which is clearly a product of the so-called playground of abstract considerations, Wittgenstein, it seems somewhat meditatively, renounces the idea of sense impressions *as* the ultimate building blocks for language. Thus, he does not renounce sense impressions themselves but the way we talk about these things in philosophical reflection. We strongly tend to talk about them in a highly specific way and, to be sure, Wittgenstein poses no exception in this very respect; he, too, feels the powerful influence that sense impressions exert on the philosophical mind. He, too, feels the urge to contemplate their nature in terms of them being private objects, in terms of them exhibiting an immediacy beyond comparison, and of them posing an exclusiveness of mind-boggling proportions. But having developed a very sensitive nose indeed for everything that philosophers tend to take to as constituting the *ultimate* thing in the world, Wittgenstein indulges in these ruminations with more tenacity, fascination, and critical reflection than all those philosophers who seek to pin their hopes if not their entire lives on such things. He asks: 'But aren't sense impressions what we are immediately aware of? Aren't they the immediate objects to which everything we say must finally refer?'

Indeed, sense impressions are hard to resist and there is real *Pathos* in the questions and the answers that seek to give them a proper place in our philosophies. Do *they* not provide us with an order, the only possible order in our vision of the world at large? *There is* an order out there, a principle that *we* do not need to impose on language and the world but that knocks on our doors as a free and generous offer! Pity on them who fail to embrace it! Blush for them who decline the bargain!—And now the *Pathos* retreats to the problems. The true fascination that 'sense impressions' exert on us sparkles off, for Wittgenstein, the moment he brings his real *need* into account. The *urge* is there, on his own part no less, the philosophical *urge* to bring language to bear upon sense impressions; the urge is there, but so is his need—for *complete clarity*.

So why believe, as Wittgenstein would ask, that there are objects out there to which everything we say must finally refer [*am Schluß beziehen muß*]?—to a certain set of objects and these objects only. Whence this idea? What is your conception of language that this idea does not fail to exert its fascination on you? Is

192

it a conception that leaves open *which* objects language ultimately must refer to, and you, in your philosophical moments, upon coming across sense impressions, find precisely these things perfectly suited for the job? Is that your conception of language with which you enter the philosophical stage? Or is it rather owing to the peculiar way sense impressions enter the stage of your mind that you begin to alter your conception of language, to the effect that sense impressions *must* be the ultimate things in the world, come what may? But what about their so-called immediacy? Is it because they strike you as *more immediate* than anything else in the world that you find them so attractive? But why think it all right to *speak* of them thus, if nothing in the world could ever be *compared* with them? Perhaps you want to say that you *feel* their immediacy.—A feeling that mediates between you and the sense impression? So this feeling is even more immediate than the most immediate things around?

If sense impressions lay claim to exclusiveness, if this is the ultimate attraction that they exercise on us philosophers, then Wittgenstein criticizes our talk about them all the more so. But this critique is brought to bear on *everything* that seeks to lay an exclusive claim on our philosophical minds; that is, Wittgenstein treats all these claims with the utmost care and fascination, only to expose them as the foundation of just another house of cards. And this way of treating has every-thing to do with the *form* of his later approach to language, with his uncommon way of looking at things. We talk here about a form that has been shaped to the core by Wittgenstein's critical treatment of the *Tractatus*, of the role of the *Und-ing* there. It is the kind of critique that he developed vis-à-vis this incomparable essence that went straight into determining the form of what became his later approach. Wittgenstein's uncommon way of looking, then, is shaped by a mo-ment of relativity, that is, by his notion that the constitutive parts in language *must* not ultimately refer to some *Unding* or other. His criticism of Tractarian logic as the ultimate thing in the constitution of every language determined the form of his later vantage point, in that *it* must never allow anything to take a part in his thinking that emulates the role that logic once played in the *Tractatus*. This criticism, rather than flowing from his new way looking at language, established its form and foundation from the first moment on.

Indeed, if Wittgenstein does not deny the existence of sense impressions, but rejects only our way of talking about them in moments of philosophy, how does *he* talk about them? Well, he pays attention to how *we*, in the daily course of life, talk about sense impressions. And paying attention to this daily talk, he pays at-tention to something that he wants to *leave as it is*. Wittgenstein does not mean to talk about sense impressions in a way different from how we do it in the daily course of life, but for all that he pays attention to how we talk about these things from his vantage point on language: '[W]e talk about it as we do about pieces in chess when we are stating the rules for the moves, not describing their physical properties.'[122] Of course, as one wants to say now, by *representing* our daily talk on the model of chess, as Wittgenstein suggests here, he does not seem to leave everything as it is after all. And yet, the point here is that *that* is precisely what his way of leaving everything as it is amounts to. For talking *thus* about language, he answers to his own critique of the Tractarian *Unding*: our way of talking about sense impressions *is* the way we do it, but other ways are imaginable. *This* is our way of talking about sense impressions, but we need not necessarily do it thus and so. So the point for us to see here is that the kind of possibility that Wittgenstein intimates here—inheres in his uncommon way of looking at language. It is not everyone's possibility; it surely is not.

The way *philosophers* talk about sense impressions is *Rohmaterial* for Wittgenstein's mind: he attends to this kind of talk, i.e. to how a given claim arises, and to how it tends to lend further support to our common way of looking at things. If we feel drawn in a definite direction on account of its alleged exclusiveness, it is Wittgenstein who seeks to let himself be drawn along, only to learn from these sojourns and to let the results teach the kind of descriptions he craves for. It thus appears that sense impressions, for all the specificity they exhibit in our way of talking about them in moments of philosophy, are much treated *like* the Tractarian *Unding* in one important respect, namely that Wittgenstein, in order to break the spell of uniqueness these things exert on us, does not place so-called other possibilities, that is, other 'building blocks' (cf. above passage) alongside the sense impressions themselves. He rather treats the way we talk about sense impressions in daily life as a building block, as what signifies one language-game among other language-games, as one possibility among other possibilities.

The above passage nicely illustrates Wittgenstein's rejection of Empiricism. That is, it nicely illustrates what his rejection of this philosophy ultimately traces back to. It is the idea that *any* philosophy in quest of 'the absolute' rests on a false picture. In Wittgenstein's eyes, the empiricist makes himself vulnerable to a form of criticism that he, Wittgenstein, once brought to bear upon his *Tractatus* in the 1930s. So what this form of criticism feeds on is the possibility of contrasting various possibilities with each other. It is at last the difficulty of this contrasting that Wittgenstein intimates when he writes 'Not empiricism and yet realism in philosophy, that is the hardest thing' (RFM, 325). It is the difficulty of his

---

122   Part of a boxed passage between *PI* §§108–09, cf. below.

194

uncommon way of looking at things. Thus, on the playground of abstract consideration, Wittgenstein may well promulgate 'Not empiricism and yet realism in philosophy', it is what he needs to *achieve* by *describing* our language-games as possibilities among other possibilities. Unless Wittgenstein succeeds in describing our own language-games by means of one variation or another on their *logical* themes, he might well have promulgated anything on his famous playground of abstract consideration.

These variations, then, are *logical* possibilities, to be put alongside our own language-games as *logical* possibilities themselves. The *Unding*, in whatever guise it forces itself upon us, should be overcome by a Realism in which the heir to Tractarian *logic* now rules the philosophical game.

Let us return to Wittgenstein's words (which in the 4th edition of the *Investigations* no longer appear as part of §108, but as part of a boxed passage closed in by §108 and §109): 'We're talking about the spatial and temporal phenomenon of language; not about some non-spatial, atemporal *Unding*.' This remark, as we have been suggesting, features an important shift of attention in Wittgenstein's turn from the *Tractatus* to the *Investigations*. But what are we to make of the notions that see themselves placed against each other there? What kind of polar contrast is at issue here?

In *PI* §92, Wittgenstein ascribes to his *Tractatus* the view that it saw the essence of language lying '*beneath* the surface. Something that lies *within*' (emphasis mine). Now this is a remarkable ascription as this essence is also deemed a 'non-spatial and atemporal *Unding*'. But if logic, according to later Wittgenstein, no longer lies beneath the surface of language, but is perfectly open to view, how does *logic* pertain to the spatial and temporal phenomenon of language? Could we say, as we did above, that logic 'partakes' of the spatial and temporal phenomenon of language? But, then, how could *logic* partake of this phenomenon? But why, indeed, is Wittgenstein so much at pains to talk about the spatial and temporal phenomenon of language at all?

Indeed, how could *he* as a philosopher be concerned with the spatial and temporal phenomenon of language, and with this phenomenon only, with something that arouses the minds of scientists and evokes a good stirring in many a philosopher alike? The spatial and temporal aspects of language are part of a world in which scientists feel at home and do their work. Is this the world in which Wittgenstein now feels himself obliged to do his daily stint as well? On the other hand, what else could Wittgenstein talk about, now that he has uncovered the real nature of the *Unding*, i.e. the ground on which it stood? Not talking was no option for him, for his criticism of the *Tractatus* did not mean the end to philosophy but the founding of a novel conception of logic at once. What is more, the spatial and temporal phenomenon of language was never absent from early Wittgenstein's mind, as our comment on *TLP* §5.557 suggests. It played its role there already, and did not cease to play 'a role' in Wittgenstein's philosophical life.

But what does this phenomenon amount to, according to the *Tractatus*? To begin with, it is the counterpart of the non-spatial and atemporal *Unding*. Early Wittgenstein cut up the whole of 'language and the world' in two sections, namely *das Unding* and *die Dinge* (things). The *Unding* is logic, the very essence of each and every language; a *Ding* is an application of logic, something that transpires within the same spheres in which we eat, drink, and die, the very setting of human life with its spatio-temporal extension. Although early Wittgenstein entertained both notions, the *Unding* and the *Dinge*, he talked but very little about the latter. However, he must nonetheless have invoked both notions, for they form a pair of logical counterparts. The *Unding*, without its spatio-temporal counterpart, would remain unreified, would fail to come true. In other words, the application of logic makes up a system, one possible system among other possible systems. The *Ding* is always the particular, the individual; it is not a degenerate possibility like the *Unding*, but 'the soft', truly one thing among other things, something that draws on logic, 'the *hardest* thing there is.' There is ample room for the particular: there *must* be, if the *Unding* leaves no room, no 'individual' choice, in each and every language.

Although the *Unding* endowed Wittgenstein's early investigations with the awe and importance he thought philosophy must have, its sole concern was at last the thing he talked about conspicuously little in the *Tractatus*, namely what language amounts to within the spatio-temporal extensions of human life. Wittgenstein committed himself to articulating the *Unding* only, but in so doing he could not but commit himself to a conception of its polar counterpart, the common spatio-temporal reality of human life, in which language finds its application and acquires the awe and importance it has for a community of users. Of the latter reality he acknowledged such things and aspects as that '[c]olloquial language is a part of the human organism and is not less complicated than it' and that '[t]he silent adjustments to understand colloquial language are enormously complicated' (TLP: 4.002). So the *Unding* is not 'part of the human organism', unlike colloquial language. Not being part of the spatio-temporal extensions of the world, the *Unding* drops out from them as what renders the application of language possible at all. Wittgenstein, in the *Tractatus*, did not let himself be tempted to saying *more* than he deemed absolutely necessary to say about the spatio- temporal extensions of our language. Indeed, why should he, now that he

196

had committed himself to articulating the crystalline purity of logic, feel committed to clear up something that is merely a possibility among other possibilities, owing to the part it takes 'of the human organism'? A commitment to the execution of that *entirely* different task would not have added any lustre to the *Tractatus* as a work of art. And yet, however much Wittgenstein abstained from performing that task, in the *Tractatus*, he left a clear and inalienable Tractarian stamp on it, for there is no evading the conception of elementary propositions. A future concern with the application *of logic*, of the *Unding*, of the incomparable essence of language, could not avoid these things.

The eye through which Wittgenstein looked at the spatial and temporal phenomenon of language, in the *Tractatus*, was the eye that committed itself to articulating the *how* of the *Unding*. *Later* Wittgenstein saw himself again committed to articulating ('describing') a *how*, but this time it was the spatio-temporal phenomenon of language itself that came to lie under his elucidations. That is, this phenomenon *not* seen through the eyes of Tractarian logic, but seen through the eyes of a logic that has ceased to be an *Unding* without having ceased to be 'prior to every experience—that something *is so*.' It is all done now in language, in the spatial and temporal phenomenon of language, but not because that is how Wittgenstein discovered it one day, but because *that* is what his way of looking at language is. It is a way of looking that commits him to articulating *how* it is all done there. It is all done in this phenomenon: a clear allusion to his Tractarian outlook, according to which it is not all done in language, for the *Unding* is not *language* itself, but the essence of each language, something lying beneath the surface of language. Language, then, according to later Wittgenstein, should not be viewed as what is *in the end* rendered possible through the mediation of whatever *Unding*. (The *Unding* of the *Tractatus* was an *Unding* not so much on account of its ingredients as on account of its being the only 'thing' underlying each and every language.) In other words, the possibility of the application of language—in a most important sense of the word "possibility"—must not lie 'outside' the spatio-temporal extensions in which the application of language actually transpires itself. But if later Wittgenstein is now at pains to talk about the spatial and temporal phenomenon of language *in which it is all done*, there is still the question of what he means to talk about.

The boxed passage should not be taken to suggest that Wittgenstein *now*, i.e. in the *Investigations*, wants to talk about the spatial and temporal phenomenon of language, *rather* than about its non-spatial, atemporal *Unding*. That is, Wittgenstein's suggestion is not that he, after having spent so much time contemplating the *Unding* in the *Tractatus*, now intends to take to task the spatial and temporal dimensions of language. To be sure, he does intend to focus on the spatial and temporal phenomenon of language now, but he wants to look at it as the only thing in the world, now that the *Unding* in whatever form has dropped out from his philosophical *Betrachtung*. But the dropping out of this thing did not leave the Tractarian conception of the spatial and temporal phenomenon of language unscathed. For without the *Unding* there is no longer any support for idea that the application of logic transpires via the application of elementary propositions, and these things only. So what goes out the window with the *Unding* is the spatio-temporal phenomenon of language as Wittgenstein conceived it to be in the *Tractatus*. But, then, if the *Unding* drops out from Wittgenstein's considerations as the counterpart of the *Dinge*, where does this leave us as regards the *spatial and temporal* phenomenon of language that Wittgenstein now intends to talk about, namely as the kind of setting *in which it is all done*? What motivates this question is also a point as the following: Wittgenstein does not mean to talk about the spatial and temporal phenomenon of language in *any* of the ways in which scientists, and many philosophers alike, are interested in it. As he says in the boxed passage: '[Only is it possible to be interested in a phenomenon in a variety of ways.] But we talk about it as we do about pieces in chess when we are stating the rules for the moves, not describing their physical properties.' Indeed, although Wittgenstein is at pains to talk about the spatial and temporal phenomenon of language, he is not committed to talk about it the very way scientists do. His suggestion is that, although the spatial and temporal phenomenon of language is as much given to us, philosophers, as to anyone else, *it* does not commit us to talk about it in one definite way rather than another. True, it *compels* us to look at it in highly specific ways, among which the empirical mode is perhaps uppermost.—Some one thing inheres in Wittgenstein's *Betrachtung*, for it is his real need, and this thing only, that commits him to look upon, and talk about, the given in the way he expounds in the boxed passage.

It is all done in language, within the spatial and temporal phenomenon of language. This means, first and foremost, that Wittgenstein looks upon this phenomenon *as* autonomous. The autonomy of this phenomenon inheres in his uncommon way of looking at things, hence in his conception of logic, in something that must be settled and articulated before it comes to an investigation of the phenomenon itself. If logic has ceased to be an *Unding*, if it must now come as one possibility among other possibilities, it is strictly speaking not logic itself that must be thus, but language, the spatio-temporal phenomena of language that are being looked upon through the eyes of logic. The autonomy of these phenomena is not a feature *of* these phenomena themselves, something that stands on the same level with, say, the enigmatic workings *of* the human brain.

This picture is to be contrasted with the Empiricist's, for in his eyes, the spatial and temporal phenomenon of language is perfectly continuous with the rest of the spatial and temporal world. So what the spatial and temporal phenomenon of language is for him is not what it is for Wittgenstein, which is another way of saying that what the latter tries to describe is not what the former has ever tried to explain. But, of course, what does the spatio-temporal world amount to in the eyes that look upon the spatio-temporal phenomenon of language as autonomous? How they do relate to each other? Well, the use of language does not come to pass in a sterile kind of autonomous space, in a dimension which 'ignor[es] friction and air-resistance', but precisely *against* the background of a world that is *not* being looked upon *as* autonomous. Language is looked upon *against* the background of a world of customary events and recurring facts that together make up the non-autonomous counterpart of the spatial and temporal phenomenon of language. The *Unding* has dropped out from Wittgenstein's picture and the kind of thing that has taken its place is the non-autonomous world of facts and events. Of course, we shall need to return to this issue.[123]

It has thus become apparent that Wittgenstein charts the spatio-temporal phenomenon of language in a special way, one that is essentially different from how empirical scientists go about the matter and how philosophers tend to proceed in emulation of the scientific example. To look at language as autonomous means to treat certain parts of it as possibilities among other possibilities; *parts*, that is, which are not such possibilities *tout court*—hence are not given *without more* ado. The empiricist likewise draws boundaries in the spatio-temporal phenomenon of language, but not along Wittgenstein's uncommon lines.[124] All the same, the empiricist's way of approaching the phenomenon of language is of considerable interest to Wittgenstein, who comments: 'But we talk about it as we do about pieces in chess when we are stating the rules for the moves, not describing their physical properties.' *Wittgenstein* wants to talk about the phenomenon of language thus, but not *tout court*, not out of the blue, but because of the urge to explain *in philosophy*. We cannot help feeling that looking upon

---

123 Cf. Chapters 5 and 6 for more on this point.
124 Cf. 'But if we wish to draw boundaries in the use of a word, in order to clear up philosophical paradoxes, then alongside the actual picture of the use (in which as it were the different colours flow into one another without sharp boundaries) we may put another picture which is in certain ways like the first but is built up of colours with clear boundaries between them' (PG: 76).

the spatio-temporal phenomenon of language in any but the empiricist's way is illusionary and unfounded.

But why should the spatio-temporal phenomenon of language as a given succumb to Wittgenstein's uncommon way of looking? Why should it give way to his interest that looks upon philosophical problems as (dis)solvable without exception? Wittgenstein aims to arrive at descriptions of our language, and these things only. But why should the spatio-temporal phenomenon of language, which Wittgenstein needs to come to terms with the way it is, and seeks to leave as it is, give way to the daily grindings of his dialectical machinery to turn out descriptions of language? Admittedly, these are curious questions, but they allude to the difficulties expounded in the second chapter, and my present suggestion is that they should be seen in close connection with other difficulties engendered by Wittgenstein's dialectical machinery, namely the ones he faces on the playground of inventing and collating fictitious language-games. Tractarian logic held out one major advantage over Wittgenstein's later conception of logic, for the *Unding* had no need to bother about appearances. True, it had to be simple; it had to be absolutely transparent and clear. But these demands rather set the standards of clarity and transparency. Basking in its own glory, the *Unding* resided below the surface of every language, beneath their perpetual contingencies and far beyond human judgement, which tends to discard things if they fail to comply with the current fashion. But now that Wittgenstein looks upon the spatio-temporal phenomenon of our language from a vantage point that overlooks its parts—called 'language-games'—as autonomous, thus at its spatio-temporal parts as possibilities that are the way they are but need not be the way they manifest themselves in our language; now that he looks thus upon language he faces the perpetual contingencies of life and human judgement: *This* is what we call doing mathematics and nothing could ever win us over to recognize any deviation from our own practice as a way as doing *mathematics* as well! As we shall see, the phenomenon of human language is somewhat recalcitrant in that it does not give way effortlessly, if at all, to the more interesting kinds of fictitious language-games that Wittgenstein seeks to set up alongside our language-games, parts of the spatio- temporal phenomenon of our language as they are, possibilities among other possibilities.

Having said that later Wittgenstein means to talk about the spatial and temporal phenomenon of language, and that he looks at this phenomenon as what 'falls apart' in possibilities that are not everyone's possibilities, we have as a matter of fact been touching upon what we had already made explicit, namely that the rationale behind Wittgenstein's fictitious language-games is not to prove or to show *that* our language-games are anything but unique, i.e. things that come the way they obtain in our *Lebensform* and that cannot possibly be different there or anywhere. They are possibilities among other possibilities as a direct result of Wittgenstein's vantage point. It is the light in which Wittgenstein looks at language-games that renders these things *describable*. Now, consider the following remark: 'Everything we can describe at all could also be otherwise' (TLP: 5.634). The suggestion of this remark is *not* that we should try to see whether something can be described or not, only to pronounce that it cannot possibly be otherwise in case we fail to describe it. Thus, Tractarian logic, i.e. the *Unding*, is not thrown up in the book as what we, readers, should *try* to describe only to discover for ourselves that it cannot be done so and to conclude that it is not a possibility among other possibilities. That is not its purpose.

The *Unding* cannot be described; *its application* is up for description. But the *Unding* has been dropped from Wittgenstein's picture, and what remains, the so-called given, is now being considered through a conception of logic that is heir to his early conception of logic. So the spatial and temporal phenomenon of language is being looked upon as what is *describable* and what one needs to describe, in order to solve philosophical problems. But what if one finds it so difficult to describe the describable? What if one fails to describe the describable? Wittgenstein says: 'If we find it so difficult to describe, why then do we also describe such cases which do not obtain at all?—The description of fictitious cases is part of the description of the real ones.'[125] Wittgenstein, as we saw in Chapter 2, appears to have serious difficulties in describing our own language-games. But now, to prey on his words in the quoted passage, if fictitious language-games are part of the description of our language, the question arises how we should evaluate the situation in which Wittgenstein tries to produce such entities, as his way of looking at language commits him to, tries—but fails, again and again? He looks at our language-game as a possibility among other possibilities, but not in order to prove or to show *that* it is a possibility, but in order to expose the *how* of its possibility—by seeing it alongside other possibilities. But how should we proceed when these other possibilities refuse to materialize? When the fleshing out of fictitious language-games turns out to be a highly problematic affair? When we find it utterly difficult to acknowledge the fictitious possibility as a variation on what *we call* doing mathematics, on what *we call* doing 'pain-things' with

---

125 'Wenn es uns so schwer fällt zu beschreiben, warum beschreiben wir dann auch noch solche Fälle//Zustände//, die es gar nicht gibt?//die gar nicht vorkommen? – Die Beschreibung der fiktiven Fälle gehört zur//ist ein Teil der// Beschreibung der wirklichen' (MS 130: 229).

words? It appears that Wittgenstein had serious difficulties, not just in giving descriptions of our own language-games, but also in describing fictitious ones, in the more extended sense of the word.

Merely trying to *describe* our own language-games, Wittgenstein already treats these things as possibilities that need not manifest themselves in the way we find them in our *Lebensform*. But if he now tries to set up alongside these language-games such fictitious ones so as *to earmark* this way (see below), that is, tries but fails: should we then not say that these language-games *cannot be described—in spite of* his way of looking upon the spatio-temporal phenomenon of language as describable? This question brings us again to that famous passage in *On Certainty*, where Wittgenstein writes: 'Am I not getting closer and closer to saying that in the end logic cannot be described? You must look at the practice of language, then you will see it' (OC: 501).[126]

Wittgenstein, in the first clause, does not say that *he* cannot describe logic, but that logic (in the end!) cannot be described. He may well have thought of himself as a complete duffer at the business of describing language (logic), but anyone with sufficient sense and imagination will find the same: *logic...cannot* be described. Is this not irony? Wittgenstein, ever since the early 1930s, tried to describe logic, whereas there is no such thing as trying to *describe* logic (the *Unding*) in the *Tractatus*. In this work, he looked at logic as being not a possibility among other possibilities itself, but as what presents *the* order of possibilities. What can be described, can be described on account of the very *Unding*, which drops out from what can be described at all. But that it drops out in this dramatic respect just lies in the *Tractatus'* recitation, for that is how Wittgenstein had laid down the internal connections among its key terms.[127] There had been no attempt on his part to limit the world and to set it in relief; and he would have ridiculed any such attempt as revealing a grave misunderstanding of what logic is and how it connects with the world as a whole. But now, from the early 1930s on, Wittgenstein looks upon the spatio-temporal phenomenon of language as the sphere in which it is *all* done, which means that there is no *end* to logic that cannot be described. Yet, not *everything* of logic can be described; there appears to be something about logic that resists Wittgenstein's efforts to take language-games apart from tip to toe, as one possibility among other possibilities. Later Wittgenstein excluded from language, right from the beginning, the possibility

---

126   More on *On Certainty* in the Chapter 6.
127   I.e. super-concepts (cf. PI: 97).

of the *Unding*; early Wittgenstein failed to conceive the possibility of language without such a thing.

Given Wittgenstein's conception of description, then, and knowing that ever since the mid-1930s he had definitely ceased to conceive logic as what must answer to a *Unding*, we begin to realize the dramatic dimension of Wittgenstein's exclamation in *On Certainty*: he seems to have hit upon something that refuses to give way to his efforts to limit it, i.e. to set it in relief. No longer wanting to champion the *Unding*, with which his philosophical career started, Wittgenstein seems to end up facing something that emulates this thing in a remarkable way.

> It seems therefore, that our concepts, the use of our words, are constrained by a factual framework [*Gerüst*]. But how can that be?! How could we describe the framework if we did not allow for the possibility of something else? – One is inclined to say that you are making all logic into nonsense! (RPP II: 190)

This passage may well have been part of Wittgenstein's considerations in *On Certainty*. There too it much seems to Wittgenstein that the use of our words is constrained by a factual framework. What this means, at least for him, is that the logic of a language-game is *in the end* constrained by something that, precisely because of this constraining, relates to logic. But what is said to relate or to belong to *logic* belongs to what can be described. So Wittgenstein faces the task of describing something that, precisely because of the kind of constraining it exerts on our concepts, will not readily allow for something else, although it *must* allow for something else. Wittgenstein's conception of logic requires its own describability, but the describability it calls for turns out to be resistant to *complete* description. 'One is inclined to say that you are making all logic into nonsense!' *All*—because he made logic into nonsense already in the *Tractatus*.

Above we talked about the interface between the non-spatial and atemporal *Unding*, on the one hand, and the spatial and temporal phenomenon of language, on the other hand. Wittgenstein's turn, as one might say, has given to rise to another interface, namely between the spatial and temporal phenomenon of language *as* an autonomous entity and its spatial and temporal counterpart. It seems that there is something utterly unclear about this interface, even in Wittgenstein's eyes, something that has given rise to serious troubles, something we shall need to return to.[128]

---

128   See Chapter 5.

4.3 Light and understanding

One of the things we have been emphasizing is that Wittgenstein's fictitious language-games, as means *for his own private use*, are not meant to change *his* outlook. Rather, they are things used within an outlook already changed. Another is that Wittgenstein's changed outlook did not render him any less susceptible to the disquieting appearances that our language exerts on his mind. On the contrary, his changed outlook has not brought peace in his mind at last but precisely aims at bringing peace there, an aim that involves much piecemeal kind of work, for each disquieting appearance of our language requires its own cure and treatment. But however various these cures and treatments may be, they all answer to Wittgenstein's changed outlook as one that considers the language-game as a possibility among other possibilities. And there is much to say in favour of our suggestion that the disquieting appearances that our language acquires for a philosopher such as Wittgenstein are rather products of his own making than special effects due to our language. Language keeps obtruding upon us its strong and usual impressions, but it is against Wittgenstein's way of looking that it begins to sport *disquieting* aspects.

That logic, our language, is *describable* epitomizes Wittgenstein's changed outlook on language. *That* logic is describable, and completely so, is not one element alongside other so-called elements of Wittgenstein's changed outlook, a kind of building block that has as it were found its way into an extant outlook only to join up there with other so-called building blocks already firmly in place and at work. Rather, *these* 'blocks' have coalesced around the pivotal point *that* logic, language, is describable. But what kind of philosophical work, if any, is there to do now? For if the kind of philosophical work to do is determined, right from the beginning, by the principle that the logic of our language is what it is but need not necessarily be the way it manifests itself in its workings, what should we make of the aim and purpose of Wittgenstein's fictitious language-games if 'the proof' that the language-game is what it is but need not necessarily be the way it manifests itself in our language—is not their business, but rather the ground on which they stand and from which they work, indeed, owe their entire purpose and sole existence? Could Russell not be right after all in his good old days, perhaps for the first time in his long life, namely with his rather caustic view on Wittgenstein that his later philosophy 'is at best, a slight help to lexicographers, and at worst, an idle tea-table amusement'?

The answer lies in the very suggestion we have just been furnishing. Thus, given that Wittgenstein's fictitious language-games take part in his efforts to give descriptions of our language, the question reduces to the one that asks why he wants to give these descriptions. And the answer to that question lies in the way we have been articulating things for ourselves so far: there is no *that* unless it gives rise to a *how*. *That* our language-games are possibilities among other possibilities commits one to seeing *how* a language-game works the way it does. The disquieting aspect that a language-game exerts on us is only the outward veneer of its real working, which is what it is but need not necessarily be the way it obtains in our *Lebensform*. It is our seeing *how* the game works that should do away with this aspect to which the *that* has added a sharp edge.

What we need to bring into account now is what we have been touching upon in the second chapter, namely that Wittgenstein wants to *understand*. He wants to understand, that is, through his descriptions of language, and through these things *only*. And not until we have grasped the point of this 'only' do we really grasp what his descriptions are like and what *his* notion of understanding amounts to. Wittgenstein aims at understanding, and it is language that he wants to understand, not any language though, but *our* language, and this language only—but then *only* insofar as it troubles him, only in opposition to the urge to misunderstand its workings. This urge and his so-called real need: they structure the entire dialectical field in which he moves philosophically, in which understanding by explanation keeps forcing itself upon him and where his need for overcoming this urge ultimately in terms of understanding by description is as obsessive a burden as the other is misleading. It is not until Wittgenstein has arrived at *his* understanding that he can be said to have done away fully with one defiant misunderstanding or another.

Of course, the fact that Wittgenstein wants to understand does not mark him down as a rather uncommon representative of the philosophical lore, any more than the fact does that it is our language that makes up the object of his understanding. His peculiarity merely is his uncommon way of looking at things, for he does not want to explain or justify, but to describe instead. Just as we have not taken Wittgenstein's notion of description for granted, we do well now to pay attention to his conception of understanding, for it is no less uncommon a thing than his notion of description.

Although Wittgenstein does not want to explain in philosophy, but to understand by description only, he has gone to great lengths explicating what giving explanations amounts to in philosophy, an exertion that need not embarrass all those philosophers who want to find the redeeming word in terms of explanation without wanting to realize what they actually do and want so much. Wittgenstein, for his part, finds it utterly natural to explicate his own sense of understanding language and the world, and as natural as he considers this philosophical preoccupation, so lame and careless of mind, if not character, he finds it *not to take care of making one's own sense of understanding clear and explicit, no matter one's approach in philosophy*. This kind of fastidiousness pervaded all of Wittgenstein's work. And the point for us to observe here is that Wittgenstein's later notion of understanding, no less than his later conception of description, has roots tracing back all the way to his early work, where both stand in an internal relation to each other, one that the *Tractatus* forged and explicated, and which went fairly unscathed into a work as the *Philosophical Investigations*. Let us try to work this out a little.

> The 'experience' that we need in order to understand [*verstehen*] logic is not that something or other is the state of things, but that something *is*: that, however, is *not* an experience.
>
> Logic is *prior* to every experience—that something *is so*.
> It is prior to the question 'How?', not prior to the question 'What?'
>
> And if this were not so, how could we apply logic? We might put it in this way: if there would be a logic even if there were no world, how then could there be a logic given that there is a world? (TLP: 5.552–5.5521)[129]

Tractarian logic forecloses on the class of things being possibilities among other possibilities. Only when logic comes in this exceptional way did Wittgenstein conceive *its* application possible, where each application merely represents one possibility among other possible applications. The above passage bears out this point, and it is interesting to observe how the notions of experience and understanding figure in the Tractarian array of internal connections ultimately bearing to the world as a limited whole: 'The "experience" that we need in order to understand logic', Wittgenstein say, 'is not that something or other is the state of things, but that something *is*: that, however, is not an experience.' The suggestion of these words is that understanding logic does not come without more ado. What needs to come into play for this kind of 'understanding', indeed needs to come perforce, is a sort of feeling that should not be categorized among the experiences. That is, the sort of feeling is only an experience of sorts as genuine experience is what it is only insofar as it concerns something that comes as one possibility among other possibilities, whereas the 'experience' that we need in

---

129   Cf. 'Time and again the attempt is made to use language to limit the world and set it in relief – but it can't be done. The self-evidence of the world expresses itself in the very fact that language can and does only refer to it. For since language only derives the way in which it means from its meaning, from the world, no language is conceivable which does not represent this world' (PG: 80).

order to 'understand' logic is the feeling that something *is*. This something is *everything* that is the case; it is not a possibility among other possibilities. It is the *totality of facts* as a *limited whole*: the world.

(In the remaining part of the above passage, Wittgenstein undertakes as it were the impossible: to limit the world and to set it into relief. The form this attempt obtains is a rational one: the existent relation between logic and the world is *ex hypothesi* put alongside *mere* logic, an imaginary act that should render the existent relation one possibility among exactly two possibilities. But, as he suggests, no sooner has one got a grip on the hypothetical possibility than one loses one's grip on the (existent) possibility, for the former renders the latter one at once puzzling and utterly inconceivable. But this kind of attempt at limiting logic is not what Wittgenstein means to admit as what can make his point accessible to a rational underpinning—the point namely that the 'experience' that we need in order to understand logic is not that something or other is the state of things, but that something *is*. For, indeed, in that case he precisely undermines his own point. Be that as it may, Wittgenstein, in the *Tractatus*, *required* the application of logic to be the application of something that is a limited whole.)

Wittgenstein speaks of the 'experience' that we need *in order to* understand logic, only to make clear that there is no such an experience, and his suggestion clearly is that logic forecloses on the things that can be *understood*. Just a few remarks ahead in the *Tractatus*, he again intimates this 'experience'.

> Not *how* the world is, is the mystical, but *that* it is.
>
> The contemplation [*Anschauung*] of the world sub species aeterni is its contemplation as a limited whole.
>
> The feeling of the world as a limited whole is the mystical feeling. (TLP: 6.44–45)

The 'experience' that we need in order to understand logic is the mystical experience, or the mystical feeling, as Wittgenstein says; the feeling, namely, of the world *as* a limited whole. The world does not compel us to behold it in a special way, but to behold the world *as* a limited whole is the way one needs to behold it in order to 'understand' logic. To behold the world as a limited whole is to behold it as what *is*, rather than as the way it is. This way of beholding the world articulates logic as what bears a connection to what *is*, rather than to something that is *so*. Indeed, beholding the world as a limited whole articulates logic itself as a limited whole – a whole, namely, that renders *its* application possible in the first instance. So the articulation of logic as a limited whole is its articulation in which the world as a limited whole partakes. The articulation of logic as a limited whole is the articulation of 'the a priori order of the world; that is, the order of *possibilities*, which the world and thinking must have in common' (PI: 97).

The little word *as* in the phrase 'the world as a limited whole' is worth pausing upon. Wittgenstein speaks of an *Anschauung*, a way of beholding the world, one that not so much underlies his book as that it is the kind of beholding of which his book undertakes to give a perfect account. The word *Anschaung* is reminiscent of a word that Wittgenstein regularly advances within the context of his later work, namely *Betrachtung*. His Tractarian *Anschauung* is a *Betrachtungsweise*, and it is the *only* way of beholding the world that the *Tractatus* addresses and undertakes to expound. What later Wittgenstein sets over against his Tractarian *Betrachtungsweise* is not a motley of other *Betrachtungsweisen* to be exploited according to the demands or whims of the language-game under investigation, but really only one *Betrachtung* (cf. PI: 108). Later Wittgenstein no longer means to look upon the world *as* a limited whole, but only at parts of the world *as* autonomous. This much seems to be a narrow way of looking, not unlike his Tractarian way itself. And yet, it was under his Tractarian *Betrachtung* that he was able to turn his object of investigation, i.e. the *Unding*, around, making out one aspect of it after another, and treating all of them as partial difficulties of a single great problem. Thus, at one time it was the sign-versus-symbol 'problem' that occupied his attention, at another time it was the aspect of asserting, at still other times it were aspects such as inference, true and false, sense and nonsense, tautology, the elementary proposition, names, picture, possibility, necessity, et cetera.[130] When early Wittgenstein reflects that it is rewarding for the kind work *he* was performing, for that work more than any other, 'to keep on looking at questions, which one considers solved, from other sides, as if they were unsolved' (NB: 40), there is no suggestion that he advises himself to give up on his way of beholding the world as a limited whole, to give up on it for a while so as to try other points of view *instead* of his way of looking. No, he just asks himself to turn his object of investigation, which bears internally to his way of beholding the world as a limited whole, to turn that object around—around the axis that bears internally to his way of beholding the world as a limited whole. The same goes for Wittgenstein with respect to his later way of looking at things. Indeed, the remark from his *Notebooks* applies as much to his later investigations as to his early effort.

---

130   Cf. 'How can logic—all embracing logic, which mirrors the world—use such peculiar crotchets and contrivances? Only because they are all connected with one another in an infinitely fine network, the great mirror' (TLP 5.511); 'The problems of negation, of disjunction, of true and false, are only reflections of the one great problem in the variously placed great and small mirrors of philosophy' (NB: 40).

Wittgenstein, then, in the *Tractatus*, did not proffer logic as what can be understood, described. Rather, he excluded it, right from the beginning, from the sphere of things that come as possibilities among other possibilities: from the spatio-temporal extensions of any language. But he did not do all this on account of a discovery; that is, he did not first see that the world *is* a limited whole and that it cannot be understood, described, only to do his utmost best in explaining that this thing cannot be understood, described. Rather, he gave a 'perfected account' of what it is like to *behold* the world as a limited whole, and in so doing he sought to make clear what both description and understanding amount to. In the *Tractatus*, he was 'talking about the non-spatial, atemporal *Unding*' through sentences, i.e. through what he called elucidations: sentences that *he* did not *mean* to be descriptions of the *Unding* and that on his own understanding of them could not furnish a book with sentences to be understood. A book, that is, whose sentences the readers of the *book* must try to see, elucidate and to grasp for *themselves*.

Let us revisit now Wittgenstein's *Investigations* and see how its author entertains the notion of understanding there. In *PI* §92, we find: 'For if we too in these investigations are trying to understand [*verstehen*] the essence of language—its function, its structure,—yet *this* is not what that question has in view.' This remark is strongly suggestive of the later Wittgenstein being concerned with *understanding* the essence of language as his previous self once was in the *Tractatus*, even if the latter work harbours a conception of the essence of language that is radically different from what his *Investigations* harbour on that score. And yet, the *Tractatus* did not bait its hooks with an essence for its readers to swallow, that is, to *understand*. In spite of this curious twist, *PI* §92 advances more cautiously in the sequel: 'For it sees the essence of things not as something that already lies open to view, and becomes *surveyable* (*übersichtlich*) through a process of ordering, but as something that lies *beneath* the surface. Something that lies within, which we perceive when we see right into (*durchschauen*) the thing, and which an analysis is supposed to unearth.' Wittgenstein is more careful here in the sense that he does not bring the notion of understanding positively to bear upon essence as an *Unding*; he speaks instead of *durchschauen*. And in *PI* §97, he speaks of trying to grasp (*begreifen*) the incomparable essence; in *PI* §116, at last, of trying to grasp (*erfassen*) this kind of essence.

Wittgenstein brings the notion of *durchschauen* already into account in *PI* §90: 'We feel as if we had to *see right into* (*durchschauen*) the phenomena: yet our investigation is directed not towards *phenomena*, but rather, as one might say, towards the '*possibilities*' of phenomena.' He adds:

What that means is that we call to mind *the kinds of statement* that we make here about phenomena. So too, Augustine calls to mind the different statements that are made about the duration of events, about their being past, present or future. (These are, of course, not *philosophical statements* about time, the past, the present and the future.)

So what are these statements, if not philosophical statements? They are the kind of things we are so much inclined to say about the phenomena; they make up the *Rohmaterial* for a philosopher such as Wittgenstein. It is because of this material, i.e. because of what we are so much *inclined* to say about the phenomena in our philosophical moments, that Wittgenstein's own investigations are directed, as one might say, towards the 'possibilities' of phenomena. Here, too, then, Wittgenstein wants to make clear that his later concern does not come out of the blue, but is intimately tied to his Tractatarian outlook. Thus, what must take the place of his early concern is not just *some other* concern but precisely the one that is directed toward the so-called 'possibilities' of phenomena. But what should we make of these possibilities and how exactly do they bear upon Wittgenstein's Tractarian concern to enunciate the *Unding*? Well, the feeling of which Wittgenstein speaks—he brings it into account only with respect to his early way of looking at things, clearly suggesting that philosophy tends to take its turn in something that urges itself upon us—fastens one's interest not on the phenomena themselves, i.e. not on what lies open to view, but exclusively on questions concerning their possibilities, that is to say, on what renders each of them 'possible' *überhaupt*—which is not one thing for one phenomenon and another thing for another phenomenon; rather, it is one and the same thing for every phenomenon: the *Unding*. Early Wittgenstein looked through the phenomena, through the phenomena of our language in the first place, but not as if he had taken notice of, and cast aside as being of no interest to him, the kinds of possibilities of the phenomena of which his later self speaks in *PI* § 90. For he simply had no conception of *such* possibilities at the time he began to look through the phenomena of our language, to look through them—up to the point where the treatment of the possibility of one phenomenon amounts to the treatment of the possibility of every phenomenon. But later Wittgenstein, for his own part, harbours a conception of the possibility of phenomenon only to the extent that is necessary to do away with the urge to espouse the *Unding*; or, to put it somewhat provokingly, only to the extent as *he deems* necessary to find his way of out a philosophical muddle. His 'possibilities' are as open to view as the phenomena themselves, but it is all because of the *Rohmaterial* that they *are*, so to speak.

Later Wittgenstein, as we have seen, did not cease to look at language *as* a system. What he did cease to do on his way towards his later conception of language as a system is to say that each such system is in ultimo answerable to the *Unding*, that is, to whatever *Unding*. Just as his early conception of language as a system inhered in his vantage point on language, so does his present conception of language as a system trace back to his vantage point: there is no possibility for any particular phenomenon of our *Lebensform*—*not* to come out as one possibility among other possibilities. Wittgenstein, having dropped his early conception of the possibility of phenomena, is not curious to look at them in order to acquire a new *conception* of their possibility. All he can be curious about now is to see *how* a particular possibility manifests itself in our *Lebensform*. He is interested in questions such as where the boundaries of a certain phenomenon begin and where they end. He is interested in what he calls *Begriffsböschungen*[131], in the individual shading-off of the phenomena of human life, as well as in questions concerning how their possibilities bears upon the world of facts and events. And in all this, the fictitious language-games play a pivotal role; sooner or later their inchoate forms knock on Wittgenstein's door, demanding to being fleshed out as possibilities alongside the possibilities of our own language.

Let us take stock: Wittgenstein sets his sights high. He wants to *describe* our language, he wants to *understand* its workings, he wants to *(dis)solve* philosophical problems, which he regards *as* knots in our thinking about language and the world the moment we become contemplative. Wittgenstein wants to say this and that, and he wants to leave everything as it is; he wants to *destroy* the houses of cards that we build and tend to build ever again, in our philosophical moments. He wants to put bad philosophers out of business[132], and to leave everything as it is. (A bad philosopher is not necessarily one that builds houses of cards!) Wittgenstein wants a lot and my point here is that there is scarcely anything in his cravings and doings that passes for a supererogatory addition to whatever else he wants and sets his face against in philosophy. What he wants is intimately related to whatever else he wants: One may well hold that his philosophy has a negative aspect—to destroy houses of cards; and one may well hold that his philosophy has a positive aspect—to understand the workings of language. Still, these two

---

131   Cf. 'It is hard to understand and to represent conceptual slopes (LWPP I: 752); The phenomenon, that is, the ethnological phenomenon of mathematics, and which of its traits could be conceived as its characteristics, is difficult to describe, especially the transitions (slopes) from characteristic mathematical performances to such ones of a different kind' (MS 123: 11).

132   'A bad philosopher is like a slum landlord. It is my job to put him out of business' (Drury1981:133).

aspects are bound up with each other in the most intimate way. Wittgenstein wants to describe and this craving is certainly no supererogatory addition to his efforts to (dis)solve philosophical problems, any more than his efforts to invent and collate fictitious language-games are. He wants to invent these things and to flesh them out, not for his own amusement, but exactly in order to understand, by means of descriptions of language, and by these things only. They, the fictitious language-games, possibilities as they are meant to be *alongside* the ones that our own language-games symbolize, belong necessarily to his conception of language description, to his conception of understanding language. 'Nothing is more important than the construction of fictitious concepts, which will teach us *at last to understand our own*' (CV: 85).[133] No description of our language is in the offing without fictitious concepts; and nothing comes of understanding our own logical predicament either: without them.

Everything depends in the end on the fictitious language-games, on Wittgenstein's efforts to arrive at proper means of comparisons. This, to be sure, is not to say that everything depends in the end on Wittgenstein's conception of logic, that is, *whether* our language *can* be described or not, for this conception precisely lays down what describing language amounts to and what is involved in the very effort. But once this conception has been laid down and articulated, it is possible to say, in Wittgenstein's case, that everything depends in the end on the fictitious language-games. Logic, according to his lights, is not so much describable itself as that *language is describable* on account of one's logic. Logic, as we might as well say, is not so much *understandable* itself as that our *language is understandable* on account of one's logic. To say that Wittgenstein looks at the language-games as *describable* entities is to say that he treats them as possibilities among other possibilities. But to say that he looks at them as *describable* entities also means that he takes great care to understand them. To commit oneself to them as *describable* entities and to leave it at that, i.e. to go through all kinds of efforts but the one that describes them at last, is no option for *him*, but the kind of *Pathos* on which the bad philosopher feeds like a slum landlord. The ultimate source of stipulations such as 'being describable' and 'being understandable' is Wittgenstein's conception of logic, his vantage point, from which he operates in order to solve philosophical problems. Problems, that is, he looks at, *not* with an irresolute sentiment as to whether they are *solvable*, but, rather, with as resolute

---

133 Emphasis added. Cf. 'Why is it important to depict anomalies accurately? If someone can't do this, that shows that he isn't quite at home yet among the concepts' (RPP II: 606).

a determination as ever before to hold on to them as plain knots in our thinking, come what may.

Wittgenstein's fictitious language-games, his clear and simple language-games, 'are meant to throw light on the *Verhältnisse* in our language' that is, 'through similarities and dissimilarities' (PI: 133). Indeed, it is poss*ible* to set up and to flesh out such language-games alongside one or another language-game of our language. And that *that* is possible is not an *assumption* on Wittgenstein's part, any more than the proposition is that our language-games are describ*able*, understand*able*, or that philosophical problems are solv*able*. But now, if it is possible to set up and to flesh out fictitious language-games alongside our own language-games, the former ones need to appear in a recogniz*able* way. They need to be recognizable *as* possibilities alongside the possibilities that our own language-games pose, as alternative[134] ways of doing things with words. Our language-games are compar*able* pieces of language, on account of Wittgenstein's conception of logic, on account of the eye through which he looks at our language. But that seems to mean that if his fictitious language-games are means of comparison, with respect to our language-games, that the latter are means of recognition, with respect to the fictitious possibilities. Unless the latter is the case, there is no comparison, and without comparison, that is, without the possibility of making comparisons, *everything* comes to naught. But it comes to naught, that is, Wittgenstein is again making nonsense of logic[135], if making comparisons *turns out* to be impos*sible*. But, importantly, *what* decides whether it is impossible? Wittgenstein's difficulty on the playground of inventing and collating language-games may well be said to concern the question whether *he* should let things *count against* his own stipulations.

A clear asymmetry is intimated, as Wittgenstein does not aim at *understanding* the fictitious language-game, but 'merely' calls upon these things as means of comparison so as to understand our language-games. Our own language-games are stipulated as understandable, ultimately on account of what the fictitious language-games are: *recognizable* possibilities; the fictitious language-games are not *understandable*, by us, users of our own language. The fictitious language-games are stipulated possibilities, which is to say that they need to reify as *recognizable* possibilities with respect to our language-games. The agent of their

---

134   Though not necessarily alternative to our own way of playing the game, in the sense that we could in principle play these alternatives *instead* of our own games.

135   An allusion to RPP II: 190, quoted above.

reification is ultimately our own language; or, for that matter, our ability to recognize these things as other possibilities.

If our language-games are *describable* things in the way Wittgenstein's conception of logic stipulates them to be, then the fictitious language-games *must* have an attribute whose stipulation traces back to *this same conception of logic.* What else could this attribute be, but their recognizability? Unless they are recognizable as possibilities alongside the possibilities of our own language-games, the latter ones do not count as describable entities. The question is whether Wittgenstein, in the 1930s, realized all that is involved in the stipulation of such a logical attribute as recognizability, that is, *with respect to the phenomenon of language.* The indeterminacy in his conception of logic, as I should like to say, is ultimately determined by the kind of logical attribute concerning those things on which everything depends at last. But, if true, is recognizability not too strong a determination, not readily 'comprehensible' by a mere abstract reflection on an attribute such as the solvability of the philosophical problems? Well, it depends ultimately on how one *wants* to look at language, on the kind of work on oneself, on how one *wants* to see things, which is not to say that one can do philosophy as one pleases.

What I am hinting at here is the following. If you let loose the dogmatic requirement that nothing counts as language unless its logic comes thus-and-so, as Wittgenstein did in the early 1930s, then you are left with something undecided as to what is to count as *language* now. Put differently, if you stipulate that logic need not necessarily come in the way it figures in our own language-games, you have left something important undetermined. Thus, if you do not determine positively that logic *must* be so-and-so, the resulting image that language under that condition presents becomes relevant, to say the least. In the extreme case you need not *accept* any construct other than your own language as a language. At the other extreme you find yourself having no scruples to *accept* nearly everything alongside your own language as another language. And if you want to occupy a position somewhere between these two extremes, as I think Wittgenstein *wants* to, you need to *determine* what counts as another language alongside the possibility of our own language. But this determination, and that is the whole point, should not be a matter of *pre*determination; it should not be decided in advance, that is to say, long before you enter on the playground of inventing and collating language-games.

The point to observe, then, is that Wittgenstein's later conception of logic does not determine which 'languages' count and which do not count as language. But it has not failed to lay such a determination down. Rather, this conception of logic 'merely' determines that it is making comparisons between language-games that determines which constructions count and which do not count as a way of doing something particular with words. Logic only sets the stage for making comparisons, and once the stage has been set it is not up to *logic* again to determine which constructions count and which do not count as a way of doing something particular with words. But that means that there can be no escape from making comparisons, from the playground of inventing and collating language-games, and to think that there is such an escape is to misunderstand Wittgenstein's conception of logic. Now notice the kind of logical indeterminacy at issue in the following stipulations.

> Language is not defined for us as an arrangement fulfilling a definite purpose. Rather "language" is for us a name for a collection, and I understand it as including German, English and so on, and further various systems of signs which have more or less affinity [*Verwandtschaft*] with these languages. (Z: 322)

> I want to say: it is *above all* the apparatus of our ordinary language, of our word-language, that we call "language"; and then other things by analogy or comparability with it. (PI: 494)

> How did I arrive at the concept 'sentence' or 'language'? Surely only through the languages that I have learnt.—But they seem to me in a certain sense to have led beyond themselves, for I am now able to construct new language, e.g. to invent words.—So such constructions also belong to the concept of language. But only because that is how I want to fix the concept. (Z: 325)

What Wittgenstein wants to fix—for reasons of philosophy—is *that* certain constructions also belong to the concept of language. But that means that this fixing of the concept of language cannot fix *which* constructions count as language and which do not. And that only means that the fixing of the former concept is no fixing unless there is a determinate way to fix, on the playground of inventing and collating language-games, *which* constructions count as language and which do not. There is a clear indeterminacy in Wittgenstein's later conception of logic, but if the indeterminacy of the kind intimated here now governs the philosophical game, there is a real danger for the philosopher to become dogmatic through the backdoor, so to speak. For while indeterminacy precisely *means* to open the front door for considering alternative ways of doing this or that thing with words, the philosopher might well want to *insist* now, for each of our ways of doing something particular with words, on the possibility of at least one fictitious construct as exemplifying a way of doing it *differently* from how we do it ourselves. He might well want to *insist* on such possibilities, that is, in the face of his own difficulties in realizing them.

But, of course, where this dogmatism-via-the-backdoor tends to creep in—and we can well imagine why Wittgenstein would not easily give way to such critics who claim that *any* attempt to invent a truly alternative way of doing mathematics is doomed to fail and that *any* such attempt concerning the field of psychology is likewise doomed to fail—, where this dogmatism tends to creep in, it precisely points towards the kind of determination that should ultimately atone for the indeterminacy in Wittgenstein's conception of logic. For what else could atone for it but the determination saying that it *depends on us*, that is, on our conceptual inventiveness together with our *willingness* to recognize alternative ways of doing things with words? There is no recognition, as one wants to say, without any willingness to recognize. On the other hand, what is this willingness without our language, without our faculty of building words and using sentences? But let us also ask what this faculty amounts to itself, without our willingness, this capacity for room and manoeuvre, without our conceptual inventiveness, which seems to come to naught unless *language* puts limits to it? But, perhaps, one now feels that all this intimated dependency cannot be claimed without more ado. A philosopher needs to investigate the matter first! Very well; but what if Wittgenstein takes up the challenge? He will find himself inventing language-games, sooner or later, putting one fictitious alternative alongside our own possibilities.

In the above passage, Wittgenstein says that the languages he has learned seem to him in a certain sense to have led beyond themselves, *for*, he adds, 'I am now able to construct new language, e.g. to invent words.—So such constructions also belong to the concept of language. But only because that is how I *want* to fix the concept' (emphasis mine). Indeed, *that* languages lead beyond themselves gives every appearance of being an objective fact, one that philosophers had better recognize before long and build their way of looking on. And yet, the point is precisely this: *that* languages lead beyond themselves is the kind of determination with which *Wittgenstein wants* to enter the philosophical stage. His words remind us of what we have seen him promulgating in the second chapter: 'Work on philosophy – like work in architecture in many respects – is really more work on oneself. On one's own conception. On how one sees things. (And what one demands from them.)' The *that*, then, i.e. the concept of language with which Wittgenstein enters the philosophical stage, is the means with which he *wants* to work on himself. The invention of fictitious language-games concerns the *how*. The *how* should make good the indeterminacy of the *that*. But there is no *how* unless *someone* determines the making good. Thus, trivial as it seems to be, Wittgenstein speaks of *languages* that lead beyond *themselves*, but this leading beyond is a matter that lies in charge of their users. Our language may well be said to lead *beyond* itself, its concept may be determined thus, but from what moment on a fictitious deviation from our language-game lies *beyond our recognition* is what one needs to find out, to work on. So our language should be said to lead beyond itself with respect to us, users of our language, Wittgenstein included. Unless there are limits of recognition, there is no room for Wittgenstein to work on how he wants to see the world. He may well say *that* languages lead beyond themselves, as a *determination* of his concept of language to work with, it is still to be seen how much freedom there is for him to do philosophy. In other words, if our language is determined as 'intrinsically' leading beyond itself, it should be clear that this leading beyond is vacuous unless it is made dependent on a certain capacity of its users, but then this capacity cannot be anything in which our language fails to play a determinative role itself. Our ability to recognize does not lie beyond the nature of our language and the extent in which our language leads beyond itself does not lie beyond our ability to recognize. It might be true that our language puts such restraints on our ability, or, for that matter, willingness, to recognize other constructions as possibilities *alongside* the possibilities that our own language-games signify that no significant construction passes our judgement as representing an alternative way of doing this or that with words. In that case we should say that Wittgenstein is making all logic into nonsense. Whether it will turn out to be nonsense is not apparent when one fixes one's concept of language: one just needs to go into the field and *look and see*. Needless to say, there is no going into field unless one fixes one's concept of language first, be it thus or so. For without the latter one cannot even be said to make all *logic* into nonsense; one is just muddled.—Once more Wittgenstein's words in *PI* §130:

> The language-games are rather set up as objects of comparison which, by similarity and dissimilarity, are meant to throw a light on die *Verhältnisse* of our language.

The indeterminacy of which we have been speaking resides in the clause 'similarity and dissimilarity'. Wittgenstein has not stipulated what counts as similar and what does not count as similar. It was not until he moved to the playground of inventing and collating language-games that he began to write remarks such as: '[o]ther concepts, though akin to ours, might seem *very* queer to us; deviations, namely, from the usual in an unusual *direction*' (RPP II: 693). Thus, a fictitious language-game may well strike us as very *similar* indeed to one of ours, and yet, we are not compelled to accept it as an *analogue*. And *would* we accept tennis without a ball

as an *analogue* of tennis with a ball?[136] Tennis without a ball: What is the point of
the language-game? That is, what is the point of the fictitious language-game, on
which so much depends at last? Indeed, what the indeterminacy in Wittgenstein's
conception of logic leaves open is the *Witz* of the game; it does not determine what
a language-game looks like. And this indeterminacy, which is precisely the kind
of thing to overcome (*überwinden*) on the playground of inventing and collating
language-games, gives rise to considerations such as the following:

> Could we imagine that people might have a concept of pretence that doesn't coincide
> with ours? – But would it then be the concept of pretence? – Well, it could be a concept
> related to ours [*ein dem unsern verwandter Begriff sein*].
>
> But aren't some of the traits of (such) a concept more essential, others less so? That is: if
> one changes this trait it will still be called "pretence" – but no longer if one changes *that*.
> And here *naming* [*Benennen*] means an attitude]. (LWPP I: 224–225)

The crucial question here, I think, is this: *Whose* attitude: the attitude of us, users
of our own language, or the attitude of the philosopher who wants so much as to
see other possibilities alongside those of our own language. The philosopher may
well *want* this or that, but our language is not without its own requirements, so
to speak. Of course, we shall need to return to his issue.

What I have been emphasizing is that the following is not an *assumption* in Wittgenstein's philosophy: *That* language-games need not be shaped by the kind of
logic that actually shapes ours. It is not an assumption, and yet, it is more often
than not looked upon as such. Consider, for instance, the following passage from
Malcolm Budd's book *Wittgenstein's Philosophy of Psychology*.

> Now the fact that the use of the words 'believe', 'expect', 'fear', 'hope', 'intend', 'think' is
> variegated means that it is possible to distinguish within the employment of a single
> psychological verb different kinds of use. It would therefore be possible for there to be
> a language in which these different kinds of use are marked by the employment of dif-
> ferent words, so that where in our language a single word is used in a number of ways,
> in this other language a number of words are used, each with a unitary employment. If
> this were so, then:
>
>> Perhaps the concepts of such a language would be more suitable for understand-
>> ing psychology than are the concepts of our language.[137]
>
> But Wittgenstein showed no interest in the construction of a language of this kind. The
> reason for this was not that he held a special brief for the concepts of our own language.

---

136   Here I exploit Wittgenstein's example 'tennis without a ball' for my own purposes.
137   Cf. PI: 577.

We have just seen that he did not regard our own psychological concepts as being specially suitable for understanding psychology, and a language in which people as it were thought more definitely than we do would make the task easier. Moreover, he believed that it is important not to assume that the concepts of our own language are the uniquely *right* ones for intelligent human beings to use. On the contrary, he argued that if we imagine certain general facts of nature to be different from what they are, then concepts different from our own will appear *natural* to us. Nevertheless, his own investigations in philosophy were directed towards the concepts we actually operate with. And the reason for this should be clear: he was interested in language only in so far as it is the source of philosophical difficulties. Philosophical problems about the nature of the mind arise, Wittgenstein believed, from the confusion about the use of our own psychological vocabulary, and this confusion can be dissipated only by gaining a synoptic view of our own language of psychology.[138]

This passage commingles truth, error, and misunderstanding. Budd writes that Wittgenstein 'believed that it is important not to assume that the concepts of our own language are the uniquely *right* ones for intelligent human beings to use. On the contrary, he argued that if we imagine certain general facts of nature to be different from what they are, then concepts different from our own will appear *natural* to us.'[139] But what Budd enunciates here as an assumption, namely that the concepts of our own language *are* the uniquely right ones, is what in Wittgenstein's own concern and presentation forces itself upon us in the form of a powerful *urge* that keeps troubling our minds *time and again*. And that it comes in this hard and cunning way, at least so according to Wittgenstein's lights, is not in the least trivial, for, as we have been emphasizing, *he* seeks to describe the workings of our language precisely *in opposition to* 'an urge to misunderstand them' (PI: 109). Budd, though, takes Wittgenstein to be suggesting that if we imagine certain general facts of nature to be different from what they are, we would soon stop *assuming* that our concepts are uniquely right. A few prompts of the imagination—and we could direct our investigations towards the concepts we actually operate with. But what, as Budd had better ask, should we say of these *investigations*? What are the possibilities that our concepts signify, now that we no longer assume that they are 'uniquely right'? What does describing our language-games amount to, now that we no longer assume that they are 'uniquely right'? Why describe them at all, now that we no longer assume that they are 'uniquely right'?

---

138 Malcolm Budd, *Wittgenstein's Philosophy of Psychology* (London and New York: Routledge, 1989), 6f.

139 Budd refers here to RPP I: 45–9 and PPF: 366, to which we shall draw our own attention in the next chapter.

Budd's muddled view on the role of Wittgenstein's fictitious language-games is also evident from the following: 'Nevertheless, his own investigations in philosophy were directed towards the concepts we actually operate with. And the reason for this should be clear: he was interested in language only in so far as it is the source of philosophical difficulties.'[140] The trouble with this way of rendering Wittgenstein's view is that his fictitious language-games drop out as irrelevant, i.e. as supererogatory additions to his sustained efforts to dissipate what Budd calls philosophical confusions. For the relevance of the fictitious language-games is now confined to help us see *that* the concepts of our language are not the uniquely right ones. And Wittgenstein's interest in these fictitious concepts, according to Budd, *is* really confined to this specific task because it is *our* language that is the source of our philosophical confusions. 'Philosophical problems about the nature of the mind arise, Wittgenstein believed, from the confusion about the use of our own psychological vocabulary, and this confusion can be dissipated only by gaining a synoptic view of our own language of psychology.' But the irony here is that Wittgenstein is interested in other languages, including fictitious ones, precisely because he is interested in our language only insofar as it troubles him. Wittgenstein's 'synoptic view of our own language' draws on fictitious language-games. The fictitious hides the real workings of our own language as long as the fictitious is not real, i.e. actually fleshed out.

Budd is right to harp on Wittgenstein's concern with our own language, and yet he fails to see the necessity of fictitious language-game to participate in a synoptic view, in what Wittgenstein calls an *übersichtliche Darstellung*. We have seen Wittgenstein emphasizing that 'Nothing is more important than the construction of fictitious concepts, which will teach us at last to understand our own.' The intimacy of connection that Wittgenstein brings into account here between the notion of understanding and the construction of fictitious concepts, i.e. fictitious language-games, is what his concept of an *übersichtliche Darstellung* lays down and commits us to exploit.

> A main source of our failure to understand is that we don't have *an overview* of the use of our words. – Our grammar is deficient in surveyability. A surveyable representation produces just that understanding which consists in 'seeing connections'. Hence the importance of finding and inventing *intermediate links* [*Zwischengliedern*].
>
> The concept of a surveyable representation is of fundamental significance for us. It characterizes [*bezeichnet*] the way we represent things [*our Darstellungsform*], how we look at matters. (Is this a 'Weltanschauung'?). (PI: 122)

---

140   This clause paraphrases Wittgenstein's words from the early 1930s, namely that he is 'interested in language only insofar as it gives [him] trouble' (AWL: 97)

Not surprisingly, there is much to say about this famous remark, if only because there is much confusion about it in the secondary literature. For now, though, I will confine myself to a few fundamental observations, beginning with another famous remark: 'Philosophy must not interfere in any way with the actual use of language, so it can in the end only describe it' (PI: 124). Indeed, if it is description *only* that sees the end of the day, it is precisely one or another *übersichtliche Darstellung* that sees it. As we remarked in Chapter 2, descriptions make up the coping stone in Wittgenstein's dialectical edifice, and we might well add now that they do so as constituting items in one *übersichtliche Darstellung* or another. Wittgenstein's concept of an *übersichtliche Darstellung* is a descriptive concept par excellence; it is the only *descriptive* concept that he has and harbours. It relates internally to his dialectical edifice. Speaking of the fundamental importance that the concept has for philosophers, Wittgenstein clearly suggests that although there are various *übersichtliche Darstellungen*, they are all answerable, in his philosophical approach, to one and the same concept. There is no such thing as *the* surveyable representation, for how a representation will turn out to be depends on the kind of aspect troubling one's mind. It may be one aspect, it may be another aspect, but more often than not it is an array of closely interrelated aspects that troubles a mind such as Wittgenstein's. Be that as it may, Wittgenstein works his way up, time and again, only to see in the end some connections, to have before him an order, not *the* order (PI: 132). Surveyable representations come in various forms, but this is not to suggest that there is no end to their variety.

What I am suggesting is that everything of importance in Wittgenstein's approach to language culminates in his *concept* of a surveyable representation. It shows us how he seeks to describe our language as well as how he thinks about understanding its very workings. All types of a surveyable representation fall under one and the same concept, and Wittgenstein's stipulation is that his uncommon way of looking commands no means of *understanding* our language-games but by surveyable representations. There is understanding only at the end of the day—that is, only when the language-game under attention *is being* seen, described, as one possibility alongside other possibilities. Thus, his words 'a surveyable representation produces precisely that *kind* of understanding which consists in "seeing connections"' should not be taken to suggest that, within Wittgenstein's approach, there are kinds of understanding *alongside* the form that his fundamental concept of a surveyable representation stipulates. The exclusive character of Wittgenstein's concept of a surveyable representation ultimately inheres in the exclusive character of his conception of a logical possibility. This brings us once more to the question of how his fictitious language-games bear on his concept of a surveyable representation.

Wittgenstein's surveyable representations *exploit the limits* of his way of looking at things. What they exploit, and are committed to do, is *that* the language-game is looked upon *as* one possibility among other possibilities. What Wittgenstein's *concept* of a surveyable *representation* earmarks is a *that*; what a surveyable representation earmarks itself is the *how* of a language-game as a possibility among other possibilities. Just as Wittgenstein's *concept* of a *Begriffsschrift* (*Tractatus*) characterizes a point of view, namely his beholding of the world as a limited whole, so does his concept of a surveyable representation characterize a point of view, *one* point of view.[141] A surveyable representation aims at taking away from the language-game under investigation the disquieting appearance it exerts on us as soon as the philosophical mood has dawned upon our minds, and these appearances may be various.[142] *The* disquieting appearance, though, which has crucially added to the characterization of Wittgenstein's *concept* of a surveyable representation is that our logical predicament is the way it is *and cannot possible be otherwise*. Hence the *fundamental* importance of fictitious language-games.

To be sure, the fictitious language-games intimated here are not to be confused with the fictitious concepts of which Budd speaks in the *first* part of the passage quoted above, the ones that Wittgenstein addresses as follows:

> We could imagine a language in which different verbs were consistently used in these cases. And similarly, more than one verb where we speak of 'believing', 'hoping', and so on. The concepts of such a language would perhaps be more suitable for understanding psychology than are the concepts of our language' (PI: 577)

The fictitious language addressed here still draws on the same kind of logical indeterminacy as does our own language. True, some boundaries are more definite in the fictitious language, but there is still indeterminacy as that there is no general agreement whether a person is e.g. in pain or not. That is why Wittgenstein writes 'perhaps' in the above passage. The fictitious concept as the polar opposite of our own indeterminate concept, however, is not stipulated as *perhaps* possible.

---

141   'Every particular notation stresses some particular point of view' (BB: 28).

142   'I group language-games around certain parts of language, fill up as it were gaps, so as to moderate the remarkable character of the particular appearances and to take it away from them' (MS 123: 45).

4.4 From without

One prominent feature of Wittgenstein's concept of *eine übersichtliche Darstellung* is that it stipulates the comparing of language-games with each other as an activity of looking at them *from without*. Trivial as this observation may be, it is precisely the kind of thing to latch onto if we wish to understand Wittgenstein's troubles on the playground of inventing and collating language-games. Wittgenstein moves as it were over this playground, looking at the language-games to be compared *from without*, rather than at their workings *from within* one of them. Of course, only with respect to a characterization such as that he looks at our own language-games from without can we, users of these games, be said to look at them from within. And that means that Wittgenstein, the philosopher, should make clear what *he* means by looking at our language-games *from without*, which is precisely what he does. Consider, for instance, the following remark: 'If you want to understand the nature of mathematics, do not look out of its windows into the open but at it from without.'[143] To look at mathematics from without is not to look at it as a mathematician. Yet that is precisely what mathematicians do, and find so difficult to withhold themselves from doing, when they think about the nature of mathematics: to look at their own practice from a *mathematical* point of view, that is, from the same point of view from which they do mathematics. It is for that reason, as Wittgenstein regularly puts it, that mathematicians disqualify themselves as capable philosophers. 'What the philosopher needs is patience with his suffering from uncertainty. Mathematicians, while addressing a philosophical problem, are too impatient with bearing the lack of clarity. They want to be freed from it as soon as possible, which is why they cannot solve the problem, but only cover it up.'[144]

Wittgenstein looks at mathematics from without, which is what he does as well with respect to the psychological sections of our language: he looks at their language-games from his uncommon way of looking at things, the same vantage point from which he considers *all* language-games exercising a disquieting influence on his mind. He could not possibly look at mathematics from without only to look at our psychological language-games from within, for then he might not be said to be doing in the latter case what he might well be said to be doing in the former case, namely to guard himself against being toppled over into considering the language-game from a point of view determined by its features, or what he

---

143 'Wer das Wesen der Mathematik verstehen will, muß nicht aus ihrem Fenster heraus, sondern von außen hinein schauen' (MS 123: 18).
144 MS 162b:35rf.

takes its features to be. We would only invite confusion if we were to look upon certain language-games from without and upon certain others from within. There is nothing more confused than that, save for thinking that this difference of approach is obligatory because of the differences between the language-games.

If looking at mathematics from without means *not* to look at it as a mathematician, how should we look at mathematics in our capacity as philosophers? Not looking at it in the capacity as mathematicians does not yet determine a point of view. Moreover, if we look at the language-game from without we do not stop being users of our language. We can cast off the mathematical skin, we can perhaps cast off another skin, but it has to stop somewhere. Wittgenstein is clearly aware of this when he says:

> If we use the ethnological approach, does that mean we are saying that philosophy is ethnology? No, it only means that we are taking up our position far outside, in order to see things *more objectively*. (CV: 45)

Wittgenstein regularly turns to the notion of the ethnological approach, or, for that matter, to that of the anthropologist,[145] but in so doing he does not articulate anything new in regard to his *fundamental* concept of an *übersichtliche Darstellung*; he merely puts some grammatical glosses on that concept. Thus, in the above passage, he again avails himself of the inside-outside metaphor, which finds further articulation here in terms of seeing things *more objectively*. The suggestion is that to take up a position 'far outside' is to move away from the bewitching influences that language keeps exercising on the philosopher's mind, but so the suggestion is that in thus moving away one also leaves behind the sphere from which, as a user of one's colloquial language, one looks upon its workings and the world at large. It *seems* simple enough: just take up your position far outside and you render your view on language and the world as objective as you like. Yet what Wittgenstein intimates, here and elsewhere, is precisely the *clash* between how he as a philosopher *desires* to see things and how he, as a user of his own language, sees things and cannot help seeing them whenever language begins to exert its disquieting influences on him. This calls to mind once more Wittgenstein's dictum that work on philosophy is actually more of a kind of work

---

145   Cf. 'We shall see contradiction in a quite different light if we look at its occurrences and its consequences as it were anthropologically—than if we look at it with a mathematician's exasperation [*Entrüstung*]. That is to say, we shall look at it differently, if we try to *describe* how the contradiction influences language-games, than if we look at it from the point of view of the mathematical law-giver' (RFM: 220; amended translation).

on oneself: 'On one's own conception [*Auffassung*]. On the way one sees things. (And what one demands [*verlangt*] of them)' (PO: 160f.). He *wants* to see our concepts as possibilities among other possibilities, a need that already makes itself felt on the playground of describing language-games, where he keeps staring at the *Tatsachenkörper* as what he *wants* to see right side up, that is, *against* his own accustomed way of doing so, *against* the urge to misunderstand it, and *against* the tendency to deceive himself.[146]

To be sure, Wittgenstein, as we have seen in second chapter, is as deeply interested in enunciating how our language strikes us in the daily walk of life as he is in enunciating how our language strikes us in our pursuit of philosophical chimeras. But at long last Wittgenstein wants to see what our language looks like to him, in *his* capacity as philosopher, working on himself as he *wants* to do. What does our language look like once *freed* from the disquieting appearances that are associated with contemplation? For what appears so essential to us, as users of our language-games to begin with, is more often than not *not* at all essential to their workings, and what we, in the same capacity as users, have always deemed irrelevant, or not even deigned a glance, may well be decisive for how we play our language-games from the 'anthropological point of view'.

> But why did I say that consensus is '<u>essential</u> for arithmetic'? It is not essential to me while doing arithmetic, but that is what it is for the anthropological phenomenon of arithmetic.[147]

Consensus does not look essential to me when I use my language: I just calculate as I have always done, and if people around me begin to raise objections to my findings, well, I perhaps should feel sorry for *them*. Thus, for me 12×12 makes 144, no matter whether people around agree with me or not. However, consensus is essential for the practice of calculating if I look at my own language from without, from a point with respect to which my status as a user of my own language forfeits all title to be called an objective point of view on the workings of my language. What is true here for mathematics also holds true for our psychological ways of doing things with words. The *lack* of consensus is as essential

---

146   The demands of which Wittgenstein speaks in his remark on philosophy as work on oneself are clearly brought out in the following: 'Let me hold on to <u>this that I do not want to deceive myself</u>. That is, a certain demand <u>which I acknowledge as such</u> I want to admit to myself again and again as a demand' (PPO 2003: 175). Cf. 'The art of the philosopher is not to be cheated out of his puzzlement before it's really cleared up' (MS 157b: 30vf.).

147   MS 162b: 30r.

for *these* ways as consensus is for our ways of doing mathematics. The so-called 'laws of evidence'[148] at play with respect to our concept of pain are just as objective as consensus is for $12 \times 12 = 144$. And *that* is what renders it possible to compare utterly different language-games with each other, a possibility that Wittgenstein did not pass over in silence.

Wittgenstein looks at our language-games from without—and it is from without that he must look at the *fictitious* language-games as well, for only then does it become possible to *compare* them with each other. The point is simply this: It is *language-games* that are being compared with each other, rather than anything else. The subject-matter under Wittgenstein's *final* comparing activities is not how our own language strikes us *as users* in the daily course of life with how a fictitious language strikes *its very users*, any more than how the world strikes us as users of a language with how the world strikes the (fictitious) users of a fictitious language. It is ultimately *language-games* that are under Wittgenstein's comparing activities: not pictures, nor points of views, nor impressions, nor our subjectivity with other people's subjectivity, but *language-games*. What matters is these things, at least for Wittgenstein, and anything else has simply not been stipulated by his *fundamental* concept of an *übersichtliche Darstellung*. Language-games, I emphasize, thus *not* minds or brain processes, any more than our subjective point of view with such ones of the fictitious stripes and colours; language-games, *not* sentences or grammatical remarks, however nicely polished they are, however impressive we may at times find Wittgenstein's prose to be. Speaking of language-games, we speak of the depth-grammar of our language-games with the grammars of the language-games *to be invented*. So it is the comparing of language-games with each other that determines the position of the philosophical observer from without. In other words, the sense of looking at language *from without* is ultimately determined by *fictitious language-games* as objects of comparison, and any other sense is *not* provided for by Wittgenstein's fundamental concept. It is a sense that is *internal* to the language-games as objects of comparison; any other sense is sheer confusion.

What is it like to be a bat? What is the feeling like of having absolute pitch? These are the kinds of questions that Wittgenstein does not try to answer but treats as *Rohmaterial*: questions that quickly lead us astray and require a thorough philosophical treatment rather than an answer.

> Let us imagine men who express a colour intermediate between red and yellow, say by
> means of a fraction in a kind of binary notation like this: R, LLRL and the like, where we

---

148   Cf. Chapter 5.

have (say) yellow on the right, and red on the left.—These people learn how to describe shades of colour in this way in the kindergarten, how to use such descriptions in picking colours out, in mixing them, etc. They would be related to us roughly as people with absolute pitch are to those who lack it. *They can do* what we cannot. (Z: 368)

And here one would like to say: "But then, is it imaginable? Of course, the *behaviour* is! But is the inner process, the experience of colour?" And it is difficult to see what to say in answer to such a question. Could people without absolute pitch have guessed at the existence of people with absolute pitch? (Z: 369)

'But is the inner process [imaginable], the experience of colour?'—This, then, is not the kind of question for which Wittgenstein sees himself setting out for the playground of inventing and collating language-games. On the contrary, it is the kind of question that he treats with utter suspicion, with a philosophical nose trained to smell a very fishy air about the question and the like.

We are here describing a language-game that we cannot learn' (Z §339); "In that case something quite different must be going on in him, something that we are not acquainted with."—*This shews us* what we go by in determining whether something that takes place 'in another' is different from, or the same as in ourselves. This shews us *what we go by* in judging inner processes' (Z: 340).

Wittgenstein, in the quoted passage preceding this one, writes: '*They can do* what we cannot.' David Cerbone, in his contribution to the *Oxford Handbook of Wittgenstein*, writes: 'Because this community "can do what we cannot do", the question arises as to how far we can go in imagining such beings in terms of imaginatively occupying their point of view on the world.'[149] Perhaps this question arises, perhaps because we feel urged to raise such questions, but imagining certain beings in terms of *imaginatively occupying their point of view on the world* is not the kind of exercise that Wittgenstein's fundamental concept of an *übersichtliche Darstellung* asks us to go through, just to compare that point of view with our own. It does not ask us to do *that*, nor should any *übersichtliche Darstellung* give rise to the urge to go through such a cerebral ceremony. An *übersichtliche Darstellung*, in Wittgenstein's sense of the word, is truly a place where matters should finally come to rest. It should not give rise to questions and troubles of its own, disquietudes that the philosopher needs to address in turn. *If* Wittgenstein feels troubled to raise such questions as Cerbone brings to the fore, he seeks to find peace in his mind by seeing *language-games* alongside *language-games*, ours

---

149   David Cerbone, 'Wittgenstein and Idealism', in Oskari Kuusela and Marie McGinn, eds., *The Oxford Handbook of Wittgenstein* (Oxford: Oxford University Press, 2011), 326.

alongside fictitious ones. And if, after the comparison done, he still feels the need to raise such questions, or if the sight of his *übersichtliche Darstellung* prompts him to raise them for the first time, he has done a poor job indeed.[150]

Now although Wittgenstein moves over the playground of inventing and collating language-games in his capacity as philosopher, he is and remains a user of his own language for all that, a user of the language under comparison. His position from without is that of the philosopher, but he is not a philosopher without position in the objects under his comparison. What is to be compared are still languages, rather than for instance chairs or tables, objects to which the philosopher might add a fictitious possibility of his own making. It is *language-games* that he compares with each other, ours with ones of his own making, ones in which he participates as a user himself with ones in which he does not or cannot participate. It is his own language with its ramifying connections and bewitching influences that prompts him to comparing activities in the first place, for *it* bewitches him and forces his mind to think along certain characteristic lines in moments of philosophical reflection. Recognizing that his own language does do such curious things with him, Wittgenstein, rather than turning his back on it, turns to its means and authority as what should finally free his mind from its influences and bewitchments, thus turns to his own language as the resource *under comparison* as well as to it as the resource that should provide him with the *objects of comparison*. He is anxious to free his own mind, but *only* 'by the resources of our language' (PI: 109). True, Wittgenstein could avail himself of a medicine, he could avail himself of another medicine should the first be to no avail, but that is not the method of redemption that he seeks. It is deceit, it is a sham; it is to cut things short, and Wittgenstein cannot walk with such a facade through the aisles of a philosophical college.

---

150 Cerbone often gets it wrong in his contribution. Cf. 'This is not to say that Wittgenstein is not *troubled* by the possibility of other-mindedness in terms of wondering how far we can go in envisaging such a possibility. […]. What troubles Wittgenstein is the idea that our capacity to describe practices involving "quite different concepts" is severally limited owing to the rather straightforward fact that our descriptions and attempts at imagining will naturally be couched in terms of our own' (*ibid,* 327f.). I want to say: if our own means to describe were not *that* 'severally limited', were so to speak broader than they actually are, it is *with respect to* these 'broader' means that the notion of "quite different concepts" arises again—as well as a Wittgenstein that would be interested in them *in order to describe our concepts*. (More on this issue in part II of the present study.)

And the question now is: What does it mean to say that Wittgenstein *exploits* the means and authority of the language he uses, of the language that bewitches his mind, so as to free himself from his bewitchment? We need, I think, to draw several important distinctions. The first point concerns Wittgenstein's saying that he takes up his 'position far outside, in order to see things *more objectively.*' *More* objectively with respect to what? Wittgenstein may try as he might to see things more or less objectively within the same frame of mind in which he uses his own language all day long. But that is not the kind of frame ('spirit') in which he aspires to find the redeeming word (see above). He may also try as he might to see things more or less objectively within that frame of mind that conceives of the language-game as autonomous, but in that frame he does not look upon his own language *more* objectively with respect to the frame of mind in which he avails himself of his daily language. Taking up his position far outside, all he should be said to have done is to have *changed* his way of looking at things.

Second, Wittgenstein appears to exploit nothing but the resources of our language for his philosophical purpose. But what he primarily exploits is his own vantage point on our language. Our language furnishes the *material,* whereas Wittgenstein's way of looking at it furnishes the *means* to exploit that *material* for his philosophical purpose. What he exploits, and must exploit, is precisely the simile underlying his vantage point on language, the thing that he has laid down in the beginning (cf. § 1.5). Of course, speaking of our language both as the resource *under comparison* and as the resource that should furnish the objects of comparison, we are suggestive of our language as what leads beyond itself *simpliciter,* that is, of it being an institution that just possesses a kind of elasticity that the philosopher can exploit so as to avail himself of the objects of comparison which he requires to cast a light on his own language and 'innate' elasticity. But the *kind* of elasticity that Wittgenstein exploits lies precisely in the simile, in what he has laid down in as articulated a form as possible, and on whose articulations his uncommon way of looking at things builds and thrives. On the other hand, and that is actually the second point, one can well change one's frame of mind in any desired direction or for any desired purpose, but each frame remains ultimately answerable to the frame in which one uses one's own language in the daily walk of life. Wittgenstein may well provide himself with the kind of simile that he *wants* to exploit for his philosophical purpose, he cannot help but that the frame of mind in which this exploitation should come to pass, the frame through which he looks at his own language, and in which the simile should find its application, is ultimately rendered possible by the daily workings of his own language. Our language furnishes the material that Wittgenstein seeks to exploit philosophically, through the simile underlying his way of looking at language, but our language provides him also with the means to exploit that simile in the first place. If we ask what these means are, all we can say is that is our language itself, or that is constituted by our language, the language *we use* in the daily course of life, rather than the language that we want *to make use of* at a particular occasion. It is Wittgenstein's own language that allows him to have and to cultivate the frame of mind in which he seeks the redeeming word, that frame or spirit through which he looks at language in his capacity as philosopher. In other words, there appears to be something *transcendental* about our *colloquial language*, about its *subjective character*, about the way we operate with it—and it on us—in daily life. That is to say, there appears to be something transcendental about our own colloquial language with regard to Wittgenstein's *comparing activities*, with regard to his position far outside. It is the language that he uses all day long that renders that position ultimately possible. Indeed, all this would be trivial, were it not so obscure.

Third, the *comparing* institution on Wittgenstein's playground of inventing and collating language-games is not an element *from without* itself; rather it is Wittgenstein *together with what his own language is for him, for us, users of our language*. Wittgenstein wants to see language from without but the institution that does the seeing and recognizing in the end, from that so-called position, is *not* what he calls the dept-grammar (see also below). It is the *liveliness* of his own language, his familiarity with his own language, including its capacity for suggestion and undertone, for bewitchment and influence. It is not entirely up to him, Wittgenstein, in his capacity as philosopher, to 'decide' whether a fictitious language-game is still a way of doing *this* or *that* particular thing with words. His own language has an important part to play here: in the way he sees things as a user of his own language, and, to continue the play on Wittgenstein's own words here, in what he demands from himself as a philosopher, thus as someone who does not want to deceive himself. *We*, users of our own language, have no demands on the way we *want* to see the world, except for the 'demands' that our own concepts symbolize as the means that railroad our daily way of looking at things. There is perhaps some irony in the fact that Wittgenstein, in his capacity as philosopher, seeks to underscore the importance of the railroading character of our own concepts. But in this same capacity as a philosopher, user of his own language as he remains for all that, he also tries to describe fictitious possibilities alongside the possibilities that our concepts are and symbolize; that is, he cannot but try to see these fictitious possibilities by exactly those means that railroad his own way of looking at things in the daily course of life, or by exactly those means

230

in which the railroading capacities of his own concepts have not lost their life and importance.[151]

Wittgenstein *wants* to see the *Tatsachenkörper* right side up; he wants to see the thing thus because he wants to see how language really is. To see the thing right side up is to see the *so-called* objective side of our language. He *wants* to see it right side up because anything less than seeing it thus is to face a (potentially) misleading image. To see the thing right side up is to see how our language really is; to see the thing the way we see it in the daily course of life is not to see the thing right side up. The latter way of seeing it, which is our accustomed way, is a hindrance to seeing the thing right side up, and a sure-fire path towards building houses of cards in philosophy. But if the ultimate source of the divide between the so-called objective and the subjective side of the *Tatsachenkörper* is the divide between *wanting* to see the thing right side up and our *being accustomed* to see the thing the way we do as users of our own language, and if the ultimate source of this divide is ultimately Wittgenstein's demand of not *wanting* to deceive himself, how then, I wonder, could there be such a thing as right side up? For the so-called objective side of language has thus far only been defined

---

151   I shall return to this complicated matter in the second part of the present study, for now the above, admittedly rather vague discussion, should do for what follows. Still, one thing should be made explicit right now. Speaking of the railroading character of our concepts, I am somewhat suggestive of a great difference between Wittgenstein's notion of surveyability of proof in mathematics and his notion of surveyability as enunciated in *PI* §122. In fact, I do think that there is a great difference between these two notions. The defining feature of the former surveyability, as Wittgenstein endorses it, is that it sees only *one* possibility; the defining feature of the latter is that it aims at seeing more than one possibility, namely the one that our own language-game embodies alongside fictitious possibilities. But although the former notion endorses the importance of seeing one possibility only, it does not exclude other possibilities. But then these other possibilities are not part of the surveyability of the proof itself, thus at the level where the mathematician plies his trade. These so-called other possibilities come into account only when a philosopher of Wittgenstein's inclinations endeavours to understand what mathematics *is*: by looking at its grammatical commerce from without, by looking at it as one possibility among other possibilities. In other words, the defining feature of the surveyability of a proof is a feature that Wittgenstein presents as what is operative at the level of our language itself, at the level where we use our (mathematical) language (cf. RFM: 243f.; more references and discussion in part II); the defining feature of the other kind of surveyability, however, is what Wittgenstein precisely seeks to bring into account at the level of his playground of inventing and collating language-games, because our grammar is deficient in surveyability.

by Wittgenstein's demand on himself of not *wanting* to deceive himself, of not wanting to let the accustomed image of the *Tatsachenkörper* count as the objective side of language in one's philosophical moments. His not wanting to accept the accustomed image of the *Tatsachenkörper* as the objective side of our language only leads him to look upon matters of language from a view under which they strike him as queer and utterly unfamiliar. On the other hand, to let our accustomed image of the *Tatsachenkörper* count as the objective side of our language only leads us to building houses of cards in philosophy. But from this it does not follow that there is anything like an objective side of our language, in the sense in which Wittgenstein seeks to pursue it. Our building of houses of cards in philosophy is not revealed through the objective side of the workings of language, that is, through the image of the *Tatsachenkörper* right side up. It is revealed through a certain way of looking upon language, a way that involves all kinds of movements of thoughts. This is not to say that Wittgenstein, in his efforts to see the *Tatsachenkörper* right side up, is himself in pursuit of a chimera, but it remains to be seen if he is not.

Wittgenstein wants to see the *Tatsachenkörper* right side up, and it is alongside that orientation that he should place his fictitious language-games. The *Tatsachenkörper* is a possibility, one among other possibilities, but a possibility for Wittgenstein only when it stands right side up. The image of the *Tatsachenkörper,* seen right side up, should give Wittgenstein peace of mind, in the light of the disquieting influence that it otherwise exerts, namely when it strikes him as representing a degenerate possibility. So it is the image of the *Tatsachenkörper,* seen right side up, alongside which the fictitious language-game should be placed as representing another possibility. But the image of the *Tatsachenkörper,* seen right side up, does not strike us as particularly familiar. It is exactly because of that lack of familiarity that is so difficult to see the thing right side up. So why demand from the part of the fictitious language-game so much recognizability, or transparency, if the image alongside which it is to represent another possibility is already beyond our familiar grasp? A curious question, but what it points to is the central role played by our familiarity, by our being so much accustomed to seeing things in a certain way, in daily life. What Wittgenstein demands from the things he wants to describe is that they show him their right sides up; it is a demand *on* objectivity, a demand ultimately deriving from his deepest self, not to deceive himself; a demand that, strictly thought through, leaves him ultimately watching *Fremdköper* alongside *Fremdkörper*—as so-called possibilities alongside other so-called possibilities of language. And how, one well wonders, could that be redeeming: the image of the *Tatsachenkörper* right side up?

232

Wittgenstein says that he does not want to learn *anything new* in philosophy (cf. PI: 89), but something new is precisely what I think his search for *understanding* the objective image of our language amounts to. He *wants* 'to establish an order in our knowledge of the use of language: an order for a particular purpose, one out of many possible orders, not *the* order' (PI: 132). So why should *an order* in our knowledge of the use of language not itself be a *new* piece of knowledge, or, for that matter, understanding? New: *because* it is an order, one that does not obtain in our language, for the order is to be attained for a particular purpose that does not hold sway in our everyday hold on language; new, indeed, *because* it involves the construction of fictitious language-games, of anomalies. 'Why', Wittgenstein asks, 'is it important to depict anomalies accurately? If someone can't do this, that shows that he isn't quite at home yet among the concepts' (RPP II: 606). Wittgenstein *wants* to feel himself at home, within the landscape of our concepts, but not in the way we are at home there as users of our language, but, rather, home in the sense that he *knows* his *philosophical* way around in a landscape of all kinds of influences that are only potentially bewitching in our everyday moments. Should Wittgenstein finally know his way around in one section of our language or another, it is not the kind of knowledge or understanding that is at work in the daily *use* of our language. He wants to know what e.g. mathematics *is*; we, though, users of our language, apply mathematical concepts and *call* this and that doing mathematics. Wittgenstein wants to feel himself at home in *the landscape* of our language, but at times it appears as if that fixed determination on his part only distances him from his own language in a way reminiscent of how his Tractarian self once distanced itself from it, namely under the spell of a bewitching influence.

4.5 Analogies

Having so much talked about, or rather alluded to, Wittgenstein's troubles on the playground of inventing and collating language-games, we now do well to consider some further remarks he made as regards these troubles. For what these remarks signify is indeed a kind of trouble that is anything but a loose impediment to his later thinking, a little snag that can be overcome rather parenthetically. Having a direct bearing on the ground on which Wittgenstein's later philosophy stands, they appear to concern a structural impediment to the redeeming word in the character of language descriptions. The contrast between the following two remarks will give us some interesting material to reflect upon.

> Nothing is more important though than the construction of fictitious concepts, which will teach us at last to understand our own. (CV: 85)

But I have kept on saying that it's conceivable for our concepts to be different than they are. Was that all nonsense? (RC III: 124)

The close juxtaposition of these two remarks reveals, I think, a tension in Wittgenstein's later thinking, a tension of which he became increasingly aware in the course of especially the last few years of his life and with which we, commentators, should acquaint ourselves as soon as we can. A concern with this tension will contribute to our understanding of his thinking. To begin with, both remarks are couched in completely general terms. Wittgenstein makes no mention of certain concepts for which he wishes to make an exception as regards the point of either the first or the second remark. It is this fact that renders the two remarks so interesting, for they have different motivations. The generality of the first remark just 'is' the overarching character of Wittgenstein's movement of thought asking for one *übersichtliche Darstellung* or another; the generality of the second remark, however, concerns a certain trouble that he faced on the playground of inventing and collating language-games. In other words, the tension concerns the relation between this playground and the playground of abstract consideration. The movement of thought that asks for an *übersichtliche Darstellung* concerns not so much some method falling *within* the philosophical framework in which Wittgenstein operates, as that it has added so much substance to the establishment of this framework in the first place. But this framework is called into question when such unreserved worries are nurtured as the second remark does.

One might as well focus on the second remark and notice that it already gives vent to a growing worry on Wittgenstein's part that there is something out of kilter with his later philosophy. For the worry expressed by 'Was that all nonsense?' begins to develop *on* the playground of inventing and collating language-games, a playground that exploits what his playground of abstract consideration has kept on saying, namely 'that it is conceivable for our concepts to be different than they are.' So the worry impinges directly on the aforementioned movement of thought itself, hence ultimately on Wittgenstein's uncommon way of looking at things. The worry expressed by 'Was that *all* nonsense?' is of a piece with 'One is inclined to say that you are making *all* logic into nonsense!'[152] Both exclamations express that our own *logical* predicament cannot be put *into relief*. Consequently, we had better begin to take such utterances as indications that there is something uncompromisingly awry with Wittgenstein's philosophical approach. For if it is indeed *all* nonsense, he does not face a hurdle, however big, *within* his later thinking, but something that lies at the bottom of it: his later conception of logic.

---

152   Both emphases mine.

Still, the above passage covers a detail that we have perhaps not given the attention it deserves in our general assessment of Wittgenstein's exclamations. For does he not speak of *our concepts*? If it is indeed all nonsense to think that it is conceivable for *our* concepts to be different from what they are, this does not need to affect the conceivability of every concept. Not every conceivable possibility, as one wants to say, is a possibility that our language could ever entertain *instead* of one of its own possibilities. Each concept of ours is a possibility in our language, with each contributing its share in its own characteristic way to its texture and array of ramifying connections in which we ourselves stand and thrive. To try to conceive one of our concepts to be different from what it is, seems to attempt the impossible, precisely due to the complex array of connections in which the concept lies, and to which it contributes its own share. One simply fails to see all the consequences that a different concept *instead of ours* involves and brings along. But that means that one might still be able to conceive of a concept different from our own, one that need not necessarily be thought of as one *instead* of ours. So what remains untouched in Wittgenstein's gloomy remark is the fundamental point that fictitious possibilities are conceivable, i.e. that certain possibilities can indeed be fleshed out as objects of comparison and put alongside the possibilities that our own concepts signify. One can well imagine a concept *simpler* than ours, one to be set up and fleshed out alongside our own complex concept so as to throw that famous light on the logical predicament of our own language. To conceive of such a concept does not necessarily mean that one should think of it as being a concept that our own language could ever entertain *instead* of its own complex concept.

The philosophical issue is surely complicated. Perhaps we are taking Wittgenstein's words in far too general a sense. On the other hand, and by way of a first rejoinder, if it is due to the inconceivable *consequences* that e.g. a simpler concept instead of our own one has in our life and *Lebensform*; that is, if it is due to this inconceivability that it is nonsense to think that it is conceivable for *our* concepts to be different than they are, what then does it mean to conceive of such a simpler concept *as a possibility to be set up alongside our own concept?* For what is a simpler concept without whatever consequences it may have in a certain *Lebensform*? If we do not know what such a concept would ever look like in our *Lebensform*, what then does it look like in a *Lebensform* in which it should pass for a simpler concept *with respect to ours*? If we can imagine such a *Lebensform*, how then *not being able* to conceive of a simpler concept instead of our own? If no concept is a concept without consequences in a certain *Lebensform*, what then is it like to imagine the consequences of a simpler concept without constant reference to the consequences that our complex concept has in our own *Lebensform*? I want to ask: If the consequences *in our own Lebensform* of a concept different from ours are inconceivable, and if this inconceivability need not necessarily affect the conceivability of the consequences of a concept different from ours, how then could this not also affect Wittgenstein's uncommon way of looking? For if it does *not* affect his later way of looking at things, what then does it mean to look at *our* language-games as autonomous *even so*?

But what did actually prompt Wittgenstein to jot down a remark as the second in the passage quoted above? What trouble did he encounter, on the playground of inventing and collating language-games, that he felt compelled to phrase his predicament in such far-reaching terms? Before attempting to articulate the kind of trouble at issue here, I propose to first consider the more extended context in which the latter remark arises. Let us see what other remarks and statements from this context have come along and might come to our aid in giving ourselves some clues about the nature of 'the trouble'.

The context is Wittgenstein's preoccupation with our colour language-games in the *Remarks on Colour*, and the remarks at issue are, in contrast to those quoted above, couched in terms clearly exemplifying an exclusive concern with the eccentricities of these language-games alone. And yet, although his whole attention is indeed directed towards these language-games, and these only, Wittgenstein sooner or later seeks to turn to that movement of thought that enables him to understand, by the authority of his playground of abstract consideration, any of our way of doing things with words at all. This movement, of course, is the inventing and collating of fictitious language-games. Thus, irrespective of the kind of language-game under consideration, it sooner or later comes to an engagement with this movement, and, apparently, given the eccentricities of our colour language-games, to a consideration such as the following.

> "Can't we imagine people having a different geometry of colour than we do?" – That, of course, means: Can't we imagine people who have colour concepts which are other than ours; and that in turn means: Can't we imagine that people do *not* have our colour concepts and that they *have* concepts which are related to ours in such a way that we would also want to call them "colour concepts"? (RC III: 154)

This is a truly fascinating passage, but its true point, I think, tends to escape us should we read Wittgenstein's words too much against the backdrop of his struggle to come to terms with our colour words alone, and not enough, I want to add, against the backdrop of his philosophical approach in general. True, it is this particular struggle that prompts Wittgenstein to raise several intriguing questions, but the kind of struggle that he wages still inheres in his manner of approach, in his uncommon way of looking at things. Another point here is that the above questions are quite unlike the one we have seen him raising above: he, now, *is not* wondering whether it is conceivable for *our* concepts to be different than they are. Rather he wonders whether we can imagine *people* having a different geometry of colour than we do. Still, the two questions are related, as we shall shortly see. So what are we to make of the number of questions just quoted? The first one clearly sets the tone, and the rest seems to denote a mere explication of the first. Now suppose we cannot imagine people having a different geometry of colour than we do. Being unable to do so, we have no way to limit our own way of doing things with colour words, no means to set it in relief. We will forever fail to *understand* our way of doing things with colour words: it presents itself to us as the only way in which such words can be operated on. This is a logical predicament that Wittgenstein faces but which his playground of abstract consideration does not consider possible; that is, it *stipulated* it as *not* possible.

Wittgenstein's way of explicating the opening question is not some way. It certainly is his concern with colour words in the first place that prompts him to step back for a moment only to ask a number of probing questions. Still, he avails himself of a mode of explicating *the point* of the first question that applies just as much to any other concept. It is a modus operandi that Wittgenstein did not contrive on account of his difficulties in understanding our way of doing things with *colour words*.

My concern here is that *the point* of the opening question is effected in terms of a movement of thought that Wittgenstein's playground of abstract consideration has enunciated and promulgated long before he bumped straight into a serious struggle with the eccentricities of—*whatever* language-game. Thus, I repeat, there are fictitious language-games to be set up alongside our language, ones that should, for one thing, draw on a logic ('geometry') that *is* not ours; hence should deviate from the logic of our own concepts in one direction or another. For another thing, the logic of the fictitious language-games should not deviate too much from the one constituting our own language-games. For in that case we run the risk of facing a way of doing things with words that we are not readily prepared, if at all, to let pass under the designation 'doing things with *colour* words'. But, again, an explication as this one concerns Wittgenstein's efforts to get a handle on the logic of each and every concept falling under his philosophical interest. Alternative logics are not *merely* possible; we must precisely see these alternatives *at work*, that is, as genuine *objects of comparison* so as to understand *our* logical predicament. And that is exactly what renders the actual passage so fascinating. For although it does not add anything new to Wittgenstein's playground of abstract consideration, the mere fact that it raises certain questions in exactly these terms and stipulations, precisely so in the face of Wittgenstein's obvious struggle to set up certain fictitious language-games, seems to hint at a serious problem.

So Wittgenstein's elucidatory words do not come out of the blue but arise in the midst of his prolonged struggle to describe and understand our way of doing things with colour words. While entrusting his familiar words to paper, he is not on the verge of setting out for the playground of inventing and collating language-games; that is, for the first time. He has rather tried his hand there already many a time. And while trying hard again at attaining the kinds of fictitious language-games for the task at issue, he, obviously, feels strongly prompted to raise the above questions. It is the failure of his prolonged efforts that throws him back upon asking, not some questions, but precisely the quoted above. These questions do not so much signal a reminder of what it means to enter upon such an enterprise as imagining logics different from ours as that they signify an unequivocal need on Wittgenstein's part to subject the meaning of such an enterprise to some probing questions.

This brings us to the following few passages, which are extracted from the same context:

> Can't we imagine people having a geometry of colours different from our normal one? And that, of course, means; can we describe it, can we immediately respond to the request to describe it, that is, do we know *unambiguously* what is being demanded of us?
>
> The difficulty is obviously this: isn't precisely the geometry of colours that shows us what we're talking about, i.e. that we are talking about colours?
>
> The difficulty of imagining it (or of filling out the picture of it) is in knowing when one has pictured *that*. I.e. the indeterminacy of the request to imagine it.
>
> The difficulty is, therefore, one of knowing what we are supposed to consider as the analogue of something that is familiar to us. (RC III: 86–88)

These few passages again cut deep into the heart of what we have been calling Wittgenstein's playground of abstract consideration. The question 'Can't we imagine people having a geometry of colours different from our normal one?' *makes itself felt*, not in the early 1930s, from which time on his considerations begin to reveal themselves increasingly in that fine-grained and steady form so characteristic of his later philosophy, but afterwards, at a time he really tries hard to invent those things that his playground of abstract consideration stipulated to be crucial: fictitious language-games. The question makes itself felt as these games must appear, not in a mere evocative mood, as rickety skeletons vouching to take on more flesh and feathers in the near future, but, rather, as true *objects of comparison*. Within Wittgenstein's realm of abstract considerations, however, it is the mere notion of 'other possibilities' that counts—a notion of which he constantly avails himself, and on which he has been building with conviction, in e.g. his criticism of philosophers who do not compare 'their building blocks' with other ones (cf. above). So, then, I repeat: What Wittgenstein's playground of abstract consideration bears out as a point of pivotal importance is something that he cannot but must bring to bear upon the playground of inventing and collating language-games. The deep-seated intricacy of the difficulties that Wittgenstein addresses in the above passages did not seem to have dawned upon him at the time he began to enunciate his later philosophy on the playground of abstract consideration—an intricacy, that is, which did not arise within this abstract realm and whose sheer absence might well be said to have played a crucial role in the formation of the playground of abstract consideration, hence in the defining of the *possibility* of the playground of inventing and collating language-games, not to mention the other playground here.

Wittgenstein speaks of the indeterminacy [*Unbestimmtheit*] of the request to imagine people having a geometry of colours different from our normal one. The request is not to describe a geometry of colours different from our normal one; rather, it is to describe *people* having a geometry of colours different from our normal one. The request is to describe some fictitious *language-games*, to flesh out objects of comparison so as to understand our own logical predicament. The request is not to describe such fictitious language-games in order to understand *them*; the request is to describe a physiognomy that is different from the one that our logical predicament displays in our own *Lebensform*. The request is to describe it and to *recognize* the result as a different way of doing things with words. It is precisely due to what the request involves that Wittgenstein characterizes it as *indeterminate*. The indeterminacy at issue, as he has obviously felt necessary to explicate, is that one does not know *what* we are supposed to consider as the *analogue* of something that is *familiar* to us. The request is: to invent a fictitious language-game; the indeterminacy of the request: not knowing, while trying one's hand on the playground of inventing and collating language-games, whether or not the request has been met at one stage or another. The request is what Wittgenstein conceived on the playground of abstract consideration, but its indeterminacy is what he learned to face on the other grounds. But that means that the request has a built-in feature of something that he concocted himself. Wittgenstein did not anticipate that his request would give rise to more than teething troubles.

The passage is unmistakably diagnostic, with a Wittgenstein availing himself three times of the notion of a difficulty [*Schwierigkeit*]; but, I think, not altogether unequivocally. All uses do relate to each other, and most intimately so; and yet, I think we should set the first occurrence somewhat apart from the remaining two, because it seems to signify a *problem*, whereas the two following occurrences circumscribe a *difficulty* which Wittgenstein faces: on the playground of inventing and collating language-games. Thus, *if* it is 'precisely the geometry of colours *that* shows us what we're talking about, i.e. that we are talking about colours'— well, *that* will give rise to a serious difficulty on the playground of inventing and collating language-games, namely that of 'knowing what we are supposed to consider as the analogue of something that is familiar to us.' On the other hand, an ongoing struggle with this kind of knowing may well prompt us to step back from the playground, only to wonder 'isn't precisely the geometry of colours that shows us what we're talking about, i.e. that we are talking about colours?'.

The indeterminacy of Wittgenstein speaks in the above passage has been hinted at already in *RC* III §42:

> We will, therefore, have to ask ourselves: What would it be like if people knew colours which our people with normal vision do not know? In general this question will not admit of an unambiguous answer. For it is by no means clear that we *must* say of this sort of abnormal people that they know other colours. There is, after all, no commonly accepted criterion for what is a colour, unless it is one of our colours.
>
> And yet we could imagine circumstances under which we would say, "These people see other colours in addition to ours."[153]

What is so interesting about this passage is that Wittgenstein, notwithstanding the difficulties hinted at in the first part, expresses in the second part what he had long been enunciating, namely, *that* we could imagine circumstances under which we would say "[t]hese people see other colours in addition to ours".

The difficulty, then, of which Wittgenstein speaks is something that impinges directly on his concept of an *übersichtliche Darstellung*. He wants to characterize *how* we deal with colours, *how* we talk about them. But precisely this very *how*—or motley of *hows*—is what Wittgenstein finds most difficult to produce on the playground of inventing and collating language-games. His recurring efforts to integrate, into a surveyable representation, fictitious language-games that present a deviating geometry *concerning colours* seem to be limited by the geometry of our own concepts. Anything that fails to display *this* geometry is in danger of falling short of our approval, of our recognition; we begin to demur, to

---

153   Cf. RPP II: 700, Z: 390.

240

raise serious doubts whether the deviating form is a form *concerning colours*. Of course, the philosopher sooner or later loses his grip anyway on his own inventions, should he push the deviation from our own logical predicament too far. But what Wittgenstein hints at in the above passages is that, at least in the case of colours, this loss of control comes far too early: the geometry of our colour words sets such limits that *only* in its own case does it show that there is talking about colours.

Wittgenstein's problem (or difficulty, for that matter), then, seems to have much if not everything to do with our ability to *recognize* fictitious language-games as variations on the themes set in our own *Lebensform*. He, at the time of his reorientation in philosophy in the 1930s, paid rather little attention to what the *effort* of recognizing (or conceiving) a deviating logic comes to. His central concern at that time was rather abstract, namely with questions such as what fixes a piece of language as one possibility among other possibilities. He had our own logical predicament as one possibility among other possibilities supervised in the first place by this abstract thing: *that* 'it is conceivable for our concepts to be different than they are.'[154] But this leaves open *how* this conceivability is to be conceived itself, that is, how the abstract idea works out in practice. Wittgenstein might be said to have left this conceivability as what should take care of itself. It was only when he began to try to invent his fictitious language-games that he began to ponder over how this conceivability *can* take care of itself. It is one thing to say that our concepts are possibilities among other possibilities; it is an altogether different thing to say that it is *conceivable* for our concepts to be different from what they are. In the latter case you have made the possibilities a function of conceivability, that is, of our conceivability. But this conceivability is a human capacity, itself a function of the concepts that we use. It is one thing to say that it is conceivable for our chairs to be different from what they are; it is an altogether different thing to say that it is conceivable for *our concepts* to be different from what they are. The former is among the kinds of things we say, in the daily course of life; the latter seems to be a kind of simile, *eine Analogiebildung*, perhaps one on which the Wittgenstein of the early 1930s might be said to have slipped into his later philosophy.

Let us return to Wittgenstein's remark 'The difficulty is, therefore, one of knowing what we are supposed to consider as the analogue of something that is familiar to us.' This remark deserves our special attention as it brings the notion

---

154   Another notion he uses in this respect is intelligibility: Other concepts are intelligible. See also next chapter.

of familiarity into account in a way that, I think, is remarkable. The analogue of which Wittgenstein speaks is a language-game of the fictitious type, to be set up alongside the logic (geometry) of our own language-game, in the present case the logic at work in our colour language-game. The difficulty that Wittgenstein faces, indeed purposely enunciates at present, is that one does not know when one has fleshed out the fictitious language-games, that is to say, an analogue *of something that is familiar to us.* But this clause is a remarkable effort to state things more precisely as it brings the notion of our being familiar to bear upon something with which we are rather *not* familiar, that is, according to Wittgenstein's own account. Recall, for instance, the following words:

> It is difficult to put the body of fact [*Tatsachenkörper*] right side up: to regard the given as given. It is difficult to place the body differently from the way one is accustomed to see it. A table in a lumber room may always lie upside down, in order to save space perhaps. Thus I have always seen the body of fact placed like *this*, for reasons of various kinds; and now I am supposed to see something else as its beginning and something else as its end. That is difficult. It as it were will not stand like that, unless one supports it in this position by means of other contrivances. (RFM: 254)

To be sure, the *Tatsachenkörper* of which Wittgenstein speaks is not a fictitious language-game, but the kind of thing that is constituted by what he calls the depth-grammar. His efforts to see the depth-grammar of our colour concepts pose no exception with respect to the kind of difficulty discussed in the above passage.

Wittgenstein speaks of the analogue of something that is familiar to us, but *if* that something is *not* the so-called depth-grammar of our colour words, he seems to want to see an analogue alongside the surface-grammar of these words, i.e. the kind of grammar that we are accustomed to see in daily life and that leads us astray in our philosophical moments. And that, to say the least, is queer. Recall: 'In order to overview these concepts, you must compare them differently than their surface grammar suggests. You must conceive other parts as homologous: One must compare what look looks like a jawbone with a foot. Concepts are concealed.' The logic of the *Tatsachenkörper* is difficult to excavate for precisely such reasons as Wittgenstein evokes in the above passage. Though difficult, it is exactly this logic, the depth-grammar, which, strictly speaking, should be said to be the kind of thing alongside which an analogue is to be set up, a thing with which we cannot be said to be particularly familiar.[155] But, as we have been

---

155 But suppose that it is precisely due to our being so much familiar with the depth-grammar that we find it so difficult to notice it in our more reflective moments? Well,

suggesting, when it comes to our *recognizing* the fictitious language-game as an analogue of our language-game, it seems to be precisely our familiarity with our own way of doing things with colour words, far more than the unfamiliar and imprecise impression of their depth-grammars, that plays the predominant if not the exclusive part in our acceptance of the fictitious language-game as an analogue. Although it is the depth-grammar that ultimately counts in the comparison, we do not attempt to recognize out of our unfamiliarity with this grammar an analogue of something that is familiar to us.

in that case, as I would say, Wittgenstein operates with at least two different notions of being familiar. His troubles remain all the same.

5. What do our neighbours look like?

5.1 Why play the game the way we do?

Let us start with the following remarks: 'Language [...] relates to a *way* of living' (RFM: 335) and 'Language is just a phenomenon of human life' (RFM: 351).[156] Both remarks are what they are: genuine *remarks*, hence not *descriptions* of the language-game themselves. Both remarks emerged on what we have called Wittgenstein's playground of abstract consideration and both bear an intimate connection to Wittgenstein's conception of language description, being of the grammatical type as they are. Neither the one nor the other states a thesis about the essence of language, and if we want to know what they aim at: we may commence by observing that both put a very fine gloss on the grammar of the expression "language". One of the important things the present gloss intimates if not brings out clearly is that our concepts need not be the way they are. The concept of pain, for instance, really need not be the way it is, that is, it need not necessarily come in the shape it actually does in our present life. It relates to our way of living, and, Wittgenstein suggests, we are well able to imagine this way to be different from what we are used to. Hence we may well imagine a different concept of pain, one that differs from the actual one in one respect or another. Having said this much, let us recall here the following passage.

> Of course this is not a common way of looking at things. It is a purely geometric way of looking at things, as it were. One into which cause and effect do not enter.
>
> That is, I look at this language-game as autonomous. I merely want to describe it, or look at it, not justify it. (LWPP II: 40)

I bring this passage up here merely in order to remind ourselves of this: Wittgenstein *does not want* to justify the workings of language-games. He is *not interested* in giving *explanatory* accounts of language; he merely *wants to describe* our language. But, as we have seen, and contemplated at length so far, he does not want to describe its workings *tout court*, for it is precisely owing to our being so much urged as to justify, explain, our language that he is at pains to come out with descriptions at the end of the day, and these things only. There is a conscious striving on Wittgenstein's part, precisely because he himself feels the pull and danger to be led astray by the bewitching force of our language. The common lore has fallen prey to this force, unendingly, to the urge to explain, in philosophy. Of

---

156   Cf. 'And to imagine a language means to imagine a form of life' (PI: 19).

course, there is a conscious striving on the part of the partisans of common lore too, but this striving is the urge to do what our language suggests us to do. The conscious striving as codified in the common lore is the cognisant adhering to a cataleptic power, invariably mistaken for the true and only philosopher in us.

From our common way of looking at things, we may well wonder why Wittgenstein merely *wants* to describe our language and steadfastly declines to make one step further, that is, to append to his descriptions the finishing touch of a revelatory account by means of explanations. Why constrain your interest, Wittgenstein, in such a weighty matter as our language? Why not concede to us, your peers and honourable thinkers, that our concepts pertain to something that goes far beyond a mere *Lebensweise*? For are we not *human* beings? Should our concepts not reflect what *we* are? Should they not reflect an innermost and tangible nature far less volatile and wavering than—a mere way of living? Do you not see that our innermost nature must come true in the workings of our language-games? Do you not see that our human nature sets limits to how language can be used, just as it sets limits to every way of living? Is it not precisely this nature that language ultimately relates to, hence what we, philosophers, need to heed and focus our efforts on? Indeed, have you not always evinced a deep interest in those limits? So why not join us, Wittgenstein, why not grant that e.g. our concept of pain reflects something highly significant about us and the world at large? Our uncertainty about whether someone is in pain hangs intimately together with what we *are*, rather than with anything as exterior and shabby as our way of living! For it is really what we are and have always been and what the world is and will be tomorrow that forms the bedrock of our *Lebensweise*, indeed all human *Lebensweisen*. We may well imagine our own *Lebensweise* to be different from how it transpires today, in one or more ways, but such imaginings must be weaved—don't you see?—around certain, hard and stalwart facts of our lovely human nature. To think that language relates to a *Lebensweise*, and to think of this relation as what counts ultimately, is just to cut language short of what it relates to *in the end*. So why not board our train of common thought, Wittgenstein, why not append to your description of the language-game an explanation, a universally acceptable account that calls upon these sublime facts?

'Because I do not *want* to explain in philosophy. I want to do work on myself, on how *I* see things, and there is a great demand at work in that effort of mine, for *I* do not *want* to deceive myself.'

One of the things we have been considering is that Wittgenstein was not prompted to adopt his uncommon way of looking in consequence of his having made a rather uncommon discovery. More specifically, it was not upon his having discovered that language works autonomously that he began to look at the language-game *as* autonomous. There is no such discovery; Wittgenstein did not *find out* anything of that sort. It is true that his uncommon way of looking at things involves a commitment, but this commitment harks back, ultimately, not to what he *found out* language to be in the early 1930s, but to what he then *made out* of his Tractarian way of looking at language. And not having found out *that* language operates autonomously, Wittgenstein did not *find out* either that language can in the end only be described, any more than we, advocates of the common lore, have *found out* that it can indeed be explained. That language can in the end only be described *points* towards a way of looking at things.

Wittgenstein's way of looking at the language-game is, he says, a *purely geometric way* of looking at things; it is a *Betrachtungsweise* that he entertains with respect to language first and foremost. The word 'entertain' serves to emphasize that there is an active element at work in his way of looking. Thus, when he says that he does not want to justify the language-game, it is significant that he does not look at the language-game *as* autonomous as soon as he suppresses the urge to justify it. By the same token, and more generally, where this urge does not even take hold of our minds, as is the case in the daily course of life, we, on that account, do not look at our language *as* autonomous. There really is a kind of positive element at work in Wittgenstein's way of looking at things; an element that, in his case, comes alive all the more so in the light of *his* own urges to explain. This element, as I want to say, delineates the boundaries, which do not just spring into being the moment you suppress the urge to explain. These boundaries arise from the kind of commitment that Wittgenstein's way of looking incorporates. He wants to understand, but his commitment does not represent an element that he has already *understood* and on the basis of which he wants to understand *more*. But to say that he has not understood that element is not to suggest that Wittgenstein is ultimately aiming for understanding *that* the language-game works autonomously. On the contrary: *that* it works thus drops out, in a most important sense of the word, from his efforts to understand the workings of our language. What remains is the *how*: how a language-game works, *how* it works in contrast to other possible workings. The *that* does not subsist *alongside* the *how*, i.e., alongside the *hows* to which it bears internally; it does not denote an understanding *alongside* the understanding that Wittgenstein is ultimately looking for. He looks at the language-game as autonomous and there is no language-game that poses an exception *in respect of this way of looking*. (To be sure, to look at the language-game as autonomous is not to look at it *as if* it operates autonomously.) In other words, *that* the language-game works autonomously is not itself a possibility among other possibilities. The *that* determines a space of possibilities, rather than a possibility itself, and this space has its ultimate source in the way Wittgenstein once went to work in his *Tractatus* as well as in what he, in the 1930s, considered to be its severest mistakes and blunders.

If I seem to be belabouring the point, it is because of the central importance of the following question: if Wittgenstein looks at the language-game *as* autonomous, had we then not better ask what his search for *understanding* its workings actually amounts to? Where Wittgenstein looks at the language-game *as* autonomous, there is something to be said in favour of the picture that whatever piece of understanding he may have gathered at the end of the day, as regards the workings of some particular language-game or other, it traces back ultimately to what he himself has brought to bear on language in the form of his uncommon way of looking. If you look at the language-game as autonomous, a good many things and interesting facts, as one wants to say, simply drop out from your considerations altogether, whereas other things, it is true, obtain importance and need to be heeded as making up the language-game. Thus, Wittgenstein's eagerness to understand is not allowed to reach out to e.g. the workings of the human brain; these he indeed *ought to* dismiss as being of no interest to him in the final analysis. But this means that whatever obtains relevance for him, thus within his way of looking, it should be worked out and articulated alongside other relevant things and items as ultimately conspiring to add up to an autonomous edifice. They should add up to what *we* call doing this or that, in the daily course of life. But why then call Wittgenstein's efforts to understand the workings of an autonomous whole as the language-game his efforts to *understand*? To be sure, it is Wittgenstein himself who has not missed the opportunity to avail himself of this common notion, thus in connection with his uncommon way of looking at things. But how much family resemblance does *his* use of the term bear to how we use it in science and in the daily course of life? We raise all kinds of questions and our concept of understanding bears strong grammatical connections to such utterly common a question as "Why?"

Indeed, one wonders whether Wittgenstein should not altogether refrain from asking as common a question as "Why?" Why do we play the game with "pain" the way we do? Whence the involved asymmetry between the first- and third-person as regards the interesting point of certainty? Why at all play the language-games thus-and-thus and not so-and-so? But what are we to make of such questions *if* language is being looked at *as* autonomous, that is, if you do not want to explain its workings, but merely to describe them, or look at them? If language is being looked at as relating to a *Lebensweise* rather than to our human nature as an enduring quality (as we, 'commoners', are wont to say), it much seems that Wittgenstein has cut himself off from considering the more interesting questions. Thus, should he refrain from asking the why-question: what then gives him cause to go on believing that he really seeks to *understand* the workings of our language?

The following remarks seem to lend support to our worry. Indeed, Wittgenstein at one point even speaks of suppressing the why-question, clearly intimating the importance of doing so in philosophy.

> In philosophy we do not want to give explanations – precisely because no explanation can satisfy us. What we want to give and what we must give is, in the end [*am Schluß*], only a description. *Our method is the method of perspicuous representation.* Everything that looks like an explanation is already falsified and *ought not* completely to satisfy us. We never ask why. (VoW: 121).

> Often it is only when we suppress the question "Why?" that we become aware of those important facts, which then, in the course of our investigations, lead to an answer. (PI: 471)

Wittgenstein's uncommon way of looking at things, or so the suggestion of these remarks, has no place reserved for the why-question. Description comes to full blossom only when the urge for explanation is being suppressed. So where our eye should behold *certain* facts, there is no beholding, and no further consideration either, as long as the why-question keeps blurring our vision, keeps taking the place where, apparently, other questions should arise and lead us to mere descriptions of language. Whatever the indicated important facts are, they seem to be among precisely the things to which language, from Wittgenstein's vantage point, is related. But bringing language to bear upon such facts and no further than such facts, rather than pushing it beyond their contingent nature up to the point where matters become more fixed and enduring, is, as one wants to say, just to deprive one's philosophical investigations of what should render them deep and interesting. If language *relates* to a way of living, then, as one wants to say, language is as much part of this way as any other part is to which it relates and answers. Hence seeing language in relation to our way of living, and to this way only, is to bring it in connection with something that cannot be thought of without our language itself. And, one wants to ask, how can *that* throw light on one's anxiousness to understanding how that language works?

And yet, Wittgenstein does raise the question "Why?" And if *he* does not raise it he sees himself confronted with its arising, sooner or later, *within* his uncommon way of looking at things. And why not? If language is being looked at as autonomous, that is, if our language, from that vantage point, relates to something as 'malleable' as our *Lebensform*[157] might be said to be, why then *is* our language the way it is? Why play the game with "pain" the way we do? If it is conceivable for our concepts to be different from what they are, why then engage in the native ones rather than in any set of others? Before considering some examples of the why-question that Wittgenstein was indeed spurred on to raise, we do well here to realize first that this question enjoys a perfectly respectable status in his uncommon way of looking at things. *His* question is indeed not to be confused with the one that rocks our common tongue and that Wittgenstein, in *PI* §471, asks us to suppress.

> There is a 'why' to which the answer permits no predictions.[158] That's the way it is with animistic explanations, for instance. Many of Freud's explanations, or those of Goethe in his theory of colours, are of this kind. The explanation gives us an analogy. And now the phenomenon no longer stands alone, it is connected with others, and we feel reassured. (LWPP II: 86)

In this passage, Wittgenstein expounds a why-question that is anything but the one that *we* feel urged to raise, in moments of philosophy; or, for that matter, in the daily course of life. Indeed, the type of question is as uncommon as his uncommon way of looking, which is no coincidence, of course. Expounding the grammar of his question, Wittgenstein employs those elements that come into view in his own expositions of his uncommon way of looking. Thus, describing it as 'a purely geometric way of looking at things', a way 'into which cause and effect do not enter', he surely wants to make it clear that his why-question, which 'permits no predictions', is just as much a geometric construct. When the why-question rocks our common tongue, we seek to reassure it, that is, the question if not the tongue itself, by answering in the Empirical mood. Wittgenstein, on the other hand, finds reassurance *only* when he beholds 'the phenomenon no longer stand[ing] alone': a clear allusion to his concept of an *übersichtliche Darstellung*, which aims precisely at understanding through seeing things no longer standing alone, by seeing them connected by analogies. Fictitious language-games, as we have been considering, are indispensable, but nevertheless worthless if none of them manifest themselves as *analogies*. Only when an *übersichtliche Darstellung* draws on analogy is it really capable of inoculating reassurance in us, of removing from the phenomenon under investigation the disquieting aspect it exerts on

---

157   The difference between *Lebensform* and *Lebensweise* should not bother us here.
158   Cf. 'We are not pursuing a natural science; our aim is not to predict anything' (RPP I: 46).

the philosophical mind, namely that the phenomenon *cannot* but 'stand alone', that it *could not possibly* have been otherwise, or it is done for.

A typical concern on Wittgenstein's part is expressed by questions such as are raised in the following passages.

> If you consider the reasons someone might have for stifling pain, or simulating it, you will come up with countless ones. Now why is there this multiplicity? Life is very complicated.
>
> There are great many possibilities.
>
> But couldn't other men disregard many of these *possibilities*, shrug them off, as it were? (RPP II: 639)
>
> There can be a dispute over the correct result of a calculation, for instance, of a rather long addition. But such a dispute is rare and is quickly decided if it arises. This is a fact that is essential for the function of mathematics.
>
> There can also be a disagreement about what colour an object is. To one person it appears as a somewhat yellowish red, to another as a pure red. Colour blindness can be recognized by specific tests.
>
> There is no agreement over the question whether an expression of feeling is simulated or genuine.
>
> *Why* not? – What do you want to know?
>
> We are playing with elastic, indeed even flexible concepts. But this does not mean they can be deformed *at will* and without offering resistance, and are therefore *unusable*. For if trust and distrust had *no* basis in objective reality, they would only be of pathological interest.
>
> But why do we not use more definite concepts in place of these vague ones? (LWPP II: 23f.)

These are intriguing words, for several reasons. Perhaps the first point to notice is that they demonstrate a highly characteristic movement of thought, one that Wittgenstein frequently exercises so as to acquire a kind of first grip on the phenomenon under his attention. The movement of thought is that he takes to mathematics *as a background* or standard against which the phenomenon under his attention is to reveal a distinguishing feature of its practices in our *Lebensform*. True, in the above passages, Wittgenstein's attention is on expressions of feelings, on one subgroup of the motley of psychological phenomena, but he clearly signifies that what he draws out as a characteristic of this subgroup obtains for *our* psychological practices *sans exception*: *we* play them with *elastic* concepts, with *vague* ones. It appears that Wittgenstein, rather than *claiming* that we play our psychological language-games with elastic concepts, is attempting to obtain traction for his efforts to give a descriptive account of these games at long last. To this end, he needs a kind of standard in order to characterize that we perform our psychological practices with *elastic* tools, and my suggestion is that he regularly takes mathematics as this background or standard for the characterization. He brings a certain characteristic into play, of what he conceives to be *essential* for the function of mathematics, only to suggest that *the lack* of this characteristic epitomizes an essential cachet of all *our* psychological language-games. But in thus positing his matters over against each other, Wittgenstein contrasts the latter language-games with our way of doing mathematics, rather than with mathematics *simpliciter*. It is essential for the function of our way of doing mathematical things with words that agreement prevails, that it does not come to blows over the (correct) result of a calculation. But where this agreement prevails, 'there is no agreement over the question whether an expression of feeling is simulated or genuine.' And Wittgenstein asks *why* there is no agreement here—only to append to it another question: 'What do you want to know?'

Now what is so interesting about Wittgenstein's obsession with the why-question is that it seems to trouble him especially in connection with our psychological language-games, and conspicuously little if at all when he turns his attention to mathematics.[159] This is all the more interesting as Wittgenstein wants to understand what mathematics is, no less than he wants to understand our ways of doing psychological things with words. He is keen to see fictitious analogies alongside our psychological concepts in much the same way that he wants to perceive fictitious analogies alongside our own way of doing mathematics. He raises the question 'Why is there is no agreement over the question whether an expression of feeling is simulated or genuine?', but a parallel question such as 'why is there is *no lack* of agreement over the question whether a result of calculation is correct or not' should be no less interesting, or legitimate, within his uncommon way of looking at things (see also below). In any case, there is an asymmetry at play in the above passages, in that mathematics adopts the part of a background or standard, against which Wittgenstein measures as it were the logical predicament of our psychological language-games. This measurement, as we shall see in more detail below, provides him with a kind of first grip on our psychological language-games; it is the light in which he considers these language-games henceforth to the effect that they *lack* general agreement. Of course, his question 'Why is there no agreement over the question whether an expression of feeling

---

159   Cf. 'But am I really trying to say that the certainty of mathematics is based on the reliability of ink and paper? *No.* (That would be a vicious circle.) —— I have not said *why* mathematicians do not quarrel, but only *that* they do not' (PPF: 343).

is simulated or genuine?' seems utterly natural, a perfectly valid and permissible thing to ask, and yet we should realize what is stake here: Wittgenstein simply has no conception *at all* of what general agreement amounts to in the *psychological* dimensions of our language, apart from what it means and amounts to in *mathematics*. He derives his 'conception' from an area like mathematics and it is now transferred, in the form of a question in the first place, to the arena of our psychological language-games. He seems to suggest that the question makes perfectly good sense, which is to say: you *can say* (without speaking nonsense) that there is no agreement over the question whether an expression of feeling is simulated or genuine. So it should make sense to set up a fictitious analogy in which there *is* general agreement over the question whether an expression of feeling is simulated or genuine. Still, what Wittgenstein seeks to have before him is not *mathematical* agreement in our psychological language-game.

Let us return to the question 'Why do we not use more definite concepts in place of these vague ones?'Our natural inclination is to answer this question by alluding to something immutable in our human constellation, which will eternally prevent us from having more definite concepts. Our vague concepts reflect this immutability and more definite concepts *are* conceivable only when the immutable can be conceived as imposing a less exacting regimentation on us and our lives. Thus, as we want to say, only *I know* that I am in pain or not and *you cannot* possible peer into my mental world. It is only when our psychological concepts build upon 'cannots' of this category that they can perform the kind of job they do in our *Lebensform*. We, human beings as we are, to put further emphasis on this, partake of both the mental and the physical world and the first thing that our vague concepts epitomize is this immutable constellation in our human condition. And why should all this not be obvious enough? Why sit pondering half a life over these things? Whence Wittgenstein's desire to see them differently?

Well, that's precisely why Wittgenstein *is* so much troubled by the aforesaid question, for he is not free from the *urge* to see things along such lines as circumscribed here. However, in his case this natural urge is thrown into relief by his resolve to look at our concepts as possibilities, as tools that are the way they are but need not be the way they appear in our *Lebensform*. For him, our vague concepts do not epitomize an immutability of metaphysical grandeur. What they relate to is our *lebensform*, or, for that matter, our *Lebensweise*. Hence his recurring motif as exemplified by 'Why do we not use more definite concepts *in place of* these vague ones?' (emphasis added). It is within Wittgenstein's way of looking at language that this question arises and strikes him with such mighty and disquieting aspect. Now, if we consider this question in the light of the passage quoted above, i.e. the one in which Wittgenstein contemplates the grammatical cachets of his why-question, the answer should be quite straightforward and promising. All he needs to do is to set out for the playground of inventing and collating language-games so as to try to invent 'more definite concepts'. All Wittgenstein needs to do is to invent a fictitious analogy and behold the outcome as part of *eine über-sichtliche Darstellung*. Of course, the niggle remains that these analogies do not come effortlessly, for they should show up in the shape of *recognizable* variations on what we *call* doing this or that with words. Otherwise, the question seems perfectly alright and answer*able*.

For Wittgenstein, then, the 'phenomenon no longer stands alone' only when he sees it placed alongside an analogy. And the phenomenon does not shed its disquieting aspect, which precisely *is* that of standing alone, as long as he fails to set up the fictitious language-games alongside the phenomenon in the required form. To be sure, the phenomenon of which *we* speak when we say that it can-not but *must* stand alone is not to be confused with the kind of phenomenon of which Wittgenstein speaks when he faces the trouble to behold it no longer standing alone. For before setting out for the playground of inventing and col-lating language-games, Wittgenstein, as we have seen in Chapter 2, first needs to draw the boundaries of the phenomenon differently from how we feel urged to do it in our philosophical moments. He needs to see the *Tatsachenkörper* right side up, as we have seen him giving expression to the task and difficulty. Of course, this thing, seen right side up, still stands alone, but once seen thus, it allows of various possibilities alongside itself as the very kind of possibility obtaining in our *Lebensform*.

To see the *Tatsachenkörper* right side up is to look at it as a possibility among other possibilities. To see the *Tatsachenkörper* right side up is to take the elastic-ity (see passage above) as the characterization of a possibility as it obtains in our *Lebensform*. In other words, to see the *Tatsachenkörper* right side up is to look at its elasticity[160] as a possibility within a series of possibilities whose ends bear to each other as polar opposites: a certain measure of definiteness stands out against a certain measure of indefiniteness (how much depends on the particular concept). Wittgenstein *characterizes* our psychological concepts as elastic tools and it is conspicuous that his desire to see them no longer standing alone is first and foremost directed at seeing them alongside (fictitious) concepts of the more definite type, rather than at concepts that are even less definite than ours. Be that

---

160   To keep to the example of psychological concepts here.

as it may, it means that Wittgenstein needs to have a firm grip on the concept in the first instance, a grammatical characterization that allows him to talk about it and its variations in such terms as being *more* or *less* definite, which is precisely what the characterization 'elasticity' allows him to. But what does it mean for a concept to be elastic? Well, as Wittgenstein hastens to qualify in the above passage, to be elastic for a (psychological) concept does *not* mean that it 'can be deformed *at will* and without offering resistance.' It means that the concept is endowed with a certain measure of elasticity in our *Lebensform*, something that we exploit and through which the concept obtains the kind of *Witz* and significance it has for us. We, players of our language-games, do not so much deform the elastic concept at will as that we exploit its very limits—limits that render the concept usable for us. You can be certain that someone is in pain, whereas I may have my doubts, perhaps because I know the person so well and more than once he has shown himself to be a real phoney. But to see someone writhing on the floor with his arms cut off should for both of us be sufficient evidence that he is in real pain and danger. To doubt here is sufficient evidence for those who do not even dream of doubting that we are unaccountable, to say the least.

> Given the same evidence, one person can be completely convinced and another not. We don't on account of this exclude either one from society, as being unaccountable and incapable of judgement. (RPP II: 685)

> "I am *certain* that he's in pain." – What does that mean? How does one use it? What is the expression of certainty in behaviour, what *makes* us certain?
> Not a proof. That is, what makes me certain doesn't make someone else certain. But the discrepancy has its limits. (LWPP II: 21)

> I am sure, *sure*, that he is not pretending; but some third person is not. (PPF: 353)

Here Wittgenstein says that 'the discrepancy has its limits', an expression that reminds us of his words quoted above: 'We are playing with elastic, indeed even flexible concepts. But this does not mean they can be deformed *at will* and without offering resistance, and are therefore *unusable*. For if trust and distrust had *no* basis in objective reality, they would only be of pathological interest.' But this must give us cause, since we do not know whether 'objective reality' means the same to Wittgenstein as it means to us. For *he* looks at the language-game as autonomous. Perhaps we should rephrase the question as follows: Objective for whom? For Wittgenstein? Or for us, users and participants of our language-games as we are?

It is easier to characterize what 'objective reality' does not mean for Wittgenstein than what it does. It is not what the Empiricist thinks it is. That is, it does not build on the relationship of the Inner and the Outer as *he* conceives it and takes its immutability to be.

> It is not the relationship of the inner and the outer that explains the uncertainty of the evidence, but rather the other way around – this relationship is only a picture-like representation of this uncertainty. (LWPP II: 68)

> But *not*: objective certainty does not exist because we do not see into someone else's soul. This expression means that. (LWPP II: 25)

> We don't need the concept "mental" [*seelisch*] (etc.) to justify that some of our conclusions are undetermined, etc. Rather this indeterminacy, etc., explains the use of the word "mental". (LWPP II: 63)

> "Mental" [*seelisch*] for me is not a metaphysical, but a logical epithet. (LWPP II: 63)

The elasticity of our concepts is a logical characterization. Wittgenstein's attention is directed at the description or explication of the so-called 'laws of evidence' (see below) *as they obtain in our Lebensform*. Now these laws, as he makes clear in the above passage, are not what they are owing to the relationship of the Inner and the Outer, a sublime reality that tends to hold sway in our philosophical moments. We think that our psychological concepts are what they are because of what *we are* in our relations to one other: my mental episodes are hidden from your eyes and ears, which is what your own episodes are in relation to my own eyes and ears. So, we think, there is something essentially immutable about us in our relations to one other, something that is the way it is and that cannot possibly be otherwise, a fixed constellation in our human condition in which our psychological concepts are deeply rooted and from which they work, and that they cannot but symbolize at the level of language. But all this, according to Wittgenstein, is just deeply mistaken and confused, for the relationship of the Inner and the Outer is rather a matter of various pictures laid down in the forms of our language—pictures that keep obtruding themselves upon us in our philosophical thinking and that lead us astray before long. So to appeal to the so-called relationship is not to appeal to some kind of objective reality, to something that lies beyond the concepts themselves and that render them the way they are. Rather, it is to appeal to what does no more than picturing a certain characteristic of these concepts, namely their elasticity, indeterminacy or indefiniteness.[161] But now, if the relationship of the Inner and the Outer is not what we tend to take it for in our philosophical moments, does that mean that there is not anything objective, a reality that lies beyond the concepts themselves and to which they

---

161 Cf. Z: 554.

relate nonetheless? Well, Wittgenstein says: 'if trust and distrust had no basis in objective reality, they would only be of pathological interest.'

Now what this remark suggests is that language not only relates, as Wittgenstein says, to a *Lebensweise*, but also to what he calls objective reality. The relation that language bears to a *Lebensweise* does not obtain in a self-contained dimension that leaves the world for what it is and that does not take issue with its course should unheard-of things supervene. On the contrary, the relation that language bears to a *Lebensweise* transpires against the background of a world of *regular* happenings. Ours is a steady world, in which we operate with definite *and* elastic concepts.

When Wittgenstein speaks of trust and distrust *having a basis in objective reality*, he appeals to a sphere that he conceives to reside outside the language-game, but not outside the logical space in which the language-game passes as autonomous. One might say: our concepts are not indifferent to how the world is, but the sense in which they are not is a matter of *logic*. Trust and distrust are part of the language-games looked at as autonomous constructs, but it is the non-autonomous part in the shape of the spatial and temporal world that sets limits to the language-games as *logical* possibilities among other such possibilities. It is only against a background of a non-autonomous whole that it makes sense to look at the language-game as autonomous; that is, only against a background of regular happenings does it make sense to look at the language-game as an autonomous whole displaying a clear and distinctive identity. To be sure, then, there is on Wittgenstein's part only one way of looking: the world is not being looked at as a non-autonomous whole with respect to the language-game that is being looked at as an autonomous whole, that is, *on a second occasion*. Rather it is all done within one and the same logical space; only then does it make sense to speak of trust and distrust having a basis in objective reality; only then do the language-game and the objective world bear the kind of logical coordination to each other that they have. And it is not so much the world that is being looked at as non-autonomous as that the language-game is being set *as* autonomous, for reasons of philosophy, and it is owing to that direction and setting that the world sets off against the language-game as *its* non-autonomous counterpart. But this world *must* be a *regular* thing, a requirement of no small proportions in Wittgenstein's uncommon way of looking at things.

Wittgenstein does not look at the language-game as a causal entity, but as a logical possibility. However, not looking at it as a causal possibility does not mean that the causal is beyond his scope of consideration. The language-game reifies as a logical possibility 'in' a causal world; it reifies in a world of *regular* happenings, that is, it cannot reify but against the background of a steady world of spatial and temporal dimensions. To look at the language-game as a logical possibility is not to look at it as a mere *game*, but at something that obtains true spatial and temporal dimensions, in whose make-up we stand ourselves as players of our own language and that operates on us no less than we on it. So the language-game must point beyond itself. There is no reification of its possibility without this pointing; only when it points thus does it individuate as a logical possibility.

It is through seeing the language-game in connection with other language-games, through seeing it 'no longer standing alone', to recall Wittgenstein's own expression here, that the language-game under investigation *individuates*, to use the same expression here as before. But this kind of individuation is something of which an *übersichtliche Darstellung* takes charge, something that needs to be worked out on the two playgrounds mutually responsible for such an overview. The former kind of individuation is what this working out 'presupposes', namely that the possibility of the language-games is a *stable* affair on account of its co-ordination with the regular world. The possibility of the language-game reifies, not in a logical space whose elements are only language-games, with whatever connections they might bear to each other in terms of similarities and dissimilarities, but in a logical space of which the non-autonomous counterpart of language-games partakes necessarily in the nature of a steady world. The possibility of the language-game is a stable affair on account of the regular actions of its non-autonomous counterpart. In other words, the possibility of the language-game *individuates* with respect to other language-games; its *reification* transpires in the more encompassing space in which these things prevail as autonomous elements. The possibility of the language-game cannot be reified at the level of the language-games alone, at the level where these things only *manifest* themselves as individual possibilities among other possibilities. Unless the language-game points beyond itself, it is not clear of what kind its possibility is. It is precisely owing to these things pointing beyond themselves to the world as their common, non-autonomous counterpart that Wittgenstein's comparing activity obtains its uncommon character.

In the preceding chapter we saw that *we* are more than players *of* our language-game; we are also part of it. We pervade the spatial and temporal phenomenon that each language-game is, just like the language-game pervades us and our lives. And it is this phenomenon that should point beyond itself. Language points beyond itself, but according to the above abstract picture it is the language-game, in its spatial and temporal dimensions, that does do so. It points thus, not because it is language that must point beyond itself, which would be the naïve expectation, but because the language-game in its spatial and temporal dimensions is being looked at as autonomous. The autonomous part in *Wittgenstein's* picture is fulfilled by the language-game and the non-autonomous part is fulfilled by the so-called spatial and temporal world of recurring facts and events. But what should we say now as regards calling this world, as Wittgenstein does, 'objective reality'? My point is this: when Wittgenstein speaks of trust and distrust having a basis in objective reality, all he does is to point at some items of the language-game as what must point beyond the language-game itself for it to pass for a firm and stable affair, a possibility. In other words, all he does is to entertain the abstract picture in terms of objective reality. And if we have been asking what *Wittgenstein* means by the notion of objective reality, we do perhaps well now to reduce this question to the following: objective *for whom*?

Objective for us, common users of our own language as we cannot help being? Or objective for Wittgenstein, in his capacity as philosopher, common user of his own language as he remains to be in spite of that uncommon role? The relevance of these questions should become clear in the light of the passages quoted below in which Wittgenstein addresses the relationship that language bears to its *non-autonomous* counterpart: the world, or, for that matter, objective reality. He, as we do well to recall here, looks at the language-game *from without*. But so he looks at the language-game *as* autonomous, which means that the non-autonomous counterpart of the language-game cannot fail to be looked at from without 'as well'. He looks at the language-game as autonomous, hence at something else—the objective world—*as* non-autonomous. But unless he looks at the world as the sum total of *regular* happenings the language-game fails to attain the status of a stable possibility. Autonomous, non-autonomous, regular happenings, stable logical possible—these interconnected points are all condensed into that droplet 'as' of Wittgenstein's uncommon way of looking at things. And that should give emphasis to the relevance of the questions just raised. For Wittgenstein did not adopt his vantage point in order to give a so-called rival account of objective reality, in fact he did not mean to give a rival *account* of anything at all. He entered the philosophical stage 'merely' in order to (dis)solve philosophical problems. Not all problems, perhaps, but still problems considered from a vantage point that considers them as solvable *sans exception*. And it is from such a point of view that Wittgenstein begins to formulate matters also in terms of objective reality. But for us, users of our own language, the world does not count as a non-autonomous *counterpart*, simply because we do not look at language as an autonomous construct.

To sum up: If you look at the language-game from without, you also look at its relationship to the world from without, which means that this world is being looked at from without in no lesser degree. We, users of our language, look at the world from within our own language—*within*, that is, *with respect to* the very sense in which Wittgenstein *says* that he looks at language from without. He, though *saying* that he takes up his position 'far outside' the language-game, is nonetheless not a philosopher without any position in the languages under comparison. He cannot but describe their similarities and dissimilarities in terms of the language *he* uses to describe his daily world. Of course, his saying that he, in his capacity as philosopher, looks at language and the world from without only endorses our statement that he tries to solve philosophical problems within a frame of mind that is far removed from the one in which he uses his daily language.[162] And if Wittgenstein's frame of mind is to be one in which all philosophical problems can *in principle* be solved, there remains perhaps one puzzle, to solve or not, namely the idea of this frame of mind as one in which he exploits 'the resources of our language' (cf. PI: 109), exploits them but cannot do so unless he *puts them to use* within that frame of mind aimed at solving problems—problems that do not arise in that frame of mind in which this language *is being used* in the first and, perhaps, only instance. When Wittgenstein says that 'What *we* do is to bring words back from their metaphysical to their everyday use' (§116), we might well interpret his words to the effect that he brings the *alleged* use of words within a metaphysical frame of mind, *not* into that frame of mind in which we use our daily language, but into an alleged frame of mind in which this language is being taken to, considered and—at last, *put to use* itself. Is there not something illusionary, perhaps even delusive, about the idea of taking up one's position 'far outside' the language-game? If this question is motivated by our abstract picture, we should also realize that it is ultimately motivated by Wittgenstein's own statement that he looks at the language-game *as autonomous*. And that looking is in turn, as far as Wittgenstein himself is concerned, no doubt motivated by the kind of wonderment with which *he* looks at our language and the world at large. The very frame of mind in which one cultivates one's own enduring wonderment, or disquietude, is perhaps something to marvel at itself, as an irresolvable remainder. Leaving these points aside, I propose to turn to the passages that we have been alluding to a moment ago.

---

162 Recall: 'Their/our answers, if they are correct, must be <u>homespun</u> and <u>ordinary/</u> trivial. But one must look at them *in the proper spirit*, and <u>then it doesn't matter</u>' (PO: 166, emphasis mine).

What then does this belief that our concepts are the only reasonable [*vernunftigen*] ones consist in? That it doesn't occur to us [*daß wir uns nicht vorstellen*] that others are *concerned* with completely different things [*an ganz anderem liegt*], and that our concepts are connected with what interests us, with what matters to us. But in addition, our interest is connected with particular facts in the outer world. (LWPP II: 46)[163]

Perhaps the first thing to notice about this passage is that Wittgenstein speaks of a *belief*, i.e., the belief that our concepts are the only reasonable ones. It is important to notice this because, if we ask what it is that Wittgenstein harbours himself concerning his criticism of this belief, we should say that it is not a *belief*, namely that our concepts are *not* the only reasonable ones. His is a *Betrachtungsweise*, rather than a belief; but not a *Betrachtungsweise* that is ultimately based on a *belief*, namely that our concepts are *not* the only reasonable ones. The second point to notice is that the deeply ingrained character of our belief, according to Wittgenstein, has much if not everything to do with the sheer lack of a ruminative moment on our philosophical parts, a moment asking for what our concepts ultimately bear upon. If we only hold our horses a moment in our *urge* to think the way we normally do in our philosophical moods, we would see and realize, Wittgenstein suggest, *that* 'our concepts are connected with what interests us, with what matters to us'—and, in addition, *that* 'our interest is connected with particular facts in the outer world.' So the third point to notice is how provocative the above passage actually is, for, seen from our own naive *Betrachtungsweise*, Wittgenstein has simply failed to see and to realize how our concepts are really connected with the world, hence that our concepts *are* the only reasonable ones. He ruminates from his own point of view and comparing his results with ours, he had better guard against attributing the difference to a lapse in *our* ruminative moments.

---

163   Cf. 'I want to say: an education quite different from ours might also be the foundation for quite different concepts. For here life would run on differently.—What interests us would not interest *them*. Here different concepts would no longer be unimaginable. In fact, this is the only way in which essentially different concepts are imaginable' (RPP II: 707–708); 'Do I want to say, then, that certain facts are favourable to the formation of certain concepts, or again unfavourable? And does experience teach us this? It is a fact of experience that human beings alter their concepts, exchange them for others when they learn new facts; when in this way what was formerly important to them becomes unimportant, and *vice versa*. (It is discovered, e.g., that what formerly counted as a difference in kind, is really *only* a difference in degree.)' (RPP II: 727).

But that is not all. Realizing that our concepts are *not* the only reasonable ones does not necessarily mean to nurture a belief. But neither does it mean that we have freed ourselves from the urge to believe *that* our concepts are the only reasonable ones. Realizing that our concepts are *not* the only reasonable ones means acknowledging that there is work to do, namely to see *how* e.g. our concept of pain reifies as a *logical* possibility, that is, in opposition to the urge to look at it as a causal contingency. It is to see and describe this against the urge to see it as a possibility that could not possibly have been otherwise. And to see how it reifies as a logical possibility is to bring the concept of pain to bear on precisely such 'nodal points' as Wittgenstein mentions in the above passage: our concerns and interests—which in turn need to be seen in connection with 'particular facts in the outer world'. And that is the fourth point to notice: at first blush one might be tempted to think that Wittgenstein, in the above passage, is merely mentioning a number of points—that is, elements that contribute to the reification of the language-game as a logical possibility. However, Wittgenstein is mentioning *all* the elements that could play a role in that very respect, that is, *all* the elements that could make a difference on the playground of inventing and collating language-games. The above passage makes indeed an important distinction: between a *that* and a *how*: *that* the concept ('language-game') reifies along the points mentioned there—is a matter that traces back to Wittgenstein's *Betrachtungsweise*; *how* a modification of one of these points could make a difference for a concept is a matter of great interest and importance for Wittgenstein, and the source of a slew of disturbing questions on the playground of inventing and collating language-games.

Of course, the kinds of interests and concerns that Wittgenstein mentions in the above passage are not private notions, entertained by a person as opposed to another person of the same community. On the contrary, they are public, i.e. shared by a community of language-users in the sense expressed by a remark as that *we* are not interested in playing the language-game with *more* definite concepts. The *Wichtigkeit* of the language-game, or its *Witz*, for that matter, is what it is for *us*, users of our language. It something that Wittgenstein tries to see in connection with *our* concerns and interests, i.e., with something on the part of the language-game as an autonomous edifice *in connection with* something on the part of the 'outer world' as its non-autonomous counterpart. The connection that the *Tatsachenkörper*, seen right side up, bears to the outer world is different from what it bears according to our accustomed way of looking at it. And if we compare with each other these two altogether different ways of bearing a connection to the world, we should notice that Wittgenstein has not come up with any kind of connection of his own mind and discovery. He has not, because he perceives no need to defend a *thesis* about how language is *really* connected to the world. His words in the above passage are no more than a grammatical gloss on his uncommon way of looking at things. It is a way of looking that is *not* ultimately grounded on a thesis about how language really bears upon the world, a thesis that he needs to defend against the odds occasioned by our dogmatic way of thinking about language and its relation to the world. Even so, it is a way of looking that cannot pretend to be a feasible enterprise, namely *a way of looking* that Wittgenstein brings into account in opposition to *the urge* to misunderstand the workings of our language, unless he articulates *in advance* what the notion of the language-game amounts to as an autonomous edifice. The above passage is an exercise in that articulation and, to that extent, no more than a grammatical gloss on Wittgenstein's uncommon way of looking at things.

Rather than substituting a connection of his own discovery for the one we think *must* obtain between language and the world, Wittgenstein, in a passage as the one quoted above, does not ask us to give up on that *must* in one of our more ruminative moments—as if such a moment suffices to do away with the undue influence that language exercises on our minds while we philosophize. Rather, he asks us to sense that dogmatic influence as it were for the first time, by seeing the relation of language that we think it *must* bear to the world in the light of such considerations as the following one. We measure, but the world does not force us to measure the way we do, *any more* than it forces us to do it at all. More provokingly, we are interested in the so-called inner states of people, but the world does not force us to harbour *such* an interest, any more than it forces us to harbour it at all. The break-through does not entail realizing how language really bears to the world. It concerns, rather, the feasibility of a way of looking that tries to oppose the urge to misunderstand the workings of our language, only to do away with it at last. So the important thing to observe here is that the *lack*, in Wittgenstein's way of looking, the lack of a dogmatic thesis about language and the world, a thesis to the effect that the world's imposition on the range of possible concepts is such as leaves us no room and choice but to operate on the concepts we actually have, is not anything to which his own way of looking testifies by means of a substitute *thesis* in the guise of, say, a grammatical clause telling how language really bears upon the world. All Wittgenstein does is to look at the language-game as autonomous, for all he wants is to understand by means of mere descriptions.

Confronted with how Wittgenstein conceives the connection between the *Wichtigkeit* of the language-game and the outer world, we might well wonder what kind of connection it is. For according to his lights, the possibility of the language-game reifies as an autonomous edifice with respect to a steady causal world as its non-autonomous counterpart. In other words, he cannot be interested in the relation between the language-game and the world as a causal entity itself. So what *is* the relation you are talking about, Wittgenstein? It looks so elusive if not downright mysterious. Of course, this question shows us how deep seated our dogmatic belief is.

The curious thing about our raising this question is that Wittgenstein has as a matter of fact already answered it, namely in the passage quoted above. *We* are at present pressing for an answer, without seeing that it already lies in that passage. *We* think that if the language-game reifies no longer as a causal edifice in the world that the causal relation that we in our deep-seated belief hold as what excludes the possibility of reasonable concepts *other than our own ones*— requires in Wittgenstein's *Betrachtungsweise* a genuine substitute *relation*, one that precisely allows for such concepts to obtain. My point here is that there is no so-called third element at work in Wittgenstein's *Betrachtungsweise* mediating between the language-game as an autonomous edifice and its non-autonomous counterpart. It is all done by the two items themselves: the language as an autonomous edifice and its non-autonomous counterpart, the world.

> If concept formation can be explained by facts of nature, shouldn't we be interested, not in grammar, but rather in what is its basis in nature? — We are, indeed, also interested in the correspondence between concepts and very general facts of nature. (Such facts as mostly do not strike us because of their generality.) But our interest is not thereby thrown back on these possible causes of concept formation; we are not doing natural science; nor yet natural history – since we can also invent fictitious natural history for our purpose.
>
> I am not saying: if such-and-such facts of nature were different, people would have different concepts (in the sense of a hypothesis). Rather: if anyone believes that certain concepts are per se the correct [*schlechtweg die richtigen*] ones, and that having different ones would mean not realizing something that we realize – then let him imagine certain general facts of nature to be different from what we are used to, and the formation of concepts different from the usual ones will become intelligible [*verständlich*] to him. (PPF: 365–66)[164]

These words, too, are no more than a grammatical gloss on Wittgenstein's *Betrachtungsweise*. The point to guard against here is the misapprehension that these words provide for anything novel, an additional element to how Wittgenstein sees the language-game as an autonomous edifice in relation to the world as its non-autonomous counterpart. The key word is 'intelligible' [*verständlich*].

---

164 Cf. RPP I: 643, LWPP I: 209.

If the formation of concepts different from the usual ones will become intelligible to us, this does not render the philosophical activity on the playground of inventing and collating language-games obsolete. For our task on this ground is not to see *that* the formation of concepts different from the usual ones will be intelligible to us, let alone *that* 'certain concepts are not per se the correct ones'. Rather it is to see what such concepts look like, that is to say, what *our own* concepts look like, in contrast to other possible concepts. And how different concepts, up to 'essentially different concepts', could be conceived: indeed, *that* is what Wittgenstein enunciates in the passage quoted above. Thus, it is not with reference to anything like our reputable intelligibility [*Verständlichkeit*] that Wittgenstein seeks *to convince* a couple of inveterate philosophers who '[believe] that certain concepts are per se the correct ones, and that having different ones would mean not realizing something that we realize'—that is, to convince them *and* to leave it at that, as if no work remains to be done on the playground of inventing and collating language-games. Rather, it is with reference to that notion of intelligibility that Wittgenstein lays down how *he* conceives of the possibility of different concepts and, to that extent, gives rise to his playground of inventing and collating language-games. So it is all arbitrary? Is 'logic' contingent in the final analysis? Wittgenstein anticipated that reaction and addressed it as follows in his *Investigations* (formerly called part II):

> Compare a concept with a style of painting. For is even our style of painting arbitrary? Can one choose one at pleasure? (The Egyptian, for instance.) Or is it just a matter of pretty and ugly? (PPF: 367)

Wittgenstein does not substitute a connection of his own discovery for the one we think *must* obtain between language and the world, but, instead, a kind of blank so to speak. A blank that leaves us, it is true, more or less groping in the dark for a firm hold in our thinking about the connection between language and the world, for we are anything but accustomed to think about this 'connection' as Wittgenstein articulates it. There is no technique now, no *method*, nothing of the sort comparable to what we have at our disposal when we think about language and the world in our accustomed way. Giving up on this way of thinking about language's connection to the world strikes us as giving up on thinking about language altogether. And yet, Wittgenstein says: '[A]nd the formation of concepts different from the usual ones will become *intelligible* to' us. Wittgenstein wants to say that there *is* way of thinking about language and the world, one that we need to accustom ourselves to, a way to which we have access on account of the fact that the formation of concepts different from the usual ones is *intelligible* to us. Interestingly, Wittgenstein did not always take to the notion of intelligible, for he writes that 'if you believe that our concepts are the right ones, the ones suited to intelligent human beings; that anyone with different ones would not realize something that we realize, then imagine certain general facts of nature different from the way they are, and conceptual structures from our own will appear *natural* [*natürlich*] to you' (RPP I: 48).

The word "natural" seems to have been less apt for Wittgenstein's objective; for nothing, as he must have come to realize, appears more *natural* to us than that our concepts are the only reasonable ones. So, then, if concepts other than ours appear far less natural to us, they are at least *intelligible* to us, Wittgenstein wants to say. In other words, he appeals to a faculty on our part on which a whole new way of thinking about language and the world can be trained and practised. This is not to suggest that he has discovered a new faculty. The irony rather is that he appeals to our concepts so as to have *them* admit the possibility of concepts other than themselves. Of course, 'intelligible' is perhaps still not a common notion to acclaim for one's uncommon way of looking at the world. It is a very fundamental notion for all that, that is, *for Wittgenstein*.

*

We have been saying that the *Tatsachenkörper*, seen right side up, bears a connection to the world that differs radically from the one that is accorded by our deep-seated belief in causal items and connections. What we have also been saying is that to see the *Tatsachenkörper* right side up is not to try to *establish* a different connection but to *explore* the intelligibility of which Wittgenstein speaks in the above passage, by focussing on *hows* rather than on a *that*. Now several points deserve our attention as regards the above glosses on Wittgenstein's uncommon way of looking. The first point concerns the fact that the latter gloss speaks of *certain* concepts that are per se the correct ones, of such concepts rather than of concepts *tout court*, as the former gloss does. This restriction seems reasonable as it appeals to our feeling that certain concepts are more basic than others and that the less basic ones are more easily conceivable to be different from ours. It also ties in with Wittgenstein's slogan that he is interested in language only insofar as it troubles him. And what could trouble him more than these so-called basic concepts? They exert on him, more than anything else, the disquieting pull that they are what they are and cannot possibly be otherwise. Now notice the following passage:

> Could a legislator abolish the concept of pain? The basic concepts are interwoven so closely with what is most fundamental in our way of living that they are therefore unassailable. (LWPP II: 44).

Wittgenstein speaks of basic concepts, among which he reckons a host of concepts from both the mathematical and the psychological branches of our language. Speaking of basic concepts, he implies the existence of less basic concepts, but the sense in which concepts are said to be basic and less basic with respect to each other is not the same for every way of looking at language. Wittgenstein looks at the language-game as autonomous, regardless of the concept under his attention, be it basic or not, hence the question of what renders a concept maximally basic for *Wittgenstein*. According to our common way of looking, concepts are basic because of the way they root in our lives, in a certain immutable constellation of our human condition, rather than in anything as ephemeral as our *Lebensweise*. It is precisely because of the first, as we want to say, that basic concepts are interwoven so closely with what is most fundamental in our way of living.

Not so for Wittgenstein. As is his wont, he turns matters around: *another* importance (i.e. *Wichtigkeit*) of the concept is to be discerned and to be seen in connection with particular facts in the outer world. It is 'still' concerns and interests that are at issue when Wittgenstein, in the above passage, speaks of what is most fundamental in our *Lebensweise*; it is 'still' these things, *rather* than things like human *necessities* such as food and sleep. In other words, the determinants of the basic concepts are still concerns and interests, i.e., matters that might well have been different and that can be thought of as different. However, with respect to the so-called basic concepts these matters are of such fundamental importance that different concepts are not easily thinkable. This brings us to the following point: the more basic our concepts are, in Wittgenstein's sense of the word, the more difficult it is to stake out the particular concerns and interest that these concepts reflect in a *Lebensweise*. In *PI* §570, Wittgenstein does not distinguish between basic and less basic concepts when he writes that 'Concepts lead us to make investigations. They are the expression of our interest and direct our interest.' This grammatical remark is very general indeed, but what are the particular interests and concerns that our indeterminate concepts reflect, our psychological ones, for instance? What are the particular concerns and interests that our determinate concepts reflect, our mathematical ones, for instance?

What I am signifying is a fundamental problem in Wittgenstein's later philosophy: the particular concerns and interests connected with the so-called basic concepts are very difficult to identify. Consider in this connection the following passage and notice: in how *general* a term he places his own way looking against our deep seated belief that 'our concepts are the only reasonable' ones.

The main difficulty arises from our imagining the experience [*das Erlebnis*] (pain, for instance) as a thing, for which of course we have a name and whose concept is therefore quite easy to grasp.

So we always want to say: We know what "pain" means (namely this), and so the difficulty only consists in simply not being able to determine this in someone else with certainty. What we don't see is that the concept 'pain' is only beginning to be investigated [*daß hier der Begriff 'Schmerz' erst untersucht wird, sehen wir nicht*]. The same is true of pretence.

Why don't we form a simpler concept? – Because it wouldn't interest us. – But what does that mean? Is it the correct answer? (LWPP II: 43)

Here it is again: Wittgenstein's why-question: 'Why don't we form a simpler concept?' But, indeed, he does *not* set out for the playground of inventing and collating language-games, that is, in order to answer it. He remains instead where he is *and*, not knowing with what interest or concern we play our language-game, answers it as follows: 'Because it *wouldn't* interest us.' Nearly everything in the above passage remains at a conspicuously abstract level. Wittgenstein does not first stake out the interests with which we play our indeterminate language-games, only to answer that a simpler concept would not interest us. There is no mention of any particular interest first, not because it is of no relevance here, but because Wittgenstein just has no answer ready for the question what the particular interests are with which we play our own basic language-games. This mode of schema-thinking is prevalent in Wittgenstein's later philosophy. Not knowing the particular interests or concerns, then, or the *Wichtigkeit* for our doing this or that, in short: the *Witz* of the game, he takes to placeholders of these particulars in his argumentation, in his enunciations, in his remarks and statements[165], only to push the matter a little further into the direction of concrete descriptions, which ultimately seem to fail.

What is our concern or interest, i.e., *woran liegt es uns?*—with respect to e.g. an indefinite concept as pain? Moreover, how are we supposed to distinguish conceptually between a particular concept, on the one hand, and the kind of interest 'underneath' it—on the other hand?

Wittgenstein says: 'What we don't see is that the concept 'pain' is only beginning to be investigated.' But whatever an investigation brings to light, in Wittgenstein's hands it must take the form of a concept that is a possibility among other possibilities. The possibility of the concept is to be framed by precisely such determinants as Wittgenstein can imagine being different on the playground of

---

165　Remarks and statements that owing precisely to their high level of abstraction tend to obtain a pleonastic or, for that matter, tautological character.

inventing and collating language-games: determinants whose change makes a difference for the concept. One type of such determinant, then, inheres in the language-game itself, in the shape of our interests and concerns: things that we just have and harbour, though not in empty space, that is, not with an absolute indifference to how the world is, but in connection with particular facts in 'the outer world'. It is in the shape of these so-called general facts of nature in which the second type of determinant enters upon Wittgenstein's playgrounds.

But one wonders what it is to say of these determinants as things that can be imagined to be different if the *consequences* of a change on their part are more than just difficult to imagine. Without these determinants there is no philosophy for Wittgenstein in his later sense of the word, but then what *is* his philosophy if he finds it more than just difficult to think its own determination through?[166]

The unassailability of which Wittgenstein speaks (LWPP II: 44, see above) concerns the question whether we could play the game differently. To be sure, then, it is not owing to the unassailability of the basic concepts that they are interwoven so closely with what is most fundamental in our way of living. That is, Wittgenstein means that it is because of the latter that they are unassailable: nothing will remain the same; everything will be different, so much so that a simpler concept *instead of ours* is virtually inconceivable. In other words, although the unassailability should in the first instance be said to be a feature of how certain concepts are 'connected with what is most fundamental in our way of living', it seems to be a feature of the powers of imagination of the users of these very concepts *no less* than of these concepts themselves.

Just to close the present section:

> Our concept is of such a kind. – But could we have a different one then? One that brings behaviour, occasion and experience [*Erlebnis*] into a necessary connection [*in zwangsläufige Verbindung*]? Why not? But in that case we would have to be made in such a way that all of us or almost all of us in fact would react in the same way under the same circumstances. For when we believe that the expression of his feelings is genuine, in general we behave differently from when we believe the opposite.
>
> But this correspondence does *not* exist, and therefore we would not know what to do with a necessary concept [*zwangsläufigen Begriff*]. (Heap of stones/sand.)
>
> Therefore because different things speak for the truth of his statement, and the statement has different consequences. (LWPP II: 23)[167]

In this passage, Wittgenstein entertains the phrase *einen zwangsläufigen Begriff*, which is one of his expressions for a definite concept. His suggestion is that in

---

166   We shall return to this point below.
167   Cf. RPP II: 712.

order to have such a concept *in place of* our vague one, 'we would have to be made in such a way that all of us or almost all of us in fact react in the same way'. But, according to him, given that such a common way of reacting does not exist among us, we would not know what to do with a *zwangsläufigen Begriff*. So it seems that the way we react to certain things should be reckoned among what Wittgenstein calls objective reality. Be that as it may, Wittgenstein again appears to have answered his why-question without the mediation of his playground of inventing and collating language-games.

Of course, there is some sort of answer when Wittgenstein says that 'we would have to be made in such a way that all of us or almost all of us in fact react in the same way'. But where he intimates a fictitious language-game in relation to a *possible* constellation of facts, he brings a possible language-game into play of which he does not yet have a clear idea at all. The question 'What does a fictitious language-game look like in which people operate with a *zwangsläufigen Begriff*' defies Wittgenstein's ability to answer right away. Yet, in a typical passage as quoted above, he *capitalizes* on the notion that a question such as the present one makes perfect sense and can be answered. Wittgenstein is clearly suggesting that there are two key conditions to be imposed upon the fictitious language-game, namely that 'different things speak for the truth of his statement, and the statement has different consequences'. Indeed, a fictitious language-game in which people operate with a *zwangsläufigen Begriff* is not a *generalization* of one such juncture in our *Lebensweise* at which all of us, or almost all of us, *factually* react in the same way. 'Only the whole is the instrument, the concept' (LWPP II: 37), Wittgenstein says.

5.2 Polar opposites and contradiction

I have been suggesting that what Wittgenstein seeks to set up alongside our psychological language-games is not *any kind* of fictitious language-game but, first and foremost, ones of the *more* definite type.[168] The disquieting appearance of our psychological language-games resides in their elasticity, in their clear and palpable indeterminacy: in a characteristic that appeals to us as what could not have been otherwise or these language-games are futile. We feel that their elasticity is our human predicament, that it somehow inheres in our nature, a feeling that soothes the Empiricist but haunts Wittgenstein as he looks at the language-game as autonomous, as a possibility that is the way it is but need not necessarily be

---

168 Indeed, *generally*, for he raises also such questions as: 'What would it look like if everyone were always uncertain about everyone else's feelings?' (LWPP II: 87).

the way it instantiates in our *Lebensform*. More generally, the fictitious language-games that Wittgenstein seeks to set up alongside our own language-games are primarily of the polar opposite type, that is, the polar opposite with respect to *his* grammatical characterization of our own game as elastic, definite, simple, complex, and indeterminate. Not being descriptions of these language-game themselves, then, such characterizations, as we have been suggesting, provide Wittgenstein with a first purchase on our own language-games, a primary *orientation* so to speak *within* his uncommon way of looking. There is work to do once a language-game has been endowed with a grammatical stamp. Though presenting no more than a way station on Wittgenstein's way towards descriptions, these stamps make a decisive contribution to the course to take.

So, then, it is *Wittgenstein* who supplies such predicates as 'elastic' and 'determinate'; *he* employs such characterizations for reasons of philosophy. On the other hand, is not up to him to determine how *we*, in the daily course of life, *call* a certain way of doing things with words. *This* is what *we* call doing mathematics and *that* is what *we* call recognizing pain in a person. *We call* it so-and-so, and *Wittgenstein proceeds by characterizing* the concept at stake as definite (mathematics) or elastic (psychology). It is important to pay heed to what *we* call doing this or that with words and how *Wittgenstein* characterizes these doings grammatically, for two meet each other at the playground of inventing and collating language-games. Thus, '[T]hat is our game – we play it with an *elastic* tool' (LWWP I: 243) is above all a type characterization, and as such prompts Wittgenstein to set out for the playground of inventing and collating language-games where he seeks to set up the polar opposite of an elastic tool. Wittgenstein wants to see what is involved in the kind of elasticity of the language-game under attention; he wants to compare it with other language-games of the elastic type, only to be pushed more and more towards the question of why we play the language-game the way we do. We need not play the game the way we do, but what does the opposite way of doing it look like? – a way of doing *psychological* things with words that for all its definiteness should not keep us, players of our own indefinite language-games, from calling it a way of doing e.g. 'pain-things' with words.

So whatever the polar opposite looks like, it should be a recognizable way of doing *it*. The *definiteness* of the fictitious language-game should not present a hindrance to our ability to recognize *it* as a variation on our own language-game, as a variation on what we call doing *this* or *that*. But how definite is the polar opposite? How sharp are its borders? What should determine them? We speak of something that Wittgenstein's uncommon way of looking deems possible, namely, a language-game *more definite* than ours. But so we speak of something that, according to this same way of looking, makes sense only when it comes as a means of comparison. The fictitious language-game should throw light on the workings of *our language*, and unless we recognize it as a variation on these workings, no light is forthcoming. So, perhaps, are the borders of definiteness defined by our capacity to recognize things as variations on our own way of doing it? But what are we to make of these capacities themselves? How do they bear upon our own language, upon the concepts we use? That is, concepts that railroad our way of looking at things. We may well be *willing* to call this or that a variation on our language-game, but why call it thus, if we are doomed to fail to recognize it as such?

Does the definite case lie within our reach of recognition? Does it lie *beyond* our reach? But *what* lies beyond our reach? Why should we call *it* anything if it lies beyond our *recognition*? So why not call the definite case the last one in a series of cases running from our indefinite concept to its so-called polar opposite, i.e., the last one that *we* recognize as a way of doing *this* or *that* with words? Wittgenstein says: 'You can vary the concept, but then you might change it beyond recognition' (RPP II: 691). But what if the polar opposite to be fleshed out implies a change that renders it beyond recognition *before long*? The game is lost the moment you attempt it in earnest.

These questions bring us back to what we have said about Wittgenstein's grammatical characterizations of our language-games and their polar opposites. For as far as *only* these characterizations are concerned, the fictitious opposites are easily realized, i.e. *defined*. Recall here that Wittgenstein formulates his first hold on our psychological language-games in the light of a grammatical characteristic that he deems essential for the function of mathematics. He does not characterize our psychological language-games as elastic without more ado, but precisely so against the background of such images of definiteness that mathematics provides, that is, our way doing mathematics. Interestingly, Wittgenstein does not take to these images as a foil only for his investigations of our indefinite way of doing things with words, but also, and most conspicuously so, with respect to the kind of definiteness that he seeks to describe in *On Certainty*, with respect to the peculiar logical role of the propositions rendered famous by Moore: 'I have two parents', 'I have never been on the moon', 'This is my hand'. Be that as it may, mathematics often obtains a *paradigmatic* status in Wittgenstein's investigations, and his characterization of mathematics as a field where rigidity rules and definiteness prevails is, on that account, different from what his characterizations of our psychological language-games amount to as a field of 'elastic rules and rulers'. Mathematics, our way of doing so, provides for paradigmatic pictures of definiteness: *this* is what it is like to operate with definite or rigid things. How influential this paradigmatic status is can be gathered from the following passage:

> -this particular and not at all simple pattern in the drawing of our life.
>
> And what would the opposite now look like? – How well defined would the borders of evidence be?
>
> One would recognize only with the possibility of error that someone was, for example, sad. But what kind of concept of sadness is that now? The old one? (LWPP II: 26f.)

The opening move of this passage furnishes a phrase that Wittgenstein repeatedly appeals to in the years in which he is nearly exclusively concerned with our psychological concepts, namely, 'a pattern in the drawing of our life'. It is not so much that these concepts *together* display a recognizable pattern in the drawing of our life as that each type of them does so, and each one in its own peculiar way. It is not always a simple pattern, but a pattern nonetheless; which is to say: this is how matters *strike* Wittgenstein with respect to our psychological concepts. What they have in common is that 'there is no agreement over the question whether an expression of [psychological x] is simulated or genuine' (see above passage). This absence does not render the use of these concepts an altogether chaotic thing; on the contrary, in the fullness of time, Wittgenstein suggests, you will certainly recognize a certain pattern in the drawing of *our life* and so in each of the uses of concepts having such a pattern as its basis. Such uses, then, involve an indeterminacy (indefiniteness), for the pattern of life, Wittgenstein articulates, 'is not one of exact regularity' (LWPP I: 211). Now, importantly, what belongs essentially to the constitution of the grammar of these uses is what he calls 'the borders of evidence'. There is a lack of agreement, for each of our psychological concepts, but this lack is not without limits. And for concept x these limits run thus-and-so, and for concept y these limits run thus-and-so, which is precisely what renders these patters so *particular*, and comparable for all that.

I pay attention to Wittgenstein's notion of the borders of evidence as it provides him with a firm point of departure as regards his activities on the playground of inventing and collating language-games. Thus, in the above passage, he first asks: 'what would the opposite now looks like? – How well defined would the borders of evidence be?', only to continue as follows: 'One would recognize only with the possibility of error that someone was, for example, sad.' This phrase, then, being a clear reference to the kind of grammatical *condition* in which Wittgenstein seeks to frame the polar opposite of our own psychological language-games, is a clear allusion to mathematics, to our definite way of doing mathematical things with signs. Indeed, the phrase 'One would recognize only with the possibility of error that someone was, for example, sad' had better alert us to the fundamental importance of the role of making mistakes in mathematics, in our way of doing mathematics. (I shall return to it in the next chapter.)

There is the possibility of error, in our way of doing mathematics, but no possibility of disagreement, which raises the interesting question of how Wittgenstein conceives of the polar opposite of our way of doing mathematics. What would the opposite look like *here*? Obviously, the polar opposite of doing mathematics should display an indeterminacy that, qua grammatical characterization, is comparable to the ones that our psychological language-games bear. It is a way of doing mathematics in which there is, besides the possibility of error, the possibility of disagreement, which brings us to Wittgenstein's attitude towards the central role of contradiction in mathematics. For the polar opposite of our way of doing mathematics concerns precisely a series of fictitious language-games in which the law of non-contradiction, as we would say, does *not* govern the grammatical commerce of these games, in a sense comparable to the present situation in our psychological language-games. In other words, Wittgenstein, as the above passage suggests, is interested in seeing fictitious language-games in which the law of non-contradiction *does* govern the use of psychological verbs. It is again important to notice here what it is with which Wittgenstein sets out for the playground of inventing and collating language-games: a mere skeleton, something that is of no use at all in a comparison with the logical predicament of our own language as long as it has not been clad by a certain amount of flesh. Should Wittgenstein manage to produce the fictitious language-games intimated here, he would present language-games in which the fictitious people play the psychological games with rigid rules, as we currently do in mathematics, and the mathematical games with 'elastic rules', as we currently do in our psychological languages-games.

Wittgenstein wants to understand what mathematics is, i.e. he wants to understand our way of doing mathematics, our mathematical predicament, and he wants to understand it no less than any other predicament of our language troubling his mind. And that means, in the case of mathematics, and from his uncommon way of looking at things: to be interested in fictitious ways of doing mathematics *less definitely*. As suggested, it is precisely with respect to an interest as this one that Wittgenstein's attitude towards contradiction mathematics comes to the fore.

'But a contradiction in mathematics is incompatible with its application.

'If it is consistently applied, i.e. applied to produce arbitrary results, it makes the application of mathematics into a farce, or some kind of superfluous ceremony. Its effect is that of non-rigid rulers which permit various results of measuring by being expanded and contracted.' But was measuring by pacing not measuring at all? And if people worked out rulers made of dough, would that of itself have to be called wrong?

Couldn't reasons be easily imagined, on account of which a certain elasticity in rulers might be desirable?

"But isn't it right to manufacture rulers out of ever harder, more unalterable material?" Certainly it is right; if that is what one wants!

'Then are you in favour of contradiction?' Not at all; any more than of soft rulers. (RFM: 377)[169]

This passage is awash with interesting markers concerning Wittgenstein's uncommon way of looking at things. Thus, he does *not strive after* a practice of doing mathematics that merits contradiction and draws on it. He wants to leave everything as it is; he only means to *describe* the present situation in our language, and our way of doing mathematics is no exception in that respect. But that means that Wittgenstein wants to describe it in opposition to the urge to misunderstand mathematics, and one outstanding misunderstanding concerns our general attitude towards mathematical concepts: *we* look at them as what could not possibly have been otherwise or mathematics is finished. The conspicuous lack of indefinite concepts in mathematics, we claim, is certainly not a contingent characteristic of our way of doing it, for contradiction definitely *destroys* the calculus. *We* think that it destroys the language-game; Wittgenstein, on the other hand, does not actually think or claim the contrary. However, he does seize upon our thinking as providing him with some choice pieces of *Rohmaterial* to ponder philosophically. Far from favouring a replacement of our own way of doing mathematics by one in which we openly engage in contradiction, Wittgenstein countenances contradiction in mathematics as a genuine *possibility*, as a constituent of a possible way of doing mathematics, to be seen alongside our own way of doing it. So it is in particular with an eye towards the role of contradiction in mathematics that Wittgenstein, in the above passage, merely expresses his uncommon way of looking at things. He

---

169   Cf. 'But isn't contradiction forbidden by the law of contradiction? – At any rate "Non (p and non p)" doesn't forbid anything. It is a tautology. But *if we forbid* a contradiction, then we are excluding forms of contradiction *from our* language. We expunge these forms' (RPP I; 44; both emphases mine).

does not claim anything there, any more than in a remark as the following: 'The laws of logic, e.g., excluded middle and contradiction, are arbitrary. This statement is a bit repulsive but nevertheless true' (AWL: 71).[170]

Another interesting marker, in the above passage, of Wittgenstein's uncommon way of looking is the one that addresses the point of interest or concern: Certainly is it right to manufacture rulers out of ever harder, more unalterable material—'if that is what one wants!', Wittgenstein adds. Of course, there would seem to be little if anything for us to wish for in mathematics in respect of the rigidity of rules, which would appear to be the essence of mathematics itself. Wittgenstein, as the mathematician might say, is clearly begging the question. Mathematics is prior to our wishes and concerns! 'You can have your wishes, I allow you your concerns, but not as things on which mathematics builds!' Of course, Wittgenstein, for his own part, would not say that he has *claimed* anything. In contrast to mathematicians, he does not find it repulsive at all *to say* that the laws of logic are arbitrary. For what he *says* here is said, not in the assertive mood, but in the grammatical mode; and, as Wittgenstein well knows, matters of philosophy are certainly not settled by promulgating merely grammatical statements. *He* looks at the language-game as autonomous, for reasons of philosophy, because of our deep-seated urges to think along certain characteristic lines there. He has not investigated the situation in mathematics first so as to make an exception there, any more than he has investigated the situation in psychology first, so as *not* to make an exception there—so as to tell the world that he always looks at the language-game as autonomous, except for the mathematical one. That should help us to see what it is like to look at the language-game as autonomous. To say that mathematics poses no exception here is to say that doing mathematics is certainly not beholden to our way of doing it; other ways are imaginable. So when the mathematician claims that 'contradiction destroys the calculus', Wittgenstein is quick to retort with an uncommon question such as the following: 'what gives it this special position? With a little imagination, I believe, it can certainly be shaken' (RFM: 376).

The conviction that contradiction destroys the calculus, as the mathematician says, need not be shaken at all *as far as Wittgenstein himself* is concerned. But that it need not be done in his own case is not because it has once been done.

---

170   Cf. 'The propositions of logic are "laws of thought", "because they bring out the essence of human thinking"—to put it more correctly: because they bring out, or shew, the essence, the technique, of thinking. They shew what thinking is and *also shew kinds of thinking*' (RFM: 90, emphasis mine); 'Logic, it may be said, shews us what we understand by "proposition" and by "language"' (RFM: 134).

276

Wittgenstein has never gone so far as to picture in detail, for himself, one or more fictitious language-games in which the law of non-contradiction has been broken (as we would say); *that is to say*, Wittgenstein has never done anything to that effect, only to be shaken thereupon in his attitude to this law. He may well be said to have been shaken, in the 1930s, in the 'belief' that the possibility of language must come in the shape of the so-called *crystalline purity of logic*. But to have been shaken in that respect does not mean that Wittgenstein ended up looking at the mathematical language-game as autonomous *because* it was ultimately his 'belief' in the law of non-contradiction in which he was shaken. But now that he looks at the language-game as autonomous, the law of non-contradiction may well be said to pose a special challenge to his imagination. As he often emphasizes, it really is a matter of finding appropriate examples, of making exceptional comparisons.

> To resolve these philosophical problems one has to compare things which it has never seriously occurred to anyone to compare.
>
> It goes *via new* examples and comparisons. The hackneyed ones don't shew us it. (RFM: 376)

Wittgenstein says that 'with a little imagination' the common attitude towards the law of contradiction 'can certainly be shaken', but the above words seem to suggest that redemption is not easily had 'with a little imagination'. As a matter of fact, it has turned out to be utterly challenging to set up fictitious language-game as possibilities alongside our own way of doing mathematics—fictitious language-games, that is, in which contradiction belongs 'reasonably' to the essence of their workings. So we should draw a clear distinction between the following two things 1) Wittgenstein's attitude towards contradiction in mathematics, an attitude that is to be elucidated with reference to his uncommon way of looking; 2) the severe difficulties he faces in coming to terms with what mathematics is *by* seeing our definite way of doing so as a possibility alongside such (fictitious) ways of doing it in which contradiction plays an *essential* role.

If Wittgenstein wants to rouse not so much the mathematicians themselves but rather that formidable part of them responsible for their firm hold on the idea that contradiction destroys the calculus, he should not be taken to suggest that contradiction poses no great challenge to his own mind. On the other hand, if the challenge that mathematics poses is that of seeing indefinite ways of doing mathematics alongside our own definite ways of doing so, the challenge should in substance be analogous to the one Wittgenstein faces in psychology, namely that of seeing definite ways of doing psychology alongside our own indefinite ways. In both cases, the challenge is what Wittgenstein is committed to take on, owing to his way of looking at language, which says *that* (our) language-games are possibilities among other possibilities. And if mathematics poses an exception in the sense that it must be done in the way we do it, that is, if it is an *Unding* in the sense that it does not allow deviations from its core determinacy, the question arises why our way of doing mathematics should turn out to be an *Unding*, and why our way of doing psychology is a possibility among other possibilities, i.e. is *not* an *Unding*.

'What gives it this special position?', Wittgenstein asks (see above); and we might well add now: *for* or *within* Wittgenstein's uncommon way of looking. That contradiction poses a real challenge to Wittgenstein's mind is clearly shown by the close alliance of the following three questions:

> "Why should contradiction be disallowed in mathematics?" Well, why is it not allowed in our simple language-games? (There is certainly a connexion here.) Is this then a fundamental law governing all thinkable language-games? (RFM: 255)

In this passage, Wittgenstein answers the ubiquitous question 'Why should contradiction be disallowed in mathematics?' with a less ubiquitous question: 'Well, why is it not allowed in our simple language-games?' He suggests that it is indeed not allowed in simple language-games, but so he suggests that if we see why it is not allowed in such language-games: Well, that should help us to answer the first question. Bringing the notion of contradiction to bear upon that of simple language-games, he suggests that the relationship among these notions is more perspicuous than between contradiction and mathematics. But the problem, I think, with this move is that it does not render the notion of simple language-games any clearer. For now he cannot, without begging the question, characterize it in turn it by invoking the notion of contradiction.

Wittgenstein speaks of *thinkable* language-games, a notion that we have been dealing with in the preceding chapter, where we have seen its pivotal importance for his uncommon way of looking at things. A thinkable language-game is a somewhat pleonastic expression, for no language-game *counts* as unthinkable, at least not in Wittgenstein's approach and way of thinking. An unthinkable language-game is an *Unding*, a degenerate 'possibility', which is not a possibility among other possibilities. But there are no such language-games, for each one is being looked at as describ*able*, as think*able*, and the philosophical challenge is precisely to describe their actual occurrences as possibilities among other possibilities. No language-game is unthinkable, but *not* because that is what Wittgenstein has discovered one day, only to lay this supposed revelation down as an attractive and trustworthy foundation for a new way of looking of looking upon the world. No, *that* the language-game *is* thinkable, *is* a possibility among other possibilities, constitutes his way looking at language. He looks at the language-game *as* thinkable, and only through this way of looking at language does he now come to face the difficult question whether the law of contradiction is *a fundamental law* governing all thinkable language-games.

If there is such a law, Wittgenstein did not commit *knowingly* to it as a cornerstone in his new way of looking. In the early 1930s, he rather began to look at the language-game as a thinkable affair, and not until later did he feel irked by the question as to whether there is as a fundamental law governing *all* thinkable language-games. Wittgenstein's way of looking at the language-game is silent on the question of what counts as another possibility with respect to a particular language-game. All he laid down by way of a determination is that language-games should be compared with each other and that the *comparison* should tell us whether a particular language-game counts as a variation on our language-game or not. It is the lack of a *pre*determination on the part of Wittgenstein's way of looking that should vouch for its being essentially undogmatic. So where does this leave us as regards that alleged fundamental law governing all thinkable language-games? Is it something that does not sit well with the kind of silence 'governing' Wittgenstein's way of looking at the language-game? A law governing all thinkable language-game is a law that puts limits on the extent to which variations on a particular language-game can be had and expanded on. (One might think of our own language being such a law.) So the law appears to pose a serious problem for Wittgenstein's way of looking, but only if it puts such restrictions on the language-games that not *all* of them can be described as representing possibilities among other possibilities. *Some* language-games are not thinkable and the simple ones seem to present themselves as serious candidates on that very score.

Wittgenstein speaks of the law as what he seems to have 'discovered' in the course of his investigations. His suggestion is that it might well turn out to be something that he had better take up as a pivotal determinant in the formulation of his new way of looking at things. As part of such a formulation the law determines that simple language-game do not count as possibilities alongside possibilities as simple as themselves. The simple language-games are not describ*able by variations on their themes*, that is, by other language-games as simple as they are themselves. On these terms, the simple language-game represents a possibility only within a series of possibilities the extreme end of which is the complex language-game, one in which contradiction might be said to hold sway. But *if* these alleged complex language-games *do not count* as possibilities either, that is to say, alongside the simple language-games as possibilities, then the simple language-game is a truly unthinkable affair, as perfect an *Unding* as anything can be. The simple language-games are just there, in our *Lebensform*, being what they are and representing a certain human condition that cannot be otherwise. And that, in turn, means that if each of our language-games is either a simple language-game or a mere extension of one of these things—things on which *everything* then ultimately builds in our language, that logic *in the end* cannot be described, to recall Wittgenstein's dramatic words here from *On Certainty*. For to describe logic *means* to describe the language-game as a possibility among other possibilities; it means to describe language to that effect, *without any leftovers*.

However, our language does not build on so-called simple language-games only, for recall what Wittgenstein said concerning our psychological concepts: 'The basic concepts are interwoven so closely with what is most fundamental in our way of living that they are therefore unassailable.' These concepts are indeterminate with respect to the grammatical characterization that stipulates our simple language-games as definite, determinate. But that seems to mean that our simple language-games *and* the ones in which indeterminate concepts figure have something important to share: namely, that they are both unthinkable in a sense of the word that Wittgenstein, given his present way of looking at things, repudiates.

What Wittgenstein needs to imagine, in the case of mathematics, is the so-called polar opposite of our own determinate way of doing mathematics. In the above passage, he has a fervent advocate of the common way of looking at things claiming that contradiction 'makes the application of mathematics into a farce, or some kind of superfluous ceremony. Its effect is that of non-rigid rulers which permit various results of measuring by being expanded and contracted.' Whether contradiction destroys the calculus or makes the application of mathematics into a farce: Wittgenstein should pay attention to such modes of talking as they give him a basis to challenge the attitude that mathematicians have respecting contradiction. And so it is: he builds upon such talks, precisely because they are among the first that come to mind. When he says that with a little imagination 'it can certainly be shaken', he, obviously, wants to exploit what he feels the mathematician has done very little if at all, namely, *imagining* language-games in which contradiction plays an essential role. The mathematician does not see why he should indulge in such a time-consuming activity. Contradiction destroys the calculus, the possibility of the language-game, and, as the mathematician should like to emphasize, a mere adding of details does do little beyond lending colour to the image of the language-game as a complete farce. So where the mathematician dismisses contradiction out of hand, he writes off any effort to see for himself that details might matter and could bring about a thorough shaking on his own part. For Wittgenstein, details do matter greatly, but, to be sure, not as means *to prove* that contradiction need not necessarily destroy the calculus. *That* contradiction need not necessarily do that expresses merely his grammatical attitude towards language-games, an attitude that traces back to his uncommon way of looking at things.

If the effect of contradiction is that of non-rigid rulers permitting various results of measuring by being expanded and contracted, then, Wittgenstein wants to say: set out for the playground of inventing and collating language-game and picture such rulers for yourself. Ask: What does a language-game look like in which such rulers obtain? – And here it is important to notice the following: the kind of language-game that Wittgenstein is anxious to see alongside our own one(s) is first conceived in terms of a rather abstract picture itself. He is interested in seeing the polar opposite of what our own language displays on the subject of its grammatical characterization. Thus, the picture of non-rigid rulers is not itself grammar, but a *prototype* of the kind of grammar (logic) of the language-game in which he is interested. There is flesh to be put on the abstract bones of the picture. The picture must come alive, and to do so is to bring in human beings *with* particular interests and concerns. In short: What is the *Witz* of a language-game in which contradiction (as we would say) is constitutive of its very essence? It is rather not the *Witz* of *our* language-game that prompts Wittgenstein to set out for his playground, but his interest in seeing the polar opposite of our own language-game, whose *Witz* remains more often than not in the dark. So he enters upon his playground of inventing and collating language-games with a *prototype* of grammar and it is with respect to such a prototype that he needs to come out with a specific interest, one that should morph *the prototype into a token* of a language-game. The prototype has no physiognomy; and only the language-game *as a token* is an object of comparison; only in that shape does it do its job, and can do in the first instance.

Let see for ourselves how a prototype might look like, a skeleton with some pieces of flesh on it, but without making mention of any kind of interest or concern. So let us imagine a language-game in which people operate with non-rigid measuring rods. The application of such rods gives rise to such results as that, say, a table measures 2 meters at one time (in the morning) and 2.30 meters at another time (in the evening), *and not a single soul balks* at such diverging results (as we would say). No person would for instance be puzzled at his obtaining such results, but neither does it come to blows over such 'diverging' results should they be obtained among a group of persons. This is just how the language-game is. At the same time, though, the persons playing this game might well harbour doubts as to whether the dough-rulers have been applied *correctly*, that is, without mistake, *when* someone claims to have arrived at the result of the table measuring a length of *more* than 2.50 meter, or *less* than 1.80 meter. That is, we can well imagine (as Wittgenstein would say) that within this practice of measuring objects the length must fall within a certain margin and that any recorded measure falling outside it will be treated with more or less suspicion up to this point: you have made a mistake! Thus, within this measuring practice, there is besides the possibility of making a mistake also ample room for disagreement over whether an object measures this or that length. Here disagreement, as one would say, does not jeopardize the language-game; on the contrary, it belongs to its essence. This is how the game is played; they play it with elastic tools. What makes one person certain does not make another certain. 'But the discrepancy has its limits'.

Our own manner of measuring objects—or doing mathematics, for that matter—is characterized by the application of rigid rulers, or rules. *This means* that there is, besides the possibility of making a mistake, *no* room for disagreement over whether the outcome of a calculation is right or not. Should disagreement supervene, calculating would lose its *Witz* (RFM: 200). This is how the game is played; *we* play it with rigid rules. Of course, the logical skeleton underlying such fictitious language-game as circumscribed above is precisely such one as can be distilled from our indeterminate way of doing psychological things with words. Indeed, what Wittgenstein wants to have before his eyes are fictitious tokens of indeterminacy *comparable* to ones in which our psychological language-games take root—and so the other way around.

But what are we to make of the interest of our fictitious people? What is the *Witz* of the language-game? Why should we call what they do *measuring*? Of course, our purpose was to portray people who use non-rigid measuring rods, people whose measuring practice diverges radically from our own practice but who *measure* nonetheless. But this setting of our purpose should not influence the way we judge the fictitious language-game. Indeed, even if we grant that their measuring rods are somewhat reminiscent of ours and that their practice of operating on them bears a certain resemblance to what *we call* measuring, there is still the question: Why on earth should we call that *measuring*? What particular concern or interest do our fictitious people connect with their practice? How does their practice connect with the rest of their *Lebensweise*? Should we not bring to bear upon the above sketch *much more* than we thought necessary at the beginning of our imaginary act? But, of course, what about *our own* interest: we play our (mathematical) language-games with rigid rules, and if this predicament is something 'connected with what interests us, with what matters to us', if that is 'what we want', what then *is* our interest? How is it expressed, if not in the rigidity of the rules themselves? How can we tell what our interest is, without telling a story in which these rules are not already mentioned? Intimately connected with these questions is the following. Above we have said that our fictitious people do not balk at attaining such diverging results as depicted. The words 'do not balk' were meant to be a placeholder, something that needs to be filled in, and can be done so in one way or another. For we grant our fictitious people sight and acumen; they are not envisaged as a bunch of deranged troglodytes. We want to portray people who measure, rather than some lunatics who render measuring 'into a farce, or some kind of superfluous ceremony'. So, starting from our language, we should like to raise all kinds of questions: how should they not be bothered by the diverging result, how could they ever get so far as to *accept* one particular measure at one time and a different one at another time? And now it *seems* that if only if we bring a certain kind of interest into account, a *Witz*, such questions would cease to trouble us. But what might such a *Witz* be if not a thing to calm our worries?

The above sketch: a farce? Wittgenstein would say: picture any such farce for yourself and put it alongside such a language-game as sketched above; picture it and let the differences and similarities between a farce and an indeterminate way of doing mathematical things take part of an *übersichtliche Darstellung*.

We do well here not to sidestep Wittgenstein's famous wood sellers:

> Suppose I had said: those people pay for wood on the *ground of calculation*; they accept a calculation as proof that they have to pay so much.—well, that is simply a description of their procedure (of their behaviour). (RFM: 93)

> Those people—we would say—sell timber by cubic measure——but are they right in doing so? Wouldn't it be more correct to sell it by weight—or by the time that it took to fell the timber—or by the labour of felling measured by the age and strength of the woodsman? And why should they not hand it over for a price which is independent of all this: each buyer pays the same however much he takes (they have found it possible to live like that). And is there anything to be said against simply giving the wood away. (RFM: 94)

> Very well; but what if they piled the timber in heaps of arbitrary, varying height and then sold it at a price proportionate to the area covered by the piles?
>
> And what if they even justified this with the words: "Of course, if you buy more timber, you must pay more"? (RFM: 94)

David Cerbone, in his contribution to *The New Wittgenstein*, writes the following about the wood sellers:

Frege's logical aliens were meant to provide a case of beings who think and speak and yet contradict the laws of thought; they were meant, that is, to be beings who are "capable" of illogical thought. What I take Wittgenstein to be doing with the wood sellers is showing how any attempt to get beyond the mouthing of the words "beings who think according to laws of thought contradicting our own," any attempt really to imagine such creatures, breaks down, because no beings we imagine of whom we would be willing to say that they are thinking would answer to this initial description.[171]

Cerbone's reaction to Wittgenstein's wood sellers is of a piece with the mathematician's reaction to contradiction, precisely the reaction that Wittgenstein seeks to shake. Indeed, Cerbone's reaction shows us how difficult it is to be shaken. But this difficulty is not to be confused with Wittgenstein's attitude towards the mathematician's claim that contradiction destroys the calculus, an attitude that inheres in his uncommon way of looking at things. Cerbone's way of presenting Wittgenstein's wood sellers makes us forget about this attitude, for Cerbone believes that Wittgenstein's wood sellers exemplify his attitude towards contradiction.

When Cerbone says that 'What I take Wittgenstein to be doing with the wood sellers is showing how *any* attempt to get beyond the mouthing of the words "beings who think according to laws of thought contradicting our own," *any* attempt really to imagine such creatures, breaks down' (emphases mine), he takes to Wittgenstein's wood sellers as a kind of knockout proof in his extensive repertoire of fictitious language-games, a kind of rarefaction that should silence, once and for all, any attempt to demonstrate the possibility of such radical a variation on the theme of our thinking as the utmost bound: "beings who think according to laws of thought contradicting our own". But if that is what Wittgenstein has *wanted* to show with his wood sellers, he should be said to have been doing something that goes radically against the grain of his later conception of logic. For he looks at our own logical predicament, on each of its themes, *as* one logical possibility among other such possibilities, and our way of thinking makes no exception in that respect. There is, in a most important sense, nothing exceptional about Wittgenstein's wood sellers: they are truly of a piece with all his fictitious language-games in that they are put to work *because* of his conception of logic—things that should show the *how* of our own logical predicament. The *that* of Wittgenstein's conception of logic is one thing, the story of its *hows* an altogether different thing. For the effort of showing the *how* of our own logical

---

171   David R. Cerbone, 'How to do things with wood: Wittgenstein, Frege and the problem of illogical thought', in Alice Crary and Rupert Read, eds., *The New Wittgenstein* (London & New York: Routledge, 2000), 304.

predicament, with respect to one or another theme, is not without trouble and difficulties, as we have been suggesting again and again. Cerbone seems to conflate the two stories.

In this regard the following passage, in which Wittgenstein enunciates his conception of logic, is relevant:

> Isn't it like this: so long as one thinks it can't be otherwise, one draws logical conclusions. This presumably means: so long as *such-and-such is not brought in question at all.*
>
> The steps which are not brought in question are logical inferences. But the reason why they are not brought in question is not that they 'certainly correspond to the truth'—or something of the sort,—no, it is just this that is called 'thinking', 'speaking', 'inferring', 'arguing'. There is not any question at all here of some correspondence between what is said and reality; rather is logic *antecedent* to any such correspondence; in the same sense, that is, as that in which the establishment of a method of measurement is *antecedent* to the correctness of incorrectness of a statement of length. (RFM: 96)

Here is Cerbone's comment on the above passage:

> Wittgenstein's talk of *antecedence* here is another way of saying that logic provides a kind of framework or background to what we call thinking, speaking, inferring and arguing, but if logic does provide such a framework, then there is no sense to be made of thinking, speaking, inferring and arguing in ways that "contradict logic." (*ibid*, 307)

The whole burden of this passage is laid down at the door of the word "framework". Not that there is anything wrong with *that* word, but in the above passage it is an empty shell. Would logic, if Wittgenstein had talked about it differently, not also have been 'a kind of framework or background to what we call thinking, speaking, inferring and arguing'? Indeed, why call it *logic* if it had not been such a background? How, I wonder, could Cerbone have prevented his conclusion—'there is no sense to be made of thinking, speaking, inferring and arguing in ways that "contradict logic"'—when nothing worth the name of logic could fail to prevent 'to provide a kind of framework or background to what we call thinking, speaking, inferring and arguing'? Would Cerbone's interpretation of Wittgenstein's wood sellers' scenarios have been different in case Wittgenstein had been championing a different conception of logic? Can it not be that Cerbone's interpretation of Wittgenstein's wood sellers has added a little too much determination on what Wittgenstein's conception of logic *must be* lest Cerbone fall into a contradiction? Or is it rather the other way around? But *if*, according to Cerbone, 'there is no sense to be made of thinking, speaking, inferring and arguing in ways that "contradict logic"', that is, if we see and understand that there is no such sense to be made once we see what Wittgenstein's conception of logic amounts to, what then is the use and significance of his wood sellers? If they reveal us no more than what we can already uncover through a little reflection on Wittgenstein's conception of logic, should this not embolden the impression on the part of many a commentator that Wittgenstein's fictitious language-games are mere pomp and embellishment?

For Wittgenstein it is exactly because of logic being *antecedent* (in the way enunciated above) that it comes to such grammatical notices as '[o]ther concepts, though akin to ours, might seem *very* queer to us; deviations, namely, from the usual in an unusual *direction*' (RPP II: 693)[172]—and, to mention one more remark here, 'an education quite different from ours might also be the foundation for quite different concepts. For here life would run on differently.—What interests us would not interest them. Here different concepts would no longer be unimaginable. In fact, this is the only way in which *essentially different* concepts are imaginable' (RPP II: 707–08, emphasis mine). Wittgenstein's own comment on his wood sellers should be heeded.

> How could I shew them that—as I should say—you don't really buy more wood if you buy a pile covering a bigger area?—I should, for instance, take a pile which was small by their ideas and, by laying the logs around, change it into a 'big' one. This *might* convince them—but perhaps they would say: "Yes, now it's a *lot* of wood and costs more"—and that would be the end of the matter.—We should presumably say in this case: they simply do not mean the same by "a lot of wood" and "a little wood" as we do; and they have quite a different system of payment from us. (RFM: 94).

That communication breaks down with the wood sellers is no reason for Wittgenstein to deny us right away any such predicate as 'they simply do not mean the same by "a lot of wood" and "a little wood" as we do; and they have quite a different system of payment from us.' But the possibility of such a predicating is precisely what Cerbone seems to deny when he says that 'any attempt really to imagine such creatures, breaks down, because no beings we imagine of whom we would be willing to say that they are thinking would answer to this initial description.' Cerbone draws a conclusion from the breakdown of communication with the wood sellers that Wittgenstein does *not* draw, namely a further breakdown on us or our willingness to recognize in their practice anything such as that 'they have quite a different system of payment from us.'

Cerbone writes:

> The cogency of Frege's description presupposes the availability of a notion of inference apart from our actual practices of inferring. The wood sellers' scenario, via examination of the concept of measuring, undermines the intelligibility of this notion. Any practice

---

172   Cf. Z: 373.

which appeared consistently to yield such contrary results is not one, Wittgenstein is reminding us, that we would call inferring at all. (*ibid*, 303)

True, *we* would not *readily* call *that* inferring at all—but *that's* why Wittgenstein reminds us of such scenarios as the wood sellers: in order to break the hold which that spell has on us. On the other hand, *that* Wittgenstein faces serious troubles on the playground of inventing and collating language is a story that one misses completely if one fails to keep these troubles apart from his stance towards language, logic. How severely Cerbone fails to do precisely that is also apparent near the end of his paper, where he writes with reference to Wittgenstein's remark *OC §501*:

> The very first entry of his *Notebooks 1914–1916*, which contain preliminary formulations of the remarks which make up the *Tractatus*, is the sentence 'Logic must take care of itself' and this too suggests an attitude that in the end logic cannot be described, and that it must instead be seen in the practice of language. Both remarks, that 'logic cannot be described' [sic] and that 'logic must take care of itself', present the kind of quietism that I take Wittgenstein to be recommending, a kind of quietism that simply leaves us where we are, with our thinking and our language, and with all confused and misleading talk of limits 'withdrawn from circulation'. (*ibid*, 309)

Cerbone thinks that what Wittgenstein gives expression to in *On Certainty*, §501, presents his so-called quietism. But what Wittgenstein gives expression to in that passage is a man in trouble. There is something highly disquieting about Cerbone's recommendation to see in *OC §501* Wittgenstein's quietism.[173]

5.3 What a strange method!

One might think as follows: It is not until Wittgenstein has furnished a description of our own concept that he sets out for the playground of inventing and collating language-games. One might think thus, because what comes to lie under his comparing eye is such a description and not until he has finished with furnishing this part of the representation does it make sense to make for a description of a fictitious language-game. Wittgenstein, however, as we have seen in the Chapter 2, more often than not runs aground in his sustained efforts on the playground of describing our language. But his difficulties there do not prevent him from going, every now and then, to the playground of inventing and collating language-games. On the contrary, one gets the firm impression that his activities on the latter playground come to his aid in respect of his realizing what

---

173   See also next chapter for *On Certainty* §501.

is involved in the effort of describing the workings of our own language-games. That is, while attempting invention, he sees himself as raising *questions* that seem to sharpen his wits as regards the workings of our concepts. Indeed, one gets the firm impression that there is *de facto* no hard and fast separation among Wittgenstein's activities on the two playgrounds, for, it is true, he keeps moving vehemently to and fro between them, between his difficulties on the one playground and his difficulties on the other playground; between his running aground here and his running aground there. For, it is true, he gets stuck all over the place.

Let us be interested in seeing what is involved in Wittgenstein's efforts to flesh out a fictitious language-game in which there is agreement over the question whether an expression of feeling is genuine or not. Thus, it is by means of working out this *logical* possibility that he is anxious to understand our own logical predicament. There is no uncertainty in the fictitious language-game whether someone is e.g. in pain or not: people all treat the moaning person as someone having pain; or they all treat the bleeding person as someone having pain, but only when the person bleeds. Many a variation is thinkable and Wittgenstein is clear about what he seeks to set up.

> The capacity to pretend therefore resides in the ability to imitate, or in the ability to have this intention.
>
> But we must assume that a subject can say the words "I am in pain". Therefore it is a matter of having the capacity to intend. Is it possible, for instance, to imagine people who cannot lie because for them to lie would be nothing but a dissonance. I want to imagine a case where people are truthful not as a matter of *morality*, but rather see something absurd in a lie. Whoever lies would be viewed as mentally ill.
>
> Or better: lying or pretending would have to appear to these people as perversity. (LWPP II: 56).

Wittgenstein, having settled on a certain logical skeleton of the fictitious language-game, faces the difficult task to see and work out what belongs to its grammar. He finds himself confronted with questions such as what facts now obtain (more) significance and what facts now, again compared with our own language-games, abate in significance [*Wichtigkeit*]. He needs to be concerned with the *Witz* of the fictitious language-game. What *is* the *Witz* of recognizing only with the possibility of error that someone is having pain? What is the *Witz* or what could it be? But, of course, wherein does the *Witz* of our own language-games lie? What do we actually know when we know that someone is in pain? *Woran liegt uns?* We know when someone is in pain in daily life. That is to say, I know it, but you may well have your doubts, and when in a certain situation we both know that someone is in pain, the *Witz* of the language-game we play is still beholden to such possible situations in which one of us has its legitimate doubts.

My present elaboration hardly goes beyond the mere broaching of the topic, yet it does add, I think, strongly to the general impression that Wittgenstein was in deep trouble on the playground of inventing and collating language-games. The topic concerns the following remark.

> But what a strange method! – I form a concept and ask myself how one might follow through with it consistently. What we feel would deserve to be called that. (RPP II: 491).

This remark concerns the fleshing out of the fictitious language-game, on the basis of the kind of logical skeleton that Wittgenstein carries to the playground of inventing and collecting language-games. Here the logical skeleton is the measure of fictitious deviation from our own language-game that Wittgenstein wants to see alongside its workings. So he conceives of one aspect of our language-game as changed, in some direction or other, only to wonder how one 'might follow through with' the conceived change 'consistently'. The strange method, then, is not a certain method among various kinds of methods of inventing fictitious language-games. Rather, it concerns whatever effort Wittgenstein brings into play so as to earmark the *how* of our language-game by a fictitious deviation from its present workings. The strangeness at issue is intimated in many a passage that we have quoted so far and perhaps we do well here to recall the following.

> We say: "Let's imagine human beings who don't know *this* language-game". But this does not give us any clear idea of the life of these people, of where it deviates from ours. We don't yet know what we have to imagine; for the life of these people is supposed to correspond to ours for the rest, and it first has to be determined what we would call a life that corresponds to ours under the new circumstances.
>
> Isn't it as if one said: There are people who play chess without the king? Questions immediately arise: Who wins now, who loses, etc. You have to make *further* decisions that you didn't anticipate in that first determination. Just as you also don't have an overview of the original technique, and are only familiar with it from case to case. (LWPP II: 71)

Setting out for the playground of inventing and collating language-games with no more in his rucksack than the logical skeleton of the fictitious language-game to be fleshed out, a skeleton as e.g. 'one recognizes only with the possibility of error that someone is in pain', Wittgenstein *immediately* faces questions on this ground which he *did not foresee* the moment he settled on the logical skeleton.

Indeed, the whole point of the above passage is this: 'Questions immediately arise'. It is a point that, once seen against the background of Wittgenstein's philosophical record, bears out the following: where these questions now arise *immediately* they did not do so at the time Wittgenstein realized the *importance* of the method that he now deems strange. That is to say, at that time the questions did not so much arise *gradually* as that they did not arise at all. It was only *after* Wittgenstein realized the importance of fictitious language-games and began to try his hand at the invention of these things, that he saw himself systematically thrown back on the effort to realize what *inventing* these things actually involves. Here is another interesting passage:

> What forms of mental defects actually exist is of no concern to us; but the possibilities of such forms do concern us. It is not whether there are men incapable of thinking "At that time I wanted to …", but how this concept can be followed through.
>
> How could this assumption be followed through consistently? What would we call a consistent follow-through? [*Was würden wir eine konsequente Durchführung nennen?*] – If you assume that someone cannot do *this*, then how about *that*? Is he also unable to do this? – Where does this concept take us? (RPP II: 578–579)[174]

The strangeness of Wittgenstein's method concerns this fact: 'I form a concept and ask myself how one might follow through with it consistently. What we feel would deserve to be called that'—a fact that he clearly intimates in similar terms in the above passage: 'How could this assumption be followed through consistently? What would we call a consistent follow-through?'

Now why would Wittgenstein say that the method is strange? Because it concerns *concepts*, rather than items of the physical world. In the latter case, you can think of some change in e.g. the mechanism of an artefact and, by dint of your knowledge of physical laws, *think through* the consequences this change will have for the mechanism as a whole. There really is a method here: a technique of seeing how a certain change leads to a deviation from the status quo. The method can be taught and, of course, is actually taught and applied in virtually every corners of our present society. But when the change is to be thought through in the 'mechanism of concepts', in the language-game, in a *Lebensform*, we find ourselves confronted with a situation that has little in common with the situation in physics. There is no technique now, nothing of the sort, no law- or rule-governed practice whose results can be brought to our attention and agreed upon by us, philosophers. We scarcely know how our concepts relate to each other, how they connect with us and the world in which we live; and when we know it one day, it does not seem likely that we will know anything comparable to our knowledge of the physical world. 'If you assume that someone cannot do *this*, then how about *that*? Is he also unable to do this? – Where does this concept take us?' Wittgenstein faces these questions as their answers make up the fictitious language-game, the obligatory object of comparison. The interesting point

---

174   Cf. Z: 183.

as regards the above passage is that Wittgenstein asks how the assumption could be followed through *consistently*.

Strange, then, the method is, for what Wittgenstein invented was not really a *method*. The best he can be said to have invented (in the 1930s) was a movement of thought, one that *stressed* the importance of setting up fictitious language-games alongside our own language. But to stress this importance does not automatically mean to possess a *method* of inventing fictitious language-games, a technique of putting flesh on the bones of one logical skeleton or another, on e.g. 'the rock-bottom' of the polar opposite of our own way of doing things with words. The logical skeleton needs to be turned into a type and this type needs to emerge ultimately as a token of some way of doing things with words. Wittgenstein needs to flesh out fictitious language-games out of an array of ramifying connections obtaining among first- and third-person parties. He needs to flesh out something highly specific. And yet, it is rare to see him watching the kind of thing for which he ultimately set out for the playground of inventing and comparing language-games. It is as if he, while wearing himself out in the effort to describe our language, finds himself constantly thrown back on the activity of furnishing grammatical *remarks*.

> "The uncertainty as to whether another person is in pain" – is it based on the fact that he is he and I am I? [...]. No, *here* I'm deceived by a picture. The uncertainty is a matter of the particular case and of the vacillating of the concept. But that is our game – we play it with an elastic tool. (LWPP I: 243; amended translation)

> The uncertainty is not founded on the fact that he does not wear his pain on his sleeve. And there is not an uncertainty *in a particular case*. (RPP II: 621).

> The *uncertainty* whether someone else…is an (essential) trait of all these language-games. But this does not mean that everyone is hopelessly in doubt about what other people feel. (LWPP I: 877)

> "But you can't recognize pain with *certainty* just from externals." – The only way of recognizing it is by externals, and the uncertainty is constitutional. It is not a shortcoming.
>
> It resides in our concept that this uncertainty exists, in our instrument. Whether this concept is practical is really not the question. (RPP II: 657)

And, to add two more passages here:

> What we attend to is not that the evidence makes someone's feelings merely probable, but the fact that we consider *this* as evidence for something; that we construct a statement on *this* involved sort of evidence, and hence that such evidence has a special

importance [*Wichtigkeit*] in our lives and is made prominent by a concept. (RPP II: 709; amended translation)[175]

If it is said, "Evidence can only make it probable that expressions of emotions are genuine", this does *not* mean that instead of complete certainty we have just a more or less confident conjecture. "Only probable" cannot refer to the degree of our confidence, but only to the nature of the justification, to the character of the language-game. Surely this must help determine the constitution of our concepts: that there is no agreement among men as to the certainty of their convictions. (Compare the remark about agreement in colour-judgements and agreement in mathematics.) (RPP II: 684)[176]

It will be noticed that Wittgenstein deploys the notion of *Wichtigkeit* in the above passage as a placeholder in a certain *Denkschema*. The last passage I have added so as to make sure how Wittgenstein conceives the sense of the phrase 'only probable', namely *not* as the Empiricist takes it. It refers, Wittgenstein says, to the nature of the justification, i.e. to the *character* of the language-game. In other words, it refers to something that is the way it is, but need not necessarily be the way it is. 'Surely this must help determine the constitution of the concept: that there is no agreement among men as to the certainty of their conviction.' So if we now ask what must *help* determine the constitution of the *fictitious* concept, i.e. one that poses the polar opposite of our own logical predicament—'for, as has been said, it would be quite possible [*wohl denkbar*] for this recognizing [whether someone is in pain, say] to be much more certain than it is' (LWPP II: 69)—, we might well think along such lines as Wittgenstein does in the following passages:

> Sufficient evidence passes over into insufficient evidence without a borderline. A natural foundation for the way this concept is formed is the complex nature and the variety of human cases [*Fälle*].
>
> Then given much less variety, a sharply bounded conceptual structure would have to seem natural.[177] But why does it seem so difficult to image the simplified case? (RPP II: 614)

I want to say: unforeseeability must be *an* essential property of the mental. Just like the endless multiplicity of expression. (LWPP II: 65)

The *important* fine shades of behaviour are not predictable.

---

175   Cf. LWPP II: 89.

176   Cf. 'I am trying to describe the laws of evidence or rules of evidence for *Erlebnissätze*: does one really characterize what is meant by the mental in this way' (LWPP II: 61); '"In investigating the laws of evidence for the mind, I am investigating the essence of the mental." Is that true' (LWPP II: 64).

177   Cf. PPF: 365–66, quoted above.

But does that mean: If they could be foreseen, we wouldn't speak of an inner and an outer in the case of human beings? —— Are we really imagining this kind of predictability clearly? Does it imply, for instance, that we wouldn't ask for a decision? (LWPP II: 65f.)

We are to *imagine* something of which we have no clear idea *yet*. And while imagining it we do not know for sure whether we are imagining it clearly. What is yet unclear in the realm of our imagination should be clear at last, for the clarity sought should cast that uncommon but crucial light on our own logical predicament, which is unclear in the first place, the rationale behind our search for clarity, and the source of the darkness in the realm of our imagination at the same time. But if our logical predicament is unclear right from the beginning, it is all due to the light in which Wittgenstein looks at it, for this light renders it a *logical* predicament in the first place and *defines* the task of seeing this predicament as one possibility among other possibilities. It is a light that cries out for the kind of light that other possibilities should throw on our logical predicament, a crying from which there is no escape. But this light, as soon as it begins to define and enunciate our predicament as a logical one, does not *foresee* what is involved in the task it defines and commits us to. It looks at our language as autonomous, rather than as a piece of mechanical workings, perfectly continuous with the rest of the world. It looks at our language as autonomous, *and yet* it commits us to a task that seems to have been conceived on the model of a task as that of *thinking through a change in the mechanical world*. In other words, the light that Wittgenstein casts on language, the light of his later life and philosophy, seems to trace back to *a simile*, one of which it is not clear yet whether it works at all. It might have been as slippery as the one that occasioned his early philosophy. True, it need not necessarily be a deceptive one. But as for now, it is not clear whether *this* works: We are to *imagine* something of which we have no clear idea *yet*. The problem, then, is not that we are to imagine something of which we have no clear idea yet; rather, the problem is that this juxtaposition of words evokes the idea of a task that might well be an illusionary one after all.

The logical skeleton that Wittgenstein carries to the playground of inventing and collating language-games *does not foresee* what sort of flesh is to be put on its bones. Questions immediately arise, Wittgenstein says, his suggestion being that once a question has been answered, that is, once one piece of flesh has been put on the logical skeleton, other questions still remain unanswered. But the answers to these questions need to be *decided* and that is an intriguing problem. For now the question arises how such decisions are to be taken. The fictitious language-game is being conceived on the model of a *composite* whole, and yet it is not a mechanical whole. It is not anything whose nature can be spelled out on the strength of one single item alone: the components do not relate to each other, e.g. in that the one implies the other. This is an important aspect of fictitious language-games and it mirrors a kcy fact of our own language-games. For recall that Wittgenstein, on the playground of describing our language, needs *to look* at our language in order to make out what is to be reckoned among the constituting items of a language-game. Thus, having for instance seen what makes up the beginning of a language-game, he really needs to *look and see* what comes in the wake of this beginning. The beginning makes up only one so-called building block of the language-game, only *one* stone in the building called the language-game. Given this building block, it does not imply what comes in its wake on the subject of additional building blocks. And yet, Wittgenstein, interestingly, while forming a concept, asks himself how one might follow through with it *consistently*.

'Can one imagine people who don't know pretence and to whom one cannot explain it? Can we imagine such people', Wittgenstein asks. 'Can one imagine people who cannot lie? – What else would these people lack? We should probably also imagine that they cannot make anything up and do not understand things that are made up' (LWPP II: 56). It is a recurring theme. Yet, the coping stone in Wittgenstein's dialectical edifice, i.e. the fictitious language-game as integral part of the descriptions of our language, *is meant* to throw light on our logical predicament, is *meant* to clear away the last questions, rather than to give rise to new ones.

6. A big gap in Wittgenstein's thinking

I should like to finish the first part of this study with some considerations on Wittgenstein's *On Certainty*. Indeed, having regularly referred to §501—'Am I not getting closer and closer to saying that in the end logic cannot be described? You must look at the practice of language, then you will see it'—it would be rather odd to leave the context in which these words arise and loom so large for what it is.

Up to the present day Wittgenstein's fascinating words have met with a profound lack of interest on the part of his commentators, which is all the more remarkable given the despair that Wittgenstein evinces over a central concern in his philosophical thinking, namely giving description of language, its logic. As for myself, I think that this lack of interest is of a piece with the general lack of interest on the part of his commentators for what philosophy can do *in the end*, namely giving descriptions of language, its logic. This general lack of interest is quite puzzling—if only in the light of *On Certainty* §501. But, of course, why be so negative, if not outright cynical? If commentators are prone to be completely absorbed in all aspects of Wittgenstein's philosophy with the exception of his final concern, why not suppose that it is all for the benefit of future commentators who will be able to devote themselves entirely to this final concern?

Well, why not? 'Philosophy must not interfere in any way with the actual use of language, so it can in the end [*am Ende*] only describe it' (PI: 124): Wittgenstein does not say here that *all* there is for philosophy to do is to describe language. He does not say *that* and his own manner of practising philosophy gives ample evidence that he is involved in more than giving descriptions alone. Wittgenstein is not averse at all, as we have seen, to mounting arguments every now and then: every so often he finds himself engaged in such diverse activities as elucidating philosophical views, drawing the physiognomy of error, enunciating statements, and excavating nonsense. He also indulges, we had better not forget, in habitual reflections on the nature of his own philosophy, that is, on his own need and interest in this 'discipline' in contrast to the need if not the powerful urge to explain there. In other words, Wittgenstein has given us, commentators, plenty of things to think about. And yet, whatever activity Wittgenstein means to undertake in philosophy, its point ultimately bears upon giving descriptions of language. It is just not arguments that should take the place of all explanation, and Wittgenstein's latest excavated piece of nonsense will not do either on that score. It is descriptions, and these things *alone*, that must take the place. Whatever worth Wittgenstein's various remarks and activities may have for us, they have really lost their merit and lasting significance for him, that is, once cut off from his final notches in the character of language descriptions.

My suggestion is that Wittgenstein's 'in the end' [*am Ende*] in *PI* §124 corresponds to the 'in the end' [*am Schluß*] in *OC* §501.[178] Wittgenstein, in *On Certainty*, does do an awful lot, is engaged there (as ever before) in a miscellany of closely related activities, but he seems to have severe difficulties in reaching the concluding moment: *descriptions* of our language. My purpose in this chapter is to explore why he despaired so thoroughgoingly of putting the coping stone on his dialectical edifice.

6.1 Surprise and a first grip

'Here there is still a big gap in my thinking. And I doubt whether it will be filled yet.'[179] This remark, clearly confessional in character, makes a good beginning. Perhaps the first thing to notice is that Wittgenstein does not say that there is something *wrong* with his thinking. He deems his thinking generally in order, save for the big gap that he, shortly before his untimely death, has come to recognize in it—and not without surprise, as it seems. But, of course, what is Wittgenstein's thinking?

It is not one particular strand of thinking: not one single *Gedankenbewegung* within the overall dialectic of his philosophical thinking. Rather, it is this dialectic itself, which is intrinsic to his uncommon way of looking at things and which stands in sharp contrast to e.g. Ramsey's way of looking at things. Ramsey, as we have seen, represents in Wittgenstein's eyes the bourgeois type of thinker. He, like Wittgenstein, wanted to establish an order in our knowledge of things; but he, unlike Wittgenstein, strived after establishing *the* order in this knowledge. To think that the present state—Wittgenstein's own example—'might not be the only possible one partly disquieted him and partly bored him' (CV: 24).[180] The opposite is true for Wittgenstein: to be confronted with the present state of affairs (i.e. of our language) as what might be the only possible one disquieted him more than anything else—precisely so because his

---

178 Cf. 'In philosophy we do not want to give explanations – precisely because no explanation can satisfy us. What we want to give and what we must give is, in the end [*am Schluß*], only a description' (VoW: 121).

179 OC p. 62.

180 Cf. Wittgenstein's German!

approach to language was that of looking at its workings *as* a possible state of affairs, as one possibility among others. Here I merely recall a pivotal point of Wittgenstein's thinking and my reason for taking to Ramsey by way of a contrast should become clear in a moment.

Wittgenstein's remark that there is still a big gap in his thinking has found its way to paper, not out of the blue, but near the end of his life, much struggling as he then was with some highly interesting *Rohmaterial* that Moore had been supplying in the shape of *the claims* he made on behalf of certain common-sense propositions, which I shall hereafter call Moore-type propositions.[181] Unlike Moore himself, Wittgenstein discerned something *logical* about these propositions, a number of highly curious aspects that prompted him to scrutinize them carefully. However, his investigations, as they have come down to us in the form of *On Certainty*, did not prompt Wittgenstein to carry his conception of logic to the melting pot. On the contrary, it was precisely this conception that enabled him to discern something logical about Moore's propositions. His thinking was really in order, save for the gap *in it*, a gap that this thinking itself recognized, in its own head as it were and through its efforts to come to *descriptive* terms with such propositions as Moore had brought to the fore. It did not fall to any other kind of thinking, one that Wittgenstein was still to develop, to fill the gap in his thinking. Although time was running out for the gap to be filled, it could be filled all the same, and his uncommon way of thinking, Wittgenstein suggests, would no doubt survive the effort unscathed.

When writing remarks such as the following

> When Moore says he *knows* such and such, he is really enumerating nothing but empirical propositions which we affirm without special testing; propositions, that is, which have a peculiar logical role in the system of our empirical propositions (OC: 136)[182],

Wittgenstein appeals to a conception of logic that is anything but a novelty in the kind of philosophical approach with which he entered his final stage. This conception, as we have seen in this book, has found numerous expressions with Wittgenstein. The particular phrasing in whose light I should like to consider some aspects of Wittgenstein's investigations in *On Certainty* can be found in *Remarks on the Foundations of Mathematics*, in the form of the following words:

---

181   Cf. Moore's 'A Defence of Common Sense' and 'Proof of an External World', in T. Baldwin, ed., *G. E. Moore: Selected Writings*.

182   Amended translation!

Following according to the rule is AT THE BOTTOM of our language-game. It characterizes what we call description.

This is the similarity of my treatment with relativity-theory, that it is so to speak a
consideration about the clocks with which we compare events. (RFM: 330)[183]

In this passage, Wittgenstein not only tells us what is at the bottom of our language-game; he also wants to make clear how this bears, obviously most intimately, on the way he treats the language-game. *That* "following according to
the rule" takes such a significant position in the language-game harks back not
so much to the language-game 'itself' as to his way of looking at it. Wittgenstein
speaks in this regard of the similarity of his treatment with relativity-theory, and
in *On Certainty* he is undoubtedly mindful of this similarity when he speaks in
terms of a particular step, namely 'a step like the one taken in relativity theory'
(OC: 305). In what follows, I shall draw repeatedly on the latter formulation as
well as on what I take its central point to be.

The step that he compares to relativity theory (hereafter: the Step) has been
no small step in the history of Wittgenstein's own philosophy, as one might say.
It added much to his characterization of the language-game as autonomous and
to that extent determined what a description of language is like when it 'receives
its light, that is to say its purpose, from the philosophical problems' (PI: 109). In
broad terms, the Step is Wittgenstein's uncommon way of looking at things. That
is to say, Wittgenstein's point of view on language could well be couched and
enunciated in terms of the Step. So, then, as one might say, the Step had begun to
inform Wittgenstein's conception of logic from the early 1930s onwards and did
not cease to do so until the end of his life. It informed his conception of logic in
On Certainty and in so doing it added substantially to the form of Wittgenstein's
struggles, that is, there as much as elsewhere.

What does it mean for the Step to inform Wittgenstein's conception of logic?
It means to practise a philosophy that sets its face against dogmatism right from
the beginning. It means that Wittgenstein can draw all kinds of distinctions in
language, that is, *to the extent as the Step allows him to do*. Consider:

There is no doubt at all that *in certain language-games* mathematical propositions play
the part of rules of description, as opposed to descriptive propositions.

But that is not to say that this contrast does not shade off in all directions. And *that* in
turn is not to say that the contrast is not of the greatest importance. (RFM: 363)

---

183   I have substituted the words 'at the bottom' for 'fundamental', which I think catches
       Wittgenstein's *am Grunde* better. Cf. also OC: 204.

Wittgenstein, in his own typical way of couching an importance, wants to make it clear that there is an important contrast at work *in his way of looking at language*, a contrast between two poles: rules of description and descriptive propositions. The contrast, he says, shades off in all directions. But *that* does not mean that the contrast, as Wittgenstein wants to emphasize, is not of the *greatest* importance. This importance, then, traces back to Wittgenstein's way of looking things, that is, traces back to the Step. One might be inclined to say that the Step is a one-sided way of looking at things. However, this is precisely what Wittgenstein wants (cf. PG: 68), and what he wants is anything but a dogmatic view. He wants to compare language with rules of the game, which means that he is operating on a contrast between two poles formed by rules of description and by descriptive propositions. As a result, Wittgenstein is committed to being attentive to what the contrast brings along in respect of those shading-offs *in all directions*. We misconstrue what he means by his one-sided way of looking at things if we fail to see that it gives him a first grip on language with respect to which he becomes able to make even the finest distinctions. Speaking of *all* directions, Wittgenstein's formulation might be said to have provided for the possibility of the direction that the contrast took in *On Certainty*, but that in turn does not mean he was ever aware of that direction, or that he had ever thought hard about it. So what could we say about the direction that his way of looking at language induced him to take in *On Certainty*, informed as he was by the Step ever since the early 1930s?

The direction could be represented by the following series of remarks, beginning with a memorable one from Wittgenstein's *Remarks on the Foundations of Mathematics*, from its last page:

> Every empirical proposition may serve as a rule if it is fixed, like a machine part, made immovable, so that now the whole representation turns around it and it becomes part of the coordinate system, independent of facts. (RFM: 437)

> The *truth* of certain empirical propositions belongs to our frame of reference [*Bezugssystem*]. (OC: 83)

> I want to say: we use judgments as principles of judgments. (OC: 124)[184]

> It is clear that our empirical propositions do not all have the same status, since one can lay down such a proposition and turn it from an empirical proposition into a norm of description. (OC: 167)

---

184   Cf. RFM: 435.

> Isn't what I am saying: any empirical proposition can be transformed into a postulate—
> and then becomes a norm of description. But I am suspicious even of this. The sentence
> is too general. One almost wants to say "any empirical propositions can, theoretically, be
> transformed…", but what does "theoretically" mean here? It sounds all too reminiscent
> of the *Tractatus*. (OC: 321)

> I want to say: propositions of the form of empirical propositions and not only proposi-
> tions of logic, form the foundation of all operating with thoughts (with language).—This
> *Feststellung* is not of the form "I know…". "I know…" states what I know, and that is not
> of logical interest.
>
> In this remark the expression "propositions of the form of empirical propositions" is
> itself thoroughly bad; the statements in question are statements about physical objects.
> And they do not serve as foundation in the same way as hypotheses which, if they turn
> out to be false, are replaced by others. (OC: 401–2)

When Wittgenstein, in *On Certainty*, detects logic in the Moore-type propositions, and begins to talk about them in terms of logic, it is all owing to the Step. However, his talk about these things in terms of logic does not establish them *as rules*. Indeed, Wittgenstein gives a nice example in *On Certainty* of what it is like to deal with language *from* his one-sided way of looking at language. Thus, the Step informs his conception of logic as ever before, but rather than conceiving Moore-type propositions as 'rules *in the language-game*', he begins to regard them as playing a logical role that is rather *like* that of rules in the *Bezugssystem* (system of reference).

Wittgenstein, notwithstanding his strong reservations, refers throughout *On Certainty* to the Moore-type propositions every now and then as propositions of the form of empirical propositions. The items in question, as he wants to make clear, are statements about physical objects (*Aussagen über Gegenstände*). The prominence given to the notion of *physical objects* in Wittgenstein's contemplations is indeed remarkable, as is the enormous diversity of range that these entities come to have in the course of his work: tables, chairs, violets, hands, the earth, brains, arms, trees, mountains, staircases, parents, etc. Equally *diverse* are the types of 'propositions of the form of empirical propositions' to which Wittgenstein turns his attention in *On Certainty*. This fact is extremely important and it cannot be emphasized too much.[185] The enormous diversity of Moore-type propositions provides ample room for us to recognize the importance of the directions in which the contrast between the aforementioned poles can shade off.

The fact that Wittgenstein keeps referring to Moore-type propositions as propositions of the *form* of empirical propositions might be taken as indicative

---

185   Notice, for instance, Wittgenstein discussion in OC §§654–57.

of how he used to look at them himself up to the moment he began to scrutinize them carefully. Acknowledging a big gap in his thinking, he seems to have *taken* these propositions – I don't say: treated – as genuine empirical propositions for a long time. They seem to have been residing in his mind without much philosophical attention, let alone philosophical treatment, which suggests that Wittgenstein hardly bothered to look *at their use,* as if their form prevented him from taking a closer look at them.[186] But now that he, in *On Certainty,* has at last become attentive to them, he notices that Moore-type propositions are scarcely put to use in the daily course of life, *and yet,* they are not without use in our *Bezugssystem.* Here we have two aspects that seem to have contributed to Wittgenstein's recognition that there is something amiss with countenancing on Moore-type propositions the possibility of doubt, that is to say, on them as *genuine empirical* propositions. Consider also the following two remarks, which are clearly redolent of surprise as well:

> Compare with this 12 × 12 = 144. Here too we don't say "perhaps". For, in so far as this proposition rests on our not miscounting or miscalculating and our senses not deceiving us as we calculate, both propositions, the arithmetical one and the physical one, are on the same level.
>
> I want to say: The physical game is just as certain as the arithmetical. But this can be misunderstood. My remark is a logical and not a psychological one. (OC: 447).
>
> I want to say: If one doesn't marvel at the fact that the propositions of arithmetic (e.g. the multiplication tables) are 'absolutely certain', then why should one be astonished that the proposition "this is my hand" is so equally? (OC: 448)

Notice that Wittgenstein, in the above passage, has apostrophised the notion of absolutely certain. The rationale behind this derives from how he treated propositions of arithmetic in the years preceding *On Certainty,* and in keeping with this treatment still looks at them in this work, namely on the model of the step like the one taken in relativity theory. The certainty pertaining to these propositions, then, is not treated as absolute, a matter that finds regular expression in the following way: Propositions of arithmetic operate within the language-game as the *hinges* on which its entire traffic turns (more on this imagery below). But now notice what Wittgenstein says in the above passage: *'in so far as* [12 × 12 = 144] rests on our not miscounting or miscalculating and our senses not deceiving us as we calculate, both propositions, the arithmetical one and the physical one, *are*

---

186 Cf. 'If I had to say what is the main mistake made by philosophers of the present generation, including Moore, I would say that it is that when language is looked at, what is looked at is a form of words and not the use made of the form of words' (LA: 2).

on the same level' (emphases mine). If you gravitate towards an 'observation' like this one, as Wittgenstein does do in *On Certainty*, you do so on account of the step like the one taken in relativity theory, which means that you commit to a certain way of looking at things, one that does not amount to treating 'physical propositions' as mathematical ones, but one that seeks to treat the former propositions on the same model on which the latter ones are being conceived to play a mathematical role in our language-games. Both kinds of propositions, in short, are being looked at as hinges in the *Bezugssystem*. But, then, *in so far* little has been said about the language-game itself, that is, about its traffic: *that* what keeps the hinges fixed and renders them the kinds of thing they are in the language-game. In other words, the language-game has not yet been *described*. There is still work to do, every kind of work, as Wittgenstein well realizes.

In order to put Wittgenstein's big gap in his thinking into further relief, we do perhaps well to contrast his words in *OC* §401–2 (see above) with those famous ones in *Philosophical Investigations* §242:

> It is not only agreement in definitions, but also (odd as it may sound) agreement in judgements that is required for communication by means of language. This seems to abolish logic, but does not do so. – It is one thing to describe methods of measurements, and another to obtain and state [*aussprechen*] results of measurement. But what we call "measuring" is in part determined by a certain constancy in results of measurement.

What my present suggestion implies is that Wittgenstein had been carrying about a big gap in his thinking, that is, half his life. So what my present suggestion is likely to provoke on the part of the proverbial dogmatic commentator is a response along the following lines: 'Wittgenstein cannot possibly have been carrying about a big gap in his thinking half his life! He *must* have settled with it already in his *Philosophical Investigation* and his focus in *On Certainty*—can't you see?!—is on notions such as certainty and doubt!' Yet, a little reading and patience should suffice to make clear that the judgements of which Wittgenstein speaks in *PI* §242 are genuine *judgements*: one measures, obtains and *states* [*aussprechen*] the result. The peculiarity of Moore-type propositions, on the other hand, is that they are emphatically not among the kind of things that we *state* in the daily course of life, and that something queer if not downright funny is at issue when we do. Here again I make mention of an aspect that has been of a great interest to Wittgenstein in *On Certainty*, and that should be considered in combination with this: these propositions do nevertheless play a role in the *Bezugssystem* of our language.

Do I know that I am now sitting in a chair?—Don't I know it?! In the present circumstances no one is going to say that I know this; but no more will he say, for example, that I am conscious. Nor will one normally say thus of the passers-by in the street.

But now, even if one doesn't say it, does that make it *untrue*??

It is queer: if I say, without any special occasion, "I know"—for example, "I know that I am now sitting in a chair", this statement seems to me unjustified and presumptuous. But if I make the same statement where there is some need for it, then, although I am not a jot more certain of its truth, it seems to me to be perfectly justified and everyday.

In its language-game it is not presumptuous. There, it has no higher position than, simply, the human language-game. For there it has its restricted application.

But as soon as I say this sentence outside its context, it appears in a false light. For then it is as if I wanted to insist that there are things that I *know*. God himself can't say anything to me about them. (OC: 552–4)

There is wonder at work here, one that lends Wittgenstein's philosophy its dialectical edges, its characteristic movements of thoughts and less characteristic turns. But the overall dynamic of his philosophy would have been altogether different if it was not *all* for the fact that he wants to reach the finishing post with descriptions of language. In other words, there is work to do and that there is still work to do can also be gleaned from the following expressions of interest.

"I believe I know" would not need to express a lesser degree of certainty.—True, but one isn't trying to express subjective certainty, any more than the greatest certainty, but rather that certain propositions seem to underlie all questions and all thinking. (OC: 415)

What interests us is that about certain empirical propositions no doubt can exist if making judgements is to be possible at all. Or again: I am inclined to believe that not everything that has the form of an empirical proposition is one. (OC: 308)

Wittgenstein does not *claim* that no doubt can exist about certain empirical propositions if making judgements is to be possible. All he does is to give expression to what takes so much hold of his present *interest*. And, indeed, we have already met with such an expression of his interest, namely the one that avows that there is still a big gap in his thinking. Wittgenstein does not *claim* that no doubt can exist about certain empirical propositions if making judgements is to be possible, that is, he does not claim it in the above remarks nor at any other place in *On Certainty*: he does not claim such things nor does he mean to claim such things—and to take his words to the contrary is to misconstrue nothing less than his precious Step, which is no small sin indeed as this thing is at work in every piece of Wittgenstein's writings from the early 1930s onwards. Of course, one may well be so bold as to consider *On Certainty* through the eyes of an epistemologist; one may even go so far as to think that Wittgenstein solved a big problem *there*, say, the so-called regress-problem in epistemology. But whatever Wittgenstein did in *On Certainty*, he did not solve anything of the sort. *On Certainty* is a study in logic, as are all of Wittgenstein's works, and what mileage we think we could get out of *On Certainty*, it fails to live up to being an interpretation of *On Certainty*, let alone an interesting one, as long as it fails to connect up with the dialectic of Wittgenstein's Step.

Let us add here one more exemplification of my point that there is still every piece of work to do for Wittgenstein. It is indicated by his frequent use of the phrase 'I want to say' in remarks such as quoted above. Here is another remark in which the phrase marks the opening tune.

> I really want to say that a language-game is only possible if one trusts something (I did not say "can trust something"). (OC: 509)

If we look at this remark, that is, in isolation from the context in which it is at home, we may well think that Wittgenstein merely repeats here, or reminds himself of, what he has been saying already long before *On Certainty*. But we really ought to consider the remark against the background of his sayings, long before *On Certainty*, about rules. If we keep this in mind, then, the sort of thing that Wittgenstein *wants to say* in *On Certainty*—in the sense of what his thoughts tend to turn to again and again—is also what a remark such as the following one says:

> Every language-game is based on words and objects being recognized again. We learn with the same inexorability that this is a chair as that $2 \times 2 = 4$. (OC: 455)

If this is what Wittgenstein wants to *say* in *On Certainty*, it is not the sort of thing in which *his* philosophical activities reach their fruition. For the very thing is not a description of the language-game but a so-called grammatical statement. Wittgenstein himself emphasizes that what he wants to say – 'the physical game is just as certain as the arithmetical' – is 'a logical and not a psychological [*Bemerkung*]'. A *Bemerkung* is not a description of language, and Wittgenstein does not seek redemption in *Bemerkungen*, but in descriptions of the language-game. (The point to realize here is what such descriptions involve.) If we overlook this we are sure to cut *On Certainty* short of the typical struggles that come in the wake of Wittgenstein's first hold on the workings of our language in terms of such *logische Bemerkungen* as quoted above. If we overlook this, or have failed to realize it ever since our first encounters with Wittgenstein and his work, we may well fill our scholarly papers with nicely polished remarks and statements from Wittgenstein's own hand, bulked up with our comments on them, only to think that we have thereby got a step or two further than our academic peers and colleagues on the question of what a work as *On Certainty* is 'really all about'. For Wittgenstein, though, mere remark and statements are not descriptions of language, any more than substitutes for such things—things that in his non-academic philosophy '*alone* must take the place' of all explanation.

The final notching of Wittgenstein's philosophical beans, then, does not come in the shape of *Bemerkungen*. Of course, this is not to diminish the role of *logische Bemerkungen*, or grammatical enunciations as we have called them. On the contrary, they add most decisively to Wittgenstein's first hold on the Moore-type propositions. And, as we have been observing as well, there is a most important step at work in attaining this first hold: the step like the one taken in relativity theory. This Step, as we better register for ourselves now, is exactly the one by means of which Wittgenstein once acquired his first hold on rules, that is, on such things that were to pass for rules on account of the Step in the first instance. But when the Step credits rules with such a pivotal role in the language-game, then, *as far as the Step itself is concerned*, Moore-type propositions cannot be denied such a role in the language-game either. So what about Moore-type propositions with respect to the idea of what is fundamental to the language-game? Should we credit the language-game with an additional sense of what is fundamental to it, one besides the sense provided by the rules? As far as the Step *itself* is concerned, there is no possibility to install a new or additional sense of what is fundamental to the language-game. On the other hand: why distinguish at all between rules on the one hand, and Moore-type propositions on the other hand? For, *as far as the Step itself is concerned*, we cannot go so far as to distinguish between these items. But that is exactly what Wittgenstein does do in *On Certainty*, among other things: emphasizing differences *and* similarities between rules and Moore-type propositions. But, then, his doing so does not render giving *descriptions* of our language superfluous. On the contrary, Wittgenstein's first hold on the Moore-type propositions by dint of the Step precisely commits him to give descriptions of our language, a commitment that is not revoked on account of the way he distinguishes between rules on the one hand, and Moore-type propositions on the other hand. This brings us to the following passage:

> The propositions describing this world-picture might be part of a kind of mythology. And their role is like that of rules of a game; and the game can be learned purely practically, without learning any explicit rules. (OC: 95)

In this passage, Wittgenstein speaks of the Moore-type propositions having a role *like* that of rules of a game. The qualification *like*, which corresponds to the adjective *peculiar* in *OC* §136 (see above), is of pivotal importance and not to be overlooked. Thus, although it is logic that Wittgenstein recognizes in the Moore-type propositions by dint of the same picture that renders rules constitutive elements in the so-called *Bezugssystem*, this recognition does not prompt Wittgenstein to hurl rules and Moore-type propositions onto one and the same heap. In other words, Wittgenstein must appeal to *additional considerations* so as to distinguish between the logical roles of rules on the one hand, and those of Moore-type propositions on the other hand. We shall shortly pay attention to some of these additional considerations. If we ignore the *like*, i.e. the so-called peculiarity of the logic of the Moore-type propositions *in comparison to* the logic of the rules, we are bound to miss the whole point and dynamics of Wittgenstein's struggles to come to *descriptive* terms with the Moore-type propositions. The difficulties he faces have *everything* to do with his fixed efforts to come out *in the end* with nothing but *descriptions*, with such things, and with such things in the light of his first hold on the Moore-type propositions in terms of the Step. It is these efforts that have brought him on the verge of despair: 'Am I not getting closer and closer to saying that in the end [*am Schluß*] logic cannot be described? You must look at the practice of language, then you will see it' (OC: 501).

6.2 A closer look at the Step

Logic, I said, is not in the melting pot in *On Certainty*. Wittgenstein, upon smelling a rather peculiar but nonetheless genuine scent of logic in the Moore-type propositions, did not begin to reconsider his *conception* of what logic should amount to in his philosophical approach. On the contrary, it was precisely his 'good old grasp' on language that enabled him to avail himself of his nose in such differentiating a way as *On Certainty* puts on display. Not going into the melting pot there itself, his conception of logic once emerged from such a pot in the early 1930s, when Wittgenstein acknowledged that logic does not come in the once-for-all shape of crystalline purity as his *Tractatus* enunciated. I make mention here of his Tractarian conception of logic because the very step like the one taken in relativity theory is not what Wittgenstein felt in love with out of blue. Rather, he began to expound it precisely against the backcloth of his recognition of what his early conception of logic was ultimately founded on. The Step, then, seen from a systematic point of view, is Wittgenstein's lasting reply to this Tractarian conception. It encompasses a good deal on the subject of grammatical attributes and, indeed, its internal connection to Wittgenstein's conception of language description is not to be overlooked.

Now Wittgenstein employed various metaphorical portrayals of the rather abstract- resonating phrase 'the step like the one taken in relativity theory', prominent among them the one for which *On Certainty* is, we may well say here, most famous: propositions as hinges on which the language-game pivots. What this picture means to bring out is that it is not, say, a fact 'out there', or a sublime version thereof, that holds the rule fast. It is rather the language-game itself, i.e. *our* manner of employing words and sentences, that does so.[187] Of course, in *On Certainty* it is precisely Moore-type propositions on which Wittgenstein now tries to bring this metaphor to bear.

> The child learns to believe a host of things. I.e. it learns to act according to these beliefs. Bit by bit there forms a system of what is believed, and in that system some things stand unshakeably fast and some are more or less liable to shift. What stands fast does so, not because it is intrinsically obvious or convincing; it is rather held fast by what lies around it. (OC: 144)
>
> The *questions* that we raise and our *doubts* depend on the fact that some propositions are exempt from doubt, are as it were like hinges on which those turn.
>
> That is to say, it belongs to the logic of our scientific investigations that certain things are *in deed* not doubted.
>
> But it isn't that the situation is like this: We just *can't* investigate everything, and for that reason we are forced to rest content with assumptions. If we want the door to turn, the hinges must stay put. (OC: 341–343)[188]

The above remarks present Wittgenstein's first grip on the Moore-type proposition in terms of his conception of logic. It is a grip that renders these things *merely* eligible for partaking of the *Bezugssystem* of *our language*. Nothing has been described so far; there is still much work to do.

Wittgenstein's Step epitomizes a way of looking at language and *as such* it does not give expression to an *insight* into the workings of any language. He wants to understand, but not an abstract idea such as the Step might be said to be. He wants to understand, namely the workings of our language, precisely so on account of the Step, by taking himself through the several stages that the Step involves. The first round of the Step finds, typically so, expression in *Bemerkungen*, in remarks such as quoted above. The last round of the Step, on the other hand, should furnish precisely those things for which it is being employed in the first instance: descriptions of our language. So we do well to keep a good many things apart, if only with respect to what the Step involves on the subject of various rounds and stages of employment. Consider, for instance, the following remark: 'This axis is not fixed in the sense that anything holds it fast, but the movement around it determines its immobility' (OC: 152). Strictly speaking, this remark only stresses the rather *abstract character* of Step. It does not entertain terms such

---

187   Cf. RFM: 96.
188   Cf. OC: 144.

as 'doubt' or 'certainty'. It is the mere idea itself that is at issue here, i.e., *before* it is brought to bear upon—in Wittgenstein's case—(our) language. But if we now look in what terms the first round of application of the idea comes, we encounter formulations such as this one: 'The *questions* that we raise and our *doubts* depend on the fact that some propositions are exempt from doubt, are as it were like hinges on which those turn' (OC: 341). A turn of phrase such as 'as it were' is not to be overlooked: it could never characterize the *abstract* idea of the Step; what it characterizes, or indicates, is that the Step has gone through its first round of application. Another point, not a small one either, is that Wittgenstein brings the Step to bear on *our* language, rather than on language *simpliciter*. He speaks of the questions that *we* raise and of *our* doubts. It is our language that troubles him and we should guard against thinking that his remarks are meant to reach out to all languages. We shall return to this point in a moment.

By drawing a clear distinction between the abstract idea of the Step and the kind of flesh that Wittgenstein means to put on it throughout *On Certainty*, we will be able to see better, or perhaps even for the first time, what counts as genuine observations in this work and what adds so much to the initial structuring of these observations. What Wittgenstein observes is, among other things, that it belongs to our *Lebensform* that we *do not doubt* many an aspect concerning miscellaneous physical objects. What Wittgenstein, in contrast, does not observe, and what he does not take to be an observation proper either, is that these complete absences of doubt constitute the language-games *logically*. Whenever the Step finds application, the complete exemption of doubt, which inheres in the language-game itself, obtains a *logical* stamp. The *logical* exemption of doubt, then, which strictly speaking does not inhere in the world itself, epitomizes in the language-game precisely the kind of *rigidity* of the axis in Wittgenstein's picture.

But if the notion of doubt is an important ingredient in Wittgenstein's first grip on the Moore-type propositions, what then about a notion such as *knowing*, which poses a substantial challenge to his mind, as much as the notions of doubt and certainty? How, indeed, does the notion of knowing relate to the Step? Does it add to the flesh on the skeleton of the Step as well? Not wanting to launch into an investigation here about how Wittgenstein dealt with *knowing* in *On Certainty*, I raise these questions so as to sharpen our wits as regards the way Wittgenstein proceeds in *On Certainty*. Well, Wittgenstein's *first* hold on the Moore-type propositions, which comes by way of the Step and imparts on him the 'realization' that there is logic at issue here, does *not* entail the notion of knowing as an ingredient of the flesh on the abstract bones of the Step. Even more, once the Step has furnished Wittgenstein's first grip on the Moore-type propositions, there is nothing left as far as the Step is concerned so as to say anything about the notion of knowing. *That is*, you may well *contemplate* the Step till the end of time—the effort will not tell you how to think about the notion of knowledge. You need to go into the field and *observe* how we use it and its cognates in the first and the third person. In other words, Wittgenstein, once having secured his first grip, needs to observe what adds to the various kinds of movements that keep the axes fixed. And for this observing he needs to pay due attention to the famous particulars, which include not only how we use the word 'knowledge', but also how we use a whole train of words that characteristically swirl around the word 'knowledge' *in our Lebensform*: words such as 'belief', 'certainty', and, 'doubt' itself. The first round of application of Wittgenstein's Step means nothing unless further steps are taken that exploit the point of this first round so as to furnish descriptions of our language at last.

The first round of the Step is left idling when we fail to commit ourselves to the rounds coming in its wake. Thus, a statement such as *that* 'about certain empirical propositions no doubt can exist if making judgements is to be possible at all' does not obviate the necessity to go into the field to see *how* we use our words and sentences. But what are we to make of a remark such as the following?

> One says "I know" when one is ready to give compelling grounds. "I know" relates to a possibility of demonstrating the truth. Whether someone knows something can come to light, assuming that he is convinced of it.
>
> But if what he believes is of such a kind that the grounds that he can give are no surer than his assertion, then he cannot say that he knows what he believes. (OC: 243)

The second part of this passage is often taken to demonstrate how Wittgenstein deals with the notion of knowing in relation to the Moore-type propositions. G. H. von Wright, for instance, writes that: 'The concept of knowing does not itself apply to that which is presupposed in its use, *i.e.* to the propositions which 'stand fast' in any given knowledge-situation. This is one reason, why Moore's use of 'I know' was out of place'[189]. Now I think that this is far too general a claim: as if the Moore-type propositions stand all fast in one and the same way and as if a little reflection on the concept of knowing in relation to these propositions suffices to see how things stand in our language, if not in all languages. Von Wright is close to using the concept of knowing to characterize what it is for certain things to stand fast. Wittgenstein, on the other hands, brings the Step to bear

---

189 Georg H. von Wright, 'Wittgenstein on Certainty', in G. H. von Wright, ed., *Problems in the Theory of Knowledge* (The Hague: Martinus Nijhoff, 1972), 52.

on our language, and his first grip on such things as Moore-type propositions commits him *to look and see* how *we* use e.g. the concept of knowing in relation to one class of Moore-type propositions and how we use it in relation to another class of such propositions. You may well sit down and *contemplate* the attributes of the Step till the end of time—it will not provide you with the 'cannot' in Wittgenstein's remark, quoted above.

Just as Wittgenstein wants 'to give an account of the motley of mathematics' (RFM: 182), so he is interested in seeing how various the propositions are that 'stand fast'. And just as his Step, rather than impoverishing the motley of mathematics, accentuates it, so does his operating on the Step accentuate the differences among the Moore-type propositions. But this accentuating occurs in the wake of the first round of the Step, thus when it comes to additional rounds of *seeing and looking* at language-games. Wittgenstein's first grip on the Moore-type propositions does not make these activities redundant, i.e. this paying attention to particulars. And, again, Wittgenstein's first grip on the Moore-type propositions concerns our language, a jungle of highly miscellaneous language-games, in which finding one's way about and even surveying a small part of it present considerable challenges. And what counts for our language need not count for all languages. Wittgenstein is interested in seeing how *we* operate with the concept of knowing.

Of course, there is no denying that *OC* §243 represents a characteristic way station in *On Certainty* at large. But so do all the passages in which Wittgenstein enunciates his first grip on the Moore-type propositions in terms of the Step. And this first grip, by itself, cannot warrant the 'cannot' in a passage such as *OC* §243. Von Wright, as I want to say, ignores or otherwise downplays the import of such characteristic *struggles* as the following way stations are and put on display.

> Haven't I gone wrong and isn't Moore perfectly right? Haven't I made the elementary mistake of confusing one's thoughts with one's knowledge? Of course I do not think to myself "The earth already existed for some time before my birth", but I do *know* it any the less? Don't I show that I know it by always drawing its consequences?
>
> And don't I know that there is no staircase in this house going six floors deep into the earth, even though I have never thought about it? (OC: 397–398)

> It is part of the language-game with people's names that everyone knows his name with the greatest certainty. (OC: 579)

> "Do I know or do I only believe…?" might also be expressed like this: What if it *seemed* to turn out that what until now has seemed immune to doubt was a false assumption? (OC: 492)

> Can one say: „Where there is no doubt there is no knowledge either"? (OC: 121)

> Do I know that I am now sitting in a chair?—Don't I know it!? (OC: 552).

These passages constitute a good example, especially so in combination with the one quoted above, of how much Wittgenstein actually *struggles* to come to terms in *On Certainty* with the notion of knowing—*even after* he has got his first grip on some Moore-type propositions. As he puts it himself: 'One is often bewitched by a word. For example, by the word 'know'' (OC: 435).[190]

I suggested that the *that* is idling without a *how*. The Step, in other words, is not what it is without descriptions, which form so to speak the last layer of

---

190 Wittgenstein's remark 'if what he believes is of such a kind that the grounds that he can give are no surer than his assertion, then he cannot say that he knows what he believes' gives rise to all kinds of questions. Where, for instance, does it leave us as regards *believing* what cannot be known? Indeed, how come so far as to believe something, if we cannot possibly come so far as to know it? Is the suggested relation between knowing and believing grammatically true of all *our* language-games? If so, where does this leave us as regards those Moore-type propositions that *have been* 'hardened' (cf. OC: 96), i.e. propositions that we once treated as genuine empirical entities but that have long since made their way into the 'foundations' of our language-games: have we *ceased to know* them now that they play a different role in the language-game?—And what are we to make of being surer of *a* than of *b*? What does this mean? In which language-game? After all, notions such as 'sure' and 'surer' have a strong psychological flavour, but Wittgenstein's first and final grip on the language-game is not a foray into psychology. It may well be true that what stands fast in the language-games is also what we are surest of, in a psychological sense of the word. But the Step, which articulates our not-doubting this and that as the logical foundation of our language-games, does not say that what stands fast in these games are the kinds of things we are surest of in the psychological sense. So it seems possible that what stands fast in our language-games need not also be the kinds of things we are surest of psychologically. But, then, what does *that* look like? One thing is certain. Our not-doubting *concerns* the miscellany of physical objects that we have made mention of in the main text above. One needs to look at the practice of *our* language. A little reflection here and there on some so-called key notions is not enough, at least not for Wittgenstein.

Needless to say, the issue *is* complex and can be treated properly, I think, only in the light of other strands of thoughts and concerns in *On Certainty*, notably Wittgenstein's preoccupation with the question of why we cannot entertain the Moore-type propositions 'without more ado'. This question, if it is *one* question, concerns considerations such as that 'for each of these sentences I can imagine circumstances that turn it into a move in one of our language-games, and by that it loses everything that is philosophically astonishing' (§622) and 'that it is anchored in all my questions and answers, so anchored that I cannot touch it' (§103). Wittgenstein is *struggling* enormously with respect to each of the various strands in *On Certainty*, which explains why they are not altogether free from tensions *intra* and *inter*.

dialectical deposit filling the big gap in Wittgenstein's thinking. Of course, if we remind ourselves here of his words in *PI* §124 that philosophy 'can *in the end* only describe' language (emphasis added), we still need to see what furnishing descriptions amounts to in *On Certainty*, as the final step in the wake of Wittgenstein's first grip on Moore-type propositions. We shall return to this issue in section 6.4, for now though, and by way of a first jab at this realization, we do well to pause at the following passage.

> But why *am* I so certain that this is my hand? Doesn't the whole language-game rest on this kind of certainty?
>
> Or: isn't this 'certainty' (already) presupposed in the language-game? Namely by virtue of the fact that one is not playing the game, or is playing it wrong, if one does not recognize objects with certainty. (OC: 446)

'But why *am* I so certain that this is my hand?' Opening the above passage with this move, Wittgenstein proceeds by entertaining a movement of thought that draws on the Step: '*one is not playing the game, or is playing it wrong*, if one does not recognize objects with certainty.' Should Wittgenstein hold fast to his Step, as he is no doubt disposed to do in *On Certainty*, he needs to relegate the original move, i.e. the question, to the books of psychology. The above passage poses no exception: 'Is there a why?', he asks, 'Must I not begin to trust somewhere? That is to say: somewhere I must begin with not-doubting; and that is not, so to speak, hasty but excusable: it is part of judging' (OC: 150). Here, too, Wittgenstein at first gives free rein to wonderment, only to consider things with more sober reflection by noticing that his *not-doubting* 'is part of judging'. Relevant in this connection is also the following conditional: 'If someone wanted to arouse doubts in me and spoke like this: here your memory is deceiving you, there you've been taken in, there again you have not been thorough enough in satisfying yourself, etc., and if I did not allow myself to be shaken but kept to my certainty—then my doing so cannot be wrong, even if only because this is just what defines a game' (OC: 497).[191] Time and again, I want to say, one can find Wittgenstein setting the record straight by saying that this and that merely *defines* the language-game. And the points for us to register right now in our efforts to understand Wittgenstein's proceedings in *On Certainty* is, first, that the defining of which he speaks is one in which the Step is at work and, second, that this defining only sets the stage for Wittgenstein to *understand* the workings of our language in terms of descriptions at last. Nothing has been described yet; nothing has been understood so far. To understand, Wittgenstein must apply himself to questions *that build upon the*

---

191   See below for more consideration on so-called if-constructions.

312

first round of the Step. And to build upon it, as we shall shortly see, is precisely to exploit the point that 'one is not playing the game, or is playing it wrong.' It is a point that Wittgenstein was eager to exploit wherever he brought the Step into account. The Step, then, is clearly implied in the following remark: '[Mathematical propositions] shew *those* connexions that we regard as rigid. But to a certain extent we look away from these connexions and at something else. We turn our back upon them, so to speak. Or: we rest, lean, on them' (RFM: 243)[192]. To say that the Step is implied in a remark such as this one is only to say that mathematical propositions are about to be conceived on the model of the Step. Thus, so far almost nothing has been said. Nothing has been understood or described yet, in the sense intended by Wittgenstein. For him, to understand is to see how things *called* mathematical propositions pass for *mathematical* things in our *Lebensform*, rather than for other kinds of propositions that we consider as fixed and rigid too. In order to understand, one must address all kinds of questions that build upon the first round of the Step, questions that pay due care and attention to the ins and outs of the language-games, to details on account of which the propositions are fixed and on account of which the propositions pass for mathematical ones. What renders a remark such as the one just quoted so interesting is not what it says so much as to what it commits us, philosophers: on the subject of seeing and looking at the language-games. It involves a slew of further steps and to ignore them is to disfigure the operative level of Wittgenstein's dialectical thinking beyond recognition.

A central thesis of this book is that one perpetrates a gross deformation of Wittgenstein's thinking if one fails to see and to endorse the status of his *Bemerkungen*. For these are truly not the kinds of things that he conceived as *claims* or *theses* about language, any more than as things that can be operated on to that effect with respect to his philosophy. Wittgenstein's style of thinking went against the grain of his times, but time is currently pressing hard on his hard-won thoughts and writings. So-called social media apart, there is the torrent of university courses as well as the verdict of long-standing expectations of a philosophical tradition that now gain ascendancy over Wittgenstein's life and thoughts, raking over it all as one does over his bones and rendering interesting to schools and styles of thinking: *his* thoughts—so much opposed to these styles, schools and socials. The whole *Witz* of giving descriptions is in the end lost and what remains at last is a Wittgenstein rendered fit for a philosophical exchange in

---

192   Cf. OC: 655.

which arguments and counter arguments dictate the form of the ongoing debate. We have just seen what Wittgenstein writes in *OC* §243; the following shows us what Duncan Prichard makes of it.

> Wittgenstein's contention is [...] that it is precisely *because* of the certainty that attaches to our belief in [the Moore-type propositions] that we are unable to properly claim to know them.

> Wittgenstein's claim is that whatever would count as a reason in favour of a claim to know must be more certain than the propositions claimed as known, since otherwise it would not be able to play this supporting role. But if the proposition claimed as known is something which one is most certain of, then it follows that there can be no more certain proposition which could be offered in its favour and stands as the required supporting reason.[193]

Prichard's style of framing Wittgenstein's remarks and proceedings in *On Certainty* has many facets. Wittgenstein is consistently presented as a philosopher in the old tradition: he *contends* this and *claims* that. A second point concerns phrases such as 'the certainty that attaches to our beliefs in [the Moore-type propositions]' and 'the certainty attached to hinges' (*ibid*, 535), but also problematic transaction of the type '*if* the proposition claimed as known is something which *one* is most *certain* of, *then it follows that* there can be no more certain proposition which could be offered in its favour and stands as the required supporting reason.' With such and other seemingly innocuous styles of operating on Wittgenstein's *Bemerkungen*, Prichard appears to buy into a misleading representation of how Wittgenstein conceives the so-called 'hinge propositions'—these being propositions, according to his lights, 'which by their very nature "lie apart from the route travelled by enquiry" (OC: 88). That I have two hands is clearly a hinge proposition for Wittgenstein, which is why Moore cannot properly claim to know it' (*ibid*, 528). Here Prichard appears to misunderstand Wittgenstein's Step, for it is not *by the very nature* of the propositions that they lie apart from the route travelled by enquiry. It is rather the other way around: it is the language-game, that is, *our way* of enquiring, asking, raising doubt, judging, reporting, stating, etc. that fixes the immobility of these propositions and shunts them 'onto an unused siding' (OC: 210). In other words, certainty is truly a matter of the whole language-game and is not 'attached' to propositions on account of 'their very nature'.

---

193 Duncan Prichard, 'Wittgenstein on Scepticism', in Oskari Kuusela and Marie McGinn, eds., *The Oxford handbook of Wittgenstein* (Oxford: Oxford University Press, 2011), 525.

314

Prichard's words 'by their very nature' are not an accidental slip of the tongue. On the contrary: '[T]he picture that Wittgenstein offers of the structure of reason now becomes relevant to help us to see that certain doubts just could not *of their nature* be grounded, and a doubt about whether or not one has hands—when one's hands are in clear view—is a case in point' (*ibid*, 527; emphasis mine). A passage such as this one demonstrates how deeply Prichard's phraseology is bound up with the kind of picture that *he* mentions. It is a picture, Prichard claims, that Wittgenstein offers us in *On Certainty*, namely 'a picture of the structure of reasons such that that which we are most certain of cannot be properly claimed as known or, for that matter, properly doubted' (*ibid*, 528). I think that Wittgenstein is not offering *such* a picture in *On Certainty*, or anywhere else in his oeuvre. Let us try to see what is going on here.

The picture that Prichard ascribes to Wittgenstein is

> the very picture that we ordinarily employ, at least when we are not in the grip of the alternative *philosophical* picture which the sceptic (and, following her, the anti-sceptic) employs. Moreover, and here is the crux of the point [sic], the philosophical picture that the sceptic uses is *completely divorced* from the non-philosophical picture that we ordinarily employ. That is, the philosophical picture is not an extension or refinement of the ordinary picture, but a radical departure from it. As we shall see, this feature of Wittgenstein's anti-sceptical view, which often goes unnoticed, has important dialectical implications. (*ibid*, 524)

These words should alert us to formulations such as 'the picture that we ordinarily employ' and 'the ordinary picture', for if '[i]t is through an examination of our practices of claiming knowledge that this picture of the structure of reasons is revealed […]' (*ibid*, 529)—and Prichard suggests that Wittgenstein should be credited with having unearthed such a picture—the question arises how *Wittgenstein* could ever have retrieved a thing in such modal a term as 'that that which we are most certain of *cannot* be properly claimed as known or, for that matter, properly doubted' (*ibid*, 528; emphasis mine). Whence *this* 'cannot'?—or, for that matter: Whence the 'should' in a formulation such as that 'an appropriate claim to know should be supported by reasons which are *more* certain than that which is claimed as known'? I again quote the above passage, this time with its sequel.

> Wittgenstein's claim is that whatever would count as a reason in favour of a claim to know must be more certain than the proposition claimed as known, since otherwise it would not be able to play this supporting role.[194] But if the proposition claimed as known is something which one is most certain of, then it follows that there can be no

---

194 Notice this clause!

more certain propositions which could be offered in its favour and stands as the required supporting reason. The propriety of Moor's claims to know are thus in doubt precisely because he is claiming to know that which he is most certain of.

One might wonder at this point why an appropriate claim to know should be supported by reasons which are *more* certain than that which is claimed as known. Why wouldn't it be enough that there is *something* compelling that one can say in favour of what one claims as known, even though what is claimed as known is more certain? A key part of the explanation for this is that Wittgenstein recognizes that claims to know are essentially tied to the practice of resolving doubts. Simply enumerating what one knows with no dialectical purpose in mind is incoherent on the Wittgensteinian picture; it just would not be clear what one was up to.[195] Rather, one explicitly claims to know something because there is some contextually relevant challenge to what is claimed—*a doubt*, broadly speaking—which this claim to know is designed to meet. (*ibid*, 525)

'One might wonder', Prichard says, 'why an appropriate claim to know should be supported by reasons which are *more* certain than that which is claimed as known.' But I, for my part, now rather wonder whether Prichard has done anything in the above passage, or elsewhere in his article at large, that might come close to being an answer, or close to becoming one, to his question. He refers at last to the alleged Wittgensteinain picture, which invokes a modal term, although the kind of modality at issue was at first raised in the form of a question. To put it differently, if Prichard, in the first part of the passage, primarily aims to enunciate what he takes Wittgenstein's picture to be, the question arises what his subsequent reference to this same picture intends to explain with respect to precisely the point that 'an appropriate claim to know should be supported by reasons which are *more* certain than that which is claimed as known.'

Prichard speaks of 'a key part of the explanation'. But why speak thus? For if 'claims to know are essentially tied to the practice of resolving doubts', there remains the question why 'an appropriate claim to know should be supported by reasons which are *more* certain than that which is claimed as known.' Indeed, what are we to make of a phraseology such as 'claims to know are essentially tied to the practice of resolving doubts'? For *if our* practice of resolving doubts *is* what it is—and Wittgenstein wants to understand *our* practice, there is still the question why *our* practice is the way it is. But Prichard seems to have another question in mind, one that speaks of *the* practice of resolving doubts, his suggestion being that nothing could count as such a practice unless it occurs by the principles operative in our own practice of resolving doubts. In other words, Prichard,

---

195   Save for the enumerating itself? If one is at least clear *that* there is *enumerating* here, why then *not* being clear about 'what one was up to'?

right from the beginning, appears to set up his interpretation of Wittgenstein's remarks and proceedings on an absolutist basis, whereas Wittgenstein *looks* at the practice of our language *as* one possibility among other possibilities. Prichard endows Wittgenstein's grammatical remarks with a metaphysical touch. And if that is the extent to which he has misunderstood Wittgenstein, it is, I think, no small extent indeed. While claiming that 'the philosophical picture that the sceptic uses is *completely divorced* from the non-philosophical picture that we ordinarily employ', Prichard appears to fail to see how much he has divorced his own non-philosophical picture from the non-philosophical picture that we ordinarily employ. The latter picture, at least so from Wittgenstein's vantage point, is one that is being looked at as the way it is in our *Lebensform*, thus as one possibility among other possibilities.

If claims to know are *essentially* tied to the practice of resolving doubts, there is still the question of what that means. If 'enumerating claims with no dialectical purpose in mind' just *means* that such an activity is e.g. 'not tied to the practice of resolving doubts', there is still the question what 'enumerating claims with no dialectical purpose in mind' means. These outstanding questions mattered a great deal to Wittgenstein as did the question whether what Moore did in his famous lecture was really 'enumerating claims with no dialectical purpose in mind'. For Prichard, though, there is a kind of universal reference, namely his Wittgensteinian picture, allegedly telling us 'that that which we are most certain of *cannot* be properly claimed as known or, for that matter, properly doubted', a picture, that is, with respect to which the meaning of a phrase such as 'enumerating claims with no dialectical purpose in mind' seems to collapse into: 'trying to do what the picture says one cannot do'. Of course, matters obtain a much more substantial and scholarly whiff when one formulates them in the way Prichard does: 'Simply enumerating claims with no dialectical purpose in mind is incoherent on the Wittgensteinian picture.'

Prichard beholds *On Certainty* under an epistemic light, rather than under a logical one first and foremost. There is little mention of logic in his considerations, and what comes as Wittgenstein's first hold on the Moore-type propositions in terms of the Step, is what Prichard misconstrues by giving pride of place to the kind of picture that speaks in terms of the structure of reasons. On the other hand, where Prichard does make mention of logic it occurs, as expected, in close connection with that picture: 'it is precisely not a mere practical limitation on our practice that certain propositions are exempt from epistemic evaluation, but part of the very logic of an epistemic evaluation. Such, indeed, is the moral of the *OC* §§341–3 that we cited above' (*ibid*, 531). These throwaway nods to logic create a void rather than fill one. Instead of trying to make clear what the notion of logic amounts to for later Wittgenstein, Prichard only makes clear how much he has misunderstood his *logical* proceedings in a work such as *On Certainty*. For if you are attentive to these proceedings, you will not pronounce this: 'Wittgenstein's *claim* is that whatever would count as a reason in favour of a claim to know must be more certain than the proposition claimed as known' (emphasis mine), any more than formulate the following: 'As the term "hinge" itself indicates, our commitment to the hinge propositions is essential to *any* epistemic evaluation – this commitment is the hinge on which any epistemic evaluation must turn' (*ibid*, 530). I want to say: If you are attentive to Wittgenstein's logical proceedings, you will be cautious with the notion *any*, just because it is Wittgenstein's conception of logic that is at work in *On Certainty*. For Wittgenstein finds it 'at any rate important to image a language in which *our* concept 'knowledge' does not exist' (OC: 562). Prichard's appeal to the notion of logic in the passage quoted above only strengthens the suspicion that he uses it in the old tradition: logic is what it is and cannot possibly be otherwise.

6.3 Rules and Moore-type propositions

Wittgenstein, then, in *On Certainty* more so than at any time before in his lifetime, realizes that there are certain elements which do not pass for rules but which nonetheless should be reckoned among the constitutive (logical) parts in the so-called *Bezugssystem*. For if rules are entitled to belong to this system on account of a certain picture that *enunciates* them as pieces of logic, Moore-type propositions cannot possibly be denied entrance to this system if this same picture obtains a perfectly good hold on them as well. But now, as I have indicated, to be a full logical member of this system involves more than merely having been seized upon by this picture. According to Wittgenstein's conception, logic is what needs to be *described*. It is what we need to see *at work in the language-game*. And we do not see logic at work in the language-game if we have merely crafted some grammatical remarks by dint of a certain picture. To be sure, the so-called *Bezugssystem* is not what Wittgenstein aims to describe[196], but if something knocks on the door of this system so as to be admitted as a full member, Wittgenstein faces the task of describing its membership by way of *language-games*. Such *is* Wittgenstein's commitment to the Step, and such *is* how he has been proceeding with respect to rules in the first instance; rules: founding members of the

---

196   Cf. OC: 102.

318

Bezugssystem as they are, and full members as they surely will remain in the face of the challenge that Moore-type propositions pose.

As the Step renders a thing only entitled to the rank of logic in the *Bezugssystem*, it is incapable to distinguish between rules, on the one hand, and Moore-type propositions, on the other hand. The Step itself cannot, for instance, tell us anything about the 'Where' of logic in the language-game. Thus, that the logic pertaining to Moore-type propositions operates in the language-game from such obscure a place as 'an unused siding' (OC: 210)—is not for the Step to determine. It is only in combination with *additional* considerations that logic can be said to work like a pivot from either this or that position in the language-game. It is important to make this point explicit if only because Wittgenstein himself is much concerned with emphasizing that Moore-type propositions are not rules but that 'their role is *like* that of rules of a game; and the game can be learned purely practically, without learning any explicit rules (OC: 95, emphasis mine). Rules, Wittgenstein says, 'leave loop-holes open, and the practice has to speak for itself (OC: 139); Moore-type propositions, however, do not leave open such kinds of things. Yet, they seem to bear an *internal* connection to the rules of the language-games precisely owing to what rules leave open. Indeed, if you pay attention to what rules leave open, to the very practice that must take care of itself, you will come up with precisely such 'propositions' as are under Wittgenstein's attention in *On Certainty*. To be sure, this is not to suggest that the stuff filling up the holes in our rules are 'propositions'—or sentences, for that matter.

For each one of the Moore-type propositions we can 'imagine circumstances that turn it into a move in one of our language-games' (OC: 622). But, as Wittgenstein continues, 'by that it loses everything that is philosophically astonishing.' One major preoccupation of Wittgenstein in *On Certainty* concerns the Moore-type proposition, not as a plain move in the language-game, but when 'it is fixed and removed from the traffic, so to speak shunted unto an unused siding' (OC: 210). True, rules are fixed too, but they are part of the traffic; they, too, render the moves in the language-game possible, but they are part of the traffic as essentially as the moves themselves. Moore-type propositions, in contrast, contribute to the logic of the language-games exactly when they are fixed *and* removed from their traffic. But, again, this is not to suggest that somewhere beneath the traffic of the language-games certain propositions are lying about, shining there with an astonishing aspect, only to lose that knack the moment they are dragged out into the open and as one move or another join in the traffic of language-games. Wittgenstein says: 'It belongs to the logic of our scientific

investigations that certain things are *in deed* not doubted' (OC: 142).[197] We just
do not call so many things into questions in daily life. These absences of doubt
do not concern one thing or another in isolation from similar absences of doubt
concerning other things, but *all kinds of absences of doubt* that together comprise
a ramifying network, a normative whole or constellation with a normative character, on which the entireties of our language-games (i.e. their traffic 'including'
rules) themselves hinge and through which they are the kind of things they are.
This network does not belong to a language-game in the same sense a rule belongs to it, for the network does not belong to a certain language-game, or to one
language-game more than to others, but it is the 'inherited background against
which I distinguish between true and false' (OC: 94). This is a point to bear in
mind, exactly so when it comes to considering Wittgenstein's difficulties in describing the logic of our language. Rules leave open loop-holes, but what they

---

197   'I want to conceive [this certainty, cf. OC: 358] as something that lies beyond being
      justified or unjustified; as it were, as something animal' (OC: 359). Pritchard says
      with respect to this and other remarks (OC: 204, 110, 148, 232, 324, 402) the follow-
      ing: 'One might extract from these remarks the thought that what Wittgenstein is
      fundamentally interested in is our hinge-like convictions [sic] to act in certain ways,
      rather than in there being certain propositions which we are convinced of. Still, if this
      is the account of hinge propositions that Wittgenstein has in mind, then it is at least
      odd that he refers to hinges as propositions throughout *On Certainty*. The proponent
      of the non-propositional view therefore has a fairly stiff exegetical task on her hands'
      (*ibid*, 535). But, here again, this just misconstrues the Step and Wittgenstein's way of
      thinking it through in *On Certainty*, not to mention what it is for *rules* to leave open
      loop-holes. Having acquired a first hold on the Moore-type propositions by way of
      the Step, Wittgenstein, throughout *On Certainty*, repeatedly reminds himself of this
      hold, probes it as it were afresh if not again. However, the terms in which he presents
      his first hold on the Moore-type propositions are not themselves *descriptive* of the
      language-games, but only determine the direction to be taken to furnish descriptions,
      the final means by way of which Wittgenstein seeks to understand the workings of
      our language. Prichard fails to see the dialectical character of *Wittgenstein's* way of do-
      ing philosophy: *his* redeeming word is not a grammatical *Bemerkung* about Moore-
      type propositions, any more than a claim, a contention or a thesis. Indeed, the very
      term 'descriptions of language-games' is a complete *Fremdwort* in Pritchard's *thinking*
      about *On Certainty* and he might himself have a 'fairly stiff exegetical task' to perform
      accommodating Wittgenstein's remark 'Am I not getting closer and closer to saying
      that in the end logic cannot be described?' (OC: 501). Of course, this does not mean
      that for so-called 'proponent[s] of the non-propositional view' *giving descriptions* of
      language-games is *not a Fremdword*. Neither does it mean that these proponents have
      not misunderstood the strong dialectical character of Wittgenstein's philosophy.

leave open does not seem to be without *normative character* itself; that, at least, is part of Wittgenstein's growing awareness in *On Certainty*, part of the big gap in his thinking as it is.

Rules and Moore-type propositions, then, are not constitutive 'parts' of the language-game in one and the same way.[198] To be sure, rules have never been allocated a so-called place within the language-game *relative to a pre-existing scheme of coordination*. It is rather they themselves with respect to which the language-game can be said to have obtained such a coordination (of sorts) in the first instance. This fact arises from the historical development of Wittgenstein's later philosophy. Whereas language-games did not appear until the early 1930s, rules were there right from the beginning, heirs as they are to particular Tractarian elements. The advent of language-games gave rules not only the kind contextual bearing Wittgenstein thought they 'deserve'; this advent—precisely owing to this contextualization—rendered rules at the same time the coordinating institutions *in language-games*. In other words, it is with respect to rules that the various elements of the language-game can be said to have a place or location there. *Not* everything of the language-game is part of its so-called traffic, but whatever belongs to it and its daily transactions is open to view. And logic has always been open to view since the early 1930s. Logic determines the sense and meaning of what it is for language's workings to lie open to view. But logic at the same time determines the sense and necessity of Wittgenstein's descriptions of language, of its workings. So, then, what about giving pronounced descriptions of these workings when a peculiar kind of logic begins knock on the door? That is, what about describing the logic of our language if one begins to take hold of a *normative quality* about the very stuff filling the loop-holes in the normative character of the rules—as if only against a normative background rules can do their normative work, and the background is not normative without the normative character of the rules of the game?

Rules are part of the traffic of the language-games as constitutive items of this traffic themselves. Indeed, one underscores the *system-character* of the language-game when one says that they are constitutive of the traffic of the language-game *through* being part of that traffic themselves. And being thus constitutive, they are, and have always been conceived to be, constitutive items of the *language-game*. Moore-type propositions, however, 'turn out' to be constitutive parts of the language-game, hence of its traffic, *without being part of this very traffic*. The fact that Wittgenstein keeps referring to them as playing a *peculiar* logical role

---

198   But neither are rules as a class.

in our *Bezugssystem* has everything to do with the fact that he has never thought of an item playing a constitutive role in *the language-game* without playing it *through being part of its traffic.* But it is one thing to notice that this logical role is peculiar; to *describe* this logic is another thing. For, of course, to describe this logic is not to describe a peculiar logic. But to describe it is not to describe it by way of any peculiar method either. For to describe the logic of a language-game is, and has always been, to describe its traffic, and to describe its traffic is to describe it as one possibility among other possibilities. That is, to describe the logic of the language-game is, and has always been, to describe the traffic of the language-game as what lends its rules the kinds of identities they have in virtue of being fixed *in its traffic* and *by this same traffic.* It is precisely through giving pronounced descriptions of the language-games that their identities should come to the fore—possibilities among other possibilities as language-games are.

Wittgenstein's first grip on rules by dint of the Step is what it is: a first grip only—and 'everything descriptive of a language-game belongs to logic' (OC: 56)[199]. What I am intimating here is that the internal connection between the Step and Wittgenstein's conception of language description was in the first instance forged by his notion of rules as constitutive parts within the *traffic* of the language-game. What is to be described is not just some aspect of the language-game but precisely the section that Wittgenstein has always conceived as its traffic: that section of which he has no grasp independently of its constituting parts in terms of rules. This is what we need to realize if we ask ourselves what it is like for Wittgenstein to furnish descriptions of the language-game with respect to Moore-type propositions, thus not as moves in the game, but precisely so when 'they do logic' in his sense of the word. Thus, if we find Wittgenstein contemplating what is 'shunted onto an unused siding' (OC: 210) or 'fused into the foundation of our language-game' (OC: 558), he should not be taken to be intimating a logic that is the way it is and that cannot be otherwise. It is logic that he is intimating, no doubt, but logic in his *later* grasp of the word.

> Giving grounds, [...], justifying the evidence, comes to an end;—but this end is not certain propositions' striking us immediately as true, i.e. it is not a kind of *seeing* on our part; it is our *acting*, which lies at the bottom of the language-game (OC: 204),

This passage underscores my suggestion that the famous end of which Wittgenstein regularly speaks is not deemed absolute. He speaks of *our* acting; we act thus-and-so, but other ways of acting are imaginable. The traffic of the

---

199   Cf. 'For if it belongs to the description of the language-game, it belongs to logic' (OC: 628).

language-game holds the rules fixed, but the traffic does do this against the back-cloth of regular ways of acting, which means that the thing called language-game hinges itself, as a whole, on the pivot of that backcloth as it were. Our way of acting represents one possibility among other possibilities, which means that the aforesaid end is describ*able* in Wittgenstein's sense of the word, hence must be described if the challenge is felt. And if the end turns out to be a most difficult thing to describe, we might as well say with Wittgenstein: 'Am I not getting closer and closer to saying that in the end logic cannot be described?'

To sum up: the kind of logic that Wittgenstein finds himself contemplating near the end of his life does not pertain to any language-game in particular but seems, in the form of a ramifying network of all kinds of absences of doubt, to be constitutive of the language-games in a way in which rules are not[200]:

> If I were to say "It is my unshakable conviction that etc.", this means in the present case too that I have not consciously arrived at the conviction by following a particular line of thought, but that it is anchored in all *my questions and answers,* so anchored that I cannot touch it. (OC: 103)

The complete absence of doubt pertaining to the Moore-type propositions is anchored in all my questions and answers: so anchored that I cannot touch it. Does Wittgenstein try to *touch* the Moore-type certainties?[201] Well, he should *describe* their 'peculiar' logic. The challenge is that of *describing* such certainties—such absences of doubt as are 'shunted onto an unused siding', 'fused into the foundation of our language-game' or that 'lie apart from the route travelled by enquiry' (OC: 88). The challenge is Wittgenstein's difficulty, because *he* enters the philosophical stage from a logical point of view, and his conception of logic, his 'good old grasp' on language, commits him to come out in the end with descriptions, and these things only.

Whereas the logic pertaining to the Moore-type propositions seems to underlie 'all my questions and answers' (OC: 103), 'all questions and all thinking' (OC: 415), 'all operating with thoughts (language)' (OC: 401),[202] in short: every

---

200   This is not to suggest that there are no transitions between rules and the items taking part of this network.

201   But are the typical *philosophical* discussions about the Moore-type propositions not themselves a respectable way of touching the Moore-type propositions, that is, without losing everything astonishing about them?—To think that philosophical discussions should *anyway* be reckoned among the language-games we play in the daily course of life, is to abolish Wittgenstein's distinction between sense and nonsense.

202   Cf. 'I cannot depart from this judgment without toppling all other judgments' (OC: 419), 'Not only do I never have the slightest doubt that I am called that, but

language-game, a rule takes part only in some language-game or other. The constitutive role of the rule is confined to the language-game in which it is 'at home'. Language-games have always been treated by Wittgenstein as being more or less independent from each other. Recall here, for instance, the way he introduces them in the famous opening sections of the *Philosophical Investigations*: 'Don't let it bother you that languages (2) and (8) consist only of orders' (§18). The blind man cannot play certain language-games, but this inability does not jeopardize his membership to the community of speakers to which he belongs. It is with respect to precisely a difference such as intimated here, between rules, on the one hand, and Moore-type propositions, on the other hand, that the interesting question arises how Wittgenstein construes the *describing* of the logic pertaining to the Moore-type propositions. It is to this point that I wish to turn now.

6.4 On Certainty §501

In order to get a feel for the difficulty that Wittgenstein intimates in §501, thus respecting his efforts to reach the end of the day with descriptions of our language only, we need to address the methods that come in the wake of his first grip on the Moore-type propositions in terms of the Step. These methods are not superimposed on the Step but pertain to it most intimately; methods, then, which Wittgenstein brings to bear on things that are constitutive of the traffic of the language-game without being items of the traffic itself. In other words, he brings these methods to bear on certain elements that, notwithstanding the Step's first grip on them, do not pass for rules and yet acquit themselves 'like that of rules of a game' and are to be described accordingly.

Wittgenstein's methods of description *exploit* the very point of the Step; that is what renders them internal to it. Their exploitation is surely no idle tea-table amusement. On the contrary, the Step is wholly idling without descriptions of the language-games. So the Step, once brought to bear on the language-game, looks at its workings, in contrast to the Tractarian conception of logic, always as one possibility among other possibilities. We do arithmetic so-and-so: *this* is what we *call* doing arithmetic, but from the vantage point of the Step ours is only one way among other ways of doing it, ways that can be imagined and set up alongside our own language-games. The same goes for our psychological language-games—on which Wittgenstein's casts his philosophical eye from

---

there is no judgment I could be certain of if I started doubting about that' (OC: 490), 'So is this it: I must recognize certain authorities in order to make judgments at all?' (OC: 493).

the same vantage point: a vantage point which renders the kind of *fictitious* determinacy that he seeks to set up alongside our own way doing psychological things with words analogous to the kind of determinacy that our *factual* way of doing arithmetic manifests. We talk here about a vantage point on language that Wittgenstein did not revoke in *On Certainty*, or start to amend, but sanctioned instead, and tried to think through as ever before, a sanctioning and trying that give rise to typical passages such as the following:

> People have killed animals since the earliest times, used the fur, bones etc. etc. for various purposes; they have counted definitely on finding similar parts in any similar beast.
>
> They have always learnt from experience; and we can see from their actions that they believe certain things definitely, whether they express this belief or not. By this I naturally do not want to say that men *should* behave like this, but only that they do behave like this. (OC: 284)

This passage is a striking example in which Wittgenstein's conception of logic comes to the fore. Making mention of certain vital actions that men have always performed without the least shadow of doubt, actions in which a great diversity of physical and biological items is involved and matters most, Wittgenstein hastens to add that he does not want to be understood as saying that men *should* behave like that. All he says, and wants to say, is that men behave thus and so.

To say that Wittgenstein's methods of description *exploit* the point of the Step is to say that the whole point of the Step is to think its business through. The Step, as we have been emphasizing, is not some kind of device to produce scholarly theses or polished remarks of the grammatical type. It is Wittgenstein's grip on the language-game, which looks upon it *as* representing one possibility among other possibilities; a grip that he needs to think through: to look and see *how* the constitutive role of a rule reifies in the traffic of the language-game in which it is at home. But now, what is it to think through the Step with respect to such peculiar things as Moore-type propositions? Once Moore-type propositions are being treated on the model of the Step, rules are about to forfeit their privileged character to lend language-games the kinds of possibilities they are. That is, if you treat Moore-type propositions on this model you seem to be about to extend the variability of the language-game beyond the limits that the constitutive role of rules bestows upon their workings. But, then, as regards the Moore-type propositions, this means that the charge of the variability is extended beyond the level where rules operate, thus beyond the traffic of the language-game and up to such margins and 'dark places' of the language-game that count as subterranean in relation to where rules find their application. This raises the question how the variability of the language-game with respect to the rule-like Moore-type propositions is to be brought out descriptively. Rules are constitutive of some language-game or other; in *On Certainty*, though, Wittgenstein faces the task to bring out constitutive aspects with respect to matters that underlie '*all* questions and *all* thinking' (emphases mine). Of course, here I am alluding to Wittgenstein's words 'in the end' in *OC* §501.

The following passages, often ignored in the secondary literature on *On Certainty*, are worth considering in the present connection:

> Here one must realize that complete absence of doubt at some point, even where we would say that 'legitimate' doubt can exist, need not falsify a language-game. For there is also something like *another* arithmetic.
>
> I believe that this admission must underlie any understanding of logic. (OC: 375)

> Imagine a language-game "When I call you, come in through the door". In any ordinary case, a doubt whether there really is a door there will be impossible.
>
> What I need to shew is that a doubt is not necessary even when it is possible. That the possibility of the language-game doesn't depend on everything being doubted that can be doubted. (This is connected with the role of contradiction in mathematics.) (OC: 391–2)

There is, as far as these passages themselves are concerned, nothing new under the sun in *On Certainty*. That is, all Wittgenstein is doing here is little more than musing over a few aspects of his conception of logic. Thus, when he admits that 'there is also something like another arithmetic', and believes 'that this admission must underlie any understanding of logic', Wittgenstein is truly not entertaining *anything new* as regards his conception of logic. For the admission [*Eingeständnis*] is what he had begun to make the most of it since the mid 1930s, upon having recognized the true nature of his Tractarian requirement that logic *must* be so and *so* only. Still, that Wittgenstein, near the end of his life, in the middle of his efforts to come to terms with the peculiarity of Moore-type propositions, reminds himself of such an absolutely fundamental thing as the 'admission' is as regards his conception of logic, is a fact worth pausing over.

The crux *concerning* the two passages is that Wittgenstein reminds himself of his conception of logic in the light of some prevalent 'urge to misunderstand the workings of our language' (PI: 109), one that forces itself upon his efforts to *describe* the logic of the Moore-type propositions. The urge in question originates in our intuiting a strong empirical flavour in these propositions, and while being wafted away on the wings of this flavour, we, before long, hold the possibility of doubt to be 'legitimate'. But where we feel that doubt is 'legitimate', we feel urged to think that the language-game cannot possibly hinge on an arithmetic (i.e. logic) that leaves this 'legitimacy' as it were untapped. It is precisely against a claim (or urge, for that matter) such as this one that Wittgenstein sets his philosophical face, in a manner that seeks to make the most of the Step: 'the possibility of the language-game doesn't depend on everything being doubted that can be doubted'. Here the *that* is important: '*that* a doubt is not necessary even when it is possible'; '*that* complete absence of doubt at some point, even where we would say that "legitimate" doubt can exist, need not falsify a language-game' (emphases mine). The 'that' is important, for nothing, as Wittgenstein well realizes, has yet been *shown* by it.

Wittgenstein speaks of the *possibility* of the language-game, of what 'doesn't depend on everything being doubted that can be doubted'. But to speak of the language-game thus is precisely to *characterize* it from the vantage point of the Step, a procedure that Wittgenstein has been going through again and again in the years preceding his struggles in *On Certainty*. His 'last work' often alludes to these past activities, for instance in the following passage:

> We say: if a child has mastered language—and hence its application—it must know the meaning of words: It must, for example, be able to attach the name of its colour to a white, black, red or blue object without the occurrence of any doubt.
>
> And indeed no one misses doubt here; no one is surprised that we do not merely *surmise* the meaning of our words. (OC: 522–3)

Here Wittgenstein reminds us of a stock-in-trade language-game where we, philosophers or not, have not missed doubt. Importantly, we not only miss it here; we are simply not surprised at all about *this* very absence of doubt either. Wittgenstein, then, by reminding us of this fact furnishes a contrast with the point where we do feel, in our philosophical moments, that doubt *is* missing ('legitimate'). But just look, Wittgenstein wants to say now, we never missed doubt *here*, that is, we have never been bothered about *this* absence and, look, the language-game has not been 'falsified' either.

The Step is idling without the methods that Wittgenstein is committed to employ the moment he brings the Step into play. That is why, in the passage quoted above, he says the following: '*What I need to shew* is that a doubt is not necessary even when it is possible. That the possibility of the language-game doesn't depend on everything being doubted that can be doubted.' What Wittgenstein needs to show is what he has *not yet* shown with his first grip on the Moore-type propositions by dint of the Step. What he needs to show are things exploiting the Step. So what Wittgenstein seeks to *show* is just the contrast that §375 and §392 intimate, namely between 'opposite' arithmetics. If the Step says that 'the possibility of the language-game doesn't depend on everything being doubted that can be doubted', the question is *what such possibilities look like* that our language does not entertain among its own workings. The suggested contrast, then, is obtained, not in theses, any more than in grammatical remarks or statements, but in terms of look-likes: *descriptions* of language-games within the purview of a perspicuous representation. The pertinent question in which the following passage ends is not to be overlooked.

> Is it essential for our language-games ('ordering and obeying' for example) that no doubt appears at certain points, or is it enough if there is the feeling of being sure, admittedly with a slight breath of doubt?
>
> The accompanying feeling is of course a matter of indifference to us, and equally we have no need to bother about the words "I am sure" either.—What is important is whether they go with a difference in the *practice* of the language. [...].
> What, then, does the case look like where someone really has got a different relationship to the names of colours, for example, from us? Where, that is, there persists a slight doubt or a possibility of doubt in their use. (OC 524–5)

The latter remark ('What , then, ... use.') is a clear allusion to Wittgenstein's reflections in §375 and §392. What Wittgenstein seeks to set up alongside the arithmetic of our language-games are *fictitious* language-games—that is, precisely those that *do* hinge on a shadow of doubt and on that account represent a way of constituting language that does not belong to the essence of our own language-games. Indeed, the kind of philosophical effort incumbent on Wittgenstein's mind in *On Certainty* amounts, as I want to say, to this: *considering fictitious language-games in which rules are followed with a shadow of doubt!* He needs to present our own logical predicament against such fictitious possibilities, and unless he manages to do so, he, as he realizes all too well, cannot be said to have *described* the *logic* ('arithmetic') of our language.

Before turning to the difficulties that Wittgenstein faces as regards these descriptive efforts, I first should like to comment on what Norman Malcolm has said about *OC* §501 and the trouble addressed there.

> *Logic cannot be described!*[203] I take this to mean that it is not appropriate for Wittgenstein to say either that he 'knows', or 'believes', or is 'certain', or is 'convinced', or 'assumes', or does not doubt, that his name L.W., or that this is called a 'hand', or that the law of induction is true. None of these terms are correct.[204]
> *On Certainty* is full of grammatical remarks. An example is this: 'The child learns by believing the adult. Doubt comes *after* belief' (*OC* §160). Wittgenstein is trying to

---

203   Notice that Malcolm leaves out Wittgenstein's words 'in the end'!
204   Norman Malcolm, 'Wittgenstein: The Relation of Language to Instinctive Behaviour', *Philosophical Investigations* 5/1 (1982), 19.

express, in this remark, something that is necessarily true about the concept of doubting – namely, that a person's behaviour and utterances can be rightly described as 'doubting', only if they occur against the background of things that the person *accepts*.

> The difficulty confronting Wittgenstein in *On Certainty* is *not* that what he is trying to state is a logical or conceptual necessity. It is instead a problem concerning *the words* in terms of which the necessary truth can be stated. Is, for example, the word 'accept', that I used just now, the right word? Can it be said that the small child 'accepts' that what he is told to sit on is a 'chair'? Isn't this too sophisticated a term to apply to him at this stage? Nor can one say that he 'agrees' that it is a chair, nor that he 'believes' this, nor even that he 'does not doubt' it. (*Ibid*, 21)

Pace Malcolm, this passage misconceives the sort of difficulty that Wittgenstein intimates in *OC* §501. For one thing, Malcolm speaks of what is 'necessarily true about the concept of doubting', rather than of what is necessarily true about *our* concept of doubting. Speaking thus about necessary truths, Malcolm's remark not only concerns our own language-games, but also those by dint of which Wittgenstein precisely seeks to contrast the arithmetic (logic) of our own language-games. What Malcolm misconstrues is nothing less than the Step. For another thing, even if we constrain the remit of Malcolm's so-called necessary truth to the confines of our own language, Wittgenstein's problem is certainly not one concerning *the words* in terms of which this truth can be stated. His problem ('difficulty') is that of showing how the abovementioned deviation from the tune ('arithmetic') underlying our own language-games goes with a difference *in the practice of language* (see above passage). Again, then, it is really *look-likes* that Wittgenstein is interested in, that is, *descriptions* of language-games within a conspicuous representation, rather than an appropriate term within a few polished remarks.

I said that Wittgenstein's methods of language description are internally related to the Step in that they exploit its point. The method presently under our consideration aims at setting up certain fictitious language-games alongside our own language-games: possibilities alongside the ones that our language entertains itself. But now, if fleshing out recognizable fictitious language-games has turned out to be so much of a trouble for Wittgenstein, as we have been seeing, where does this leave him as regards this task in *On Certainty*? The language-game should concern absences of doubt that do not underlie one language-game or another, but 'all questions and all thinking'. So how divert, in the imagination, from something as fundamental as *this* and still recognize the upshot as a language-game—as what *merely diverges* from our own way of doing it, i.e. from what we *call* doing this or that at home? That there is, to say the least, a serious difficulty here can easily be seen and exemplified by dint of the following passages:

> There are cases such that, if someone gives signs of doubt where we do not doubt, we cannot confidently understand his signs as signs of doubt.
>
> I.e.: If we are to understand his signs of doubt as such, he may give them only in particular cases and may not give them in others. (OC: 154)
>
> Doubting has certain characteristic manifestations, but they are only characteristic of it in particular circumstances. If someone said that he doubted the existence of his hands, kept looking at them from all sides, tried to make sure it wasn't 'all done by mirrors', etc., we should not be sure whether we ought to call that doubting. We might describe his way of behaving as like the behaviour of doubt, but his game would not be ours. (OC: 255)

'Doubting', Wittgenstein says, 'has certain characteristic manifestations, but they are only characteristic of it in particular circumstances.' Of course, what Wittgenstein says here is what he has been saying for a long time. What is more, he did not confine these and similar sayings to doubting alone: 'Only surrounded by certain normal manifestations of life, is there such a thing as an expression of pain. Only surrounded by even more far-reaching particular manifestations of life, such a thing as the expression of sorrow or affection. And so on' (Z: 534). Such statements are part of what might be called Wittgenstein's firm grammatical commodity. Be that as it may—try as you might: to set up fictitious language-games in the face of 'the normal manifestations of life', that is, against the backcloth of matters with which these language-games still need to *keep up* lest we end up facing something beyond our recognition—need to keep up, in spite of the stipulation to engender an anomaly. Of course, a small variation on the logical theme of a language-game need not necessarily render its fictitious counterpart unrecognizable. Such a variation may as a possibility even partake of the physiognomy that a variety of language-games manifests in our own *Lebensform*. But there are limits to such variations, limits to what we would accept as a language-game played *by us*, and Wittgenstein is interested in these limits, in what lies beyond them, however vague they are or may be. A *small* variation on the logic of a language-game is of interest to him as the inauguration of a series of *Zwischenglieder*, i.e. intermediate cases in a surveyable representation (see below), *Zwischenglieder* between our own language-games as *poles* in such a representation on the one hand, with certain far-reaching fictitious language-games representing *polar opposites* on the other hand. If Wittgenstein nourishes a profound interest in *seeing* these polar opposites thus connected to each other, it is the Step that prompts him to have that kind of interest in the first instance—an interests in possibilities which the Step as an abstract idea does not exclude

330

but whose concrete manifestations more often than not turn out to lie beyond our ability to recognize them as representing one or another deviation from our logical predicament.

So what are we to make of the task of fleshing out fictitious language-games that we should recognize as a variation on what *we call* doing this or that, in spite of these games hinging on a stipulation such as 'there persists a slight doubt or a possibility of doubt in [the] use' (OC: 525) of, say, the human hand? The signs of doubt that the fictitious counterpart is to display should be *genuine* signs of doubt in this language-game, rather than merely *like* signs of doubt for us. (Cases of the latter type are of interest even so, namely as ones in the series of deviations lying beyond the case that should display *genuine* signs of doubt.) Thus, when someone is being ordered to buy a book we should, in the case of its fictitious counterpart, really be able to say of him that he is *following* the order at stake. The signs of doubt that the person displays should not prompt us to say that he has failed to understand the order, or that he is following it wrongly—or that he is just insane. The fictitious person is merely to play the language-game *differently*, rather than to stage a man out of his mind. His signs of doubt should not suggest, *to us*, a dubious trait characterizing his personality. We should rather recognize them as being a 'legitimate' trait characterizing *the essence* of the language-game played.

Wittgenstein, in *On Certainty*, is at times clearly doubtful about the feasibility of furnishing such fictitious language-games as he deems necessary for the descriptive task at hand. But how self-assured he once was in respect of this feasibility, hence how indubitable he thought the grounds were on which his later philosophy stands! Recall here what he writes in the *Philosophical Investigations*: 'I can easily imagine someone always doubting before he opened his front door whether an abyss did not yawn behind it, and making sure about it before he went through the door (and he might on some occasion prove to be right) – but for all that, I do not doubt in such case' (PI: 84). Notice that this passage does little more than presenting the admission of which Wittgenstein speaks in *OC* §375; instead of furnishing an invention, it merely *speaks of* an invention, of a certain fictitious scenario, of someone who simply has his doubts where we do not doubt, and who, for all that, need not necessarily to be seen as out of his mind. So our own practice of not-doubting is not to be regarded as what 'falsifies' our language-games, but as one possible condition among other possible conditions. Wittgenstein, in the *Philosophical Investigations*, is really making the most of his admission, in the sense that he formulates it in a highly confident and assured way: 'I *can easily imagine* someone always doubting [...]'. The admission, though, commits one to work out language-games showing 'that a doubt is not necessary even when it is possible' (OC: 392). And it is precisely with respect to such an effort as to show what needs to be shown that it comes in e.g. *On Certainty* to less optimistic tones: '[W]e should not be sure whether we ought to call that doubting. We might describe his way of behaving as like the behaviour of doubt, but his game would not be ours.'

I just mentioned the insane, and, needless to say, this type of character displays an intriguing and recurring trope in Wittgenstein's thinking. In *Remarks on the Foundations of Mathematics*, for example, he writes: 'Frege says in the preface to the *Grundgesetze der Arithmetik*: "…here we have a hitherto unknown kind of insanity"—but he never said what this "insanity" *would really be like*' (RFM: 95, emphasis added). Wittgenstein criticizes Frege here for his mulish refusal to think in less abstract terms and considerations, suggesting that if only he had tried his hand a little at fleshing out *examples* ('look-likes') he *might* well have come to see that where contradiction looms large it *need not* always signify insanity. But if he thinks that Frege might well have seen things differently, it is because Wittgenstein thinks that examples can indeed be given that show another logic (another arithmetic). Wittgenstein invokes a pivotal movement of thought here, one that underlies his own way of philosophical thinking. And this fact renders his criticism of Frege, I think, so interesting if not notable, for what Wittgenstein seems to prey on here is this movement of thought more in the shape of an abstract idea itself than in the shape of some gripping examples. He confronts Frege's mulish abstractions, not with concrete examples *showing* the contrary of what lies at the bottom of Frege's whole thinking, but with what is contrary to it at the level of abstraction itself and what underlies his own thinking, namely his admission 'that there is something like another arithmetic'. Needless to say, Wittgenstein repeatedly tried to set up such fictitious anomalies as he thought Frege should have tried to set up for himself. But it is not these efforts themselves that had brought home to him the admission *that* 'there is also something like another arithmetic.' It is rather the other way around: his admission commits him to try to set up another arithmetic. It is Wittgenstein's steadfast adherence to his admission, rather than the success *or* failure of what it commits him to undertake, that leads him to criticize Frege for not having tried himself.

The trope of the insane person is an important instrument in Wittgenstein's efforts to obtain a *descriptive* grip on our logical predicament. He seeks to behold the insane person within the purview of a surveyable representation. He wants *to see connections*—'Hence the importance of finding and inventing *intermediate cases*' (PI: 122). The insane person is such an intermediate thing, i.e., a borderline case within a certain survey in which the difference between playing a game wrong and not playing it provides for a most pivotal exploitation of the Step. The insane person does not play the game wrong; rather, he has just ceased to play the game the way we do. But what does the difference *look like*? That is the question! – 'What is the difference between mistake and mental disturbance? Or what is the difference between my treating it as a mistake and my treating it as mental disturbance?' (OC: 73). Here we have one example of a passage[205] that raises this curious but utterly important question. And what it is suggestive of is that much is involved in working out the specified difference, for the insane person is above all someone whom *we* treat in a way that *is* just different from how we treat making mistakes.

The question that asks for the difference between playing the game wrong and not playing it is a Wittgensteinian movement of thought, intimately related to the Step. This being so, it should not surprise us to see it turning up within contexts other than *On Certainty* alone. Consider the following passage from *Remarks on the Foundations of Mathematics*:

> What is the difference between not calculating and calculating wrong?—Or: is there a sharp dividing line between not measuring time and measuring it wrong? Not knowing any measurement of time and knowing a wrong one? (RFM: 236)
>
> I have not yet made the role of miscalculating clear. The role of the proposition: "I must have miscalculated". It is really the key to an understanding of the 'foundations' of mathematics. (RFM: 221)

When Wittgenstein speaks of the role of the proposition 'I must have made a mistake' being the key *zum Verständnis* of the 'foundations' of mathematics—he has singled out, or so it appears, a rather minor if not downright uninteresting aspect of the way we do mathematics. Yet, it is precisely an aspect such as this one that provides for a most important *übersichtliche Darstellung* as it allows language-games to shade off in various directions. The aspect, once made to become the centre of such a *Darstellung*, strives to include not only the difference between not calculating and calculating wrong, but also, and most importantly, such intermediate cases as progress towards really *different* modes of *calculating*. The proposition 'I must have made a mistake' is the key as it provides for the construction of 'a continuum between an error in calculation and a different

---

205　Here is another example: 'If I believe that I am sitting in my room when I am not, then I shall not be said to have *made a mistake*. But what is the essential difference between this case and a mistake?' (OC: 195). Cf. OC: 446, quoted above.

mode of calculating'[206]. The 'foundations of mathematics' is not a kind of premise on which our way of doing mathematics stands and on which every way of doing things with signs need to stand as well lest it fall short of *being* mathematics. Rather, the 'foundation' is a combination of two things, namely *that* we do it thus-and-so—*and that* other ways of doing it so as to characterize ours should be fleshed out by making the most of the difference between not calculating and calculating wrong. Our way of doing mathematics should be characterized in the same way in which other of our ways of doing things with words should be characterized and understood, namely in the end by means of an *übersichtliche Darstellung*. The one concerning our way of doing mathematical things should be characterized by a *Darstellung* in which other ways of doing mathematical things with words participate as integral parts. Hence the pivotal importance of considering the role of the proposition 'I must have miscalculated', for the other ways of doing mathematics should be recognizable as such, rather than as ways of our having blatantly miscalculated—among other things.[207]

6.5 Another exploitation of the Step

The difference between playing the mathematical game wrong and not playing it exploits the limits of Wittgenstein's vantage point on language, but it becomes a genuine exploitation thereof only when one draws on language-games, on details, on questions of what the traffic of the language-game looks like.

Now details are of Wittgenstein's concern as well with respect to another important movement of thought in *On Certainty*, one that seeks to exploit the very Step no less than the difference does between playing the game wrong and not

---

206　'We could say people's concepts show what matters to them and what doesn't. But it's not as if this explained the particular concepts they have. It is only to rule out the view that we have the right concepts and other people the wrong ones. (There is a continuum between an error in calculation and a different mode of calculating)' (RC: 293).

207　Felix Mühlhölzer (2014: 154f) says that 'With this almost dramatic statement [i.e. Wittgenstein's remark concerning 'the key to an understanding of the "foundations" of mathematics'], Wittgenstein isn't referring to the key to his *own* understanding of mathematics, but to foundationalist endeavours like the Hilbertian one that aim at consistency proofs'. This, I think, is a truly big mistake on Mühlhölzer's part, one that is not likely to have left no deep traces in his recently published opus magnum *Braucht die Mathematik eine Grundlegung? Ein Kommentar des Teils III von Wittgensteins* Bemerkungen über die Grundlagen der Mathematik. I will return to this dramatic issue in part II of the present study.

playing it. Thus, so far Wittgenstein exploited the point that it is first and foremost the traffic of the language-game that holds the axis fixed and renders it the kind of thing it passes for in the language-game: a proposition of mathematics, for instance. Still, the language-game does not pivot on its axis in empty space. Rather, its pivoting occurs against the background of a gently behaving world. As we have seen, this 'backstage notion' of a smooth and regular running of the world's facts and affairs is an absolutely pivotal building block in Wittgenstein's Step, something that cries out for an exploitation of its very point. (Although Wittgenstein does not leave this point unexploited in *On Certainty*, it is not there that he exploits it for the first time.[208]) The following passages are precisely the ones that we need to address so as to see what this kind of exploitation of the Step amounts to.

> If I were contradicted on all sides and told that this person's name was not what I had always known it was (and I use "know" here intentionally), then in that case the foundation of all judging would be taken away from me. (OC: 614)

> If something happened (such as someone telling me something) calculated to make me doubtful of my own name, there would certainly also be something that made the grounds of these doubts themselves seem doubtful, and I could therefore decide to retain my old belief. (OC: 516).
>
> But might it not be possible for something to happen that threw my entirely off the rails? Evidence that made the most certain things unacceptable to me? Or at any rate made me throw over my most fundamental judgements? (Whether rightly or wrongly is beside the point.) (OC: 517)

> Could I imagine observing this in another person? (OC: 518)

> What if something really *unheard-of* happened?—If I, say, saw houses gradually turning into steam without any obvious cause, if the cattle in the fields stood on their head and laughed and spoke comprehensible words; if trees gradually changed into men and men into trees. Now, was I right when I said before all these things happened "I know that that's a house" etc., or simply "that's a house" etc.? (OC: 513)

---

208   Cf.: 'We learn the word 'red' under part[icular] circ[umstance]s. Certain objects are usually red, and keep their colours; most people agree with us in our colour judgements. Suppose all this changes: I see blood, unaccountably sometimes one sometimes another colour, and the people around me all make different statements. But couldn't I in all this chaos retain my meaning of 'red', 'blue,' etc., although I couldn't now make myself understood to anyone? Samples, e.g., would all constantly change their colours—'or does it only seem to me?' "Now am I mad or have I really called this 'red' yesterday?"' (PO: 267).

"Do I know or do I only believe…?" might also be expressed like this: What if it *seemed* to turn out that what until now has seemed immune to doubt was a false assumption? Would I react as I do when a belief has proved to be false? or would it seem to knock from under my feet the ground on which I stand in making any judgement at all?—But of course I do not intend this as a *prophecy*.

Would I simply say "I should never have thought it!"—or would I (have) to refuse my judgement—because such a 'revision' would amount to annihilation of all yardsticks? (OC: 492)

These passages abound in if-constructions, but not every occurrence entertains the kind of exploitation that is presently under our attention. To be sure, Wittgenstein's philosophical concern is of a purely logical nature, which is shown by his warning that he does not intend to dabble in *prophecies*. But this fact alone does not render all his if-construction of one and the same logical type. We had better interpret these *ifs* as either logical enunciations of the Step themselves or as logical exploitations of its 'backstage notion'. The following examples are all of one type:

If I *really doubt* what stands fast for me, this would drag out the language-game, or else does away with it. (OC: 370, emphasis mine)

Not only do I never have the slightest doubt that I am called that, but there is no judgement I could be certain of if I started doubting that, (OC: 490)

If my name is *not* L.W., how can I rely on what is meant by "true" and "false"? (OC: 515)

These if-constructions are to be sharply distinguished from the following:

What if something really *unheard-of* happened? (OC: 513)[209]

Both types of *ifs* are not prophecies, but not in one and the same way. The tokens of the type quoted first are all if-*enunciations* of the Step. That is, when Wittgenstein brings the Step to bear upon our language he enunciates his first grip on the Moore-type propositions as follows: 'about certain propositions no doubt can exist *if* making judgements is to be possible at all' (emphasis mine). In other words, a remark such as 'the language-games hinges on what is exempted from doubt' means that 'if I *really doubt* what stands fast for me, this would drag out the language-game, or else does away with it' (emphasis added); it means that if *doubt really* supervenes 'this would 'amount to annihilation of all yardsticks'[210]

---

209 Cf. OC: 420–421.

210 See also the last sentence in the following passage: 'If I say "I have never been in Asia Minor", where do I get this knowledge from? I have not worked it out, no one told me; my memory tells me.—So I can't be wrong about it? Is there a truth which

(see above). But stipulating this, the Step leaves untouched precisely the question whether an annihilation of all yardsticks *must* intrude *if* the world around me ceases to run in its *usual* smooth and gentle way. Wittgenstein's stipulation was never meant to pre-empt any further philosophical action; its whole point rather lies in what it cries out for:[211] Whether I should let doubt creep into the marrow of my being *if* the world ceases to look what it has always looked *to me*. In other words, what Wittgenstein's question 'What if something really *unheard-of* happened?' cries out for is an answer to the question whether I *must* so to speak go unheard-of myself should I behold things going unheard-of. What interests Wittgenstein is what stands between the (stipulated) doubt that amounts to (the) annihilation of all yardsticks, on the one hand, and the world going unheard-of, on the other hand, namely our *human reactions* to our seeing things going unheard-of.

It is important to emphasize that Wittgenstein frequently resorts to the phrase 'What if it *seemed...*' (cf. OC: 492). He does do so because only when the unheard-of circumstances strike me as such, thus as what I *for myself* construe as *contradicting* my deepest convictions, that the question arises how I will re-act to this situation. Should I say that I must be crazy? Should I say that I *was* wrong? 'Would I react as I do when a belief has proved to be false?'—Thus, if the world turns *unheard-of*, the question still is *whether* it would ever strike me *as such*—and that is an intriguing question.[212] Would I now let *doubt* creep into the marrow of the language-game—or should I refuse to do so? 'Would I simply say "I should never have thought it!"—or would I (have to) refuse to revise my judge-ment—because such a 'revision' would amount to annihilation of all yardsticks' (OC: 492). 'Why', Wittgenstein asks, why 'would it be *unthinkable* that I should stay in the saddle however much the facts bucked?' (OC: 616).—

Having no intention to prophesize, Wittgenstein conceives his if-questions as relating to the Step in such a way that the answers can be had by looking at the practice of language. But, then, here too: looking yes, but *not* without exerting

---

I know?—I cannot depart from this judgment without toppling all other judgments with it' (OC: 419).

211 Recall here Wittgenstein's words: 'What interests us is that about certain empiri-cal propositions no doubt can exist if making judgements is to be possible at all' (OC: 308).

212 Cf. 'One might also put this question: "If you know that that is your foot,—do you also know, or do you only believe, that no future experience will seem to contradict your knowledge?" (That is, that nothing will seem to *you yourself* to do so.)' (OC: 364). See also OC: 365.

the imagination. As with the other exploitation of the Step before, Wittgenstein is again deeply obsessed with polar opposites, this time concerning circumstances: with a world going *unheard-of* as the extreme end of a continuum starting with descriptions of the smoothly running world in which we live and die. The picture of this continuum will give you the kind of hold that we have on the world. The polar reactions in which Wittgenstein is interested limit the kind of sureness that keeps the whole thing together: the language-game in which we stand and through which we are the kind of human beings we are. But, as before, Wittgenstein faced serious troubles in generating such a continuum, precisely owing to his having extreme difficulties in getting a hold on its constituting pillars: the polar opposites. Witness only this question: 'Why would it be *unthinkable* that I should stay in the saddle however much the facts bucked?'——

References

Cited Works of Wittgenstein (with list of Abbreviations)

AWL   *Wittgenstein's Lectures, Cambridge, 1932–1935*, ed. Alice Ambrose (New York: Prometheus Books, 1979).

BB   *The Blue and Brown Books*, 2nd edition (Oxford: Blackwell, 1998).

CV   *Culture and Value*, 2nd edition, ed. G. H. von Wright in collaboration with Heikki Nyman (Oxford: Blackwell, 1998).

LA   *Lectures and Conversations on Aesthetics, Psychology and Religious Beliefs*, ed. Cyrill Barrett (Oxford: Blackwell, 1999).

LFM   *Wittgenstein's Lectures on the Foundations of Mathematics, Cambridge 1939*, ed. C. Diamond (Sussex: Harvester Press, 1976).

LPP   *Wittgenstein's Lectures on the Philosophical Psychology 1946–7*, ed. P T. Geach (Hemel Hempstead: Harvester Wheatsheaf, 1988).

LWPP I   *Last Writings on the Philosophy of Psychology*, Volume I, ed. by G. E. M. Anscombe, G. H. von Wright and Heikki Nyman (Oxford: Blackwell, 1982).

LWPP II   *Last Writings on the Philosophy of Psychology*, Volume II, ed. G. H. von Wright and Heikki Nyman (Oxford: Blackwell, 1992).

NB   *Notebooks 1914–1916*, 2nd edition, ed. G. H. von Wright and G. E. M. Anscombe (Oxford: Blackwell, 1979).

OC   *On Certainty*, ed. G. E. M. Anscombe and G. H. von Wright (Oxford: Blackwell, 1998).

PG   Philosophical Grammar, 2nd edition, ed. R. Rhees (Oxford, Blackwell, 1974).

PI   *Philosophical Investigations*, 2nd edition, ed. G. E. M. Anscombe and R. Rhees (Oxford: Blackwell, 1998).

     Philosophical Investigations, revised 4th edition, ed. P. M. S. Hacker and Joachim Schulte (Oxford: Wiley-Blackwell, 2009).

PO   *Philosophical Occasions 1912–1951*, ed. James C. Klagge and Alfred Nordmann (Indianapolis: Hackett Publishing Company, 1993).

PPF   *Philosophy of Psychology: a Fragment*, published in PI, 4th edition (Oxford: Wiley-Blackwell, 2009).

PPO   *Public and Private Occasions.* ed. James C. Klagge and Alfred Nordmann (Lanham, Boulder, New York, Oxford: Rowman and Littlefield, 2003).

PR   *Philosophical Remarks*, ed. R. Rhees (Oxford: Blackwell, 1975).

RC   *Remarks on Colours*, ed. G. E. M. Anscombe (Oxford: Blackwell, 1977)

RFM   *Remarks on the Foundations of Mathematics*, 3rd edition, ed by G. H. von Wright, R. Rhees and G. E. M. Anscombe (Oxford: Blackwell, 1998).

RPP I   *Remarks on the Philosophy of Psychology*, Volume I, ed. G. E. M. Anscombe and G. H. von Wright (Oxford: Blackwell, 1980).

RPP II   *Remarks on the Philosophy of Psychology*, Volume II, ed. G. H. von Wright
and Heikki Nyman (Oxford: Blackwell,1980).

TLP   *Tractatus Logico-Philosophicus*, translated by D.F. Pears & B.F. McGuinness (London: Routledge & Kegan Paul, 1971).
Tractatus Logico-Philosophicus, translated by C. K. Odgen (London: Routledge, 1998).

VoW   *The Voices of Wittgenstein – The Vienna Circle: Ludwig Wittgenstein and Friedrich Waisman*, ed. Gordon Baker (Oxon: Routledge, 2003).

WC   *Wittgenstein in Cambridge. Letters and Documents, 1911–1951*, ed. Brian McGuinness (Malden, Mass: Blackwell, 2008).

Z   *Zettel*, 2nd edition, ed. G. E. M. Anscombe and G. H. von Wright, (Oxford: Blackwell, 1998).

MS/TS   *Wittgenstein's Nachlass: The Bergen Electronic Edition* (Oxford University Press, 2000).

Other references

Baker, Gordon and Peter M. S. Hacker, *Wittgenstein: Understanding and Meaning. Part II – Exegesis §§1–184* (Oxford: Wiley-Blackwell, 2009).

Budd, Malcolm, *Wittgenstein's Philosophy of Psychology* (London and New York: Routledge, 1989).

Cerbone, David R., 'How to do things with wood: Wittgenstein, Frege and the problem of illogical thought', in Alice Crary and Rupert Read, eds., *The New Wittgenstein* (London & New York: Routledge, 2000), 293–314.

Cerbone, David, 'Wittgenstein and Idealism', in Oskari Kuusela and Marie McGinn, eds., *The Oxford Handbook of Wittgenstein* (Oxford: Oxford University Press, 2011), 311–332.

Cheung, Leo K. C., 'The Unity of Language and Logic in Wittgenstein's *Tractatus*', *Philosophical Investigations* 29/1 (2006), 22–50.

Conant, James, 'A Ladder Turns into a Fly-bottle', in David Wellbery, Hans Ulrich Gumbrecht, Anton Kaes, Dorothea von Muecke, and Judith Ryan, eds., *New History of German Literature* (Cambridge, Mass: Harvard University Press, 2004), 866–871.

Conant, James, 'Wittgenstein's Later Criticism of the *Tractatus*', in Alois Pichler and Simo Säätelä, eds., *Wittgenstein: the Philosopher and his Work* (Frankfurt am Main: Ontos Verlag, 2006), 172–204.

Conant, James, 'Continuity and Discontinuity in Wittgenstein's Philosophy', in Günter Abel, Matthias Kroß, and Michael Nedo, eds., *Ludwig Wittgenstein: Ingenieur—Philosoph—Künstler* (Parerga Verlag, 2007), 51–90.

Conant, James, 'A development in Wittgenstein's Conception of Philosophy: From "The Method" to Methods', in Stefan Tolksdorf and Holm Tetens, eds., *In Sprachspiele verstrickt – oder: Wie man der Fliege den Ausweg zeigt: Verflechtungen von Wissen und Können* (Berlin: De Gruyter, 2010). 55–80.

Conant, James and Cora Diamond, 'On Reading the Tractatus Resolutely: Reply to Meredith Williams and Peter Sullivan', in M. Kölbel and B. Weiss, eds., *Wittgenstein's Lasting Significance* (London: Routledge, 2004), 46–99.

Dummett, M., *The Logical Basis of Metaphysics* (Cambridge, Mass: Harvard University Press, 1991).

Drury, Maurice O'C., 'Conversations with Wittgenstein', in Rush Rhees, ed., in *Ludwig Wittgenstein: Personal Recollections* (Oxford: Basil Blackwell, 1981), 112–189.

Frege, Gottlob, *Grundgesetze der Arithmetik* (Hildesheim, Zürich, New York: Georg Olms Verlag, 1998).

Glock, H.-J., ed., *Wittgenstein: A Critical Reader* (Oxford: Blackwell, 2001).

Hylton, Peter, 'Functions, Operations, and Sense in Wittgenstein's *Tractatus*', in W. Tait, ed., *Early Analytic Philosophy: Frege, Russell, Wittgenstein: Essays in Honour of Leonard Lynsky* (Chicago: Chicago University Press, 1997), 91–106.

Kripke, S., *Wittgenstein on Rules and Private Language* (Cambridge, Mass: Harvard University Press, 1982).

Kuusela, Oskari, 'Gordon Baker, 'Wittgensteinian Philosophical Conceptions and Perspicuous Representation: the Possibility of Multidimensional Logical Descriptions', *Nordic Wittgenstein Review* 3/2 (2014), 71–98.

Kuusela, O. and McGinn, Marie., eds., *The Oxford Handbook of Wittgenstein* (Oxford: Oxford University Press, 2011).

Lovejoy, Arthur O., *The Great Chain of Being* (Cambridge, Mass: Harvard University Press, 1964).

Malcolm, Norman, *Ludwig Wittgenstein: A Memoir. With a Biographical Sketch by G. H. von Wright* (London: Oxford University Press, 1958).

Malcolm, Norman, 'Wittgenstein: The Relation of Language to Instinctive Behaviour', *Philosophical Investigations* 5/1 (1982), 3–22.

McGuinness, Brian, *Approaches to Wittgenstein* (London: Routledge, 2002).

Monk, Ray, *Wittgenstein – The Duty of Genius* (London: Vintage, 1991).

Mühlhölzer, Felix, *Braucht die Mathematik eine Grundlegung? Eine Kommentar des Teils III von Wittgensteins* Bemerkungen über die Grundlagen der Mathematik (Frankfurt: Vittorio Klostermann, 2010).

Mühlhölzer, Felix and Sebastian Greve, 'Wittgenstein's Philosophy of Mathematics: Felix Mühlhölzer in Conversation with Sebastian Greve', *Nordic Wittgenstein Review* (3) 2 (2014), 151–180.

McGinn, Marie, "The Single Great Problem": Wittgenstein's Early Philosophy of Language and Logic', in A. Pichler and S. Saatela, eds, *Wittgenstein: The Philosophy and his Work* (Bergen: Wittgenstein Archive Bergen), 99–132.

Moore, G. E., 'A Defence of Common Sense', in T. Baldwin, ed., *G. E. Moore: Selected Writings* (London: Routledge, 1993), 23–44.

Moore, G. E., 'Proof of an External World', in T. Baldwin, ed., *G. E. Moore: Selected Writings* (London: Routledge, 1993), 147–170.

Putnam, Hilary, *Renewing Philosophy* (Cambridge, Mass: Harvard University Press, 1992).

Prichard, Duncan, 'Wittgenstein on Scepticism', in Oskari Kuusela and Marie McGinn, eds., *The Oxford handbook of Wittgenstein* (Oxford: Oxford University Press, 2011), 523–549.

Priest, Graham, 'What is Philosophy', *Philosophy* 81 (2006), 189–207.

Russell, Bertrand, *An Inquiry into Meaning and Truth* (London and New York: Routledge, 1995).

Sacks, Oliver, *Seeing Voices: A journey Into the World of the Deaf* (Berkeley and Los Angeles: University of California Press, 1989).

Schulte, Joachim, 'Privacy', in Oskari Kuusela and Marie McGinn, eds., *The Oxford Handbook of Wittgenstein* (Oxford: Oxford University Press, 2011), 429–450.

Sluga, H. and Stern, D. G., eds., *The Cambridge Companion to Wittgenstein* (Cambridge: Cambridge University Press, 1996).

Snowdon, Paul, 'Private Experience and Sense Data', in Oskari Kuusela and Marie McGinn., eds., *Oxford Handbook of Wittgenstein* (Oxford: Oxford University press, 2011), 402–428.

Tomasello, Michael, *Origins of Human Communication* (Cambridge, Mass: The MIT Press, 2008).

Tomasello, Michael, *A Natural History of Human Thinking* (Cambridge, Mass: Harvard University Press, 2014).

Verschuren, Sebastiaan A, 'Johannes Climacus reads the *Tractatus*', *Wittgenstein-Studien* 5 (2014), 57–87.

Von Wright, George H., 'Wittgenstein on Certainty', in G. H. von Wright, ed., *Problems in the Theory of Knowledge* (The Hague: Martinus Nijhoff, 1972).

Waismann, Friedrich, *The Principles of Linguistic Philosophy*, ed. R. Harré (London: Macmillan Press,1997).